A PEOPLE'S ATLAS OF DETROIT

A PEOPLE'S ATLAS OF DETROIT

Edited by Linda Campbell, Andrew Newman, Sara Safransky, and Tim Stallmann

WAYNE STATE UNIVERSITY PRESS

DETROIT

All royalties generated by this book are going to the Transforming Power Fund to enable the work documented in this book to be continued and to purchase additional copies to be distributed without charge to Detroit-based community organizations.

ISBN: 978-0-8143-4297-8 (paperback); ISBN: 978-0-8143-4298-5 (ebook)

Library of Congress Control Number: 2019950183

Wayne State University Press
Leonard N. Simons Building
4809 Woodward Avenue
Detroit, Michigan 48201–1309

Visit us online at wsupress.wayne.edu

CONTENTS

List of Maps and Figures   ix
Acknowledgments   xi

INTRODUCTION   1

LINDA CAMPBELL, ANDREW NEWMAN,
SARA SAFRANSKY, AND TIM STALLMANN

CHAPTER 1. DETROIT AND THE LONG STRUGGLE FOR LIBERATION   10

Introduction   11

Mapping Slavery in Detroit   20

ESSAY BY TIYA MILES, MICHELLE CASSIDY, EMILY
MACGILLIVRAY, PAUL RODRIGUEZ, SARAH KHAN,
ALEXANDRA PASSARELLI, AND KAISHA BREZINA

City of Midnight: The Underground Railroad and
Anti-Slavery Resistance in Detroit   25

ESSAY BY ANDREW NEWMAN

Labor Struggles   30

LINDA CAMPBELL, ANDREW NEWMAN,
SARA SAFRANSKY, AND TIM STALLMANN

Race and the Right to Housing   35

LINDA CAMPBELL, ANDREW NEWMAN,
SARA SAFRANSKY, AND TIM STALLMANN

The Walk to Freedom   46

LINDA CAMPBELL, ANDREW NEWMAN,
SARA SAFRANSKY, AND TIM STALLMANN

1967: "Riot Is a Four-Letter Word"   56

LINDA CAMPBELL, ANDREW NEWMAN,
SARA SAFRANSKY, AND TIM STALLMANN

Speaking with Grace and Sterling   62

CONVERSATION BETWEEN GRACE LEE BOGGS AND
STERLING TOLES, ORGANIZED BY ZAK ROSEN

CHAPTER 2. THIS LAND IS OURS: TOWARD A NEW URBAN COMMONS   68

Introduction   69

"Defending the Land Is Important"   76

INTERVIEW WITH DIANNE FEELEY

Detroit-Opoly: Who Owns and Cares for Land in Detroit?   79

ESSAY BY KEZIA CURTIS AND JESSI QUIZAR

"This Is What We Call Home"   87

INTERVIEW WITH CECILY MCCLELLAN

Backyard Garden   94

ESSAY BY AMELIA WIESKE

The River Rats: Fishing, Mutuality, and Community   100
ESSAY BY ANDREA SANKAR, MARK LUBORKSY,
AND ROBERT JOHNSON

Detroit/Windsor: Building a Cross-Border Commons   106
ESSAY BY LEE RODNEY AND MICHAEL DARROCH

"We Need to Put Together a Plan That Honors People in This
Place, on This Land"   111
INTERVIEW WITH MICHELLE MARTINEZ

CHAPTER 3. GROWING A REVOLUTION   116

Introduction   117

Urban Agriculture in Detroit: A Long Tradition   120
CARTOGRAPHIC ESSAY BY ALEX HILL

"We Actually Have the Capacity to Define Our
Own Reality"   124
INTERVIEW WITH MALIK YAKINI

Resurget Cineribus   129
POEM BY ISAAC GINSBERG MILLER

"Liberated Territory Is a Means of Survival"   130
INTERVIEW WITH WAYNE CURTIS

"We're Just Beginning the Journey"   136
INTERVIEW WITH LILA CABBIL

"Poor People Are Not Some Exotic Breed of People; They're
Our Brothers and Sisters"   139
INTERVIEW WITH BROTHER JERRY SMITH

"There's a Narrative of the New Detroit, but It Doesn't Include
the Majority of Detroit"   142
INTERVIEW WITH PATRICK CROUCH

"We Are Trying to Build Foundational Relationships That
Transcend Any Issue"   146
INTERVIEW WITH LOTTIE SPADY

"Food Justice beyond Urban Agriculture"   149
INTERVIEW WITH LINDA CAMPBELL

CHAPTER 4. SUSPENDING DEMOCRACY IS VIOLENCE   156

Introduction   157

"Put Your Body and Put Your Voice into Debates"   163
INTERVIEW WITH TOVA PERLMUTTER

On Citywide Suffrage: "People who are undocumented are
human. They have rights"   166
INTERVIEW WITH GABRIELA ALCAZAR

The Detroit People's Platform   170

The Fight for a Community Benefits Agreement Ordinance in
Detroit   173

No Alternative? People's Plan for Restructuring   176

"We Believe in People Power"   181
INTERVIEW WITH JOSELYN FITZPATRICK HARRIS

United Nations Deems Water Shutoffs a Human
Rights Violation   183

"You Have Taxation without Representation" 186
INTERVIEW WITH LEE GADDIES

Election Reflection 188
ESSAY BY SHEA HOWELL

Detroit 193
POEM BY TAWANA "HONEYCOMB" PETTY

CHAPTER 5. GENTRIFICATION IS ONLY PART OF IT: UNDERSTANDING RACE AND DISPLACEMENT IN DETROIT 194

Introduction 195

Black Homeownership in Detroit 198
LINDA CAMPBELL, ANDREW NEWMAN,
SARA SAFRANSKY, AND TIM STALLMANN

Corporate Power and the Reinvention of Detroit 204
ADDRESS BY GLORIA HOUSE

Letter to Alden Park Towers Management 210
LETTER BY BETTY A. SCRUSE

The Campaign for the Griswold Seniors:
"If I had the money, I wouldn't move" 214
LINDA CAMPBELL, ANDREW NEWMAN,
SARA SAFRANSKY, AND TIM STALLMANN

Detroit Future City: Urban Sustainability as a Force
of Displacement 217
LINDA CAMPBELL, ANDREW NEWMAN,
SARA SAFRANSKY, AND TIM STALLMANN

The Riverfront East Congregation Initiative: "Do they have
our community's best interests at heart?" 222
INTERVIEW WITH KATHLEEN FOSTER, JEANETTE
MARBLE, AND DEBORAH WILLIAMSON

Hantz Woodlands Project 227–28
PHOTOS BY GREGG NEWSOM

Toward Land Justice: "When we stop dreaming, we have no
hope but to remain stuck in a nightmare. Dreaming . . . we
remember the taste of freedom" 231
INTERVIEW WITH AARON HANDELSMAN

"Most of the Work We Do Is Systems Change Work" 238
INTERVIEW WITH REV. JOAN ROSS

CHAPTER 6. THE RIGHT TO THE CITY 242

Introduction 243

The Right to Water 246
LINDA CAMPBELL, ANDREW NEWMAN,
SARA SAFRANSKY, AND TIM STALLMANN

Why I Choose to Block Water Shutoff Trucks 249
ESSAY BY JAMES W. PERKINSON

"How Do We Unite around Dignity?" 254
INTERVIEW WITH CHARITY HICKS

Charity Hicks: In Memoriam 257
LINDA CAMPBELL, ANDREW NEWMAN,
SARA SAFRANSKY, AND TIM STALLMANN

The Right to Environmental Justice   258
　LINDA CAMPBELL, ANDREW NEWMAN,
　SARA SAFRANSKY, AND TIM STALLMANN

"We Must Be the Voice That Says What the Change Is Going
to Be in Our Own Communities"   259
　INTERVIEW WITH RHONDA ANDERSON
　AND VINCENT MARTIN

"From the Organization of Youth, We Are Trying to Lay a
Foundation"   262
　INTERVIEW WITH WILLIAM COPELAND

Toxic Debt: The Detroit Incinerator, Municipal Bonds, and
Environmental Racism   265
　ESSAY BY JOSIAH RECTOR

The Right to Mobility   269
　LINDA CAMPBELL, ANDREW NEWMAN,
　SARA SAFRANSKY, AND TIM STALLMANN

Jericho Speech   271
　SYRI SIMPSON

The Right to Education   273
　LINDA CAMPBELL, ANDREW NEWMAN,
　SARA SAFRANSKY, AND TIM STALLMANN

Detroit Students Will Fight Back   279
　OPEN LETTER BY IMANI HARRIS

Humanizing Schooling in Detroit   281
　INTERVIEW WITH JENNY LEE

Creative Teaching: Key to Detroit School Reform   285
　ESSAY BY JANICE HALE

The Right to Live Free from Crime and Police Harassment   287
　LINDA CAMPBELL, ANDREW NEWMAN,
　SARA SAFRANSKY, AND TIM STALLMANN

"People Hold Power. Organized People Hold Power"   291
　INTERVIEW WITH TANESHA FLOWERS
　AND HERBERT JONES OF DETROIT ACTION
　COMMONWEALTH

"Reclaiming Our Souls"   293
　INTERVIEW WITH YUSEF "BUNCHY" SHAKUR

ANOTHER CITY IS POSSIBLE   296
　LINDA CAMPBELL, ANDREW NEWMAN,
　SARA SAFRANSKY, AND TIM STALLMANN

Notes   304
Sources for Selected Maps and Figures   315
Selected Bibliography   321
Contributors   326
Index   330

MAPS AND FIGURES

Red Sky's Migration Chart   16–17
Bellin Map of Detroit, 1764   17
Slavery Landmarks in Detroit   22
Traces of Slavery in Present-Day Detroit   24
Detroit and the Underground Railroad   26
Labor Struggles in Detroit   31
Detroit and Suburbs Historical Population   33
Housing Struggles in Detroit   38
HOLC Redlining map of Detroit   40
DGEI Map of Houses Deteriorating and Dilapidated, 1960   41
Race and Ethnicity in Detroit   42–43
Wealth and Poverty in Detroit   44–45
Globalization from Below   50–51
Everywhere in Michigan with at Least as Much Vacancy as Detroit, 2012   73
Uniting Detroiters Workshop Map   74–75
Land Speculation in the Feedom Freedom Neighborhood   84–85
Black Bottom, 1949   91
Black Bottom, 1956   93
Detroit Historical Land Cover, circa 1800   98–99
Great Lakes Watershed   104–5
French Ribbon Farms   120
Pingree Potato Patches   121
Thrift Gardens in 1930s Detroit   122
Detroit Urban Agriculture and Population Density   123
Black Farm Operators in the United States, 1900–2012   153
Michigan Cities under Emergency Management   162
The Vote on PA 436   165
Olympia Development Area   172
Detroit Water Department Top Unpaid Water Bills, 2014   184
Generations of Wealth Extracted from Detroit   191
Black Homeownership in Detroit, 1960–2010   199
Wayne County Mortgages Granted by Race of Home Buyer, 2007–15   200
Asian American Homeownership in Detroit, 1990–2010   202
Latinx Homeownership in Detroit, 1990–2010   203

Property Speculation in Detroit, 2016   208–9
Housing Insecurity in Detroit   212–13
DGEI Map of Displacement from the Trumbull Community   213
Reinvestment Fund Detroit Market Value Analysis   220–21
RECI Community Asset Map   225
Hantz Woodlands Project   227–28
Wayne County Tax Assessments as a Percentage of Market Value,
   2008–15   233
Race and Water Shutoffs   247
Water Shutoffs Timeline   252–53
Environmental Justice in the 48217 Zipcode   261
Asthma Rates and Polluters   266–67
M-1 Streetcar   270
School Closures   274
DGEI Map of Spaces for Adults and Youth in Fitzgerald, 1969   276
Spaces for Adults and Youth in Fitzgerald, 2014   277
Detroiters in Exile   288
Incarceration Rates in Detroit   289

We owe our first and most important thanks to the people of Detroit—some of whom appear in this book and many more who do not—whose creativity and resilience inspire the editors. We would like to pay tribute to those who made their transitions during the making of this book. Although Grace Lee Boggs, Lila Cabbil, Janice Hale, Kaleema Hasan, and Charity Hicks are not here to see the final book, their lights continue to guide us in our work. Grace, Lila, Janice, Kaleema, and Charity were all people who dedicated their lives' work to Detroiters in different ways depending on their distinct talents. We are honored to include their words and contributions in this book.

This project would not have been possible without funding from several sources. The Antipode Foundation, the Human Geography Small Grants Program, and the Wenner-Gren Foundation for Anthropological Research all funded different aspects of this project. The idea for *A People's Atlas of Detroit* was first discussed as a brainstorm at a Building Movement Detroit meeting in Detroit in 2012 and evolved into the book you are now holding only because of the tireless dedication of many people. Our editorial board members, Danielle Atkinson, Shane Bernardo, Wayne Curtis, Aaron Handelsman, Shea Howell, Carmen Malis King, Gregg Newsom, Lottie Spady, and Aaron Timlin gave their much-needed time and feedback from the very beginning, sitting in on meetings and calls and reviewing submissions. In addition, Gregg Newsom went above and beyond the call of duty as the manuscript moved into production by graciously helping with numerous last-minute requests for photographs and permissions.

In the project's very early stages, we also benefited from the feedback of Alesia Montgomery. We extend our gratitude to Heidi Bisson, who worked tirelessly to assist with administrative tasks related to the project, including transcription of interviews. Thanks also to Vanessa Marr and Tawana Petty for their assistance early on with transcription. Our mapping workshops required the cooperation of many people. We wish to thank all of those who attended the workshops as well as Oliva Dobbs, Emma Slager, and Jeremy Whiting for their technical help with cartography. Alex Hill, Emily Kutil, and Jessica McInchak all provided helpful cartographic assistance and graciously shared access to essential data. Ahmina Maxey provided valuable insights on doing "one-on-ones" as part of the Uniting Detroiters project. At different stages of the Uniting Detroiters project, Isra El-beshir, Jimmy Johnson, Ayana Rubio, and Dennis Sloan all gave their time and energy to collecting interviews and performing a myriad range of tasks.

We also express our thanks to several institutions who gave us permission to include historical maps and images in the book: the Bentley Historical Library at the University of Michigan, the Bibliothèque Nationale de France, the Burton Historical Collection of the Detroit Public Library, the Detroit Historical Society, and the Walter P. Reuther Library of Labor and Urban Affairs at Wayne State University. We would particularly like to thank Shirley Sorrels and the Museum of Ojibwa Culture in St. Ignace, Michigan, for allowing us to reproduce James Red Sky's migration chart in this book and Bob Vogel for his assistance with editing the file.

We would like to express our appreciation of the support of colleagues in the Department of Geography at the University of North Carolina–Chapel Hill, the Human and Organizational Development Department at Vanderbilt University, at Research Action Design, and in the Department of Anthropology at Wayne State University. At Vanderbilt, Tessa Eidelman and Ashley Bachelder provided helpful editorial support. We are also appreciative of the support given by the national Building Movement Project team: Sean Thomas Breitfeld, Frances Kunreuther, and Caroline McAndrews. We would like to thank the members of Counter-Cartographies Collective, especially Liz Mason-Deese and the Cobarrubias-Casas family. Liz Ault, Mike Dolan Fliss, Libby McClure, and Pavithra Vasudevan also gave valuable feedback at various stages.

We are indebted to those who reviewed the manuscript: Laura Pulido provided invaluable feedback on an early draft; the manuscript also benefited immensely from the generous and constructive criticism of two anonymous reviewers. In addition, we wish to thank our editor Kathy Wildfong at Wayne State University Press for believing in this project in its early stages and for seeing it through. Jude Grant, Kristin Harpster, Sara Leone, Katrina Noble, and Rachel Ross provided deft editorial and graphic design guidance, for which we are grateful. We also wish to thank Ceylan Akturk for her help and support with the permissions process for this book.

Finally, we thank our families. We relied on the emotional support, love, laughter, and sometimes editing assistance of Shaira Daya, Oskar, and Shane Ali; Noah Rubin-Blose and Zach Aliotta; and Ashley Carse, June, and Eli.

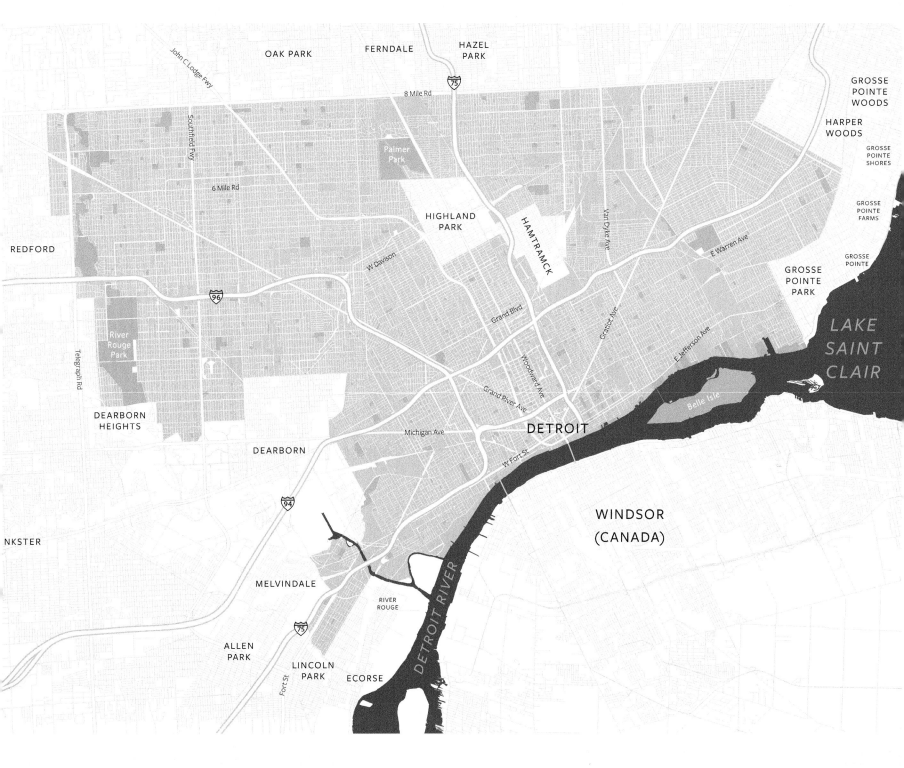

INTRODUCTION

LINDA CAMPBELL, ANDREW NEWMAN,
SARA SAFRANSKY, AND TIM STALLMANN

Detroit is a city of monumental boulevards and sprawling neighborhoods, interwoven by lives and bound with memories both proud and painful. This book tells the stories of people and places involved in political battles central to the future of Detroit and urban America. Narrating the lived experience of these struggles has never been more crucial.

In twenty-first-century Detroit, a powerful mythology threatens to crowd out the stories of many residents. In this myth, Detroit is an urban wilderness, a postapocalyptic landscape, a blank slate waiting for heroic entrepreneurs to discover, develop, and redeem it. The need to rebuke such narratives is important. Even more urgent is the question of what kinds of stories should replace them.

The racial overtones of such mythmaking loom large. Detroit is the nation's largest Black majority city, with an 83 percent African American population. Despite a dramatic loss of residents since the mid-twentieth century, Detroit remains home to 670,000 residents—and ranks consistently among the top twenty largest US cities.[1] That Detroit is continually rendered as a no-man's-land and new frontier waiting to be claimed, tamed, and resettled speaks volumes on America's stark racial divides and to an unrelenting anti-Blackness that once shaped historical disinvestment from the city and now drives its supposed renaissance.[2]

There is a large power differential between mythmakers and most Detroiters. Indeed, the myths themselves can ultimately shape the realities with which many Detroiters are forced to contend. Some of the cases discussed in this book, such as Hantz Woodlands and the Detroit Future City plan, can be thought of as struggles over whether Detroit will be *made into* an urban wilderness. In other examples, such as the redevelopment of Downtown, the Cass Corridor, and the North End, Detroiters—including many of our contributors—are contesting who benefits economically, politically, and culturally from urban revitalization. One of the greatest myths this book seeks to dispel is the idea that Detroiters are absent, silent, or disengaged from efforts to improve their city. In fact, Detroiters have been engaged in preserving the vitality of their own neighborhoods—often with little or no external support—long before real estate developers began to promote themselves as agents of the city's "revitalization."

The *Atlas* is written as a response to this crisis of representation, understood in both its aesthetic and democratic senses. It seeks to counter myths about the city and transform the way we think about governance and political power. Our focus as editors is to highlight the analyses and experiences of Detroiters and lift up grassroots responses to racism, postindustrial decline, and political abandonment.

The *Atlas* is organized around crucial problems facing residents, including governance, infrastructure, land, housing, education, the food system, and the environment. Our selection of topics pertains to broad issues facing cities around the world and, at the same time, forms one small part of a strategy to build more neighborhood-based power in Detroit itself. Following in the tradition of action research and militant cartography, this book aims to both chart and help build movements for social justice in the city.[3]

The *Atlas* has its origins in a participatory research project known as Uniting Detroiters. Uniting Detroiters was founded in 2012 during a period of intense political and economic restructuring for insolvent cities across the United States. Already reeling from deindustrialization, Detroit, like other predominantly African American cities, was hit hard by predatory lending associated with the 2008 subprime mortgage crisis. Between 2000 and 2010, the city lost 25 percent of its population. Foreclosures and out-migration combined with the downward pressures of federal funding cuts further hollowed out a decimated municipal tax base. By April 2012, the city had surrendered its fiscal autonomy with a Consent Agreement that gave the State of Michigan sweeping power over its budget. In an unsuccessful attempt to stave off emergency management and bankruptcy, the city began shedding public property, ratcheting up tax foreclosures, privatizing and cutting back public service delivery, and aggressively recruiting private investment. This led to the eviction of low-income residents and an increasingly divided city. In 2013, Detroit became the largest US city to ever declare bankruptcy.

Emerging within this context, the Uniting Detroiters project had three overarching goals: first, to challenge dominant narratives about development; second, to use collective research to strengthen the organizing infrastructure of the city's long-vibrant grassroots sector; and third, to reassert residents' roles as active participants in the development process.[4] To this end, our group, made up of activists, community leaders, scholars, students, and other residents, conducted sixty-six interviews and oral histories with individuals involved in social justice organizations and neighborhood groups. Our aim was to document and understand how Detroiters were analyzing and responding to urban restructuring. Everyone involved approached the interviews with the aim of identifying commonalities, cultivating relationships, and fostering coalitions.

As part of the project, we hosted a series of workshops to discuss the emerging development agenda in Detroit, its relationship to national and global processes, and local challenges to and opportunities for transformative social change. We saw the workshops, which over 120 residents attended, as a place for people to engage in collective analysis, grapple with hard questions about resistance, and expand the kinds of grassroots political formations that the new conjuncture required.

The *Atlas* exists thanks to the participation of over sixty contributors. Each chapter is a collage of interviews, maps, poems, photographs, and essays, as well as found objects, such as neighborhood bulletins, letters, and flyers. Many of the interviews were conducted and organized with the help of students at Wayne State University and residents with connections to the organizations profiled in this book.[5] From its inception, the *Atlas* has been a project of collective analysis and generous engagement. We've tried to maintain this spirit by approaching our role as editors as an opportunity to think with contributors. We invite readers to do the same by critically evaluating, debating, and extending the propositions put forth herein.[6] Ultimately, we hope that the *Atlas* will help illuminate the troubling times we are living through today and contribute to imagining new political possibilities.

Many of those who collaborated on the *Atlas* felt that access to important data unevenly distributed across race and class lines, making it difficult for many people in the city to know how Detroit was being represented and reinvented, let alone participate in the process. As a result, from the beginning many of us were adamant about the need to create a tangible book instead of an online project. This concern with medium was, in part, due to a recognition that many Detroiters lacked high-speed internet access. Even with the popularity of social media and prevalence of smartphones (and as web-based mapping projects in Detroit have proliferated), the digital divide regarding access to online data and maps still parallels racial and class-based divides.[7]

URBAN REVANCHISM

In 1996, geographer Neil Smith coined the phrase "urban revanchism," which refers to a violence-infused style of right-wing "revenge" politics, often with populist roots, that can emerge in direct response to visible political gains made by Black people, people of color, women, LGBTQ, and other historically oppressed groups. Revanchist politics, as Smith describes it, is embodied by "a revengeful and reactionary viciousness against various populations accused of stealing the city from [them]."[8]

Smith initially used *revanchism* to describe New York under the control of then mayor Rudy Giuliani, but revanchist shifts in American politics date at least to the era of Reconstruction, when elite whites stoked popular resentment over African American political gains with the aim of taking back power, giving rise to Jim Crow. Since we first began the *Atlas* project, we've witnessed right-wing revanchist politics grow into one of the key political dynamics of the present moment: locally, nationally under President Donald Trump, and, indeed, globally. This book suggests that activists, policy makers, and urbanites around the world have much to learn from the political inventiveness demonstrated by Detroiters when confronted by urban revanchism compounded by austerity-driven cutbacks.

Detroit can be considered a "movement town" historically shaped by a broad spectrum of mobilizations that included working-class people, indigenous communities, African Americans, LGBTQ people, and diverse immigrant groups. Emergency management policies represent a direct assault on the idea of the city as an inclusive, local democracy shaped by the distinct needs of the people who have long called it home. Detroit's loss of political autonomy at the behest of a Republican-led state government was understood across the political spectrum as a powerful symbolic act owing to the city's historical status as a bulwark of institutionalized Black political power since the 1970s. The manner in which emergency management legislation was pushed through was marked by a revanchist tendency to replace consensus politics with the undiluted imposition of political will: despite being overturned by voters in a statewide referendum, emergency management legislation lived on through the use of a procedural maneuver. Once installed, emergency managers governed by issuing orders that disproportionately impacted people of color and low-income communities. The material consequences included, but were by no means limited to, the emergence of water crises in Detroit and Flint.

While emergency management was controversial at the time, major media outlets' framing of these policies echoed the opinion of prominent Detroit real estate developer Dan Gilbert, who said, "As hard as it is to sort of suspend democracy for a short period of time if you will, my view is let's get it over with, let's get it done, let's stop talking about it, let's go through the pain and then move forward, and I think it will fade into the background."[9] Such revenge politics are particularly significant in Detroit where public institutions, local memory, and sense of place have been profoundly shaped by progressive social movements for much of the city's history.

URBAN COMMONS AND THE RIGHT TO THE CITY

Scholars who study protest politics in cities have developed and debated two important concepts to better understand social movements: the urban commons and the right to the city. Despite differing philosophical backgrounds, the two concepts describe the way urbanites make use of the physical and social terrain of the city as a way of claiming political control. The urban commons refers to sites in a city where shared control and decision-making is practiced in a variety of forms.[10] Whether by intentional political choice, such as the establishment of cooperatives, or more casual, customary uses of space, such as gardening, "commons" can have the effect of replacing an individualized, market-value logic with an economic rationale oriented toward community control of urban resources, including land. The right to the city, a concept developed by French philosopher and sociologist Henri Lefebvre, describes a process by which people re-appropriate urban spaces in order to shift the social function of the city from a profit-making engine for elites to instead serve the direct, everyday needs of residents.[11]

For all the popularity these concepts have enjoyed with scholars of social movements and radical politics, the case of Detroit illuminates the degree to which their scholarly treatment could gain from a deeper engagement with race and racism.[12] For example, in the domain of urban agriculture, well-intentioned projects focus on establishing forms of commons but are often led by white, middle-class newcomers who ignore questions of racial inequality at the heart of how land is procured, purchased, and redefined. At times, such DIY efforts enact white supremacist "frontier culture." This term has been used by anthropologist Anna Tsing to describe a worldview held by privileged newcomers that asks "participants to see a landscape that doesn't exist, at least not yet. It must continually erase old residents' rights to create its wild and empty spaces where discovering resources, not stealing them, is possible."[13] As a result, some efforts to redefine Detroit's future through new forms of land use—notably the Detroit Future City plan, discussed in chapter 5—reproduce patterns of dispossession rooted in settler colonialism, by indulging in a vision of the city as a frontier waiting to be exploited.

During discussions that took place as part of the Uniting Detroiters project, it became clear that, while scholarly conceptions of the right to the city and urban commons were helpful for understanding Detroit, many Detroiters had ideas that developed these concepts further.[14] *Atlas* contributors understand land, governance, and housing as extensions of long-term struggles against racial inequalities and for liberation. They challenge color-blind usage of the commons, contending that if anti-racism was not central to discussions of seemingly technocratic domains such as bus routes and the management of water systems, then racial inequalities would be reproduced if not worsened. It was thus no coincidence that catastrophes such as the Flint water crisis and the Detroit water shutoffs (declared an affront to human rights by the United Nations) occurred during periods when residents were conspicuously removed from the democratic process through emergency management.

CHALLENGING RACIAL CAPITALISM

One of the most important goals of the *Atlas* is to highlight and explain current visions for radical change emerging in Detroit. Those visions—and the impetus for them—can only be understood by situating the current wave of revanchism as a backlash against prior gains made by Black liberation movements, as well as part of a longer history of racial capitalism, colonialism, and dispossession.

Our analysis follows in the footsteps of political scientist and Black studies scholar Cedric Robinson, who saw racism as a fundamental part of capitalism. Racism is neither a layer of economic exploitation nor an unanticipated byproduct of market dynamics. Rather, the history of Detroit reveals racism and capitalism to be fundamentally intertwined and synergistic forces.[15] Racial capitalism emerges from white supremacy as a

pattern of exploitation that is visible in American (and Detroit's) history from the beginnings of settler colonialism to the present period and remains a driving logic of accumulation strategies, particularly in the foreclosure crisis of the late 2000s.[16]

In a similar fashion, the concept of racialized citizenship is crucial to how we understand two processes: the uneven distribution of rights in a society among people based on their membership in racialized groups and the way people draw on their experiences of systemic racism in order to organize against it. The leadership of people from groups that have been historical victims of racial oppression is also an indispensable aspect of organizing against racialized citizenship.

The current wave of revanchism sweeping the country requires us to engage in deep collective analysis about the history of dispossession and oppression on which the United States was founded. At the same time, it requires us to attend to the radical imagination: how past and present liberation movements have envisioned anti-racist and anti-capitalist futures. In particular, it demands attention to those struggling to survive at the margins who offer forms of organizing social life in ways that counter liberal parables of property, personhood, and justice. Finally, it requires that we practice an alternative ethics of care and create infrastructures to support new ways of being in this world. The *Atlas* is an offering to this project.

A PEOPLE'S ATLAS

Our use of the terms *people's* and *atlas* demands some explanation. We want to be clear at the outset that the *Atlas* does not include all peoples of Detroit, nor is it an atlas in the conventional sense. As explained above, the book captures a moment in the early 2010s, when Detroit was experiencing a dramatic political-economic and territorial reordering. It serves as both an archive of voices and an analysis of the resistance that emerged during this period. Yet by no means does it highlight all the people and organizations that were involved at this time in collective analysis, resistance, and action. There are many people, groups, and organizations beyond those included in the book that are doing important work in Detroit. Notably, this *Atlas* does not delve deeply into present-day indigenous organizing. Moreover, neither the struggles of immigrant communities in Detroit, Hamtramck, and Dearborn nor the region's rich history of gay, lesbian, queer, and trans culture get more than passing discussion.

Thus, our use of the term *people's atlas* is not intended to signal an exhaustive or comprehensive guide to the peoples of Detroit. Rather it's meant to reference a particular set of struggles, from the perspective of residents, organizers, and activists in the city, following the approach of writing "history from below," per E. P. Thompson, or a "people's history," as popularized by Howard Zinn.[17] The *Atlas* documents and analyzes how different forms of struggle, subjugated knowledges, and visions for the future are articulated in complex ways during a particular historical moment. In this way, it offers a multivocal rather than singular narrative.

Our usage of *atlas* also differs in some important ways from how the term is typically invoked. Maps form an important component of the book, as we discuss below, but the *Atlas* is more than a book of illustrations. At the time we began conceptualizing this book, mapping and spatial data had become key points of engagement for people who were struggling to survive in the city.[18] The *Atlas* emerged as a response to this dynamic. The contributors to this volume want to have a say in how Detroit is being reimagined and "put on the map" in new ways. In this regard, the *Atlas* is a new type of guide for Detroit (and other cities across the globe that are also facing revanchism) to chart its way forward during a period fraught with danger but also filled with possibilities for better, more just societies.

MAPPING AND POWER

Maps exercise a powerful grip on our perceptions of reality. Consider how maps contribute to the authoritativeness of a variety of documents: urban plans, guides to cities, social science studies, history textbooks, real estate surveys, and military plans. The traditional importance of mapping in these endeavors—and the close links between the history of cartography and the rise of territorial nation-states and empires—is no accident.

The power of mapping, especially in the era of geographic information systems, or GIS, is often linked to scientific precision. However, maps have been a source of authority since before the rise of modern computerized mapping. Mapmaking, in the Western cartographic tradition, is not just a depiction of a space but also a tool to define territory and assert governance and control over it.[19]

During the same period in which Detroit became associated with twenty-first-century "frontier culture," the city experienced a mapmaking boom. From large-scale mapping efforts supported by major foundations and city governments such as Detroit Works/Detroit Future City and the Detroit Blight Removal Task Force, to professional mapping outfits such as Loveland Technologies, to nonprofits like Data Driven Detroit to efforts such as *DETROITography*, Property Praxis, the Riverfront East Congregational Initiative, the We the People of Detroit Community Research Collective, and our own *Atlas*, the city was being mapped from a plethora of perspectives, not infrequently in conflict with one another.

In the *Atlas*, we try to redirect the "cartographic gaze" back toward the priorities and projects of neighborhood-based groups. At times, we have developed or included maps made by others in direct rebuttal to politically influential mapmaking projects. Other maps are meant to cast light on the harsh realities of segregation, income inequality, and racist foreclosure practices that are frequently avoided in many policy-related discussions of the city. At its core, the *Atlas* calls for a fundamental reordering of the way we perceive and know cities via maps. Where possible, the maps here bring the everyday life experience and tacit knowledge of Detroiters to bear on GIS data emerging from satellite views, deed books, and government censuses. In a similar vein, we have attempted to map a multiplicity of overlapping representations of the city. Mapping Detroit from the perspective of its watersheds, of children, or of Underground Railroad routes highlights the diversity of experiences, struggles, and histories that makes Detroit distinct.

In this respect, our approach is heavily influenced by the work of the Detroit Geographical Expedition and Institute (DGEI) in the 1960s and '70s. In the late 1960s, Wayne State University professor William Bunge and Detroit resident Gwendolyn Warren, along with many others, cocreated the DGEI, which combined evening college-credit classes, hosted in the neighborhood, with data gathering, conversations, and mapping about the issues most pressing to residents at the time.[20] DGEI participants developed a nuanced analysis of the city through the lenses of race and class, paying particular attention to the conflicting geographies of Black inner-city children, on the one hand, and white suburban commuters, on the other. Their work was initially collected in a series of "Field Notes" and reports and, later, in *Fitzgerald: Geography of a Revolution*, a book that, much like this one, combines maps, photos, and firsthand accounts to detail a century of transformations in one square mile in Detroit leading up to the rebellion of 1967.

ORGANIZATION OF THE BOOK

Our book has an unusual structure, combining interview excerpts, maps, essays, poems, timelines, and images. This format conveys not only a critical analysis of a key juncture in Detroit's history but also the affective and emotional landscape of a city amid profound political struggle.

The contributors come from many walks of life and include members of neighborhood block clubs, activists, farmers, artists, students, nonprofit and city government workers, clergy members, school board members, educators, and academics. While some contributors submitted essays for this volume, in other cases, we favored interviews as a way to highlight the degree to which analysis can emerge from lived experience. Others, given their talents and personal approaches, opted to share poetry, memoirs, and photography.

This book is organized around six main body chapters. Chapter 1, "Detroit and the Long Struggle for Liberation," excavates three centuries of regional history to illuminate how changing formations of racial citizenship have shaped the city. The chapter focuses not only on oppression but also struggles against inequality and visions for social alternatives.

In chapter 2, "This Land Is Ours: Toward a New Urban Commons," we adopt a ground-level view of Detroit's contemporary landscapes and highlight the meanings that land holds for residents. We demonstrate how they have developed systems to care for the land, their neighborhoods, and one another, even in circumstances in which they have no legal rights to the land or housing. In such cases, land can operate as part of an urban commons through practices emphasizing care. The chapter suggests the right to the city is not simply about accessing the right to own land or property, but it also comprises the right to define the cultural, economic, and political significance of land.

In chapter 3, "Growing a Revolution," we highlight urban farming as one of the key ways that Detroiters have been repurposing vacant land over the last several decades. Urban agriculture has received a great deal of attention as a radical way to reimagine a city. However, urban agriculture is actually a heterogeneous and contested sphere in Detroit. Some urban agriculture projects are rooted in the history of Black liberation movements, other projects aim to exploit cheap land prices for profit, and others are steeped in back-to-the-land nostalgia and frontier culture. As a result, urban agriculture can easily become a way in which white privilege and racial inequalities are reproduced and reinscribed on the landscape. In contrast, urban agriculture projects fulfill their radical political potential when projects are planned as a form of urban commons to directly confront racial capitalism in Detroit. As the words of contributors demonstrate, one of the most significant yields of urban agriculture in Detroit has been a robust conversation about race, inequality, privilege, and food justice.

In chapter 4, "Suspending Democracy Is Violence," we analyze struggles over governance and finances between the State of Michigan and the City of Detroit and other majority African American cities in Michigan, notably Flint. We push the analysis of the city-state dynamic beyond critiques of neoliberal austerity and argue that the policies amount to a revanchist assault steeped in an ideology formed by a decades-old racial and urban/suburban-rural divide. Revanchism in Michigan ultimately foreshadowed a broader American dynamic, but the responses by Detroiters suggest there are myriad ways that people can not only protest and resist but also establish alternative approaches to governing their communities.

Chapter 5, "Gentrification Is Only Part of It: Understanding Race and Displacement in Detroit," moves beyond the gentrification debate, which has been a dominant paradigm for understanding conflicts related to urban change since the 1980s. While gentrification is a visible and disruptive force for Detroiters in some areas of the city, it is neither the only nor the most important factor behind displacement. The contributors highlight foreclosures, nonprofit driven development gone awry, and large-scale property acquisitions that resemble the global phenomenon of "land grabs" more than classic urban redevelopment politics. In response, some Detroit groups have developed a land justice framework that goes beyond an anti-gentrification focus by emphasizing the racialized history of liberal property and the political importance of decommodifying land.

Chapter 6 is titled "The Right to the City," a concept often invoked by movements attempting to claim, hold, and redefine space in contested cities. By focusing on residents' plans and mobilizations to reclaim and rethink public services in the city, including water, transit, and schools, we bring the concept back to the Lefebvrian ideal of the city in which residents redirect urban energies and resources to enrich their own lives and communities instead of the economic agendas of elites. However, in contrast to Lefebvre-inspired approaches, we focus on racial injustice and demonstrate how the definition and claiming of rights emerges out of the experience of Black liberation and anti-racism politics. We conclude by using Detroit as a platform to think through urban politics in other contexts around the globe. The book ends by revisiting the voices of many of our contributors to offer a synthesis and chart a path forward to the future.

1

DETROIT AND THE LONG STRUGGLE FOR LIBERATION

Speramus Meliora; Resurget Cineribus. This motto, found on the City of Detroit's seal, is Latin for "We hope for better things; it shall rise from the ashes." The motto has its origins in the fire of 1805, which destroyed nearly all the wooden structures in what was then a settlement of six hundred people. But it also seems to foreshadow moments throughout Detroit's modern history, from episodes of civil unrest in 1943 and 1967 to current efforts to reimagine the postindustrial metropolis as a fundamentally new type of city.

At times, the desire to reimagine Detroit has been driven by radical critiques of social injustice. At other moments, it has acted as a political form of erasure. Current narratives emphasize entrepreneurship, creativity, and hard work as the ingredients that will allow Detroit to rise again from the ashes. Such stories not only obscure existing inhabitants and competing visions for the city's future, but they also erase the past. The stories we tell about places—and what we collectively decide to remember and forget—matter immensely for how we're able to read the contemporary cultural landscape. They matter for how we make sense of inequality. And they matter for how we imagine, design, plan, and fight for the future.

This chapter looks at Detroit's history with specific attention to social struggles that emerged in response to shifting dynamics of power. The chapter's historical scope is broad, extending from the precolonial era to the present. Rather than a comprehensive history, our aim is to offer a historical perspective on key forces that have given rise to and continue to shape the types of collective action highlighted in subsequent chapters.

This chapter consists of six sections: the first section focuses on the colonization of Detroit; the second, the Underground Railroad; the third, labor struggles; the fourth, housing struggles; and the fifth, activism in the 1960s. The last section is an intergenerational conversation about social transformation between DJ and music producer Sterling Toles and longtime Detroit activist Grace Lee Boggs. Each section is prefaced with a timeline that outlines events that are covered in more depth in subsequent pages.

We encourage the reader to approach the material presented in this chapter as constellations open to multiple readings. While a number of patterns can be identified, we emphasize four overarching themes: racialized capitalism and citizenship, erasure, globalization from below, and the importance of space and place in liberation struggles.

The first theme explores race as a fundamental framework through which colonization and capitalism take form; this is the idea that racism is not a by-product of capitalism but rather fundamental to its evolution. The chapter highlights the violence and racialized dispossession that have always accompanied the making of private property and capitalism in the United States. It underscores the central role of the state in perpetuating both the racialization of space and people. Throughout Detroit's history, racialized citizenship has provided a justification for dispossessing people of land and wealth as well as physically controlling their bodies and labor. The history of labor struggles in Detroit points to how race was used to undermine worker solidarity. At the same time, the chapter chronicles how people have responded to dispossession over time. Much of what makes Detroit unique comes from these responses, including the city's critical role in the Underground Railroad, its centrality in the American labor movement, and its importance as a wellspring of radical thought, especially with regard to Black politics.

The chapter also shows how the erasure of Blacks and other people of color that we see in development discourses today (as discussed in the Introduction) has roots in the persistent erasure of indigenous societies that began during the settler colonial era. When French settlers arrived in Detroit, they found villages, crops, sacred landmarks, trail networks, and indigenous societies in transformation and conflict. To redefine the region as the edge of civilization, generations of settlers erased the traces of people who inhabited the area for centuries. This happened through genocide and forced removal. It also happened through mapping. Racist violence and cultural erasure were enabled by characterizing the land as uninhabited wilderness waiting to be culturally redefined and settled by a new population. This legacy lives on, evidenced in the oft-used description of Detroit as a postindustrial frontier being settled by "urban pioneers," while the city's nearly seven hundred thousand residents are viewed as either nonexistent or passively waiting for help from outsiders.

The third theme of this chapter is what we call globalization from below. The global economic history of Detroit is well documented from the era of the French fur trade to the automotive industry. However, what's often left out of popular narratives is how responses to dispossession and racialization were also global. Not only did activists in Detroit analyze oppression from a global perspective, but their organizational networks often extended to the national and international scales, too. A few key examples include Underground Railroad conductors and Detroit's Colored Vigilant Committee, which maintained correspondence with abolitionists outside the United States; labor activists who coordinated strikes nationwide and traded information internationally; and Black radicals who faced a situation of internal colonialism in solidarity with decolonization movements across the world.

The last theme that unites this chapter is the importance of everyday space and place in activism and dreams of liberation. While early colonial maps of Detroit depicted in this chapter erased existing inhabitants and their claims to land, property, and territory, the chapter shows how people also always responded to spatial inequalities by negotiating their surroundings in ways that aided their survival. For example, the chapter points to how resistance movements have long cultivated the spaces and networks that we call commons in Detroit—from Native American land use along the straits where Detroit is now located, to Underground Railroad depots, union halls, and study groups.[1] An examination of these alternative claims to space offers insights into other possible ways of being in relationship to land, space, and one another that do not reinforce dispossession, domination, and ownership and that might allow for what Black studies scholar and cultural geographer Katherine McKittrick calls "more humanely workable geographies."[2]

Many of the Detroit activists profiled in this book have dedicated their lives to cultivating such geographies. The chapter culminates with a conversation between Sterling Toles and Grace Lee Boggs. In that section, we reflect on Grace Lee and her husband James (Jimmy) Boggs's lifework of public intellectualism and activism.

Grace Lee and Jimmy Boggs used to routinely ask, "What time is it on the clock of the world?"[3] In responding, they imagined three thousand years of human history on a clock. Every minute equaled fifty years. Decolonial struggles in the 1950s and 1960s were only thirty seconds old. The civil rights movement happened only fifteen seconds ago. Their point was that the present moment is shaped by human responses to structural conditions over thousands of years, including consent to state policies, rebellions, and the small actions that make up everyday life.

What time is it on the clock of the world? Their provocation challenges us to take a long view of history. It reminds us that because things are constantly changing, we should not assume that progressive ideas in one era will be revolutionary in the next. Instead, we must continuously reevaluate how we got here and where we want to go. In the process, we must find ways of becoming more human by advancing our creativity, consciousness, and sense of social responsibility.

THE COLONIZATION OF DETROIT

Christopher Columbus "discovers" the Americas, starting a rapid decline of the indigenous population over the next two hundred years owing to war, exposure to diseases from Europe, enslavement, and famine.

Until 1650, the Assistaronnon group (likely Algonquian) occupy much of what becomes Michigan's Lower Peninsula and the western part of Upper Canada.

Iroquois Wars between the French and the Iroquois begin and last until 1701, when the Grande Paix (Great Peace) is signed in Montreal by representatives from Native American tribes, the French, and the English. The Iroquois Wars, also known as the Beaver Wars, were a series of brutal conflicts in which the Iroquois Confederation, led by the Mohawk tribe, fought Algonquian tribes with the goal of becoming the central middlemen in the French fur trade.

The Virginia colonial assembly rules that mixed-race children will be classified as slave or free based on the race of their mother.

Antoine de la Mothe Cadillac and his party land at "Détroit" (a derivation of the French *de troit*, which means "the strait"). Native American tribes, including Wyandot, Potawatomi, and Odawa found villages next to Detroit. Miami and Ojibwe reside nearby. The French fur trade expands west and northwest.

1492   **1600**   **1641**   **1662**   **1701**

1502   **1607**   **1664**   **1676**   **1750**

The first African slaves are imported to the Americas.

Jamestown, the first English colony in the Americas, is settled. In early colonial times, notions of difference are based primarily on religious beliefs and class but not race. While differences in custom, culture, and physical appearance among Africans, Native Americans, and European settlers were salient in the early colonies, the concept of separate, fixed, and legally defined "races" of humans does not emerge until later in the century and is not fully developed until the heyday of scientific racism in the eighteenth and nineteenth centuries.

The Maryland colonial legislature passes a law classifying all Black persons as chattel slaves, one of the first codifications of race into law.

After Bacon's Rebellion in Virginia, in which European indentured servants and enslaved Africans formed alliances, Virginia lawmakers begin to divide groups by "black" and "white." Whiteness is increasingly linked with new forms of status; African ancestry, with hereditary bondage.

French authorities conduct the first census in Detroit, counting 450 free citizens and 33 enslaved people. They do not distinguish between indigenous and African slaves. Between 1780 and 1790, nearly 100 indigenous people were enslaved in Detroit.

A confederation of indigenous tribes under Ottawa Chief Pontiac launch Pontiac's Rebellion against British forces in Detroit. After two years, the British make concessions to end the conflict but retain their claim to Ohio territories.

1763

The Declaration of Independence is adopted by the Second Continental Congress, declaring that the thirteen colonies have no allegiance to the British Crown.
  On the Natural Varieties of Mankind is published, laying a foundation for scientific claims to be made about white superiority. Its author, naturalist Johann Blumenbach, proposes a racial pyramid of five human types, with "Caucasians" at the top.

1775

The Northwest Ordinance prohibits the extension of slavery in the Northwest Territories, which would become Indiana, Illinois, Ohio, Michigan, and Wisconsin. It is the first anti-slavery legislation in North America. However, the status of existing slaves is unchanged. Any move to end slavery is also thwarted by the signing of the Constitution later that year and the "Great Compromise," which involves allowing slavery in the South and promising not to interfere with the slave trade for twenty years.

1787

Representatives of the United States and the Ottawa, Chippewa, Wyandot, and Potawatomi Nations sign the Treaty of Detroit, which cedes a large swath of land in what is now southeast Michigan and northwest Ohio.
  Augustus Woodward, chief justice of the Michigan Territory, rules in favor of escaped slaves Peter and Hannah Denison who sued their former enslaver, Catherine Tucker, for their children's freedom. Woodward's ruling lays the groundwork for the eventual abolition of slavery in the Michigan Territory. When Michigan becomes part of the United States in 1837, its first constitution prohibits slavery.

1807

The US Congress enacts the Civilization Fund Act with an annual budget of $10,000. It funds partnerships between the federal government and missionaries to establish schools aimed at "civilizing" Native children and forced them to adopt Christian practices. Five years later, in 1824, the Bureau of Indian Affairs is established to oversee the fund and implementation of its programs.

1819

1764

Jacques-Nicolas Bellin publishes his *Petit Atlas Maritime*, which includes the first published map of Detroit. It demonstrates the colonial mind-set at the time, which imagined areas beyond the settlement of Detroit as empty despite being occupied by indigenous people.

1785

Congress adopts the Land Ordinance, which dictates that land parcels in the Northwest Territories should be surveyed, parceled, and sold according to the "New England township system," without regard to Native Americans already living in those lands.

1795

Following the Battle of Fallen Timbers, Native groups cede land around the fort of Detroit to the US government as part of the Treaty of Greenville. The newly established treaty line set a boundary between Native American territory and lands where European Americans could settle, even if settlers often end up breaching it. It also establishes the "annuity" system whereby the federal government gives money and supplies yearly to tribes.

1812

The United States and Great Britain fight in the War of 1812. A diverse force of Native Americans led by the Shawnee chief Tecumseh joined the British to lay siege to Fort Detroit. There, despite being outnumbered by the US Army, they strategically used Brigadier General William Hull's fear of the Native Americans gathered there to deceive him into surrendering Detroit without a shot being fired. Detroit would not be recaptured by the Americans until the following year.

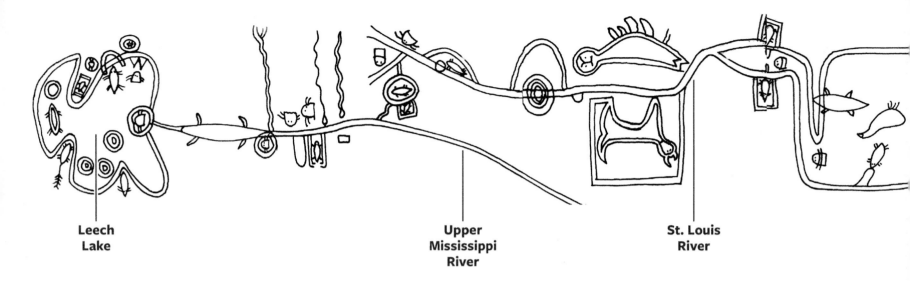

**Leech
Lake**

**Upper
Mississippi
River**

**St. Louis
River**

Red Sky's Migration Chart

This image is an adaption of a display from the Museum of Ojibwa Culture in St. Ignace, Michigan. The editors wish to thank the museum for sharing the background story associated with the map and for allowing us to photograph it.

The Great Lakes region has long been a crossroads for diverse Native American societies. The Anishinaabeg, who include the Odawa, Ojibwa, and Potawatomi, are one of these groups. This illustration, created by James Red Sky, is based on a birch bark scroll, or *wiigwaasabak*, that was approximately ten feet in length. Read right to left, it depicts a version of the migration story of the Anishinaabeg from an ancestral homeland along the Atlantic Ocean to several places that have large Anishinaabeg communities today, including Ontario, Michigan, and Minnesota. According to *The Sacred Scrolls of the Southern Ojibway* by Selwyn Dewdney, this migration chart does not depict Detroit, which is south of the route. However, some accounts emphasize multiple migrations and routes that include Lake Erie, Lower Michigan, and the Detroit River. Regardless of the paths taken, the lands that would later be called Detroit and its waterways have long been important to the trade and livelihood of the Anishinaabeg. The chart depicts not only a historical journey but also the waterways of the Great Lakes and Upper Midwest. Thus, the chart resembles a map in that it depicts specific landmarks, but it also tells a dynamic story of people moving across a landscape over time while forming relationships with particular places of importance. The migration chart is a reminder that what we choose to map—and the making of maps themselves—is based on cultural and political assumptions.

Bellin Map of Detroit, 1764

The Bellin map of Detroit, created in 1764 for Jacques-Nicolas Bellin, after an earlier survey by Gaspard-Joseph Chaussegros de Léry, is the first published plan of Detroit. It is a striking demonstration of how early colonial cartographers imagined the world. Bellin conveys his understanding of white settlement as the arrival of civilization through the careful attention he gives to enclosures around land claims, anchorages for ships, and above all, the fort. A symbol of civilization itself, the fort represented safety from all that lay beyond its walls, including the unknown wilderness, native peoples, and the threat of competing colonial powers. Within the walls, the fort conveys a social ideal, embodied by the well-ordered street grid, the

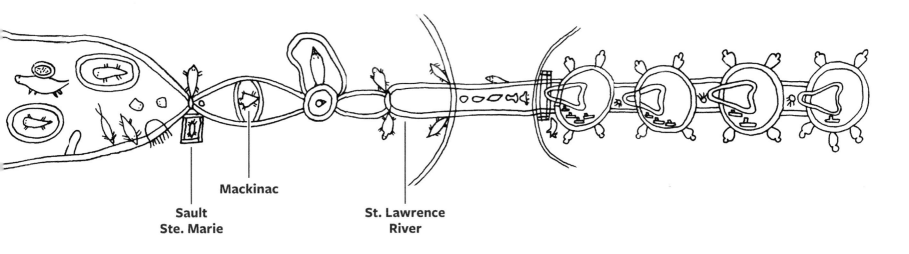

Mackinac

**Sault
Ste. Marie**

**St. Lawrence
River**

regimentation of military life, combat pre-
paredness, and the church, represented here by
A. *Logement du Commandant* (the command-
er's quarters), C. *l'Église* (the church), and D.
Magasin á Poudre (the gunpowder magazine).
As Red Sky's Migration Chart (pictured above)
suggests, indigenous ideas about the landscape often did not conform to the mind-set
of colonial mapmakers. Indeed, at the time of
the earliest encounters with the French, there
was an indigenous holy shrine located in the
rough vicinity of the area marked *la carrière*
(the quarry) downriver from Detroit (likely
near the present town of Riverview, Michigan).
Upon being discovered by two French priests,
François Dollier de Casson and René Bréhant
de Galinée, in 1670, the stone shrine was destroyed as idolatry and cast in the river.

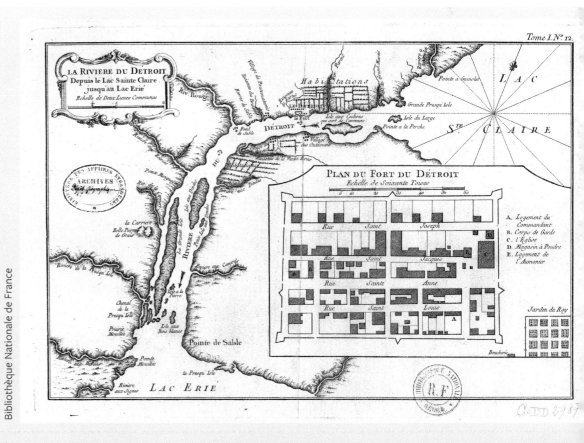

SLAVERY AND THE EARLY REPUBLIC

The first Fugitive Slave Act authorizes state officials to cooperate in the extradition of escaped slaves and criminal fugitives.

Upper Canada (present-day Ontario) bans the importation of new enslaved Africans, although it does not officially abolish slavery until 1834.

The Michigan Territory is counted for the first time in the federal census with Detroit's population totaling 1,442, including 67 African Americans.

The Indian Removal Act forces tribes to migrate west in what became known as the Trail of Tears.

A group of prominent Northern free African American men found the National Negro Convention Movement. The same year, the Blackburn incident in Detroit leads to an anti-slavery rebellion.

As part of the Compromise of 1850, the Fugitive Slave Act is amended to allow for any person to assist in capturing refugees from slavery. Later that year, an equal suffrage proposal to amend the state constitution is defeated in Michigan. Both events help galvanize anti-slavery activism. In 1855, Michigan defies the Fugitive Slave Act by refusing to hold escaped slaves in Michigan county jails and offering counsel for any who are captured by bounty hunters. During the 1850s, Detroit's Colored Vigilant Committee helps over five thousand people escape to Canada.

1793　　　1820　　　1830　　　1850

1789　　　1808　　　1827　　　1837

The US Constitution goes into effect in thirteen states. The Constitution writes slavery into law through the Three-Fifths Compromise of 1787 and the distinction it makes between "free Persons" and "all other Persons."

The United States bans the international African slave trade but continues to allow interstate trading.

The Michigan Territorial government enacts "An Act to Regulate Blacks and Mulattoes, and to Punish the Kidnapping of Such Persons." Known as Black codes, it restricts where African Americans can live, while also allowing the criminal prosecution of "slave-catchers" as kidnappers.

In June, African American members of the First Baptist Church in Detroit petition for an end to segregation within the church. The next month, several Black members withdraw from the church; the rest follow by the end of the year. They found the first African American church in the city, called Colored American Baptist Church, which later became Second Baptist Church.

1857

The US Supreme Court rules in the *Dred Scott v. Sanford* case that Black Americans are not citizens and therefore cannot sue. The *Dred Scott* decision also holds that the federal government is not allowed to deprive a citizen of property, including slaves, without due process.

1859

Seeking support for the raid at Harpers Ferry, abolitionist John Brown meets with Frederick Douglass in Detroit at the home of William Webb.

1861

The US Civil War begins.

1863

The Negro Regiment Law is enacted allowing African American men to serve in the Union army. Later that year, the War Department authorizes the formation of an African American regiment in Michigan, which becomes the First Michigan Colored Volunteers.

1865

General William T. Sherman issues Special Field Order No. 15 on January 16, decreeing that "forty acres of tillable ground" be reserved for each family of freed slaves in the Southeastern United States; the order was never fully realized.

The Bureau of Refugees, Freedmen, and Abandoned Lands (Freedmen's Bureau) is established in March to aid former slaves and poor whites in Southern states and the District of Columbia during Reconstruction.

In April, General Robert E. Lee surrenders Confederate troops to the Union, marking the beginning of the end of the Civil War.

In December, the Thirteenth Amendment is ratified. The amendment abolishes slavery and involuntary servitude except as punishment for crime. This loophole permits Southern states to pass laws that allow the "leasing" of state prisoners who work for no pay. Southern states also begin passing "Black codes" that restrict the labor and behavior of African Americans.

1866

The Southern Homestead Act of 1866 promises to redistribute land to emancipated African Americans, but many white authorities in the South refuse to comply, and the act is repealed in 1876.

1867

Black citizens begin to gain a voice in government in Southern states for the first time (15 percent of those elected to office at the state level are African American). However, a violent white backlash in the following decade reverses many of these gains.

1868

Another proposal to amend Michigan's state constitution for Negro suffrage is defeated. Three months later, the Fourteenth Amendment to the US Constitution is adopted, which gives citizenship to "all persons born or naturalized in the United States."

1870

Detroit's population totals 79,577 people, of which 2.8 percent—or 2,235 people—are African American.

MAPPING SLAVERY IN DETROIT

TIYA MILES, MICHELLE CASSIDY,
EMILY MACGILLIVRAY, PAUL RODRIGUEZ,
SARAH KHAN, ALEXANDRA PASSARELLI,
AND KAISHA BREZINA

In this piece, the historian Tiya Miles and six of her students puncture the image of Detroit as a "free city" in a Northern state. In contrast to the American South, where slavery remains central to the historical imagination, the fact that hundreds of Black and indigenous people were held in bondage in Detroit has largely been omitted from local memory.

Detroit has long been imagined as a zone free from racial slavery. In what was then the northwestern frontier of America, enslaved Southern African Americans seeking emancipated lives could reside in relative safety. If they wished for a more secure freedom—and many did—fugitive slaves could make for Upper Canada (present-day Ontario). That British province, which had ended slavery along with the rest of the British Empire in 1833, was just a liquid border away. Black freedom seekers escaping the South needed only to reach "Midnight" (the code name for Detroit) on the Michigan side to catch a "ride" on the Underground Railroad.

But there is a prehistory to the Underground Railroad in Detroit that reveals another dynamic among groups of historical actors. From the first moments of French settlement in 1701 through the War of 1812 and beyond, elite Detroiters owned slaves of Native American as well as African American descent. This was a period, as historian Gregory Wigmore has termed it, "before the Railroad," in which slavery was practiced in the Midwest.[4] Individuals who were held as slaves and who owned slaves in Detroit are less known in the public memory of the city, and yet it is their experience of defining, testing, and weakening the inhumane practice of slavery that laid a foundation for the Underground Railroad movement, which would form a century later. Hundreds of people were caught up in the net of slavery in the urban hub of Detroit, where fur traders, merchants, and military officials sought to control the fate and natural resources of the city and broader region. The following map of slavery landmarks in Detroit seeks to chart the existence of enslaved individuals and the people who owned them on the visual cityscape of present-day Detroit.[5] Slaveholders, many of whom were prominent Detroiters with streets named after them to this day, as well as enslaved men, women, and children, are represented through the designation and description of historic sites on this map. As is often the case in attempts to recover the lives of enslaved people, limited documentary evidence yields much more about the enslavers than the enslaved.

The stories of over two hundred Black and indigenous people held in bondage at the height of Detroit slaveholding in the period following the American Revolution have escaped detailed historical documentation, but they need not escape our historical imagination.[6] The settings where their lives played out, and the actions that they took in these places, are documented in preliminary form in this map of slavery in Detroit. Charting the history of slave ownership and slave resistance in Detroit indicates the deep roots and historical complexity of social hierarchy and social change in the city. Groups of disparate backgrounds have long had much to lose, and much to gain, in the City of the Straits, where slavery emerged as a defining feature of life just as it did elsewhere in early America.

Slavery Landmarks in Detroit

Map by Tim Stallmann based on research by Tiya Miles, Michelle Cassidy, Emily Macgillivray, Paul Rodriguez, Sarah Khan, Alexandra Passarelli, and Kaisha Brezina. Text by Tiya Miles et al.

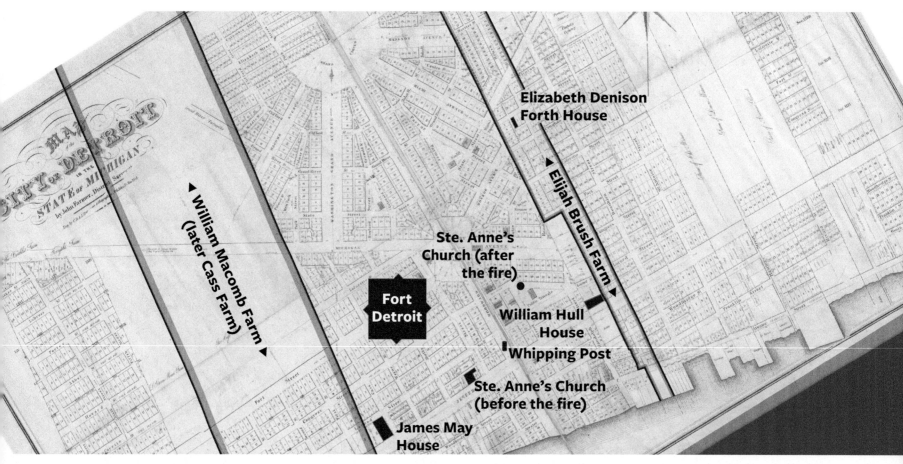

ELIZABETH DENISON FORTH'S HOUSE

Elizabeth "Lisette" Denison Forth was a slave in Detroit and the daughter of Peter and Hannah Denison, who were also born into slavery. She and her family were at the center of the first legal case that defined the parameters of slavery in Michigan Territory. After a decision from the Michigan Supreme Court that returned Lisette Denison and her siblings to slavery, she and her family escaped to Canada. Years later, she returned to Detroit and married Scipio Forth. Lisette Denison Forth was a savvy and prudent businesswoman who actively worked to control her own finances. In addition to other property, she owned a home on the corner of Brush and Macomb Streets. She was also widely regarded for her cooking in Detroit and Paris. Upon her death in 1866, she willed funds for the construction of St. James Episcopal Church on Grosse Isle to make "provisions… for the poor" in a house of worship.

ELIJAH BRUSH'S FARM (ASKIN'S FARM UNTIL 1806)

In 1806, Elijah Brush married Adelaide Askin and purchased this farm plot from John Askin, his father-in-law. That same year, Catherine Tucker "indented" Peter and Hannah Denison to Brush for one year, after which the Denisons would gain freedom. Elijah Brush became the Denisons' lawyer in 1807, when they sued for the freedom of their children: James, Elizabeth, Scipio, and Peter Jr. They lost the case and the children were ordered to stay with Catherine Tucker. The children later escaped to Canada. The former Elijah Brush farm is now the neighborhood known as Brush Park.

WILLIAM HULL'S HOUSE

In 1805, Thomas Jefferson appointed William Hull governor of the newly created Michigan Territory, a position he held until 1813. Fearing attacks from the British and their Native American allies during the war scare known as the Chesapeake Incident of 1807, Governor Hull created a Black militia (1806–7) to boost Detroit's defenses. The Black militia largely comprised runaway slaves from Canada. The three commissioned African American officers were Captain Peter Denison, Lieutenant Ezra Burgess, and Ensign Bossett.

SAINTE ANNE'S CHURCH

Because of its French origins, Ste. Anne's parish played a prominent role in early Detroit, which was a largely Catholic settlement. The records of Ste. Anne's contain the baptisms and deaths of Native American slaves and African American slaves, who were buried at the parish cemetery. This map marks both the church's original location and the site where it was rebuilt in 1818 following an 1805 fire.

FORT DETROIT

A critical landmark in the city, Fort Detroit is placed on the map to assist with visualizing the locations of other landmarks. First established in 1701, Fort Detroit continued to be a hub of military activity. The Black militia exercised military drills in Fort Detroit. According to the Askin Papers, "A Company of Negros mounted the Guard, the Cavalry Patroling every night, Batries Erecting along the settlement, and the Militia called out frequently."

WHIPPING POST (1818)

Michigan's first public whipping post, established in 1818, was at the intersection of Woodward and Jefferson Avenues. On July 27, 1818, the judges of the Territory of Michigan passed an act stating, "that any justice of the peace, on conviction, may sentence any vagrant, lewd, idle, or disorderly persons, stubborn servants . . . such as [those who] neglect their calling and employments, misspend what they earn, and do not provide for themselves or their families, to be whipped not exceeding ten stripes, or to be delivered over to any constable to be employed in labor not exceeding three months." According to the firsthand account of Ephraim S. Williams, the whipping post was, "where criminals were whipped for petty crimes, and sold for fines and costs to the one who would take them for the least number of days' work on the streets."

WILLIAM MACOMB'S FARM

(*not shown, southwest of map area*)

William Macomb was the largest slave owner in Detroit during the late 1700s. He owned an estimated twenty-six slaves at the time of his death in 1796, including a man named Scipio and his wife, Lisette, and Jerry along with his wife, Charlotte, and their two children. His farm was at the current location of Westcroft Gardens in Grosse Isle.

JAMES MAY'S HOUSE

James May was a prominent merchant and judge in the Detroit area. He is known to have owned both Black and Native American slaves, as well as indentured servants. He also hired slaves from other slaveholders, such as John Askin.

JOHN ASKIN FARM/ESTATE

(*not shown/southwest of map area*)

John Askin was a prominent fur trader and farmer in the Detroit area, who was originally a British subject. He was part of a close network of wealthy slaveholders. His power and influence can be seen through the number of slaves he owned as well as the number of indentured servants he oversaw. He owned more than twenty African and Native American slaves. His daughter married Elijah Brush, who inherited Askin's farm after Askin moved to Canada. A number of Askin's slaves worked in the shipping industry, performing dangerous tasks. For example, Toon, Pompey, and Jupiter transported, maintained, and operated the ships.

MATTHEW ELLIOTT'S HOUSE

(*not shown, southwest of map area*)

Matthew Elliott was born in Ireland and immigrated to the American colonies in 1761. In 1778, during the American Revolutionary War, Elliott fled to Detroit and became a British Loyalist. The British government gave Elliott land east of the Detroit River in gratitude for his loyalty during the war. Elliott built an estate modeled after Southern-style plantations, with separate slave quarters. He owned "dozens" of enslaved Black people, who worked on his property. Elliott was reputed to have been a harsh and violent master. To punish his slaves, Elliott would secure them to a black locust tree for whippings on his property. The iron ring to which the shackles were attached is preserved and can be viewed at the North American Black Historical Museum in Amherstburg, Ontario. Throughout his life, Elliott traded extensively among the Shawnee and had an intimate partnership with a Shawnee woman with whom he had two sons. In 1810, he married Sarah Donovan, a British woman, and they also had two sons together. Elliott's ties to Native communities and ownership of Black slaves demonstrates how racialized peoples of disparate backgrounds had much to lose and much to gain on both sides of the Detroit River in the late eighteenth and early nineteenth centuries. Elliot held several prestigious positions within the British Indian Department during his life and served in the War of 1812 before his death in 1814.

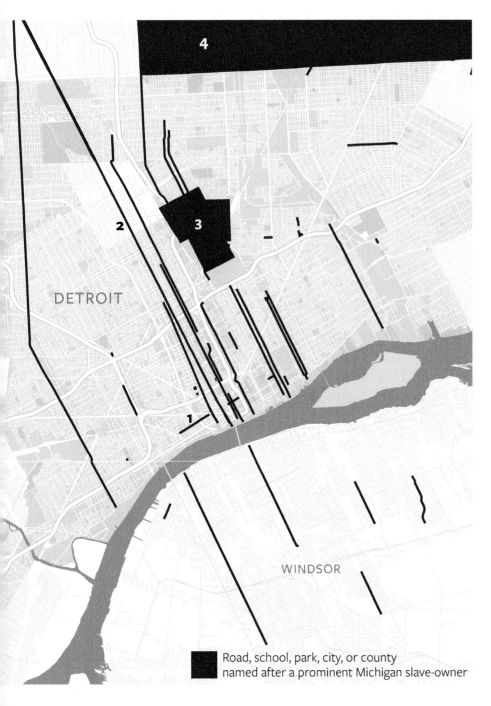

Road, school, park, city, or county
named after a prominent Michigan slave-owner

Traces of Slavery in Present-Day Detroit

Map by Tim Stallmann. Text by Tiya Miles, Michelle Cassidy, Emily Macgillivray, Paul Rodriguez, Sarah Khan, Alexandra Passarelli, Kaisha Brezina, and Tim Stallmann.

This map shows some of the many streets, parks, schools, and even cities and counties in the Detroit and Windsor area that still carry the names of slave owners.

1. ABBOTT STREET

The Abbotts were a prominent family in Detroit. James Abbott Sr. was a merchant, fur trader, and store owner. His wealth allowed him ownership of multiple slaves. Pompey Abbott was a former slave of John Askin who then worked for the Abbott family, most likely for James Abbott Jr. Pompey received a city donation lot after the 1805 fire.

2. WOODWARD AVENUE

Judge Augustus B. Woodward made important decisions on slavery in the Michigan Territory. He arrived in Detroit from Washington, DC, after the 1805 fire, and designed a street plan, similar to the DC city plan, which resembled wheel spokes. Woodward presided over the 1807 case in the Supreme Court of the Territory of Michigan that determined that Elizabeth Denison Forth and her family were slaves and the property of Catherine Tucker. He decided that "all slaves living on" May 31, 1793, "in possession of Settlers" in Michigan Territory on July 11, 1796, would remain slaves for life. Children born to slave mothers after May 31, 1793, would remain slaves until the age of twenty-five, while children born after this date would be free. In a case later that year, Judge Woodward ruled that anyone coming to Michigan Territory was free, and he refused to return slaves from Canada. Ironically, Woodward himself continued to own at least one slave until he left the Michigan Territory in 1824.

3. CITY OF HAMTRAMCK

Colonel Jean-François Hamtramck, commandant of Detroit, was known to have owned slaves. He also led attacks against the Wabash Confederacy during his time in the US Army.

4. MACOMB COUNTY

Macomb County is named after General Alexander Macomb, commanding general of the US Army from 1828 to 1841, who played a key role in the War of 1812. Although it is unclear whether Macomb himself owned slaves, both his father (Alexander Macomb) and his uncle (William Macomb) were notable Detroit-area slave owners.

CITY OF MIDNIGHT

The Underground Railroad and
Anti-Slavery Resistance in Detroit

ANDREW NEWMAN

In Detroit, the Underground Railroad was led by an African American organization called the Colored Vigilant Committee. They used direct action to create a safe space, or urban commons, to ensure community survival in the face of revanchist policies such as the Fugitive Slave Law. The Colored Vigilant Committee foreshadows the twentieth-century Black organizing in Detroit discussed in the rest of the *Atlas*.

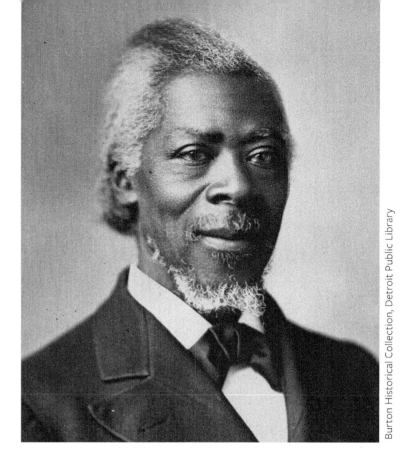

William Lambert, a tailor who moved to Detroit from New Jersey, emerged as one of the most important leaders of the Blackburn Rebellion and the Underground Railroad.

Code-named "Midnight," Detroit's role in the Underground Railroad first began to emerge after the War of 1812. It grew in importance after the British Emancipation Act of 1883 made Canada a destination for thousands of runaway slaves. Despite its common identity as a free state, Michigan had a contradictory and often-changing relationship with the legal realities of slavery during its time as a territory and a state. A so-called code noir, or "Black law," was passed in the territory in 1827. While it restricted the ability of African Americans to enter the Michigan Territory, it also enabled the criminal prosecution of slave catchers, who frequently attempted to kidnap freedom seekers and, on occasion, African Americans who had never been enslaved, and transport them to the South for sale.

In this ambiguous political climate, Detroit's African American community emerged as an energetic actor. Second Baptist Church became an important Underground Railroad station and a nerve center for anti-slavery efforts. In pre–Civil War Detroit, as in other

Detroit and the Underground Railroad

Maps by Tim Stallmann

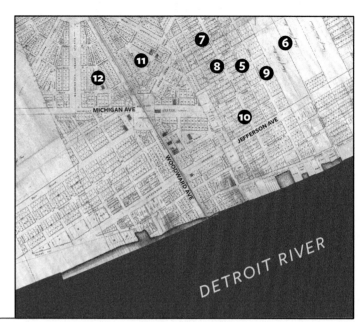

CITY OF DETROIT

DETROIT, AMHERSTBURG, AND SURROUNDS

1. St. Matthew's Episcopal Church (now St. Matthew's–St. Joseph's Episcopal Church), an important meeting place for members of the Underground Railroad. Abolitionist William Lambert was a member of the congregation.

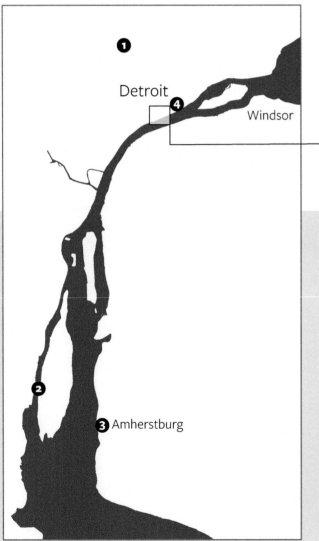

DETROIT, AMHERSTBURG, AND SURROUNDS

2. Approximate location where two freedom seekers, whom we now know only as "Ben" and "Daniel," were held aboard a boat after being recaptured by a slave catcher in 1828. They were freed in a night-time rescue by members of the Detroit and Amherstburg Black community and spirited to Canada.

3. Amherstburg, British Canada, site of large free Black community and frequent destination for freedom seekers.

4. Home of William Lambert, well-known abolitionist and conductor on the Underground Railroad who shepherded an estimated forty thousand men, women, and children to freedom.

CITY OF DETROIT, 1850S

Second Baptist Church

Detroit's first African American church and a meeting place for those involved with the Underground Railroad. To facilitate the successful resettlement of freedom seekers in Canada, the parishioners maintained connections with congregations and Baptist associations just across the border, in Amherstburg and Sandwich. The church has had three locations:

5. Fort, between Beaubien and St. Antoine (from the church's founding until 1851),

6. Fort and Hastings (1851–54), and

7. Monroe Street (1857–present).

Second Baptist was one meeting place of the Colored Vigilant Committee, which was founded by Underground Railroad conductors William Lambert and George DeBaptiste to aid freedom seekers. Modeled on the Prince Hall Masons, the exclusively African American organization had differing degrees of membership, transported freedom seekers to Canada, and provided support for those who were resettled there; in addition, they worked on issues such as voting rights and education.

8. Bethel African Methodist Episcopal Church, an important meeting place for members of the Underground Railroad, had the largest congregation of any African American church in Detroit.

9. William Webb's home (on Congress Street), site of a historic 1859 meeting between the famous abolitionists John Brown and Frederick Douglass, with William Lambert and George DeBaptiste in attendance. In the encounter, Brown revealed

Northern cities, a Colored Vigilant Committee was established to aid fugitive slaves. Detroit's committee was a Black-led organization, and two of its most important leaders were a tailor from New Jersey named William Lambert, and George DeBaptiste, an experienced underground railroad operator who purchased a steamer named the *T. Whitney*, which he used to smuggle freedom seekers to Canada. The group had connections with Underground Railroad operatives in the South and with abolitionists in other Northern cities. Long before the catchphrase "think globally, act locally" was coined among activists, Detroit's Colored Vigilant Committee maintained correspondence with abolitionists outside the United States, as well as with allies in the British government. Though a precise accounting of their clandestine activities is difficult, one scholar makes a conservative estimate that Detroit's

Colored Vigilant Committee helped more than five thousand people cross into Canada during the 1850s alone.[7]

While the group often operated in secret, at other times Black Detroiters directly opposed the efforts of slave catchers and slave owners in the open, often at considerable risk to themselves. The "Detroit and the Underground Railroad" map relates the stories of several Black Detroiters who organized themselves to rescue freedom seekers who had been captured on multiple occasions.

In one famous case, a group led by Lambert used a combination of deception and force to free Thornton and Lucie Blackburn from the Detroit jail in 1833. Many white Detroiters were so outraged by this defiant act that they burned homes in Detroit's Black community, forcing a large proportion of Detroit's early African American population to flee across the border. Political pressure led to the arrest of the Blackburns in Canada. They narrowly escaped extradition thanks to the influence of abolitionists in both the United States and Canada. Remarkably, Thornton Blackburn would secretly cross the border back to Detroit years later. From there, he rode the Underground Railroad *in reverse* to Kentucky, rescued his mother from slavery, and then fled with her back across the border to Toronto.[8]

The various sites and places associated with the Underground Railroad and the Colored Vigilant Committee represent one example of spaces created to oppose, and provide refuge from, the most extreme forms of racialized citizenship and dispossession. As with many forms of urban commons, such spaces were often kept as carefully guarded secrets to protect the lives and rights of people under direct assault. Because of these spaces and the actions that occurred there, Detroit earned a reputation as a place of defiance and resistance against slave catchers and slavery supporters.

his intentions to raid Harpers Ferry, and a heated debate ensued, with Frederick Douglass opposing the plan.

10. Home of George DeBaptiste, Black businessman and abolitionist. In the 1850s, DeBaptiste bought a steamship and used it to transport fugitive ex-slaves across the river to freedom.

11. Historic Detroit Jail, site of the escape of Thornton and Lucie Blackburn two decades earlier. The Blackburns had escaped slavery and lived freely in Detroit for a couple of years, only to be recaptured by a slave catcher in 1833. While they were awaiting their return to the South, both were freed in separate acts of bravery by Black Detroiters. Their escape becomes known as the Blackburn Rebellion. Lucie was rescued when a woman entered her jail cell to pray with her. The two switched clothes (and places), and Lucie was smuggled across the river to Amherstburg. Thornton was subsequently rescued by a group of African American Detroiters who overpowered Sheriff John M. Wilson and Blackburn's "owner" and successfully smuggled him across the river to join Lucie. In response to these acts of defiance, the so-called Blackburn riots occurred, in which angry white residents burned the homes of Black Detroiters in June and July of 1833.

12. Temperance Hotel. The hotel's white owner, Seymour Finney, allowed freedom seekers to be hidden in the stable during the day before crossing into Canada at night. At times, slave owners and slave catchers stayed at the hotel, unaware that they were just next door to runaways.

RACE, INDUSTRIAL CAPITALISM, AND UNIONIZATION

The Populist movement, a cross-race solidarity movement among Black and white small farmers in the Midwest and South, fights for greater control over the economy. The movement suffers from corporate and conservative forces seeking to undermine their solidarity by exploiting racial tensions.

Henry Ford introduces the Model T, the first mass-produced car. Migrants stream to Detroit to work on his low-cost, high-volume production lines. His assembly system becomes a model for social discipline and economic development, known as Fordism.

President Woodrow Wilson permits the segregation of the Railway Mail Service at the request of Postmaster General Albert Burleson, who reported it "intolerable" for Black and white workers to labor side by side.

The Industrial Workers of the World (also known as the Wobblies) lead a strike at the Studebaker plant in Detroit.

African Americans from the rural South join the first Great Migration to northern industrial cities, arriving in Detroit at a rate of one thousand per month.

In February, Congress passes the Immigration Act of 1917 (also known as the Asiatic Barred Zone Act), which restricts Asians, Mexicans, and other non-Caucasians, as well as people with mental and physical disabilities, from immigrating to the United States. The act remains in effect until 1952, when the Immigration and Naturalization Act eliminates racial restrictions in favor of a national quota system that strongly favors immigrants from Western Europe and the Western Hemisphere.

In April, the United States enters World War I.

Typographers and shoemakers create the first trade organization in Detroit.

1830   1892   1908   1913   1917

1883   1897   1910   1914   1920   1925

In January, the US Supreme Court upholds Alabama's anti-miscegenation statute, which prohibits and criminalizes marriage, cohabitation, and intimate relationships between whites and African Americans. Later that year, it strikes down the Civil Rights Act of 1875, which was enacted during Reconstruction in response to the violation of African Americans' civil rights.

Ransom E. Olds opens Olds Motor Works, be-ginning the automobile industry in Detroit. By this point, Detroit is an industrial powerhouse whose signature items from ships to cast-iron stoves are shipped across the world.

Detroit's population reaches 465,766, of which 1.2 percent—or 5,741 people—are African American.

In response to worker dissat-isfaction and the organizing efforts of the Industrial Workers of the World, Ford institutes the Five Dollar Day plan in his Detroit-area factories. However, Ford workers receive the full $5 only if Ford determines the worker is living "right." To determine this, he establishes a Sociological Department. A project of civic reform and surveillance, the department aims to Americanize immigrants and mold "good Ford men."

Detroit's population is 993,678. Of that, 4.1 percent–or 40,838 people–are African American. By 1930, Detroit's population will have grown to 1,568,662.

Fifty-five percent of all US autoworkers live in Michigan.

A successful sit-down strike at the General Motors plant in Flint between December 1936 and February 1937 inspires several actions by the labor movement in Detroit. Later in February, the all-female staff at Woolworth's in downtown Detroit strike in conjunction with the Flint autoworkers. The protests soon spread to other stores in the national chain. Next, in May, the UAW attempts to extend their organizing efforts into Ford's River Rouge plant in Dearborn. UAW organizers are met with violence. The beating of several of them by Ford security staff is caught on camera and becomes known as the Battle of the Overpass (see photo on p. 30). Ford employed 99 percent of his African American workforce at the River Rouge plant, which held an astounding one hundred thousand laborers under one roof.

President Roosevelt orders the internment of Japanese Americans.

The March on Washington Movement merges with the Double V Campaign to call for victory over fascism abroad and racism at home. Black workers form Victory Committees inside union locals to advocate for workers' rights.

The US Border Patrol begins Operation Wetback, an immigration law enforcement initiative in California, Arizona, and Texas aimed at curbing Mexican immigration because Mexicans are seen as "displacing domestic workers." Later that year, the Immigration and Naturalization Service extends the program to the Midwest.

Thirty percent of all US workers, public and private, are in unions. Fifty years later, only 11.9 percent of workers will be unionized.

The Big Three employ 1,530,870 union members. By 1979, membership is reduced to 840,000; by 1983, 477,000.

The stock market crashes, and the Great Depression begins.

1929   1937   1942   1954   1960   1969

1932   1940   1941   1943   1959   1968

Unemployed Councils and the United Auto Workers (UAW) in Detroit organize the Ford Hunger March.

Blacks hold only a small fraction of skilled auto industry jobs in Detroit. With the emerging wartime economy, the Temporary Negro Coordinating Committee for National Defense is formed to protest discrimination in the defense industry.

The Japanese attack Pearl Harbor and the United States enters World War II. Detroit auto factories shift to wartime production, earning the city the name the "Arsenal of Democracy." The war dramatically changes the racial patterns of employment, increasing the number of Black autoworkers and thus also their ability to protest job discrimination. The March on Washington Movement and the threat of one hundred thousand African American protesters in Washington leads President Franklin D. Roosevelt to sign Executive Order 8802, banning racial discrimination in defense industries nationwide.

White workers at Packard Motor Company in Detroit hold a "hate strike" to protest desegregation at the plant. A couple of weeks later, a white race riot erupts on Belle Isle. Thirty-four people are killed, including twenty-five African Americans and nine whites.

Black unionists establish the Metropolitan Labor Council, which along with the Victory Committees, provides a broad infrastructure for Black protest and community organizing in the plants and beyond. Leftist literature circulates in auto plants, including literature from the Communist Party, the Socialist Workers Party, the Workers Party, and the Industrial Workers of the World.

Police ride in integrated patrol cars in Detroit for the first time.

Martin Luther King Jr. is assassinated on April 4 at the Lorraine Motel in Memphis, Tennessee. He had traveled to Memphis to support African American city sanitation workers who were protesting unequal wages and unsafe working conditions.

In May, an African American wildcat strike at the Dodge Main plant in Detroit leads to the formation of the Dodge Revolutionary Union Movement, precipitating Revolutionary Union Movements in other plants and nonautomotive facilities in Detroit and beyond. The following year, the League of Revolutionary Black Workers incorporates to centralize these movements.

LABOR STRUGGLES

LINDA CAMPBELL, ANDREW NEWMAN,
SARA SAFRANSKY, AND TIM STALLMANN

Detroit is often synonymous with the labor movement owing to the strength of unions in the automotive industry. In its early years, the labor movement was at the forefront of radical calls for social change in the United States. However, the movement was also fractured from within by white supremacy. After World War II, when organized labor reached the apex of its political power, radical activists organized coalitions in Detroit to address issues of racial injustice within unions and on the factory floor.

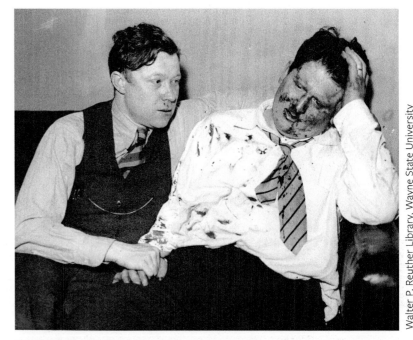

UAW organizers Walter Reuther and Richard Frankensteen after they were attacked by members of the Ford Motor Company's internal security organization, the Ford Service Department, in the Battle of the Overpass, May 26, 1937.

The workplace has long been a site where workers confront dispossession, unequal treatment, and racialized citizenship. Workers have been organizing in Detroit since at least the 1830s, when typographers and shoemakers created the first trade organizations in the city. Starting in 1913, when the Industrial Workers of the World, also known as the Wobblies, led a strike at the **Studebaker plant**, the early days of the automotive industry became associated with labor militancy.

Some of the most important moments in Detroit's union history occurred when workers took their struggles off the factory floor to claim a broader right to the city. In 1932, Detroit's newly formed Unemployed Councils led between three thousand and five thousand workers on the **Ford Hunger March**; their list of demands included the right to unionize and the right to medical care for laid-off workers, and they further called for an end to racial discrimination.[9] The march was violently suppressed by the Dearborn police and Ford's private security agents (the infamous "Ford Service Department") who fired shots into the crowd, leaving five dead and as many as sixty wounded. The

This map locates the events described in the accompanying essay, which are bolded when they are first mentioned.

Dodge Revolutionary Union Movement

White riots at Packard Motor Company

Detroit Public School sickouts

Ford Hunger March

Woolworth's sit-down strike

Studebaker plant

Battle of the Overpass

Labor Struggles in Detroit

Map by Tim Stallmann

funeral procession down Woodward Avenue for the dead drew an estimated sixty thousand spectators.

Five years later, when Walter P. Reuther and a group of organizers from the United Auto Workers (UAW) attempted to mobilize workers at Ford, they were again met with violence in an incident that later would be called the **Battle of the Overpass**. This time Henry Ford's strategy of violently suppressing the labor movement backfired. Photographs of the violence (such as the one included here) swayed public opinion to the side of the UAW, paving the way for unionization at Ford and the UAW's rise to national prominence.

While these and other UAW actions are legendary episodes in American labor history, the union—and manufacturing workers in general—were far from the only workers in Detroit to make history through collective action. Earlier in 1937, the all-female staff of the downtown Detroit's Woolworth's store, in conjunction with autoworkers in Flint, went on a **sit-down strike** by locking themselves inside their place of work. Their militancy and the sit-down tactic quickly spread to other stores in the national chain. Ultimately, their demands for higher wages, better hours, and union recognition were met, marking a major milestone in the labor struggle for retail workers.

People of color have often been faced with particularly exploitive working conditions, and, in many cases, the labor unions have enacted their own regimes of racialized citizenship. Internal migration in the United States during the 1940s, '50s, and, to a lesser extent, '60s changed the social composition of labor movements in Detroit, elevating the importance of racial and cultural difference.[10] During World War II, it took pressure

from A. Philip Randolph, the African American leader of the American Brotherhood of Sleeping Car Porters, for Franklin Roosevelt to issue an executive order opening jobs in Detroit's numerous unionized wartime defense industries to African Americans. The Black workers who obtained jobs in wartime production often faced racist hostility from whites, and on June 3, 1943, over twenty thousand white workers went on strike at **Packard Motor Company** in anger at the promotion of three African American workers to an aircraft assembly line.

Even after the civil rights movement began, African American workers felt the sting of racism within the labor movement. Black workers held the most dangerous, worst paying, and least secure jobs. In 1968, a group of African American workers held their own wildcat strike at the Dodge Main plant when management disproportionately punished Black workers after a general walkout. They declared that the UAW—which focused primarily on negotiating pay raises instead of working conditions—no longer represented Black interests. Throughout the 1950s and '60s, Detroit and other Rust Belt cities experienced a precipitous decline in employment as car manufacturing tended toward automation and responded to unionization by shifting production to other regions of the country and abroad where labor was cheaper. As a consequence, the UAW's bargaining power weakened and its leaders began to align more with the auto companies. Workers experienced a serious decline in safety conditions, with injuries and even fatalities becoming more common.

The **Dodge Revolutionary Union Movement** (DRUM), founded in 1968 in the wake of a wildcat strike at the Dodge Main plant, denounced the mainstream labor movement as racist and

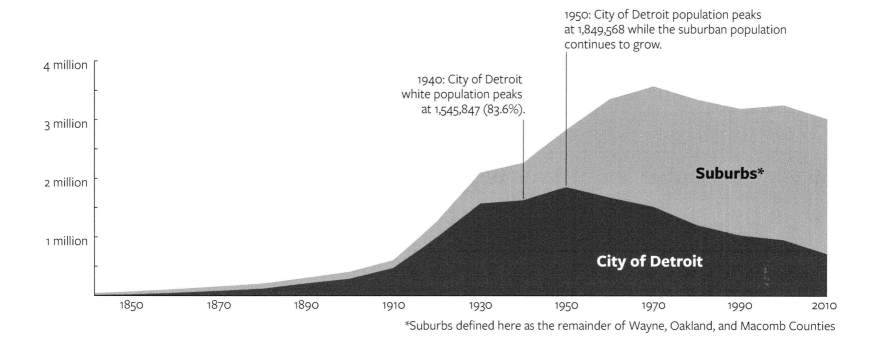

1950: City of Detroit population peaks at 1,849,568 while the suburban population continues to grow.

1940: City of Detroit white population peaks at 1,545,847 (83.6%).

Suburbs*

City of Detroit

*Suburbs defined here as the remainder of Wayne, Oakland, and Macomb Counties

Detroit and Suburbs Historical Population

The changing census figures for Detroit and the surrounding metro region illustrate the history of major shifts in labor, race, and housing. Between 1910 and 1930, Detroit's population skyrocketed due to the boom in industrial employment and African American in-migration. For the rest of the twentieth century, the population of Detroit proper and the metro region would never see such a dramatic change in total numbers, but the movements of people between city and suburbs belie struggles over race and housing discussed in this section. Before World War II, most whites could not afford to move out of the city. Afterward, not only did most whites leave the city, but homeownership increasingly came to be seen as a prerequisite for "cultural" citizenship in the white 1950s American mainstream. However, the suburban dream was not accessible to all. Institutional

and quotidian forms of racism continued. While rates of homeownership nationally rose to 18.7 percent for whites between 1940 and 1960 (reaching 64.9 percent), African Americans saw only a 14.7 percent increase for the same time period (to 38.2 percent). By 1968, when the Fair Housing Act made redlining illegal, sixteen of Detroit's richest suburbs had no Black homeowners, and most of the others had very small Black populations. Today the racial and ethnic geography of metro Detroit continues to be defined by segregated access to homeownership.

white controlled. The organizing effort created solidarity among Black workers and precipitated Revolutionary Union Movements at other plants—Ford, Cadillac, Chrysler—and nonautomotive facilities in Detroit and beyond, like the United Parcel Service and the health care industry. DRUM's fourteen demands included a reduction in work hours, safer working conditions, pay increases, a rejection of union dues, a reduction in union bureaucracy, and alternatives to the traditional union grievance process that they felt limited workers' ability to leverage their strike power to fight for changes. In June 1969, the League of Revolutionary Black Workers (LRBW) was incorporated in an attempt to organize these efforts centrally.[11]

Even though it was only in existence for a few short years, the LRBW made an indelible mark on radical organizing within the labor movement and beyond the factory floor. The LRBW sought to overthrow capitalism, reform the UAW, and bring about racial equity by organizing workers at the point of production—that is, on the shop floor. As the LRBW centralized leadership they expanded their programming initiatives into community organizing and legal defense. The league also founded a bookstore and organized book clubs. It was common for up to two hundred people, including many white suburbanite sympathizers, to attend the book club meetings. Finally, the league organized to produce and control its own media, establishing a printing press and embarking on film production. In 1970, the LRBW released the documentary *Finally Got the News*, a documentary about the league's political program that garnered international interest. With LRBW's rapid expansion, the league faced new organizational challenges related to capacity and differing views on political strategy. They were forced to contend not only with the loss of jobs from continued deindustrialization but efforts by Chrysler to diffuse their power.

By 1974, Chrysler was the only automobile manufacturing company that remained active in Detroit. The decline in jobs created additional tensions within the labor movement as union leaders sought to discredit Black revolutionaries, and auto companies attacked the bargaining power of the UAW, leading to steep declines in membership, for which workers paid greatly. In 1969, 1,530,870 union members worked for the Big Three. By 1979, membership was reduced to 840,000, and by 1983, to a mere 477,000 workers.[12] The declining membership of the UAW mirrored a national trend. In the 1960s, approximately 30 percent of all US workers (public and private) were in unions. By 1983, this figure had fallen to 20 percent and, by 2010, to a mere 11.9 percent. From 1950 to 1960, laborers staged 3,517 work stoppages compared to 201 between 2000 and 2010.[13]

The decline in union membership reshaped not only the labor landscape in Detroit but also the infrastructural support for social movement organizing and political education that was a part of radical worker movements. While municipal workers emerged in 2013 at the forefront of protests against the policies of Emergency Manager Kevyn Orr, and in 2016 Detroit Public School teachers took part in "**sickouts**" to protest deteriorating conditions under the administration of Emergency Manager Darnell Early, the face of labor militancy has changed. In discussions related to the United Detroiters project, coeditor Linda Campbell identified this as a challenge, calling activists to think about "what structures need to exist in addition to electoral politics to strengthen our neighborhoods and communities."

RACE AND THE RIGHT TO HOUSING

LINDA CAMPBELL, ANDREW NEWMAN,
SARA SAFRANSKY, AND TIM STALLMANN

While Detroit is often defined as a postindustrial city, the politics of housing and, in particular, the historical links among race, property values, and ownership rights have been as important as factory closings in shaping the city's landscape. In the early twentieth century, as African Americans arrived in Detroit seeking better-paying jobs and fleeing the racist violence of the Jim Crow South, they were confronted by written and unwritten racial restrictions related to where they could purchase homes and live. In Detroit, white residents formed property associations and vigilante groups to protect neighborhoods from the "Negro invasion." They instituted racially restrictive covenants that excluded any person with more than one-eighth of "Negro blood."[14] By 1910, these color lines were further enforced by real estate developers and economists, who had started to standardize guidelines for government appraisals and construction practices, and the subsequent emergence of all-white real estate boards in most major US cities. These boards codified rules about race and property and threatened to expel realtors who sold real estate to African Americans in all-white neighborhoods.[15]

The map on p. 38 illustrates some of the key battles that took place when African Americans transgressed the color line and fought for open housing. One of the best-known cases in Detroit is that of Ossian and Gladys Sweet, who in 1925 bought a new house in a white neighborhood on the city's East Side. Though the Sweets' economic standing afforded them a degree of mobility that most Black Detroiters did not have—Ossian was a Howard-educated physician—their home purchase prompted threats. On moving day, a small group of whites tried to scare them away. By evening, the group grew to a mob of eight hundred. The mob dispersed the next day but returned in the evening, stoning the house and chanting racial epithets. As the crowd advanced, two shots were fired by Ossian's brother and a police officer. Two white men were shot, one died, and the Sweet family was arrested.[16]

The public began passing judgment immediately, including the mayor of Detroit, John Smith, who laid down his color-line policy in no uncertain terms: "Any colored person who endangers life and property, simply to gratify his personal pride, is an enemy of his race as well as an incitant of riot and murder."[17] Smith's main contention—that what he called the Sweets' "murderous pride" in defending their social status was the true threat to society as opposed to racism itself—was a classic example of revanchism directed at individuals who asserted their equality in defiance of the racial status quo. That the Sweets were eventually acquitted makes their story exceptional. However, the hostility and retribution they faced for buying a house in a white neighborhood was not unique. At the time, the Ku Klux Klan (KKK) and its offshoot the Black Legion boasted thousands of members in Detroit and tens of thousands in Michigan.[18] Together, they

HOUSING AND PROPERTY STRUGGLES

The US Supreme Court rules that municipally mandated racial zoning is unconstitutional. In response, white neighborhood groups, homeowners, and developers begin adopting racially restrictive covenants to prevent African Americans and other people of color from purchasing homes in their neighborhoods.

1917

A white mob attacks the home of Ossian and Gladys Sweet on Detroit's East Side.

1925

Charles Bowles is elected mayor of Detroit. He begins serving in 1930 but is recalled the same year because of corruption charges and his involvement with the KKK.

1929

The National Housing Act of 1934 creates the Federal Housing Administration, which revolutionizes homeownership in the United States by creating a financial mortgaging system and lending structure that are preferentially accessible to white home buyers and neighborhoods.

1934

The Detroit Housing Commission approves plans to build a public housing project for African Americans in Detroit called the Sojourner Truth Homes.

1941

1923

The Burn Act goes into effect in Michigan, prohibiting "public gathering of masked men." It is specifically aimed at the KKK, which, in conjunction with the Black Legion, a white supremacist organization that split from the KKK and operated in the Midwest, boasted thousands of members in Detroit and tens of thousands in Michigan.

1926

The Supreme Court validates the use of racial covenants in *Corrigan v. Buckley*.

1933

The Home Owners' Loan Corporation is established with the mandate to protect urban homeowners from foreclosure.

1937

The US Housing Act of 1937 provides federal subsidies for local housing agencies.

1942

The KKK holds a rally near the Sojourner Truth Homes complex on February 27, the day before the project is supposed to open. The following day, a mob of approximately twelve hundred whites attack Black families who attempt to move in. White residents riot again on March 10.

The GI Bill provides low-cost mortgages to veterans. Of the first sixty-seven thousand mortgages that the GI Bill insured, it issues fewer than one hundred to nonwhites.

The US Supreme Court strikes down the use of restrictive covenants, although racist block-busting tactics continue to enforce de facto residential segregation. Though unenforceable, racially restrictive covenants from this time period remain on the legally recorded deeds of properties across the country to this day.

The US Supreme Court rules in *Brown v. Board of Education of Topeka* that "separate educational facilities are inherently unequal."

The Housing Act of 1954 is enacted, providing funding for 140,000 units of public housing.

President John F. Kennedy issues Executive Order 11063, banning federally funded housing organizations from discriminating against individuals on the basis of race. However, no mechanism of enforcement accompanies the order, allowing discriminatory lending practices to continue.

The Fair Housing Act of 1968 prohibits discrimination in the sale, rental, and financing of housing based on race, religion, national origin, and sex. At this time, sixteen of Detroit's richest suburbs have no Black homeowners. Most of the others have very small Black populations.

1944　1948　1954　1962　1968

1946　1949　1956　1966

Detroit mayor Edward Jeffries unveils the Detroit Plan, which slates the African American neighborhood Paradise Valley (referred to as a "slum" in the plan) for urban renewal. The plan stalls with lawsuits over the condemnation of property. Ultimately, the Michigan Supreme Court rules in favor of Detroit.

The American Housing Act of 1949 is enacted. The sweeping and contradictory legislation provides financing for slum clearance associated with urban renewal, destroying affordable housing units. At the same time, it provides funding for the construction of public housing.

White flight from Detroit accelerates with the Federal-Aid Highway Act of 1956. The highway act, in combination with the housing acts of 1949 and 1954, ignites "urban renewal" and reshapes the material and political terrain of American cities.

The Michigan Supreme Court rules in *Spencer v. Flint Memorial Park Association* that racially restrictive covenants on burial plots in cemeteries are indefensible.

Housing Struggles in Detroit

Map by Tim Stallmann

EIGHT MILE WALL

In the 1940s, a developer proposed to build a white suburb immediately to the west of the predominately Black Eight Mile neighborhood. The Federal Home Loan Bank Board refused to underwrite the development (because it was near an African American neighborhood) until this one-foot-thick and six-feet-high cement wall, known as "Detroit's wailing wall," was built to separate the two neighborhoods.

SOJOURNER TRUTH HOMES

A World War II–era federal housing project intended for Black defense workers, Sojourner Truth Homes became a flashpoint in the city, as white mobs violently opposed its construction and attempted to force out its residents. In April 1942, sixteen hundred National Guardsmen and eleven hundred police officers were deployed to protect eight Black families moving into the homes.

MCGHEE HOME

Restrictive covenants, legal language attached to property deeds restricting sale to Caucasians, were a frequent weapon used by white neighborhoods to maintain segregation. In 1944, African Americans Orsel and Minnie McGhee attempted to buy a home with a restrictive covenant in a majority white neighborhood. Neighbors sued to block the purchase, and the Michigan Supreme Court held in favor of the neighbors in *Sipes v. McGhee*. McGhee's appeal reached the US Supreme Court. Argued by Thurgood Marshall, it became a companion case to other challenges against housing discrimination. The following year, in its landmark 1948 *Shelley v. Kramer* decision, the US Supreme Court overturned previous decisions in ruling that while restrictive covenants were legal, no state or federal courts could enforce them.

POLETOWN NEIGHBORHOOD

First settled in the 1870s, this neighborhood was home to Polish, Italian, and Black residents. In the 1980s, General Motors and the cities of Detroit and Hamtramck used eminent domain to demolish over thirteen hundred homes in order to construct a Buick-Oldsmobile-Cadillac factory.

OSSIAN SWEET HOUSE

Ossian and Gladys Sweet successfully defended their home against an armed white mob in 1925.

BLACK BOTTOM NEIGHBORHOOD

The first neighborhood in which African Americans settled in Detroit during the Great Migration, Black Bottom became hugely crowded because Black people were barred from buying or renting housing in most other parts of the city. The entire area was cleared as part of urban renewal in the 1960s.

GROSSE POINTE BOUNDARY

The line between the majority white Grosse Pointe suburbs and majority Black Detroit is a stark contemporary example of housing segregation. Fences line much of the border (even cutting across roads at some places), and even where roads do continue across the border, they often run through barricades intended to restrict traffic flow.

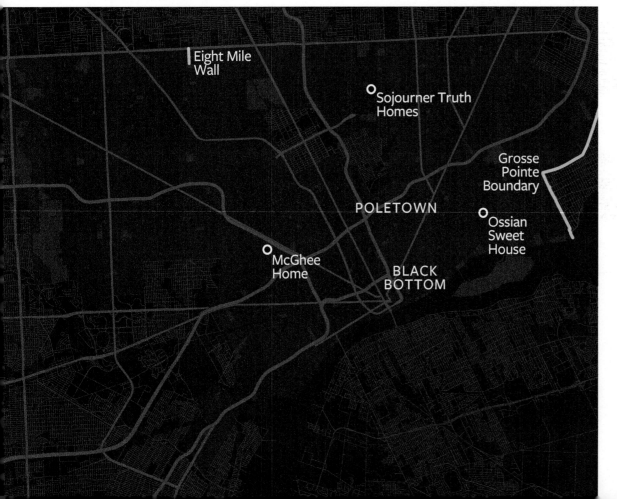

exerted a tremendous force on urban politics and municipal elections, shaped anti-unionist and racist sentiments among factory managements, and were active in housing debates. Consequently, it was not uncommon for African Americans moving into white neighborhoods to be confronted by mobs of upward of two thousand people.[19]

White hostility increased as more Black residents moved to the city. Between 1940 and 1950, Detroit's Black population doubled. With increased migration to Detroit during World War II, housing continued to be a hot-button issue. Redlining severely limited the mobility of African Africans. Financial institutions systematically used the racial makeup of a neighborhood as a standard to decide whether to offer home loans in that neighborhood. This meant that banks denied loans to African Americans and other people of color solely based on the demographics of the neighborhoods they lived in, forcing residents to either leave their neighborhoods or remain renters.

Between 1934 and 1962, the federal government subsidized more $120 billion worth of new housing. Nonwhites had access to less than 2 percent of it.[20] Moreover, the Federal Housing Administration (FHA) and Veterans Administration (VA) worked in combination with other programs that subsidized and regulated conventional mortgage markets (not covered by the FHA or VA), creating a secondary mortgage market that enabled investors to trade home finance debt. Postwar suburbanization, as historian David Freund documents, represented a shift in the socialization of consumer debt as a driver of economic change. "Suburban growth and its corollary prosperity were not just state managed but also inherently discriminatory," Freund writes, "[b]ecause the programs that subsidized the mortgage market systematically excluded racial minorities. . . . Federal housing policies did not merely 'embrace . . . [t]he discriminatory attitudes of the marketplace,' as the FHA's critics have long argued. Selective credit operations created a new *kind* of discriminatory marketplace."[21]

As new migrants contended with redlining, the practice of "block busting" became common among real estate brokers. *Block busting* refers to the process whereby opportunistic brokers sold homes to African Americans in white neighborhoods and then bought homes from whites who lived in close proximity, saving money on the purchase by taking advantage of their racial fears. As property values deteriorated, whites would take what they could get for their homes, eager to salvage equity. Brokers then profited doubly by reselling homes to African Americans at higher prices.[22]

The striking difference in racial makeup between Detroit and its suburbs (see map on p. 42) is a direct result of such practices of housing discrimination—racially restrictive covenants, white violence, racist mortgage lending, block busting, and white flight—not to mention federally funded highway construction, which led to the demolition of some of the city's most populated Black neighborhoods.[23] As more and more people, jobs, and wealth moved to the suburban fringe, the region's wealth gap grew (see map on p. 44) and Detroit sunk deeper and deeper into poverty.

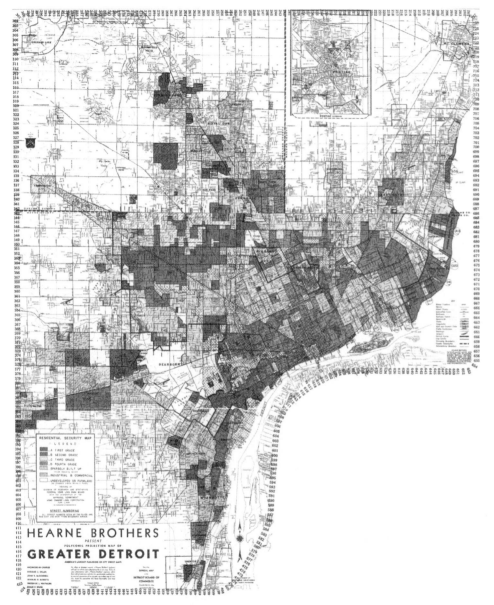

HOLC Redlining Map of Detroit

One of the most powerful and tenacious forms of housing racism in Detroit, and across the United States has been the systematic denial of credit to African Americans. *Redlining* is a term taken from the red outlines used to designate African American neighborhoods as "high risk" for lending on maps commissioned by the Home Owners' Loan Corporation (HOLC), as shown on this map of Detroit. The federal government played an instrumental role in redlining through the HOLC and its outgrowth, the FHA. In 1933 the HOLC was established with a mandate to protect urban homeowners from foreclosure. It issued long-term, self-amortizing mortgages. It also established the first countrywide appraisal system, hiring appraisers to assess the "quality" of neighborhoods in cities with at least forty thousand people. In 239 cities, including Detroit, appraisers assigned every city block a rating from A to D, which led to a color-coded risk assessment map, like the one included here. Neighborhoods with a D rating, shown in red, signified areas that appraisers thought to be high risk for lending, a designation usually based only on the presence of African American or Jewish residents.

Credit for the idea to make the comparison between these two maps goes to Alex Hill's *DETROITography* blog.

HOUSES DETERIORATING AND DILAPIDATED, DETROIT, 1960

Houses Deteriorating and
Dilapidated as Percent
of All Houses by Tract

SCALE   MILES

0-9

10-29

30-100

DGEI Map of Houses Deteriorating and Dilapidated, 1960

The legacy of redlining deeply impacted Detroit's neighborhoods, as can be seen by comparing the HOLC map with this one, produced by the Detroit Geographical Expedition and Institute (DGEI), of houses that were in poor condition. Without the financing to purchase homes, redlined areas had far fewer homeowners, and consequently residents themselves had less incentive or capacity to make needed repairs. Notably, many of these redlined areas were also the first to see large increases in Black homeownership after the Fair Housing Act passed in 1968, as can be seen in the map series on page 199.

Race and Ethnicity in Detroit

Map by Tim Stallmann

Metro Detroit's color line is the legacy of racist patterns of bank lending, housing discrimination, and white flight. This map also illustrates the locations of several ethnic enclaves that emerged throughout the metropolitan area. Southwest Detroit stands out as the most densely populated Latina/o community in the region, and Hamtramck is home to a large Bangladeshi community. There are several notable enclaves of people of color in the suburbs, including the predominantly African American communities of Southfield to the northwest and Inkster to southwest, as well as South Asian and East Asian enclaves in the northern suburbs. Because of a discrepancy between the way the US government officially defines race in the census and the way many people actually self-identify, several significant communities are invisible or muddled in this map. For example, the category "Asian" makes it impossible to differentiate among metro Detroit's Indian, Bangladeshi, Pakistani, Chinese, Filipino, Hmong, Japanese, and Korean communities, all of which have very different histories and contrasting reasons for settling in specific neighborhoods. People of Middle Eastern descent are listed in the census as white, hiding significant Arab American communities in Dearborn.

Each dot represents the approximate location of thirty people. Dots are colored by race and ethnicity, according to categories used by the US Census. These categories obscure some important distinctions. For example, the census counts people of Middle Eastern descent as white, so the immigrant communities in Hamtramck and Dearborn's large Muslim community are not visible on this map.

Asian   Black or African American   Latinx or Hispanic origin

American Indian or First Nations   White (and not Latinx)

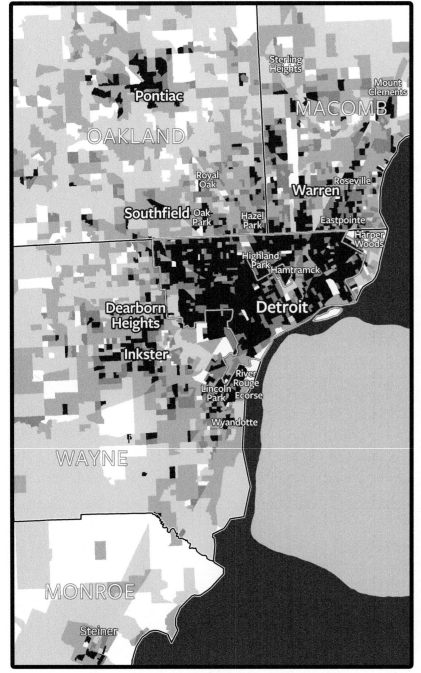

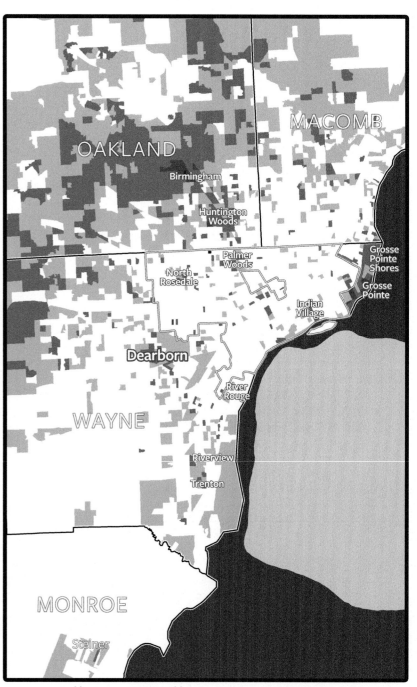

HOUSEHOLDS IN POVERTY, 2007–12

HIGH-INCOME HOUSEHOLDS, 2007–12

Wealth and Poverty in Detroit

Map by Tim Stallmann

At first glance, maps like these showing wealth disparity confirm the stereotype that metro Detroit is divided between wealthy white suburbs and a low-income African American city. But looking more closely, these maps of the spatial concentrations of wealth and poverty across the metropolitan area reveal that the situation on the ground is more complex. While Detroit is marked by the most concentrated examples of poverty, and the northwest suburbs contain the wealthiest enclaves, examples of suburban poverty and urban affluence abound, too. Portions of Macomb County and southeastern Oakland County, as well communities to the southwest of the city, vividly illustrate the degree to which poverty exists in the suburbs, offering a reminder that effects of deindustrialization are regional in scope. At the same time, Detroit has several neighborhoods, including Boston-Edison, Indian Village, and Palmer Woods, which are wealthier than significant portions of the suburban counties. While some of that wealth may reflect recent arrivals to the city, these neighborhoods have long been home to the city's most affluent residents, a number of whom never "fled" to the suburbs.

Households in Poverty
Households with income below the poverty level*

Less than 10 households per square mile

11 to 100 households per square mile

101 to 500 households per square mile

501 to 1,000 households per square mile

more than 1,000 households per square mile

Wealthy households
Households with annual income over $200,000

Less than 10 households per square mile

11 to 100 households per square mile

101 to 500 households per square mile

501 to 1,000 households per square mile

more than 1,000 households per square mile

* The income threshold for poverty varies each year by family size and number of children. In 2012 the Census considered a single parent with one child, earning less than $15,825 yearly, to be below the poverty level.

THE WALK TO FREEDOM

LINDA CAMPBELL, ANDREW NEWMAN, SARA SAFRANSKY, AND TIM STALLMANN

The civil rights movement was not merely a southern phenomenon. Dr. Martin Luther King Jr.'s visit to Detroit in 1963 underlines the importance of northern cities, where well-organized African American communities contributed to the nationwide struggle.

One of the best-known struggles against racialized citizenship in the United States was the civil rights movement of the 1950s and '60s. Though it is most famously associated with southern cities such as Birmingham and Selma, Detroit, like other northern cities, had an important role to play. The struggles against racist housing policies in Detroit described on the previous pages were understood at the time as extensions of the campaign against Jim Crow in the South. At a practical level, civil rights leaders such as Dr. Martin Luther King Jr. looked to Detroit's rising Black middle class as an important source of financial support for the movement. In many respects, the urban commons that had been long established by Detroit's Black community, coupled with its economic strength, helped provide a logistical base to sustain the battle against Jim Crow. It was this social and economic network that attracted King to Detroit in June 1963.

In the summer of 1963, Martin Luther King Jr. delivered a preliminary version of his "I Have a Dream" speech in Detroit. The recording of the speech was released by Gordy Records, a subsidiary of Detroit's famous Motown label.

One hundred and twenty-five thousand people came to Woodward Avenue to march with Dr. King and other civil rights leaders for the Great March to Freedom. The march and the speech King delivered in Detroit served as a rehearsal for one of most the famous actions of the civil rights movement, the March on Washington in August 1963.

On June 23, 1963, King led a 125,000-strong march down Woodward Avenue. The event, known as the Walk to Freedom, was the largest civil rights demonstration up to that point in time. It honored the victims of the Detroit race riot of 1943, which had occurred twenty years before. In organizing it, King sought to call attention to common links between the civil rights struggle against Jim Crow in the South and the struggles that African Americans faced in northern cities, including discrimination in hiring, wages, housing, and education. The march moved southward from the corner of Woodward Avenue and Adelaide Street to Cobo Arena on Jefferson Avenue, paralleling the route of the Underground Railroad toward Canada. The event culminated with a rousing speech by Dr. King, who spoke these words:

I have a dream that one day, right down in Georgia and Mississippi and Alabama, the sons of former slaves and the sons of former slave owners will be able to live together as brothers.

I have a dream this afternoon that one day, one day little white children and little Negro children will be able to join hands as brothers and sisters.

I have a dream this afternoon that one day, that one day men will no longer burn down houses and the church of God simply because people want to be free.

I have a dream this afternoon that there will be a day that we will no longer face the atrocities that Emmett Till had to face or Medgar Evers had to face, that all men can live with dignity.

I have a dream this afternoon that my four little children, that my four little children will not come up in the same young days that I came up within, but they will be judged on the basis of the content of their character, not the color of their skin.

I have a dream this afternoon that one day right here in Detroit, Negroes will be able to buy a house or rent a house anywhere that their money will carry them and they will be able to get a job.[24]

Both the speech and the march were intended as a rehearsal for the March on Washington, providing another example of Detroit's role as a crucible for radical ideas and actions.

Located on the corner of Cass and W. Forest Avenues, the First Unitarian Universalist Church of Detroit has a history of involvement with social justice struggles that is well over a century old. One of the most famous members of the church's congregation is Viola Liuzzo, who traveled to support the civil rights march in Selma, Alabama, in 1965. Liuzzo helped transport protesters between Selma and the nearby airport in her car. While on one trip, three members of the Ku Klux Klan followed Liuzzo's car and opened fire, killing her. She was thirty-nine years old and a mother of five.

Globalization from Below

By the 1960s, Detroit had emerged as an important center of Black radical thought. Many activists of color had grown frustrated with the pacifist approach and limited success of the civil rights movement. This new group of activists looked beyond the borders of the United States and connected inner-city politics at home—on colonized ground—with anti-colonial struggles occurring in more than forty countries around the world between 1945 and 1960. This map illustrates some of the national and transnational connections of the city's social movements.

Many African Americans who joined the Black Panthers developed their analysis of colonialism and imperialism while serving in the Vietnam War, and their thinking about strategy and tactics was heavily influenced by the conflict.

Vietnam

Oakland, California
In spring 1968, the Oakland-based Black Panther Party established a local chapter in Detroit, two blocks from the epicenter of the rebellion. Detroit was one of forty chapters, including international chapters in England, Israel, Australia, and India.

Sudan

In 1968, five hundred Black radicals convened at the Black Government Conference held at the Shrine of the Black Madonna and signed a Declaration of Independence with the aim of creating the Republic of New Afrika—an independent Black nation that would occupy five southern states within the United States (Alabama, Georgia, Louisiana, Mississippi, and South Carolina). In an attempt to garner international support, they also met with foreign governments, including those of the Soviet Union, Tanzania, Sudan, and China.

Tanzania

Jackson, Mississippi
Soon after its founding in 1968, the Republic of New Afrika moved its headquarters to Jackson. In 2013, the republic's former vice president Chokwe Lumumba (born and raised in Detroit) was elected mayor of Jackson as part of the Malcolm X Grassroots Movement.

USSR

Wilberforce, Ohio

The Revolutionary Action Movement—the first Maoist-influenced organization in the United States—was founded by Black students at Central State University in 1962, inspired by the civil rights leader and proponent of armed Black self-defense Robert Williams's experiences in Cuba, where he lived in exile from 1961 to 1969. In 1968, Williams was chosen as the first president of the Republic of New Afrika while still in exile.

Detroit

A number of Detroit-based initiatives emerged under the ideological leadership of Reverend Albert Cleage and his church, Detroit's Shrine of the Black Madonna, including the City-Wide Citizen's Action Committee, which aimed to foster Black-owned businesses and at times attracted more than two thousand people to its meetings, and the West Central Organization, an active multiracial neighborhood group, which used Saul Alinsky's model of community organizing to protest redevelopment around Wayne State University.

Indonesia

Shortly after the United Nations formed in 1945, the Civil Rights Congress, under the legal leadership of William Patterson and Paul Robeson, filed a petition entitled "We Charge Genocide: The Crime of Government against the Negro People" (1951), charging the US government with Black genocide under the Geneva Convention. A decade later, after the 1955 nonaligned movement took place in Bandung, Indonesia, the Afro-Asian People's Solidarity Organization was formed in China (1957).

China

Cuba

Black students at Wayne State University, inspired by the Chinese and Cuban Revolutions, formed a revolutionary Black nationalist/socialist action cadre called UHURU (meaning "freedom" in Swahili). They attended Socialist Workers Party forums, listened to members of the Communist Party, and studied with historian C. L. R. James, who in the 1950s made Detroit his base for intellectual and political activities. James and Grace Lee Boggs, who worked with James as members of the Facing Reality group, became important political activists in the city. In collaboration, the three produced a newsletter called *Correspondence* that sought to synthesize Black nationalism and socialism (a project they continued after they broke with James). In addition to these organizing efforts, radical labor alliances emerged from the confrontation between Black workers and white unions, notably in the example of the Marxist Dodge Revolutionary Union Movement.

THE REVOLUTIONARY '60S

The Civil Rights Act of 1964 becomes law.

President Lyndon B. Johnson signs the Economic Opportunity Act of 1964, claiming that for the first time a nation is making a commitment to eradicate poverty among its people. The act authorizes the formation of local Community Action Agencies (CAAs) to carry out the Community Action Program (CAP), which became the centerpiece of the War on Poverty. Modeled on the Peace Corps, the program encourages "maximum feasibility participation" and the devolution of political power with the aim of containing and integrating radical groups seen as a threat to the security of liberal democracy. Detroit had one of the first tactical assistance grants for training staff to work with local CAAs.

The Freedom Now Party, a Black political party founded in 1963 during the March on Washington, mounts a statewide slate of candidates for political office in Michigan, where the party's efforts were primarily directed.

The Revolutionary Action Movement is founded in Wilberforce, Ohio.

Malcolm X is assassinated on February 21.

The Voting Rights Act becomes law on August 6. Five days later, the Watts Rebellion erupts in the Watts neighborhood of Los Angeles.

1962

1964

1965

1963

The Birmingham campaign is organized by the Southern Christian Leadership Council.

Medgar Evers is assassinated on June 12.

Martin Luther King Jr. leads a march down Woodward Avenue in Detroit on June 23 in advance of the March on Washington.

Detroit activist Jimmy Boggs's book, *The American Revolution: Pages from a Negro Worker's Notebook* is published in July.

The Northern Negro Grass Roots Leadership Conference is held in Detroit in early November, chaired by Jimmy Boggs. Participants pass resolutions endorsing the Freedom Now Party and the principles of self-defense.

Malcolm X gives his "Message to the Grassroots" speech at King Solomon Baptist Church in Detroit on November 10, advocating for revolutionary Black nationalism on a global scale:

In Bandung back in, I think, 1954, was the first unity meeting in centuries of Black people. . . . There were dark nations from Africa and Asia. Some of them were Buddhists. Some of them were Muslim. Some of them were Christians. Some of them were Confucianists; some were atheists. Despite their religious differences, they came together. Some were communists; some were socialists; some were capitalists. Despite their economic and political differences, they came together. All of them were Black, brown, red, or yellow.

The number-one thing that was not allowed to attend the Bandung conference was the white man. He couldn't come. Once they excluded the white man, they found that they could get together. Once they kept him out, everybody else fell right in and fell in line. This is the thing that you and I have to understand. And these people who came together didn't have nuclear weapons; they didn't have jet planes; they didn't have all of the heavy armaments that the white man has. But they had unity.

. . . All the revolutions that's going on in Asia and Africa today are based on what? Black nationalism. A revolutionary is a Black nationalist. He wants a nation. I was reading some beautiful words by Reverend Cleage, pointing out why he couldn't get together with someone else here in the city because all of them were afraid of being identified with Black nationalism. If you're afraid of Black nationalism, you're afraid of revolution. And if you love revolution, you love Black nationalism.[26]

President John F. Kennedy is assassinated on November 22.

The Demonstration Cities and Metropolitan Development Act of 1966 funds the Model Cities Program. Detroit becomes one of the largest experiments. The program ends in 1974.

1966

Civil unrest erupts in Newark, New Jersey, from July 12 to 17. The following week, the National Conference on Black Power is held in the city. At the conference, delegates adopt a resolution that the nationwide rebellions are necessary for the freedom movement to advance.

The Detroit rebellion erupts on July 23. It is one among hundreds that take place in cities across the United States between 1964 and 1968, constituting the most extreme period of domestic violence since the Civil War.

Rev. Albert B. Cleage founds the Shrine of the Black Madonna church in Detroit, which spreads a Black nationalist interpretation of Christianity. Later renamed the Black Madonna Pan African Orthodox Christian Church, it expands to other cities in the 1970s.

In a measure widely viewed as way to limit community control over resources, Congress passes the Green Amendment. The amendment gives control of CAP funds to local elected officials, defunding local groups.

Forty-seven thousand residents (mostly white) leave Detroit in one year.

1967

1968

The Republic of New Afrika is founded at a Black Government Conference held in Detroit at the Shrine of the Black Madonna church.

The Black Panther Party establishes a chapter in Detroit.

The Kerner Commission, which was tasked by President Lyndon B. Johnson to investigate the urban uprisings, releases a report that argues that the United States is "moving toward two societies, one Black, one white—separate and unequal. . . . What white Americans have never fully understood—but what the Negro can never forget—is that white society is deeply implicated in the ghetto. White institutions create it, white institutions maintain it, and white society condones it."[27]

Eighty thousand residents (mostly white) leave Detroit in one year.

Martin Luther King Jr. is assassinated on April 4.

1969

The National Black Economic Development Conference, a gathering of Black Power activists, is held in Detroit in April. The League of Black Revolutionary Workers, in collaboration with other activists, including James Foreman of the Student Nonviolent Coordinating Committee, takes over the conference, where they issue the "Black Manifesto," the first systematic plan for reparations to come out of the Black freedom movement.

Forty-six thousand residents (mostly white) leave Detroit in one year.

These photographs taken during the summer of 1967 capture several different aspects of the ways Detroiters experienced the rebellion and its aftermath. Henri Umbaji King's photograph titled *Linwood Madonna and Child* (left) highlights the vulnerability of children and bystanders as Detroit became a militarized zone. King's photograph *Hi Boys* (right) depicts armed soldiers, a young woman smiling, and residents attempting to maintain the rhythm of everyday life while living under conditions of military occupation. The middle picture, taken by an unknown photographer, shows the word *Soul* painted on a window, a tactic used by African American proprietors to discourage arson and looting.

Detroit Historical Society

1967: "*RIOT* IS A FOUR-LETTER WORD"

LINDA CAMPBELL, ANDREW NEWMAN,
SARA SAFRANSKY, AND TIM STALLMANN

The 1967 rebellion remains a defining point in Detroit's history. It is common for the events to be described as a spontaneous, apolitical "riot." However, such myths elide the important political legacy of 1967.[25]

From 1964 to 1967, every major central city in the United States with a sizable Black population experienced civil disorders. There were 329 major rebellions in 257 different cities. Following the assassination of Dr. Martin Luther King Jr. on April 4, 1968, there were another 200 uprisings in 172 cities. In July 1967, Detroit was considered "long overdue" for major unrest. People said, "You could feel it coming."[26]

It was in the predawn hours of July 23, 1967, when the Detroit police arrived near the corner of Twelfth Street and Clairmount Avenue on what would have normally been a routine task: the breakup of a late-night party at an unlicensed bar, or "blind pig." On this occasion however, approximately eighty people had gathered to celebrate the homecoming of two African American soldiers from Vietnam, and the police decided to arrest the entire party.[27] With dawn approaching and the police waiting for so-called cleanup crews to transport the prisoners to jail, a large crowd gathered. The precise catalyst for the uprising remains disputed. Some accounts claim that people who had gathered began smashing store windows in anger immediately after the police completed the arrests. One eyewitness account maintains that an officer struck a woman with a flashlight because she argued with how he was treating her boyfriend, and in response, the bystanders began pelting the police with rocks.[28]

Regardless of the immediate cause, the unrest—which included violent protests and confrontations with police as well as looting and arson—quickly spread to other parts of the city. With the Detroit Police Department suddenly overwhelmed, Michigan governor George W. Romney called in the National Guard, but even this was seen by authorities as inadequate to control the situation. By the next night, July 24, President Lyndon B. Johnson took a drastic step normally not used for standard civil unrest. Invoking the 1807 Insurrection Act, which was meant to address a direct threat to the government from within the United States, he ordered the redeployment of active duty US Army troops intended for service in Vietnam—the 82nd and 101st Airborne Divisions—to Detroit. Within a week, seventeen thousand armed officials patrolled the city. More than seven thousand people were arrested. As one Detroiter named Jesse Davis, a recent draftee home on army leave, described the situation, it defied the standard definition of a "riot" even by the standards of the turbulent 1960s:

The word was, that they [the army] had just come from Vietnam, so they was combat-ready. . . . You could hear, every now and then, one of those tanks firing. And they were saying on the news and stuff it was snipers in the building. They evacuated the building, they got the snipers out, they let off a few rounds from those tanks and stuff. Then they had opened up Belle Isle—the people they were arresting and stuff, the jails were so full. They were just packing them all in Belle Isle. Like a camp or something.[29]

By the time the conflagration and fighting ended, Detroit had witnessed the largest civil disturbance in American history since the Civil War. Forty-three people died—thirty-three were Black and ten were white; thirty were killed by law enforcement personnel. The property damage after the uprising was extensive: over 2,509 buildings were looted, burned, or destroyed.[30] The uprising had lasting effects on the geography of the metropolitan region, the material landscape of the city, and the collective consciousness of residents.

Many Detroiters, white and Black alike, understood the 1967 uprisings as a direct confrontation with a white-dominated power structure that had been brewing for a very long time. The uprisings were not just spontaneous protests but a response to a multitude of factors that were making life in Black communities increasingly untenable, including a racist white police force, the promise and failure of Great Society programs, urban renewal, and rising unemployment. As car companies tended toward automation and outsourcing unemployment rates for African Americans nearly doubled those for whites..[31]

While frequently called the "'67 riots" by commentators outside of the city, many Detroiters call the events the "'67 rebellion," a reference to both their scale and their political meaning. An excerpt from a 1967 church bulletin from First Unitarian Universalist Church of Detroit expresses a view of the events from within the city:

> It was an interesting experience during the riot week to drive through a long-integrated neighborhood just adjacent to the doubled area. Families were sitting on their front porches, children playing in the yards, fathers working their gardens—while just ten blocks away, the nation's worst civil disturbance flared! A lot of people are saying: "Now I should think you'd want to get out of Detroit." But this is a feeble and futile reaction. Whether you like it or not, the major proportion of American people are increasingly going to be living in cities. The answer is not to desert the cities but to be concerned and active in solving their problems. . . . The answer, of course, is quite apparent. If we can afford billions to get to the moon; if, indeed, we could afford four billion dollars to reconstruct war-ravaged Berlin, we can afford it![32]

The bulletin's account captures many important themes of the 1967 rebellion that have often been erased in the memory of it as a "riot," including the degree to which the events were

Shanna Merola

The national and local news media produced thousands of photographs during the five days Detroit spent under military siege in 1967. This collage is part of a series called "Black Day in July" that combines images with testimonial. Shanna Merola enlarged archival photographs of army tanks and militarized neighborhoods to create the collages. She then placed them inside some of the homes at the site of the rebellion, on Twelfth and Clairmount Streets—homes that remain abandoned forty-five years later—and photographed them.

viewed as an intentional political act at the time, the complicated and often misunderstood role that race played in the uprising, and finally, the strange juxtaposition whereby calm and normalcy could exist in some sections of the city only blocks away from the fighting. Unfortunately, despite the church's plea, there would be no Marshall Plan for the reconstruction of Detroit—in stark contrast to Berlin.

White flight was underway prior to the uprisings—between 1964 and 1966, twenty-two thousand whites left. However, in the years following the rebellion, out-migration increased eightfold. In 1967 alone, forty-seven thousand residents left the city. In 1968, eighty thousand left, and in 1969 another forty-six thousand fled.[33] In the ensuing years, the booming white suburbs formed an economic, racial, and psychological boundary with Detroit that only became more pronounced with the election of Coleman Young as Detroit's first Black mayor in 1973, a position he would hold for twenty years.

The uprisings from Newark to Detroit presaged the rise of African Americans in political office. Young was one of 104 Black mayors elected nationwide between 1969 and 1974. While Young's platform included housing and education reform, his main campaign promise was to establish a "people's police department" and dismantle a special undercover police unit called STRESS (Stop the Robberies, Enjoy Safe Streets) that had been terrorizing the Black community since 1971. In addition to the police department, Young worked to change the racial configuration of city government by facilitating the hiring of African Americans to head and staff numerous agencies. Despite the federal government's dismantling of Great Society initiatives like the Model Cities Program for urban development, Young continued local Great Society programs, building new parks, recreation centers, and low-income housing. Yet he could not stem the tide of economic divestment from the city despite an ambitious urban renewal agenda and generous corporate welfare incentives.

After Young's election, the out-migration dwarfed earlier rushes. Whereas in 1969, 891,000 whites still remained in Detroit, by 1976, as Young began a second term, 348,000 of them had left. The mass departure threw Detroit into economic turmoil, which was compounded further by the fact that the country was entering an economic recession and new phase of multinational capitalism.

Young had to contend not only with disinvestment but, in the coming decades, major shifts in federal urban policy as well. Ultimately, the uprising in Detroit and other cities became the key justification for the reconfiguration of Johnson's Great Society program toward crime control, surveillance, and incarceration. As the drug trade swept urban communities, and welfare retrenchment continued unabated, industrial labor restructuring and financialization gave rise to cities oriented around the service economy and permanent unemployment, setting the stage for the contemporary reconfiguration of Detroit.

1960s–2000s: BACKLASH AND RESISTANCE

The Omnibus Crime Control and Safe Streets Act passes, permitting law enforcement authorities to use wiretapping and electronic eavesdropping under certain conditions. It also establishes the Law Enforcement Assistance Administration, which provides financial assistance to state and local government law enforcement.

The Organization of Petroleum Exporting Countries (OPEC) oil embargo launches the United States into an era of "stagflation." Real wage growth levels out and begins to decline, a trend that continues into the 2010s.

Between 1969 and 1974, Black elected officials across the United States increase to include 16 congressional representatives and 104 mayors. Among them is Coleman Young, elected mayor of Detroit in 1973, a position he would hold for the next twenty years. One of his main campaign promises is to establish a "people's police department" and dismantle STRESS, which was responsible for four hundred warrant-less raids and the death of twenty-two citizens.

In 1969, 891,000 whites remained in Detroit. By 1976, when Coleman Young begins a second term in office, 348,000 of them have left. The mass departure, compounded by the country's economic recession, throws Detroit into economic turmoil.

Jimmy and Grace Lee Boggs join with other activists to found the National Organization for an American Revolution, which seeks to develop a new self-governing America and invigorated concept of citizenship.

1968   1973   1976   1978

1971   1974   1980

Stop the Robberies, Enjoy Safe Streets (STRESS), a special police unit dedicated to targeting street gangs begins operations in Detroit. Operating in undercover teams with little oversight, the eighty STRESS officers kill thirteen Black men during the first eight months of the program's operation. Among those murdered by STRESS officers were Herbert Childress, a gay man, and James Henderson, a trans sex worker. STRESS, along with a similar program by the Los Angeles Police Department named CRASH (Community Resources against Street Hoodlums), which lasted until 2000, is one of the most violent and notorious examples of how, following the rebellions, urban policy shifted from an emphasis on community development to fusing antipoverty and anticrime measures.

The Supreme Court rules in *Milliken v. Bradley* that segregation of schools is allowed if it is de facto rather than de jure. The case began in 1970 when the National Association for the Advancement of Colored People sued the State of Michigan to desegregate Detroit's schools. In the initial hearing, Stephen Roth, the federal judge assigned to the case, argues with the plaintiffs that residential segregation had created school boundaries that the government could not legitimately enforce. He rules that Black students from Detroit need to enroll in suburban schools and white students from the suburbs need to enroll in Detroit schools. In July 1974, the Supreme Court overturns Roth in a 5–4 vote, with the majority arguing that segregation is allowed if the school district has not engaged in an explicit policy of segregation.

Jimmy and Grace Lee Boggs publish *Revolution and Evolution in the Twentieth Century*.

Detroit contains only 16.5 percent of the region's property wealth, reduced from half of what it had in 1960.

The Detroit region has the widest household income gap of any large metropolitan area in the United States.

1983

James and Grace Lee Boggs found Detroit Summer.

Moody's downgrades Detroit's debt from investment grade to speculative grade despite the city's efforts to respond to the credit agency's concerns by exacting "fiscal surgery."

1992

Between 1996 and 1998, Moody's, Standard and Poor's, and Fitch upgraded Detroit's credit rating five times.

1996

David Bing, former NBA basketball star, takes office in 2009, pledging to restore public trust in city government. While Bing served only one term, the changes that occurred over his four-year tenure were pivotal for the present and future of Detroit. The research for *A People's Atlas of Detroit* takes place primarily during this period.

2009

1987

Save Our Sons and Daughters is founded in Detroit to educate the public on the problem of teen violence and youth homicide. In 1986 alone, 43 children are killed in the city from street violence and 365 are shot. We the People Reclaim Our Streets also forms in the mid-1980s.

1994

After twenty years as mayor, Coleman Young is succeeded by Dennis Archer, who wins by a narrow margin. Deploying the discourse of multiculturalism and regional cooperation, Archer promises to "transcend old racial divides, work with a Republican governor, and spur new business investment." His deracialized campaign infuriates many Black Detroiters. For many political and corporate leaders in the suburbs, his election marks the dawn of a new day in Detroit.

2001

Kwame Kilpatrick, a thirty-one-year-old state congressman, becomes the youngest mayor ever elected in Detroit's history. The centerpiece of his campaign platform is demolition. While he is seen as an up-and-coming Black politician—and is being eyed by national Democratic leadership—his political career begins to unravel at the start of a narrowly secured second term when he is involved with his chief of staff in a sex scandal. Detroit is politically paralyzed as the mayor bungles his way through the controversy, refusing to resign for almost a year.

SPEAKING WITH GRACE AND STERLING

CONVERSATION BETWEEN GRACE LEE BOGGS AND STERLING TOLES, ORGANIZED BY ZAK ROSEN

Zak Rosen contributed this conversation between Sterling Toles and Grace Lee Boggs. Grace Lee Boggs (1915–2015) and her husband, James (Jimmy) Boggs (1919–93), were prominent activists in Detroit. They were married in 1953 and collaborated and debated with some of the twentieth century's most important radical thinkers, including C. L. R. James (a Trinidadian-born historian and philosopher), Raya Dunayevskaya (a Russian-born activist and founder of Marxist humanism in the United States), and Malcolm X. Throughout it all, Grace (who held a PhD in philosophy and was the daughter of Chinese immigrants) and James (an Alabama-born African American and longtime Chrysler autoworker) remained fiercely independent intellectuals whose understandings of race and capitalism were directly rooted in their experiences in Detroit. They were influential as mentors and teachers for multiple generations of activists in Detroit.

While James and Grace might be considered products of Detroit's postwar years, it is equally true that their thinking has shaped what is often called radical Detroit, through their constant search for more humane alternatives to capitalism and their emphasis on personal growth and evolution. The conversation documented by Rosen captures what many consider most distinctive about Grace's approach to radical social change: her gentle approach to teaching and, above all, her insistence, shared with Jimmy, that social movements were not only about transforming society but also about personal reflection, growth, and healing.

Grace and Jimmy began to formulate their ideas about the necessity of what they referred to as a "two-sided transformation" in the wake of the urban uprising that swept cities across the country in the late 1960s. The Boggses embraced dialectical thinking, arguing that the world is constantly changing and that progressive ideas needed to change accordingly.

For Jimmy and Grace Boggs, if ideas don't change, they become reactionary. Like many other radical activists, they argued that the uprisings in Detroit and other cities were not riots but rebellions. They saw the uprisings as a form of spontaneous collective protest against the white power structure and oppressive policing tactics that were making life in urban Black communities increasingly unbearable. Yet the rebellions, particularly the rage and urgency embodied in them, also forced them to think more deeply about the difference between rebellions and revolutions. Whereas a rebellion is short lived, they argued, a revolution involved more than protesting oppression. A revolution required people to be able to project a vision for the future. This kind of visionary organizing required human beings to become more advanced in their creativity, in their ability to practice loving relationships with one another and the planet, in their social and political consciousness, and in their confidence of their own capacity to govern. In short, it required a new concept of invigorated citizenship. It also required people to nurture communities and develop programs.

In 1974, they published *Revolution and Evolution in the Twentieth Century*, which examined movement history from the American revolution to the present and outlined their revised political philosophy. The book aimed to project a "vision for a new road" to revolutionary social change in a country that had "lost it sense of direction, its sense of purpose, its sense of history, its knowledge of where it came from and where it should be going."[34] They argued: "A revolution is not just for the purpose of correcting past injustice. A revolution involves projecting the notion of a more human human being, i.e., a human being who is more advanced in the specific qualities which only humans have—creativity, consciousness and self-consciousness, a sense of political and social responsibility."[35]

In subsequent decades, they dedicated themselves to putting their political philosophy into practice. In 1978, the founded the National Organization for an American Revolution (NOAR), which had local study groups in Detroit and across the country where members worked to deepen the concept of citizenship that the Boggses articulated in *Revolution and Evolution*. NOAR lasted until the mid-1980s. By then, they understood that the United States had entered a new stage of multinational capitalism, and rampant consumerism and materialism that was threatening cities and communities.

Over the next several decades, Grace and Jimmy (and then Grace after Jimmy passed away) worked to realize their vision of simpler living, decentralized economies, strong communities, and self-government in Detroit. They helped organize a number of groups, including Detroiters for Dignity, which organized female seniors; We the People Reclaim our Streets, which organized neighborhood groups to fight the crack cocaine epidemic; and Save Our Sons and Daughters, which sought alternatives to youth violence. In 1992, they founded Detroit Summer, which sought to bring young people from the city and country to Detroit together to collaborate on projects that would "rebuild, redefine, and respirit Detroit from the ground up" and be a pathway where they could share their ideas of radical citizenship and visionary organizing with a new generation (for current iterations of Detroit Summer, see "Humanizing Schooling in Detroit" in chapter 6).[36] The following year, Jimmy Boggs passed away, and shortly after, the James and Grace Lee Boggs Center to Nurture

Community Leadership was founded. Over the next twenty years, Grace and her comrades worked through the center to cultivate a generation of leaders that can be felt in the energy of many of Detroit's community-based organizations. The Boggs Center is an important social center where people gather to share and debate alternative visions for Detroit's future.

To know Grace Lee Boggs was to know her favorite prefix, *re-*. She called on teachers and students to *re*imagine education. She urged neighbors to *re*-create public safety. She encouraged the American people to *re*think the idea of work itself. Boggs, who passed in 2015 at the age of one hundred, was a philosopher, writer, and visionary organizer. Her work over the past seventy-plus years touched on most of the major social movements this country has known: labor, civil rights, Black Power, and women's and environmental justice. She authored several books and countless pamphlets, essays, and articles.[37] She wrote a weekly column for the *Michigan Citizen* called Living for Change (which is what she later titled her autobiography).

Boggs was born to Chinese immigrant parents in Providence, Rhode Island, in 1915 and raised in New York City. She was politicized in Chicago when, in 1940, she joined a struggle against rat-infested housing. It was then when she became active with the South Side Tenants Organization, a group affiliated with the Workers Party. In her autobiography, she writes about that period: "For the first time, I was talking with people in the Black community, getting a sense of what segregation and discrimination meant in people's lives, learning how to organize protest demonstrations and meetings."[38]

She moved to Detroit in 1953, partly because it "felt like a *movement* city where radical history had been made and could be remade again."[39] That same year, she married African American activist, writer, and Chrysler worker James "Jimmy" Boggs. They lived together on Detroit's East Side in a two-family home on Field Street. Together, they wrote books, formed study groups, organized local and national conferences, and met with countless neighbors and activists until Jimmy's death in 1993. Grace remained in the same house and talked about Jimmy all the time, for example, how he swept their front porch constantly as a way to make himself accessible to their neighbors. She also liked to invoke his aphorisms when driving home a point: "My husband used to say, we have to change things not just because we don't like what's going on, but because what's going on is making us less of a human being every day."[40]

If Boggs was the grandmother of Detroit's reimagination, Sterling Toles is the laid-back older brother. Whereas Grace, when you would visit her at home, would send you on your way with a stack of books and pamphlets, Sterling will turn you on to all sorts of music you never knew existed. A Detroit native, Sterling is an illustrator, sound sculptor, DJ, and music producer. From his home recording studio, he produces the music of established musicians, friends, and neighborhood kids, rarely charging for his services. These sessions usually last for several hours and consist mainly of Sterling and his collaborators talking, with the microphones turned off.

In 2010, I invited a group of Detroiters to Grace's house for a series of recorded, freewheeling, one-on-one conversations. Having spent the year living in the flat above Grace's, I came to understand how lauded she had become for her stirring writings, lectures, and interviews, but that she was less known for her insatiable impulse to listen. In the excerpt below, Boggs sits back and mostly directs questions to Toles. The exchange gravitates around the themes of love, youth, work, education, personal transformation, and the world of ideas.

GRACE: I've been looking forward to today.

STERLING: Oh wow, me too.

GRACE: I have a lot of questions to ask you. Tell me about what you're doing with the young people. I've heard lots of stories.

STERLING: The funny thing about it was that I had some kids that used to be at YouthVille* and kids that have recorded at other places but were censored. My whole thing was I wouldn't censor them, but I would ask them why they felt what they felt. One of the premises that I really work on is that so much of this culture is about conduct, control, and behavior control as opposed to nourishment.

I really feel that a person's actions are a reflection of their state of health. If somebody is expressing something that's less than loving, it just may be the symptoms of their own suffering. So

*YouthVille is a nonprofit institution that leads afterschool programs in Detroit.

once those symptoms are addressed, we can begin the process of healing. I think it's very important that they express the things that they express in their truest nature, then from that we can have the information in front of us that will lead us toward the things that are really affecting them. So often, they would express things initially and somebody can say, "Whoa, that's really inappropriate" or "That's wrong" or "That's oppressive behavior," or whatever else. My understanding is that, obviously if they're expressing something that can be potentially painful, more than likely, that's a process of them trying to throw up the pain within them, because there's an innate understanding that pain isn't a true reflection of who they are. The fact that it's being released verbally is just a sign of them trying to release it and get it out. From that point, we can take that energy and begin to actually transform it as opposed to dispose of it.

GRACE: When did you arrive at that understanding? And how?

STERLING: One of the moments where it really rung home for me was a kid came to record with me and he sang the lyrics, recorded the lyrics, and I'm listening to the lyrics and I'm like, "This sounds like it's about another kid." He's like, "It is," and I'm like, "Why would you make a song that's disrespecting another kid?" And he was like, "Well, he disrespected me." I told him that people often react to things when they feel they don't have the power to transform them. One mantra that I live by is, "To be lured out of your own kindness is the initiation of your own sickness." To harm him is the greatest disservice you can do to yourself. He actually went home and a few days later, he comes over and he's like, "I thought about what you said, and you know, I decided for myself that I wasn't gonna participate, that I was gonna let this kid feel about me however he wanted to, and I was gonna continue to be who I am." Then he's like, "Guess what happened? The kid called me and apologized and said the reason that he said something was because he actually admired what I did." It was like the moment that he changed his heart was the moment that circumstances changed.

GRACE: "The moment he changed his heart was the moment circumstances changed." That's extraordinary: how something you knew inwardly, changes the objective environment.

STERLING: I was having this conversation with a friend and he was like, "Man, it's so hard to get people to change." And I was thinking to myself, through my life, I've found the greatest way to get people to change is just to show them you in the process of you transforming yourself. You know?

GRACE: I've been thinking a lot about why we use the word *nurture* in describing the Boggs Center. I don't remember exactly how it happened, but after Jimmy died and they created the Boggs Center, they asked me to give it a name, and I chose to use the word *nurture* rather than *develop* because *develop* suggests a goal that you have to go to, that you haven't reached that goal. Development implies underdevelopment so that you're judging somebody. *Nurture* suggests what you just said, that there's an inner transformation that takes place that changes the external

circumstances.... When did you arrive and how did you arrive at that understanding?

STERLING: In seventh grade, I had a friend who I wasn't being very nice to that day, and another friend stopped me and said, "Why are you treating him like that?" I thought to myself, "Damn, why am I treating him like that!?..." and it really hurt me that I could be like this to my friend. I remember that summer, I thought to myself, when I come back to school I'm not gonna say anything bad about anybody else. I'm gonna just treat everybody like they're my best friend, regardless of what they even think about me or how they may treat me or whatever else. I remember going back to eighth grade, and initially certain people were like, "Why is he so open and present with everybody now?" By the end of the year, it was like, I was cool with everybody and had a wonderful relationship with everybody who was around me.

I don't joke when I say this to people.... I really got to a place where I engage with people with their life being my life. One thing that I've realized in that process, it's sort of required me to have time for silence. I internalize people's experiences as my experience, so therefore, it causes me to perpetually live in the state of healing. In a sense it's like, once you tear down those walls of identity, and the moment that you're led into a person's experience in that moment, you have a whole new set of things to embrace and become intimate with in a way in which now I can understand how to integrate it into our collective healing.

GRACE: I think all of American history, and particularly at this moment, is the overcoming of that individualism. That I-ness that cannot feel the We-ness. I think it's the most challenging secret actually to not only personal development but to this country's. Everything in the culture is organized to make you an individual. To see your separateness as essential to your being. That's what's really destroying us.

One of the most important things happened to me when I was writing my dissertation. I read George Herbert Mead,* and I wrote my dissertation on the philosophy of the social individual. I recognized at that moment how much of American culture has been based on the individual. It's the only thing that will save this country, if we can overcome that individual identity, which is satisfied by buying material things. I think that Jimmy's paragraph in *Revolution and Evolution* where he talks about the next American Revolution will be different from all other revolutions, because it will require that we give up things rather than acquire more things. And that until we do so, we're gonna face revolutionary terror. This was written in 1974. I think the last decade has really been bringing home that truth that I don't think has yet been faced. I think these are the times to grow our souls.

STERLING: What does that look like?

GRACE: Seeing with your heart instead of with your eyes. I think in the history of every individual who lives in modern society, there comes a time when you have to reject the polarization of the ideal and the material. The tendency is if you talk this way about the heart, people say you're idealistic. Then you withdraw and you don't want to be seen as idealistic. It's associated also with superstition and magic and backwardness.

STERLING: People always say to me, "you're so idealistic, you're so philosophical," and it's like, "Do you understand democracy was somebody's idea at some point? Do you understand police forces were somebody's idea, somebody's philosophy?" Everything we consider to be reality was conceived of by somebody.

GRACE: Say that again! People have such an anti-intellectualism and anti-egghead thing, they don't understand the power of ideas and how important it is to struggle.

*George Herbert Mead (1863–1931) was an American philosopher, sociologist, and psychologist.

2

THIS LAND IS OURS

Toward a New Urban Commons

ities are built on land. This point seems obvious, but most discussions of cities, which focus on housing, infrastructure, development, and similar topics neglect the land itself. This chapter's contributors make a powerful case for why a focus on land control should be placed front and center in urban politics. Furthermore, the historical, political, and often personal attachments to land described by our contributors suggest that the dominant way of talking about land—as a form of property—neglects the other ways in which people value land. While these alternative valuations of land are sometimes glossed over as "home," this chapter shows that the meanings of land are at once more complicated and more politically focused than that. In this chapter, we highlight a direct link between material access to land and the ability to effectively shape the narrative surrounding a people's past, present, and future.

At a tangible level, land is literally the foundation on which urban politics rests. As such, many aspects of the urban crisis in Detroit turn on questions of land: To whom does it belong? Who defines its uses and value? What should it become? Who has the power to decide? Today Detroit's version of the land question is part of larger discussions around the world that connect citizens of rural and urban areas, and those of the global North, South, East, and West.[1] The increasingly ethereal nature of financial markets has made amassing and commodifying land in varying corners of the world far easier than before. This is nowhere more evident than Wayne County's annual tax foreclosure auction (one of the world's largest), where investors from around the world sweep in to buy properties (many still inhabited) at rock-bottom prices. As a result, many Detroiters are fighting for the right to stay put and for control over their neighborhoods. These struggles over land are part of a global story, even if the critiques, testimonies, and visions of the future that make up this chapter are unique to the Motor City.

This chapter's contributors draw out three themes related to urgent land questions that face Detroit. The first theme is that the trend to portray Detroit as an "urban wilderness"—its lands empty and open for the taking—is a myth steeped in indigenous erasure and anti-Blackness. This visual narrative of a majority Black city depopulated and cleansed by nature is deeply linked with doctrines of white supremacy, which since the beginnings of European colonialism have sought to define lands owned and occupied by non-whites as empty and available for the taking. In the early 2010s, when research for this book was being conducted, city officials characterized approximately 150,000 parcels—one-third of the city's landed area—as "vacant" or "abandoned." This dramatic statistic led to a way of defining Detroit in the media that made vacancy and absence the primary point of emphasis. As the image on p. 73 shows, many other cities and towns in Michigan have as much vacancy as Detroit, but these places are not subject to the same obsession with "untamed" urban nature as the Motor City. This casting of Detroit as a fantasy landscape "retaken" by nature manifests itself in the abundance of clichéd images of mansions ensnarled in vines, trees growing out of skyscrapers, and neighborhoods "returned" to midwestern prairie.[2]

As our contributors make clear, the focus on nature's power to reclaim cities often ignores the role played by humans, and racism in particular, in *producing* vacancy in the landscape. Moreover, it ignores the people who live in and care for those landscapes.

In "Detroit-opoly: Who Cares for Land in Detroit?," Kezia Curtis and Jessi Quizar argue against a cliché of settler colonialism that continues to be espoused in metro Detroit—the ideology that the people who occupy the city's land are not capable of managing it effectively. Curtis and Quizar, among other contributors, counter these myths by showing how Detroiters spend an inordinate amount of time caring for land they often don't legally own. They mow yards. They plant flowers. They look out for houses. They tend public parks. In doing so, they care for Detroit. By contrast, speculators and investors lack a personal investment in the city. Neglect of housing and land is, for them, a logical choice.

The second theme emphasized in this chapter is that ongoing displacement in Detroit needs to be understood as part of a longer history of displacement that shapes people's relationship to land. Land loss and legal and extralegal segregation practices extend from colonialism and slavery to Jim Crow, urban renewal, racist federal housing policies, and the reverse redlining of the 2008–9 subprime crisis. This repeated process of dispossession and displacement has severely limited the ability of African Americans and other people of color not only to accumulate wealth through property ownership but also to claim a piece of land as home without the risk and fear of displacement. Histories of displacement and migration are integrated into the family narratives and identities of Detroiters. For example,

Cecily McClellan reflects on growing up in the old Black Bottom neighborhood, a segregated African American neighborhood in Detroit that was bulldozed as part of urban renewal in the 1960s. McClellan remembers Black Bottom as a place that in spite of its crowdedness, or perhaps because of it, benefited from a strong sense of community. Ever since she and her family were forced to move, she's been trying to re-create a similar sense of place and community in the neighborhood where she now lives.

Similarly, Michelle Martinez describes how her family's home in Southwest Detroit was taken to make way for the Ambassador Bridge. This demolition robbed her family of material ownership and continued a multigenerational legacy of displacement that fundamentally shapes her relationship to land today. Martinez argues that for her, like many Detroiters, part of this legacy entails defining land as an element of resistance. As an example, she cites *palenques* in Latin America, which, similar to maroons in the United States, are autonomous communities formed by escaped slaves and indigenous people who engaged in communal life on collective land. She suggests that Detroiters can draw sustenance from this history, which offers another way of being in relationship to land and one another. Caring for land provides one important way for many to honor these common histories, which are at once personal, intimate, and deeply political.

This map, like those at the start of chapters 3 through 6, highlights locations mentioned in the interviews and essays in this chapter. Neighborhood boundaries source: City of Detroit Department of Neighborhoods, 2017.

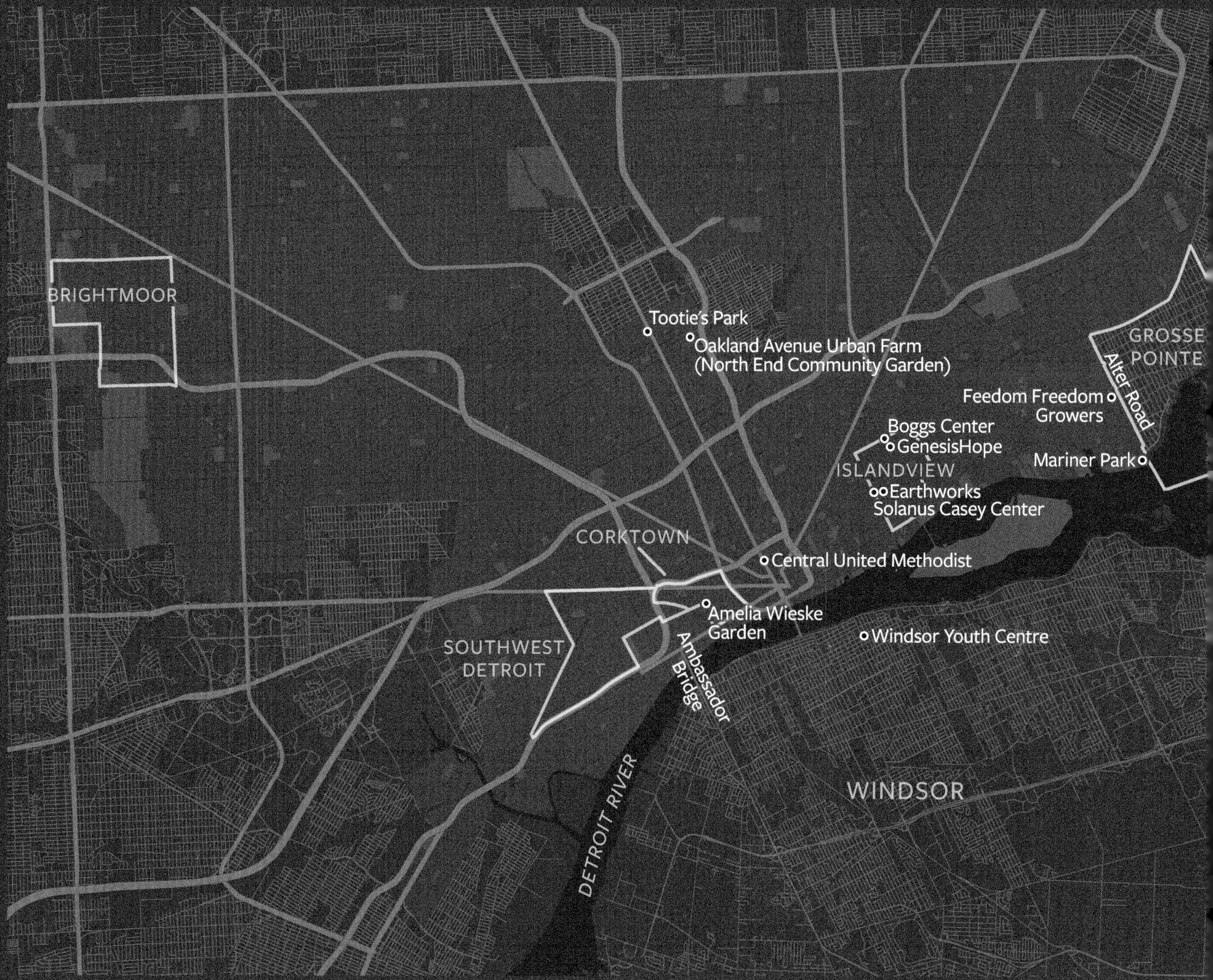
BRIGHTMOOR
Tootie's Park
Oakland Avenue Urban Farm
(North End Community Garden)
GROSSE
POINTE
Alter Road
Feedom Freedom
Growers
Boggs Center
GenesisHope
ISLANDVIEW
Mariner Park
Earthworks
Solanus Casey Center
CORKTOWN
Central United Methodist
Amelia Wieske
Garden
Windsor Youth Centre
SOUTHWEST
DETROIT
Ambassador
Bridge
DETROIT RIVER
WINDSOR

"We don't call it vacant. . . . Just because you see something that's not built doesn't mean the land doesn't have value. The word 'vacant' or 'derelict' is pejorative. We say 'open space.' . . . Land that is open space is held in the commons." **—CHARITY HICKS**

Charity Hicks was a Detroit resident, community activist, and member of the People's Water Board, which she discusses in a longer interview in chapter 6. She passed away in 2014 before this book was completed.

This connects to the third theme that emerges in the chapter: Detroiters' common care of the land is productive of alternative forms of politics and sociality. For example, Andrea Sankar, Mark Luborsky, and Robert Johnson discuss how the multigenerational sharing of fishing knowledge and skills among anglers in Detroit not only retains culture but also reaffirms values of mutual care and community. Amelia Wieske's memoir-like essay about her family's backyard garden illustrates how tending and cultivating the land gives rise to notions of belonging that connect people to a larger whole. Similarly, in an interview about eviction defense work in Detroit, Dianne Feeley argues that block clubs bring people together to care for the neighborhood. In the course of mowing lawns and taking care of vacant houses, people establish important social networks that can then be mobilized to fight, for example, against home foreclosures and school and library closures, which contribute to the destruction of the neighborhood.

Toward the end of the chapter, several of our contributors talk about the role of the Detroit River in shaping Detroiters' sense of place and the ways they interact with the environment. The river—which is really a strait between Lake Erie and Lake St. Claire—structures the topography and political geography of the region. Once a key crossing on the Underground Railroad, the strait is now the largest border crossing between Canada and the United States. Lee Rodney and Michael Darroch describe efforts to reimagine the Detroit River as the meeting point it has long been instead of as a border or terminus. They describe how activists and artists are working to reestablish a cross-border commons between Detroit and Windsor (the Canadian city directly across the strait). They emphasize the importance of such relations at a time when revanchism, nationalism, and xenophobia exert a strong pressure to keep separate the lives and struggles of residents on both sides of the border. Lauren Rosenthal's map of the Great Lakes watershed region (see p. 104) suggests the potential of organizing political communities around waterways rather than using rivers as a means of division.

The theme of transcending borders and reorganizing political geographies extends to Detroiters' relationships with land, which go far beyond ownership and access. These connections tell a broader story: who people are, where they come from, and who they seek to become are intimately linked to land. Relationships with land are therefore personal and political. To

Everywhere in Michigan with at Least as Much Vacancy as Detroit, 2012

According to the 2008–12 American Community Survey, Detroit has a residential vacancy rate of approximately 28 percent. This map lists all the places in Michigan with housing vacancy rates of 28 percent or higher as of 2012.

There are many reports, books, films, and other narratives about Detroit that focus on the sheer quantity of vacant land in the city, so it is easy to adopt the mistaken assumption that vacancy is a uniquely "Detroit" problem. This graphic shows cities and towns around Michigan (names of cities are written near to their approximate locations) that have rates of vacancy equal to or higher than Detroit's. Many towns with high rates of vacancy are located in rural sections of western and northern Michigan. This graphic is a reminder that the dramatic degree of deindustrialization and disinvestment that produced vacancy in Detroit impacts a broad region that stretches far beyond the urban areas of the state. Nevertheless, the social stigma and political blame that is associated with deindustrialization and disinvestment is overwhelmingly focused on Detroit and other majority African American cities.

White Pine, Ahmeek, Eagle River, Eagle Harbor, Michigamme, Copper Harbor, Marenisco, Watersmeet, Alpha, Crystal Falls, K. I. Sawyer, Big Bay, Garden, St. James, Cross Village, Levering, Mackinaw City, Mackinac Island, De Tour Village

Carp Lake, Pilgrim, Elberta, Frankfort, Crystal Downs Country Club, Benzonia, Beulah, Empire, Crystal Mountain, Glen Arbor, Nessen City, Lake Ann, Cedar, Leland, Suttons Bay, Northport, Omena, Elk Rapids, Norwood, Eastport, Fife Lake, Rapid City, Alden, Central Lake, Charlevoix, Bellaire, Ironton, Bay Shore, Advance, Horton Bay, Manistee Lake, Boyne City, Harbor Springs, Alba, Bear Lake, Walloon Lake, Bay View, Boyne Falls, Lakes of the North, Oden, Ponshewaing, Indian River, Wolverine, Lewiston, Canada Creek Ranch, Atlanta, Mio, Millersburg, Hubbard Lake, Presque Isle Harbor, Lost Lake Woods, Lincoln, Harrisville, Pentwater, Arcadia, Onekama, Bear Lake, Wellston, Copemish, Baldwin, Caberfae, Mesick, Harrietta, Luther, Canadian Lakes, Lake City, Harrison, Houghton Lake, Prudenville, Loomis, St. Helen, Rose City, Skidway Lake, Lupton, Prescott, Whittemore, Sand Lake, East Tawas, Bay Port, Au Sable, Oscoda, Caseville, Port Austin, Minden City, Port Hope, Forestville, Douglas, Saugatuck, Barnes Lake-Millers Lake, Port Sanilac, Lexington, Michiana, Grand Beach, New Buffalo, Shorewood-Tower Hills-Harbert, Lake Michigan Beach, Paw Paw Lake, South Haven, South Gull Lake, Colon, Manitou Beach-Devils Lake, Vineyard Lake, Estral Beach, Detroit, Highland Park

Gregg Newsom

have a firm hold on land is to have more control over one's place in the world, including the ability to self-define one's identity, the story of one's past, and control over one's future. The anthropologist Keith Basso wrote about the Western Apache that "wisdom sits in places."[3] The same is true in Detroit. The continuing threat of dispossession in Detroit drives an urgent need voiced by social movements to draw on intergenerational wisdom to look beyond the value of land as merely a commodity and, in doing so, to rethink the "racial regimes of ownership" that have defined the United States since its beginning.[4]

Uniting Detroiters Workshop Map

In August 2012, more than fifty residents gathered at the Solanus Casey Center on the East Side of Detroit for a Uniting Detroiters workshop. After a discussion of the territorial reordering of the city at the hands of planners and developers, participants broke into small groups to create their own maps of Detroit. During the workshop, one group created a map with a legend associating red dots with "stop, challenge, community detriment," which included the Hantz Woodlands project (see p. 75). They used yellow dots to identify zones of "caution," which included potential land grabs and a large "zone of gentrification" that extended from Downtown to Midtown. Blue dots, by contrast, denoted "historical memory," including sites of historical displacement like the Fox Indian Massacre, Black Bottom, the Battle of the Overpass, and Poletown. In addition to highlighting such sites of struggle, this group and others also located community assets that supported an alternative vision for the city's development, including public sites like museums, libraries, and parks; community gardens like Feedom Freedom Growers, the North End Gardens, and Earthworks; and community-based social justice institutions like the Boggs Center and Central United Methodist.

District 5

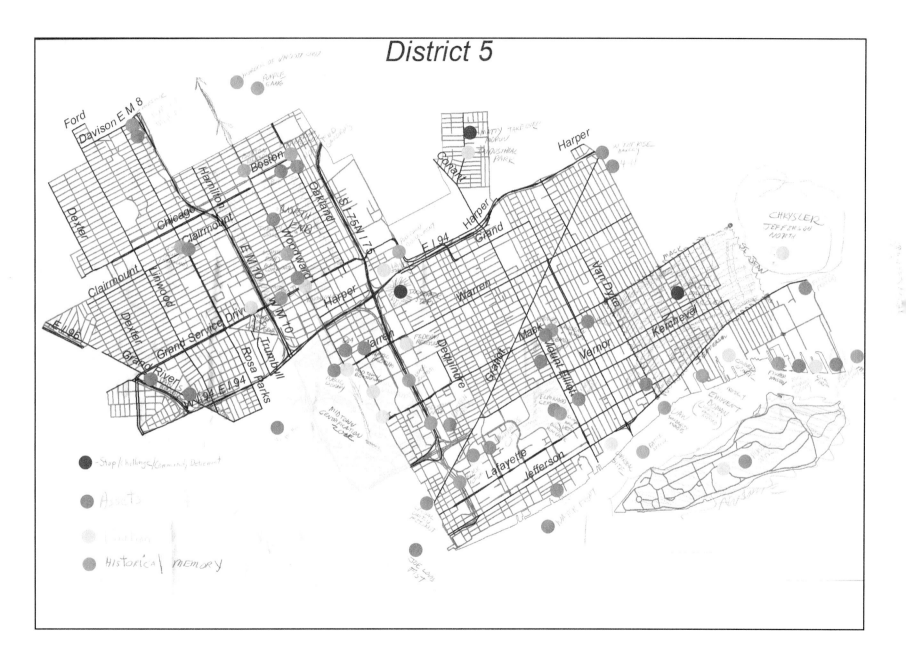

"DEFENDING THE LAND IS IMPORTANT"

DIANNE FEELEY

Dianne Feeley is a Detroit-based resident, activist, and retired autoworker. She has lived in Detroit since 1987. Over the years, seventy-eight-year-old Feeley has been involved in supporting social movements, including anti-war movements (such as US wars conducted in Central America and Iraq) and anti-apartheid struggles. At the time of this interview in 2013, Feeley was a part of Occupy Detroit's Eviction Defense Committee, working with block clubs to fight evictions and foreclosures caused by predatory mortgages backed by Fannie Mae, as well as property tax foreclosures at the city and county levels. This interview was conducted by Ayana Maria Rubio as part of the Uniting Detroiters project.

Members of Occupy Detroit's Eviction Defense Committee and neighbors defend a home from eviction.

Detroit is a city of neighborhoods. People in Detroit have a real sense of homeownership born out of housing struggles. Throughout the nineteenth century, as immigrants flocked to a continuously industrializing city, they found whatever shelter they could and then built their own homes. But with the flood of southern migration of the early twentieth century—which was not only Black but also white—the city didn't have enough housing. What housing it had was expensive, crowded, and increasingly redlined. The most remembered incident of that period is the 1925 case of Ossian Sweet, a Black doctor who bought a house in a better-off neighborhood on the East Side. He knew neighbors would oppose his family's presence, so he invited friends and relatives to help him defend his new home. The second night a crowd of three thousand whites gathered outside, throwing stones. Someone in the house shot from an upstairs window, killing one person and injuring another. Everyone in the house was arrested; amazingly, after two trials they were acquitted.

Few African Americans, however, could afford homeownership until after World War II. Then, in some neighborhoods, block-by-block fights attempted to maintain segregated housing. Whites wanted to protect their "investment." They said, "If Blacks move in, we would have to move out."

I grew up in San Francisco, but that's what my own parents said. When I asked, "Why would we have to move out?" they replied that the price of housing would drop. This was one of the first arguments I had with my mother. The racist stereotype about the "Black homeowner" portrayed the Black family as dirty, criminal, lazy, undereducated. This racist stereotype undermines any possibility of solidarity.

Detroit's history intertwines racial injustice with governmental policy. After the war, as auto corporations built new plants beyond the city limits, as government programs deliberately opened up suburban housing to the white working class, African Americans challenged segregation in Detroit. In the 1970s, African Americans became the city's majority population.

*The Occupy movement began on September 10, 2011, when protesters set up an encampment in Zuccotti Park in New York City to protest social and economic inequality. That particular protest was called Occupy Wall Street. Over the next year, hundreds of similar "occupations" occurred in downtowns across the United States and world. Detroit's was in Grand Circus Park.

You're active in fighting evictions in Detroit. Could you talk about that work?

I think the question of defending the land is important, defending the land against attempts to take it away.

The wealth that most working people have is in the home they own. That's been especially true in Detroit. The economic recession [which began in December 2007] wiped out much of that wealth, disproportionately so for African Americans. Gentrification continues to reinforce that inequality. It destabilizes neighborhoods by starving them of resources, allowing evictions and then using money that could keep people in their homes to tear them down instead. Our movement works to keep people in their homes and opposes policies that displace them.

I'm active in Occupy Detroit's Eviction Defense Committee, which began out of [the] Occupy [movement] over the last year.* It combines with other organizations and works with block clubs in neighborhoods where they exist. I see activist block clubs as a vital component in halting the destruction of neighborhoods. I think one of the secrets of Detroit is the existence of block clubs in about 20 percent of the city. They're the glue that holds much of the city together. Members often mow the lawns of vacant houses, create and maintain community gardens and parks, pressure banks to take care of vacant houses, and welcome new people into the neighborhood. They have also protested the closure of schools and libraries, sometimes successfully. It is a really important form of self-organization.

As banks threaten to foreclose, we work with the homeowner to organize neighbors, their union, or their church. We ask them to call or email the bank, or Fannie Mae, the government agency that guarantees the mortgage. Sometimes marching on the bank's local office can bring enough pressure for banks to renegotiate. If the homeowner has a court date, we accompany them. When their case is called, we all stand up so the judge sees our standing with them.

In Detroit, the eviction is carried out only after a dumpster is placed in front of the house. Generally, the homeowner then has three days to move before the sheriff and his deputies empty out the house and change the locks. If the eviction order has been given, we set up a ten-hour-a-day watch over the house. In one case, we stopped the truck from delivering the dumpster; in other cases the dumpster never arrived.

We also publicize the reality that the majority of homeowner applications for federal aid are rejected. Just as with Fannie Mae, government agencies are facilitating foreclosures!

We also want to tackle tax foreclosures. The city and county are not in compliance with the state law that requires property taxes to be calculated based on a percentage of the market value. But unlike other Michigan cities and counties, there has been no reassessment since the economic crisis hit. Further, low-income homeowners are entitled to a poverty exemption, but the city doesn't publicize its existence or make it easy to apply. Further, the city imposes an 18 percent interest rate on unpaid taxes. Clearly many of the tax foreclosures are avoidable!

Those who have been unable to pay these exorbitant taxes for three years will have their homes sold in a county auction. These are then bought up at bargain basement prices by developers and individuals. Often the former homeowner (who is barred from bidding on their own house) will be asked if they'd like to rent their home from the new owner, at a hefty rent.

We have whole neighborhoods where the majority of the houses on the block are empty. Once houses are vacant, they are stripped by scrappers. I have a friend who lives on a street where there are twenty-two houses: twelve of them occupied; ten are not. The home is vacant; the neighborhood is dying. How does the city benefit from a policy of thousands of tax foreclosures and evictions? This policy accomplishes two things: it provides cash for the government and clears out neighborhoods so developers can move in.

"Those who own the land right now or are trying to acquire it will have the power.... The homes that have been vacated as a result of the foreclosure crisis.... We feel very strongly that those houses can be repaired and put back into productive use. We have our own ideas for one of the vacant schools—to turn it into a food-processing center. There's a lot of vacant land around it, so you could grow and process your own food. We see people who live in the community engaging in that effort."**—JEANINE HATCHER**

Jeanine Hatcher is a native Detroiter and the executive director of Genesis HOPE, a community development corporation that empowers youth to organize community events, connect people to good food, and help local businesses thrive.

DETROIT-OPOLY

Who Owns and Cares for Land in Detroit?

KEZIA CURTIS AND JESSI QUIZAR

In this essay, Kezia Curtis and Jessi Quizar discuss the many ways Detroit residents maintain property they do not actually own as a way of caring for their communities. They explore the on-the-ground tensions that emerge between an atmosphere shaped by land speculation and the experiences of residents whose valuation of land transcends commodification.

Feedom Freedom is a small urban farm on Detroit's far east side, just a few blocks from Alter Road, the stark line that divides Detroit from the Grosse Pointe suburbs. Kezia's parents, Wayne Curtis and Myrtle Curtis Thompson, started the garden in 2009, inspired in part by Wayne's activist work in the 1960s and 1970s. As a member of the Detroit Black Panther Party, Wayne participated in the party's survival programs, including helping run the before-school breakfast program for Detroit children (see the interview with Wayne Curtis, "Liberated territory is a means of survival" on p. 130). When he and Myrtle moved into the neighborhood, Wayne saw the vacant lots that surrounded their house and decided to create another kind of survival program—growing food in the neighborhood.

Now Feedom Freedom has grown to include six farmed lots that yield everything from collards to snap peas to eggplants. Bees whiz back and forth to their hive, busily collecting pollen. The farm runs programs in cooking, art-in-the-garden workshops for kids, and a youth mentorship program where teenagers learn political skills like dialogue facilitation as well as how to farm.

We, Kezia and Jessi, met at the garden. Jessi was a researcher from California, working on her dissertation about food and land in Detroit. Kezia was working at Feedom Freedom, building the program with her family. We start here, at the garden, because it is precisely the kind of project that is underrepresented in many portrayals of Detroit. Feedom Freedom is Black led and run by two generations of lifelong Detroiters rather than the "creative class" who have been much publicized as moving in to "save" the city.[5] We write and work against this narrative and for the idea that longtime Detroiters have indeed built a culture of caring for and creatively shaping our city. We are writing this essay together as a Detroit-born resident with a lifelong commitment to the city (Kezia) and a new Detroiter (Jessi) who aims to work in solidarity with those who have been working for social and racial justice in the city for generations. We wrote this essay in primarily one voice. In two places, we share our personal narratives, which we signal with the narrator's name.

KEZIA

In the 1940s, my grandfather moved from Mississippi to Detroit, Michigan. He owned numerous apartment buildings on the city's

West Side and worked as a handyman inside them. I remember spending the summer when I was eight years old walking in my grandfather's shadow, filling errand requests for tenants and, most important, finding playmates who would take adventures around the building with me. One afternoon while playing with friends, we heard fire truck sirens screaming. They were so close the noise interrupted our play and sent us rushing in the direction of the closest window. A complex across the street from my grandfather's building was on fire. As we stood watching firemen climb out of the truck and put out the fire, one of the girls said, "Someone set that building on fire again." The other girls agreed, shaking their heads with their lips curled up to one side.

A part of me didn't understand what they were seeing because I had never noticed that the building was abandoned until that moment. Nor had I noticed the few other abandoned buildings and homes on the block. In that instance, my vision of the block changed. I had so many questions about the fire and the other buildings on the block. Who better to ask than my grandfather? I told the girls I would see them later and rushed to his office. I ran through his door breathing hard and spilling all the questions that had formed and were still forming in my head. He began his answer by rambling on about city politics and how things in Detroit should be better. He recalled when he first arrived in Detroit from the South. I was too young to really grasp most of what he said. However, our conversation stayed in the front of my mind for days. On the way home, I saw all the abandoned buildings I had never noticed before. It was the first time the vacancies within my city and community had affected me.

Amy Senese

Kezia Curtis (*center*) works with student leaders to prepare garden beds at Feedom Freedom for the winter months.

As I grew up, I had more interactions with abandoned spaces in the city—from huge toxin-filled automotive plants that have been left to decay by fleeing companies to abandoned homes that have become decrepit, some left standing, others bulldozed. In the decades following World War II, the vacancies and abandonment created by former residents and businesses brought about a tidal wave of changes within Detroit communities. These abandoned structures and empty lots have become dumping grounds, prime property for drug trafficking, dark spaces on neighborhood blocks, and financial burdens for the bankrupted city. At the same time, as residents of Detroit find ways to reclaim these spaces, they have become homes for squatters and places for graffiti artists to express their creativity. They have become murals that speak of what the city has been and what it will be. They have become community gardens that feed neighborhood residents, sites for cleanup initiatives that simultaneously curb public dumping and build community relationships, and pop-up businesses that help create local economies. These reclaimed spaces represent the drive of "reimagination" within Detroiters.

THE VIEW FROM THE OUTSIDE

Articles published all around the world paint Detroit as a desolate city that is falling apart at the hands of Detroiters. In a 2013 *Washington Post* article, journalist Keith B. Richburg writes, "Detroit has really been broke, broken and in decay now for decades—a shell of a city, with a small downtown and some scattered neighborhoods dissected by miles of abandoned storefronts and vacant lots."[6] He goes on to say that the lost pride of Detroiters is not only what allowed the city to spiral downward, but it is also what will keep it here.

These articles frequently feature images of buildings and homes crumbling to pieces and lots overgrown with grass, trees, and weeds. *Time* magazine has published two photo essays of the city, which ruminate on ruin—one called "The Remains of Detroit"; the other, "Detroit's Beautiful, Horrible Decline."[7] Both highlight abandoned buildings, damaged and falling. The first photograph in "Detroit's Beautiful, Horrible Decline" is the hulking ruin of Michigan Central Station with the caption "Detroit's

main train station opened in 1913, has not been used since 1988." The station looks haunted and very much abandoned. The essay fails to mention that the building has been under active speculation and is currently owned by Manuel "Matty" Moroun, a billionaire who in 2015 had wealth upward of $1.8 billion, according to Forbes.[8] It is not that there are no resources to fix the train station. Moroun, an investor who lives nowhere near the building, simply has chosen to neglect it.

However, many articles that focus on Detroit imply that Detroiters themselves are to blame for lack of upkeep of their communities. For instance, in his article "Who to Blame for the Death of Detroit?" reporter M. D. Harmon quotes an editorial from *Investor's Business Daily*: "An estimated 78,000 of the city's homes are unoccupied, and in 2011, half the occupiers of its 305,000 properties did not pay any tax."[9] It is true that many Detroiters struggle to meet basic needs, including paying their taxes. However, a statistic like this obscures, for instance, that many property owners who live outside the city list city addresses as their primary residences. These people are among those who are behind on their taxes—and indeed they risk much less by not paying taxes because their home is not at stake. Where are the articles on non-Detroit homeowners who allow their properties (homes, buildings, and lots) to become eyesores and hazards in communities all over the city? Or the articles about how Detroit residents are left with the responsibility for cleaning up the mess in the face of skyrocketing home and car insurance rates, steadily declining home values, and ever-increasing property taxes—and with all the blame?

DETROIT LAND BARONS

The case of Michael Kelly and Matthew Tartarian illustrate the problem of land speculation in Detroit. In 2013, Kelly and Tartarian, both residents of wealthy suburbs outside Detroit, together owned more land parcels than anyone in the city, over eleven hundred, three of which are in the same neighborhood as Feedom Freedom. Their vast holdings and $100,000 in city blight fines were enough to prompt a *Detroit News* investigation.[10] The report concluded that their basic investment strategy was to buy tax-foreclosed land at the annual Wayne County Tax Foreclosure Auction for $500 a parcel and then sell it at a significant markup either to developers or back to the city for development projects. Meanwhile, they sat on the land, allowing their properties to become increasingly overrun with weeds and trash. Neglect of the land was actually inherent to their investment model—the less they invested in the property, the more profit they made.

Yet activities on Kelly's and Tartarian's properties also went beyond mere neglect. The property that Tartarian lists as his home address on the tax records, 3631 Chene Street, is a double lot on Detroit's East Side, near Feedom Freedom. It contains a windowless warehouse and a boarded-up Victorian house surrounded by a ten-foot-high fence topped with barbed wire. From the outside it looks abandoned, but not too long ago it was occupied. On August 24, 2011, the Detroit police raided the building on tips from neighbors and found what Sheriff Benny Napoleon called the second-largest marijuana-growing operation ever discovered in the city, worth about $15 million.[11] Three people were arrested at the facility. None of them resided in the city but rather commuted to the city specifically to grow marijuana.

The large neglected property at 3631 Chene Street, owned by Matthew Tartarian.

Tartarian, the owner of the property, was never charged and indeed felt comfortable enough that he chose to list the former grow house as his home address on property records.

This property at 3631 Chene Street is an egregious example, and yet it is telling. The city has long been used as a dumping ground for various kinds of waste and hazards. The issue of illegal dumping, particularly the habit of nonresidents specifically driving into the city and dumping trash, has long been a public issue.[12] On a grander scale, Koch Carbon (owned by the billionaire Koch brothers) has been widely criticized for piling hills of petroleum coke right next to neighborhoods in

Southwest Detroit, coating residential areas in a fine layer of this petroleum by-product.[13] One could think of the grow house on Tartarian's property as serving a similar function. It is in this way that Detroit becomes a "dump" for undesirable industries, while the producers, and likely many of the consumers, are themselves from the suburbs.

JESSI

In 2011, I purchased a house in Detroit's East Side that had been vacant for over a year. The day after I signed the papers for it, I went over to the house, excited about the project of fixing it up. As I pulled into the driveway and began taking tools out of my car, a group of neighbors came up to me, not aggressively but certainly assertively, to question who I was, why I was there, and what business did I have going in and out of that house. They were watching out and mercy to anyone who tried to break into the house to steal the pipes. Many of my neighbors had been living on that street for more than thirty years. They knew each other, they had watched out for each other's children, and they were deeply invested in keeping the neighborhood safe, beautiful, and a good place to live. Before I bought the house, they took turns mowing its lawn, shoveling its walk, and trimming its exuberant flowering bushes.

I bought my house from Deutsche Bank, which had acquired it through foreclosure from the investment rental company that had previously owned it, which was based in Austin, Texas. Neither the bank nor the rental company had ever bothered to perform even basic caretaking tasks as the house became vacant.

But the neighbors did. While they did not own the house, they were genuinely invested in its well-being and in the well-being of the neighborhood through their history, through their relationships, and through a sense of responsibility to a place that goes deeper than financial investment.

WHO REALLY CARES ABOUT THE NEIGHBORHOOD?

In much news media and other mainstream public discourse about the city, there is a base assumption that outside investment, that is, non-Detroiters buying properties, will lead to a reduction in blight. The examples of Kelly and Tartarian make it clear that "investment" from non-Detroiters does not necessarily lead to a better quality of life in Detroit neighborhoods. In fact, it is perhaps precisely outside investors' remove from the city, their lack of personal investments, such as relationships with neighbors, that make it seem financially logical and beneficial to neglect the land that they own. This kind of impersonal monetary investment arguably *causes* blight in Detroit.

On the other hand, all over the city a different kind of investment is taking place—an investment of relationships, of time, of care. While popular images may portray Detroiters as being responsible for the neglect of properties in the city, one of the things that is most striking about Detroit is the way that so many residents and neighbors take care of so much more land than they are actually legally responsible for or to which they do not even have legal rights.

It is not easy. Even when residents are improving land, it is often difficult to gain legal title to it. For example, Feedom Freedom workers were for years unable to buy the land that they farmed, despite having the money to do so. During the first years of Feedom Freedom, few options existed for urban growers to claim the land they grew on. When Myrtle began researching possibilities, she found that the city offered garden permits. In exchange for land upkeep, Feedom Freedom was able to lease the plot of land from the city. With that lease came rules: no permanent structures could be built on a plot, and if the city sold the land, Feedom Freedom must evacuate immediately. In 2010, Feedom Freedom received donations to purchase plots that they had been farming. Myrtle was told to use the zoning code "Green Spaces" when applying for the land. At the time, there were no zoning or ordinances that specifically allowed urban gardening, so the application was denied.

In 2013, investor John Hantz signed a purchase agreement for roughly 1,550 parcels of land for an urban tree farm. In advance of the purchase, Detroit's Planning and Development Department offered residents with homes adjacent to city-owned land the right of first refusal to buy the parcels for $200 each.[14] During that time, Feedom Freedom was able to purchase three parcels. The entire process took two years. Ironically, it was only the promise of large-scale investment that compelled the city to sell Feedom Freedom the land.

DETROITERS CARE ABOUT DETROIT

All over the city, residents perform caretaking work for spaces that they do not own. They take responsibility for land owned and neglected by people who most often live outside of the neighborhood or city. In neighborhoods like Brightmoor, residents have come together to create numerous gardens, parks,

Land Speculation in the Feedom Freedom Neighborhood

In recent years, foreclosures and subprime mortgages have highlighted the racial dynamics underlying land control. According to the Michigan State Housing Development Authority, 62 percent of all mortgage loans to African Americans in metro Detroit in 2005–7 were subprime loans, compared to 28 percent for whites. Meanwhile, 87 percent of African American borrowers in Wayne County, where the City of Detroit is located, were sold subprime loans in 2006. Despite the widely publicized racial inequalities underlying the foreclosure process and the long-recognized problem of empty houses in Detroit, Wayne County foreclosed on an astounding eighty thousand houses in 2014 for failure to pay property taxes, almost half of which were estimated to be owner or renter occupied. This policy produces yet more vacant lots in Detroit while also displacing families from their homes and dispossessing them of their remaining equity. By putting the properties up for sale in one of the world's largest public property auctions, foreclosures also fuel an increasingly lucrative trade in large numbers of vacant lots amassed by investors from around the world at rock-bottom prices. As part of this process, around $100 million in federal money from the Hardest Hit Fund program has been routed to cities throughout Michigan to demolish houses and clear land for private development. The Blight Authority Task Force (cochaired by real estate developer Dan Gilbert) has compared demolition to excising a "malignant cancerous tumor." Scholars once described American cities as real estate–driven growth machines led by an alliance between business leaders and government. While we still have corporate control of the state and a focus on growth, crisis-era Detroit is also being transformed by a new kind of profit-making engine based on contraction, dispossession, and speculation. As Kezia Curtis and Jessi Quizar describe in their piece, the foreclosure auction and out-of-town speculation have a deep impact on who cares for land in the city. This map illustrates these impacts in the area that surrounds Feedom Freedom.

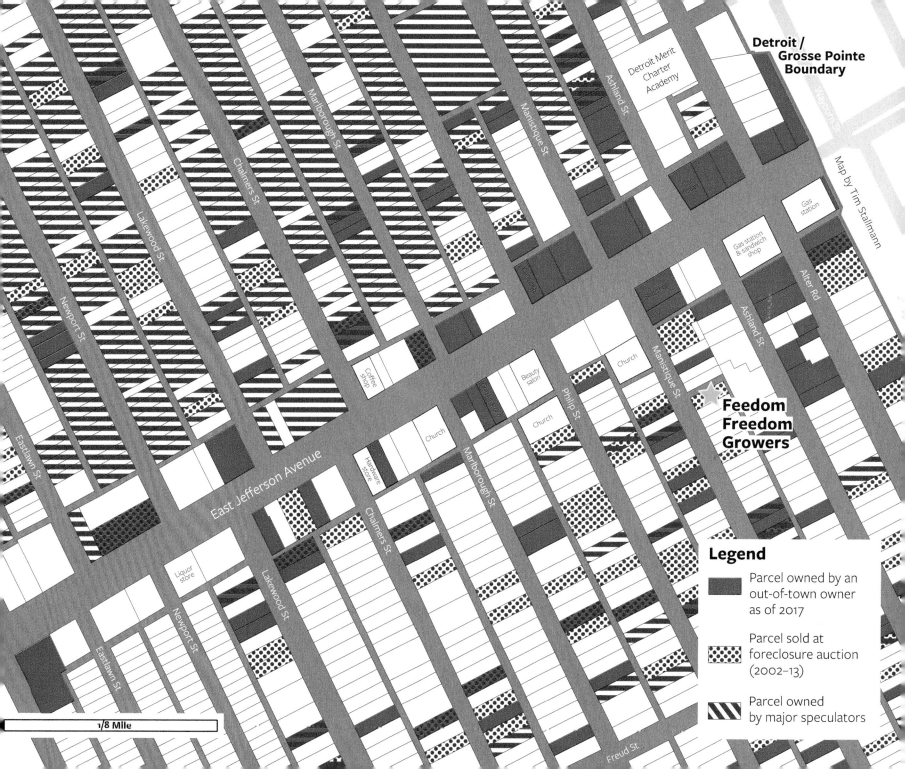

Detroit /
**Grosse Pointe
Boundary**

Detroit Merit
Charter
Academy

Ashland St

Map by Tim Stallmann

Marlborough St

Chalmers St

Manistique St

Gas
station

Lakewood St

Gas station
& sandwich
shop

Newport St

Alter Rd

Ashland St

Coffee
shop

Church

Manistique St

Beauty
salon

★ **Feedom
Freedom
Growers**

Philip St

Church

Eastlawn St

East Jefferson Avenue

Hardware
store

Church

Marlborough St

Liquor
store

Chalmers St

Lakewood St

Newport St

Eastlawn St

Legend

Parcel owned by an
out-of-town owner
as of 2017

Parcel sold at
foreclosure auction
(2002–13)

Parcel owned
by major speculators

1/8 Mile

Freud St

community pathways, and playgrounds in what had been vacant lots. Urban gardens like Feedom Freedom exist all over the city, making use of vacant land to grow food.

This, of course, does not mean that all neglected spaces in the city are taken care of by residents. But it does mean that often the most responsible, creative, and community-centered ways for combating neglect in neighborhoods in Detroit come not from outside investors but from existing residents who already live there and have family histories in the city. As neighborhood residents, we are best positioned to care for our neighborhood because its beauty, its safety, its community, and its quality of life are *our* quality of life. We should be looking much more to projects like Feedom Freedom as models for shaping vital, innovative, and useful spaces in the city.

Detroit's residents are strong and resilient. We have the ability to overcome, as we have done in the past many times before. Detroiters have survived urban renewal and the construction of freeways in the 1960s, the destruction of Paradise Valley and the Black Bottom neighborhood, and mass displacement. Just as before, Detroit will find ways to come together, to reimagine, and create community when all odds are against it.

"THIS IS WHAT WE CALL HOME"

CECILY MCCLELLAN

In 2015, Aaron Handelsman, then a community organizer and analyst with the Detroit People's Platform, spoke with Cecily McClellan at 95 Calvert Street. They met at a vacant lot that she and her neighbors converted into a park, which they call "Tootie's Park." The park is dedicated to McClellan's sister who passed away. McClellan and her neighbor fenced the park so that her two dogs could roam. They also constructed an outdoor living space that includes a tent, sitting area, and flower bed. Like many vacant lots in Detroit, a house previously stood at 95 Calvert Street. McClellan's family moved to Calvert Street in the spring of 1972 from a house they rented in Black Bottom, one of Detroit's historically African American neighborhoods. McClellan's family and so many others were displaced from Black Bottom because their houses were torn down for urban renewal. In this interview, McClellan shares her memories of Black Bottom and thoughts on neighborhood stabilization in Detroit.

My family migrated here in the late '40s from Kentucky. My grandfather (my mother's father) was a coal miner. A coal mine caved in on him. It damaged his back, and he really could not work. This accident was one of the reasons my family migrated from Kentucky to Detroit. Also, the North was believed to provide better employment opportunities and $5-an-hour auto industry jobs. My father also migrated from Kentucky and married my mother in Detroit. My father worked at Chrysler for thirty years and retired from the Trenton, Michigan plant. For periods of time during his employment he would be laid off. When he was laid off, times would be tough. If you were a renter and couldn't pay your rent, you would have to move to someplace else or move in with your relatives. We had our share of that.

You also had a lot of housing discrimination back then. There weren't a lot of places African Americans could live in Detroit. A large population of African Americans were crowded into the lower east side's "Black Bottom" or out in the Royal Oak Township Eight Mile and Wyoming neighborhood. There was also an area over on the West Side and in Southwest Detroit. But many locations had covenant deeds that restricted the sale of homes to African Americans.

What was it like in Black Bottom when you were growing up?

Everybody knew everybody. I lived in an area where within a ten-block radius you had Duffield Elementary School, which is one of the oldest schools in the city. You had Miller Junior High, which was a high school, but it was turned into a junior high, in the late 1950s. And then you had the old Eastern [school]—it used to be on the East Grand Boulevard and Mack Ave, but it was rebuilt and moved down on East Lafayette in 1966. And then, in 1968, Dr. King was killed and so the school changed its name from Eastern to Martin Luther

King Jr. Senior High in his honor. The families in Black Bottom were close knitted. Within a few-block radius, my grandmother and my mother's sisters lived—my mother had eight living siblings for a period in the Black Bottom. Therefore, it meant I could go literally a few blocks over to my grandparents' home or my mother's sister or see my uncles on Joseph Campau Avenue or Chene Street in the business areas. You grew up close to your extended family. The business area of Black Bottom had several markets (like Big Three, Marshalls, and Lauri Bros.), a small department store (Lieberman's), a theater (like the Carver), funeral homes (like Bristol & Bristol), drugstores, cleaners, barbershops, record shops, pool halls, a smoke shop, and many other businesses. Most of your needs and services were provided or available in the Black Bottom.

My family moved a lot in the Black Bottom. When I was born, we lived on McDougall and Chestnut. Our McDougall residence was said to be next door to the Joe Louis family home. It was Jay Street where we stayed the longest time—that was from '61 to '72. Prior to that we lived on Madison Street (twice, once with my grandparents), Clinton Street, Dubois Street, and Waterloo Street, all in the Black Bottom. You became familiar with your neighbors within a ten-block radius.

What caused you to move from Black Bottom to Calvert?

Urban renewal, some refer to as Black folks' removal. The city was demolishing our homes. They were literally demolishing an entire neighborhood. Roman Gribbs was mayor at the time. Only a few housing developments were built to accommodate the current residents of Black Bottom, like Ralph Bunche Co-op, Gas Light

Homes, and Martin Luther King homes. We had been hearing that they were going to demolish our area for a long time. Finally, by the beginning of the '70s, that rumor had become a reality, everything south of the Vernor Highway East, east of Chene Street, north of Jefferson Avenue and west of Mt. Elliott Street was demolished.

So, you were literally forced out?

Yeah. You had to go. By the '70s, the conditions and the quality of life in the neighborhood were deteriorating. When it was happening, it felt like it was happening fast. Although we knew and were aware of the demolition of Paradise Valley, Hasting Street, and other parts of the lower east side, urban renewal had become a personal reality. If you didn't own your own, you were offered $2,000 to move. And the folks were given small amounts for their houses, usually not enough to purchase another house. My mother and my father at that point in time were both working; she was working at the post office, and he was at Chrysler, so they were able to purchase a home on Calvert Street. By 1974, things in the City of Detroit had begun to change for African Americans under the newly elected Coleman A. Young. Many more employment opportunities and housing became available.

I'm curious to hear your personal perspective on what's happening in Detroit right now in terms of development.

You know, I think all we want are stable neighborhoods and a decent quality of life, so that once I have retired, my house is paid for, that I am going to be able to pay my taxes and enjoy my later years without having the burden of a house loan. But instead what

Residents posing in Detroit's Black Bottom neighborhood, 1949.

has happened since 2000 is the steady destabilization of neighborhoods. The destabilization and destruction of neighborhoods was brought to a crisis level with home foreclosures and school closings. In this neighborhood alone, anchor public schools were closed—Northern High School, Hutchins Middle School, and Doty Elementary School. It became very difficult for childbearing parents to stay in the neighborhood. Now parents must drive kids to school and kids take buses to schools in other neighborhoods, which often are charter schools. School closings are destroying communities. At the same time, if you are low income or need to get subsidies, like Section 8, there were none being provided in the City of Detroit. Detroit residents were encouraged to move to the suburban areas outside Detroit for lower rents, utilities, auto insurances, public education, and general city service delivery.

It's like what we talked about earlier. I lived in a community where everybody knew each other because everybody walked to school together. We all went to the same schools. Just by going to neighborhood schools, you knew your neighbors and your neighborhood. The destruction of public education and neighborhood schools have destroyed community and a whole way of life.

We all want Detroit to survive and thrive. I mean, during the late '70s and '80s, when people were working, it was fantastic! You had manicured lawns. This area and many other neighborhoods in Detroit were stable. You had the areas that were going down, largely due to the crack cocaine epidemic, but nothing like the foreclosure crisis. What happened after 2008 is totally different; it caused the destruction of once-stable neighborhoods—in 1999, Detroit had the highest African American homeownership rate in the nation. And now it's flipped. That cannot happen by mistake.

It was hard for my mother and father to get a loan in 1972, and like I told you my father worked at Chrysler and my mother worked at the post office. So, isn't it amazing that by 2002, 3, 4, 5, if your only source of income was Social Security you could get a home loan. Detroit was targeted for lucrative high-interest-rate subprime mortgages. Many lenders found creative ways to approve loans for those with credit challenges. These subprime loans were bundled together and sold as investment on Wall Street. That was a recipe for disaster and they knew it. Some investors had invested in the housing bubble bursting, which it did in 2008.

The City of Detroit during this same period took out municipal type subprime loans, called pension obligation certificates (POCs). The city had difficulty meeting its POC in 2009, and the State of Michigan did not intend to maintain agreed levels of revenue sharing. These things and others were used to justify the financial takeover of Detroit in 2012 and bankruptcy by 2013. However, the residents had been living under austerity city budgets since 2009 and city services were being drastically reduced. The banks got bailed out, but not the city or homeowners. The Hardest Hit Funds provided by the Obama Administration saved a few homes with underwater mortgages in Detroit. More neighborhoods could have been saved if more home-owners had access to the Hardest Hit Funds and other stimulus programs. The foreclosure rate for home loans and property taxes escalated in Detroit and once-stable neighborhoods became blighted and stripped overnight. After two or three houses are stripped on a block, then it can be designated as blighted and demolition begins. They [city officials] are finding resources to refurbish homes, but it's not reaching the long-term residents or low-income residents in the neighborhood. The senior citizens and low-income home improvement grant programs are now low-interest loan programs, which have challenging eligibility criteria.

One of the things that struck me at the beginning of our conversation is how you were talking about this street on Calvert and how it almost sounded like you re-created here, in this one small pocket, what you experienced growing up in Black Bottom.

I guess in some way we have. We have a street here where pretty much everybody knows everybody on the street. We don't have a

"That has become indoctrinated in our family, that you are not owners of the land, you are stewards of that land for the next generation. I see that as part of my legacy and my heritage, that I am not an owner of, to dispense with as I see fit, but I am a caretaker for the next generation. . . . I think that we have allowed somebody else's vision of success to cloud that historic mandate to us. Once upon a time it was 'Don't sell the farm,' right? 'Never sell the farm. Never ever ever ever!' I mean that was like a mantra."**—LEE GADDIES**

Lee Gaddies is a Detroit resident and community activist.

serious problem with crime because would-be criminals recognize stability in a neighborhood. We use this area [Tootie's Park] quite a bit for holiday celebrations and barbecues. Folks from the old neighborhood know they can find my family on Calvert Street, and many of the former residents know they can still drop by. Our kids are real comfortable on the street. You can say, "Okay, look, I'm a run across the street to Auntie's house, or down the street to Uncle's or cousins' house." If I need something I can borrow it from a family member or friend. The kids will remember this street and neighborhood for the rest of their lives.

My family has been here since '72. We've had people that knew the family years and years ago pull up on the street and see people out here [Tootie's Park] and not know none of the faces. Maybe somebody that knows me but they haven't seen me in ten, fifteen years. But they know we moved over here on Calvert Street and

BLACK BOTTOM: 1949

The aerial photograph on this page shows Detroit's Black Bottom neighborhood as it stood in 1949. Much of the housing in Black Bottom was built in the 1850s during an influx of German immigrants. During the Great Migration, it became one of the few places in the city where Black migrants were allowed to live. The photos included here are part of a series showing everyday life in the neighborhood just before its clearance.

1369 Clinton, September 6, 1949.

1231–35 Orleans, August 29, 1949.

Cecily McLellan childhood home (corner of McDougall & Chestnut)

Miller High School
Sidney D. Miller High (built in the early 1920s) was Detroit's main high school for African American students from 1933 until 1957. Detroit's school board closed the school in 2007 as part of a round of school closures.

Duffield Elementary School
Built in 1922, this school was closed in 2010, but reopened as Bunche Preparatory Academy in 2012.

1536 Monroe, August 31, 1949.

1483–85 E. Lafayette, July 26, 1949.

we have a lot of family on the block. So, they'll pull up and say, "Y'all know anybody that knows Cecily McClellan?" And they'll say, "Oh yeah, that's my mother or auntie." So we have created some of the elements of the old neighborhood that we miss.

I think the vision is to have a stable family-oriented neighborhood that people would be happy to come to and enjoy, and that it would be there for them as time passes. We don't want to have what happened in the Bottom—that we'd get moved and relocated and now there's no evidence that you were even there. I don't want that to happen again. I just would hope that we could have something that people would be able to say that, "These folks lived here. This family, these Black folks lived in this neighborhood."

BLACK BOTTOM: 1956

By the time this aerial photogaph was taken in 1956, Detroit's city government had already bulldozed Black Bottom homes as part of its first urban renewal efforts. In 1954, Detroit completely destroyed over 400 homes in order to build the new Lafayette Park development. Due to lack of funding, the area remained vacant and undeveloped for several years.

Expressway construction and later urban renewal projects in the 1960s eventually impacted nearly all of the land in this photo and displaced tens of thousands of Detroiters.

1954 Demolition Area
The area demolished to construct Lafayette Park development encompassed 423 residences, 109 businesses, 22 factories, and 93 vacant lots.

Areas impacted by urban renewal
Over the following years, further urban renewal projects continued to cause displacement in Black Bottom. These projects included Gratiot, Lafayette, and Elmwood Park.

Maps by Tim Stallmann, with assistance from Emily Kutil. Burton Historical Collection at Detroit Public Library and the DTE historical aerial photo collection at Wayne State University

BACKYARD GARDEN

AMELIA WIESKE

Amelia Wieske's "Backyard Garden" is a memoir-like piece that explores the social and cultural importance of maintaining a family garden. Wieske highlights the degree to which digging in the dirt and tending the land shape our sense of home and self in fundamental ways.

feel an immense privilege to live in my city. This feeling of luck is common for many Detroiters. There is a luxury to living here—of belonging to Detroit—that is often incomprehensible to people who do not know my city.

I grew up in an old two-story wooden house in Corktown at the edge of Bagley and Rosa Parks. Next door to our house was an empty parking lot where my older sister and I played. We made snow angels in the winter. We rode bikes through it in the summer. Our mom, an avid gardener, taught us to avoid the belladonna plant that grew along its border. The belladonna had dark purple flowers with bright yellow centers. She called it "deadly nightshade" and said it could poison us. While my sister and I learned to fear and avoid the belladonna, for me, it was also an object of fascination. That I recognized the simple plant that could kill, remembered its name, and knew not to eat its glossy berries made me feel wise. This was not kids' stuff. This was knowledge.

Our backyard like those of many Detroit homes was large. At its rear was a trellised cobblestone patio that my dad built with help from my uncles. A fence separated the patio from the alley. In the summertime, wild grape vines covered the fence. Their tart fruit made our mouths feel strangely hairy. A locust tree grew up from the center of the cobblestones, and thorny rosebushes bordered the rest of the patio area. A rope hammock slung between two patio beams would deliver you straight into those thorns if you swung too enthusiastically.

A huge cherry tree towered over the yard. Climbing it was a daily job, though I was mostly content to sit on its lowest branch. From there I studied the tree's marred and shiny red purple bark and listened to the ferry boats blaring their horns as they carried passengers from Detroit downriver to the now shuttered Boblo Island Amusement Park.

Right behind our house was a space for animal cages. My mom nursed injured birds—victims of her cat, Sylvester—back to health. Nearby was the only unworked bit of dirt in the entire yard where I once buried a pair of my dad's prescription glasses. On cool fall evenings we carved pumpkins in that dirt patch.

It was not only birds that filled those cages. Other animals came and went too. One day my dad discovered a matted angora rabbit in the alley. We took her in and named her "Alley." In the evenings, my mom brushed out her soft gray halo. We also kept guinea pigs in the cages. One day twenty-two of them escaped; we recovered only eighteen.

During the winter, the cages filled with ring-necked doves. They lived in the house. We released them every spring and they nested in our neighbor's yard. Generation after generation, they

Amelia Wieske's backyard in Corktown.

came back to us when it got cold, trading open air for seed and warmth. Singing to the doves was my primary winter occupation.

Over the years, our backyard filled with more trees. In addition to the cherry and locust trees, my mother planted a sweet white peach tree and a pear tree. One Christmas, we kept our tree, which was a silver pine, decorated and lit in the front room all winter long, root ball and all. When the ground thawed in the spring, we planted it in the backyard.

In the summer, we nibbled our way through the garden. Low strawberry bushes that bore jewel-sized treats lined some of our garden beds. Herbs—chives, lavender, basil, sorrel, and mint—seemed to be everywhere. Not everything was edible, of course. Irises were prized. There were dewy hostas, a pleasingly named bleeding heart, bearded snapdragons, and the old Corktown standbys of lamb's ears and alyssum. What I most remember are the things with drama or flavor.

Two cherished gooseberries, one white and one red, were planted along a fence. To reach them we walked on wooden boards. Traveling to the gooseberries on those boards was perilous. Our movements triggered a storm of wide-eyed grasshoppers that bounced erratically into the air. They landed in our hair and on our feet, bounding off of our small bodies and scaring my sister, who squeezed my arm and trembled. We got revenge by collecting them in lidded jars. Our friend Tom helped us pull off their legs. A little older than us, Tom lived next door with his grandma. He always came over with a Kool-Aid mustache. Tom used bad grammar, causing my mom to frown the same way she did when she was digging in her purse for her small hairbrush, determined to make us look presentable in spite of ourselves.

I'm just now starting to understand my mom's deep need to garden: to put things in the ground, watch over them, and wait for them to reveal themselves. My earliest memory of my mom's anger was when a city worker mowed over the flowers she had planted in the easement between the sidewalk and our street. She seethed. She swore. She wanted to drive steel spikes into the ground to break the city mower blades. I can recognize a certain inner yearning that drives one to incessantly plant. It is the type of need that drives you to plant your Christmas tree, to trade bulbs like gossip, to spend dusk watching fireflies while being nipped by mosquitoes. Her dad had it too.

My dad helped cultivate an ecosystem beyond our backyard. He bought maples from the now extinct Parks and Recreation Department nursery, where the D-Town Farm is now located. Up and down our street, he planted the trees. Every spring, we fertilized the trees with smelly fertilizer stakes that we drove into the soft earth with hammers. My father said they were a "birthday present" for the trees. As an urban beekeeper, my father has long approached the entire ecology of the city as his own personal business. Today he is working to foster a new generation of Detroit beekeepers.

My parents raised me to understand that Detroit is a place full of life. It is a place where the private rituals of families—families binding together and families falling apart—are nested among the sweetness of cherries and mulberries. It is a place where the circulating heat of anger is cooled by standing barefoot in the yard.

Over time I began to understand things about my life. I began to understand that I knew way more about gardening and cooking than my peers. I began to understand that poverty frayed my parents' marriage. I learned that our relatives had worried about our well-being. Would we get tetanus from our rusty old house? Would our house be broken into? Would we be held at gunpoint?

The deep chasm between my relatives' fears for my life and the reality of my actual life has shaped how I talk about my town to others. In the past, when I traveled, I often avoided telling people where I was from. The outsized expectation that strangers had of Detroit was irreconcilable with my own experiences of being a Detroiter. For many outsiders, like my relatives, the city seemed to appear to them as ruins. From my perspective though, the landscape looked like home.

To experience Detroit's landscape as home is to be attuned to the thousands of overlapping personal paradises that crowd the broken sidewalks and overgrown fields. The city easily embraces the complexity of its own beauty and misery. Its citizens balance continuously between the fault lines of power, freedom, and failure. We all have our own ideas of success, of love, and of beauty. Yet we are connected to the place we inhabit, connected to the land. We belong. We have without having. There is an essential personal freedom in being straight with your own street. The lack of pressure to keep up with the Joneses, the lack of Joneses,

gave me an unhampered experience of belonging in downtown Detroit. To an incredible degree Detroiters own what they know, regardless of paperwork or law.

Something about the nature of belonging makes life more valuable. It is about being both a place and a person, not just a person in a place. Belonging is about unfolding into what surrounds you, about being part of a larger whole.

My city and I, we are family. You won't read about *my city* on the front page of the newspaper. It can't be encapsulated by a slogan on a shirt. My Detroit is not catchy. It has a current, and it has roots. It runs deep below the socialized sphere of general conversation. My Detroit is hard to put into words—it is a Detroit that is about doing, living, and digging around in the muck. My Detroit is a city in which place and people are braided over time into belonging. This Detroit is a place of bounty. This Detroit is a sublime place to live and grow.

Present-day Detroit outline

Bog

Wet Prairie

Beech / Sugar Maple Forest

LAKE ST. CLAIR

Map by Tim Stallmann

Oak / Hickory Forest

ROUGE RIVER

DETROIT RIVER

Mixed Oak Savanna

Mixed Hardwood Swamp

LAND COVER, CIRCA 1800

Beech - Sugar Maple Forest

Black Ash Swamp

Mixed Conifer Swamp

Mixed Hardwood Swamp

Mixed Oak Savanna

Muskeg / Bog

Oak - Hickory Forest

Shrub Swamp / Emergent Marsh

Wet Prairie

Detroit Historical Land Cover, circa 1800

This map illustrates Detroit's historical land cover, which consisted primarily of beech and sugar maple forest, bogs, wet prairie, and emergent marsh. During the late Wisconsin glacial period, Detroit was under the waters of Lake Erie. Today the Detroit River area sits on a bedrock of limestone. Atop the limestone are glacial deposits, till plains, and lake plains, which were left behind when the glaciers retreated about fourteen thousand years ago. The Detroit River emerged about thirteen thousand years ago when water levels fell. Archaeological surveys have found at least thirty-two historic Native American sites along the river. The river has long served as a source of water, food, livelihood, and transportation. It forms an international boundary between the United States and Canada and is the busiest port in the Great Lakes. In spite of heavy industry along the riverfront and waste discharge, which create adverse environmental impacts, the river remains a vital habitat for fish and migratory waterfowl. This historical map offers an alternative perspective on land and resources in the city to conventional maps, which divide the city by political boundaries and property parcels. Streams and coastlines show present-day courses, not historical locations.

THE RIVER RATS

Fishing, Mutuality, and Community

ANDREA SANKAR, MARK LUBORSKY, AND ROBERT JOHNSON

The Detroit River has long shaped people's relationship to land in the city. Whereas the Detroit River is often thought about solely in terms of transportation, the following essay by Andrea Sankar, Mark Luborsky (both medical anthropologists at Wayne State University), and Robert Johnson (a doctoral candidate in Wayne State's anthropology department) gives a picture of the everyday life of the river and how it continues to be a vital source of livelihood and pleasure for Detroit's anglers. The essay emerged from a research project with anglers on the Detroit River. The project sought to educate public health officials on the importance of fishing for Detroit residents while also developing best practices for anglers to minimize their exposure to toxins through choice fish and strategies for cleaning their catch. The essay highlights the case of the River Fishing Association of Detroit, which is committed to multigenerational sharing of fishing knowledge and skills and taking care of public spaces along the river neglected by the city. Drawing on interviews with residents, Sankar, Luborsky, and Johnson demonstrate how for many Detroit anglers, fishing is as much about retaining culture and reaffirming values of mutual care and community as it is about food.

One important sign of spring in Detroit is the melting of the ice and snow along and on the Detroit River. The opening up of the water to the sun and warmth mirrors the opening up of public spaces, like city parks and the river walk. Depending on the season and severity of winter, one sure sign that spring is arriving is the sight of individuals and families casting fishing lines along the river. In the weeks between St. Patrick's Day and Mother's Day, anglers and their friends and families gather along the river shore to catch scores of white bass migrating from Lake Erie to spawning areas of Lake St. Claire.

One angler, Curtis, observes, "The river is Detroit's first factory." Fishing along the Detroit River has been a continuous activity for hundreds of years. Archaeologists have discovered Native American fishing campsites dating back several hundred years before the arrival of Europeans. The earliest French settlers established their homesteads in long piano-key land plots that enabled both farm and fishing production and consumption (see the French ribbon farms map on p. 120). As Detroit's riverfront became industrialized, factory workers and their children who lived near the river and local canals fished along the shore for leisure and family bonding. Most of the Detroit anglers who are fifty and older today learned to fish along the same shoreline that their parents and grandparents fished decades ago.

Given Detroit's recent industrial heritage, it seems unusual that people would continue to fish in waterways that, for many decades, were often perceived to be too polluted to swim in. From the mid-twentieth to the early twenty-first century, the State of Michigan posted "Eat Safe Fish" signs and fish consumption advisories at most of Detroit's fishing venues.

Fishing, however, is about more than finding food. For many anglers, fishing is a way to reaffirm common values of mutuality and community. Dennis, a longtime Detroit angler, reveals how fishing can provide community and mutual care when other social networks break down: "There is an energy in getting fish. Have you heard the saying 'Teach a man to fish and he will eat forever'? That's what we do here at [the river]. A few months ago, a woman came down here with her children. She had a shopping cart with her, and you know, it looked like she needed to feed her children. So, instead of keeping the fish, we took our fish and filled up a cooler with it. Then, we gave her a pole and taught her how to fish on her own."

Another aspect of fishing is being near the river itself. The river provides a contrast to the images and experiences of urban living. Marian, an angler who was taught to fish as an adult, reflects that "fishing is nerve calming": "You can come out here, and, you can have problems, but you look on the water, and you can just think. A lot of days, I don't come out here and fish. I just come out here and sit and look on the water. It makes me calmer."

A final aspect of fishing that has kept anglers coming to the river over generations is in the way fishing allows older gen-

Courtesy Andrea Sankar, Mark Luborsky, and Robert Johnson

The River Rats Fishing Association (RRFA).

erations to teach younger generations. Another angler, Remo, relates how fishing has taught him life skills that he is able to pass on to his children through fishing:

The most important thing about fishing is patience: fishing is a patient man's game. . . . You got to have patience in life, and you have to know how to get along with other people. Patience is important in life because you have to understand that everyone is different. [My son] is sixteen now and at that age where he thinks he knows everything. I have told him that he must have a lot of trust and patience with his [football] coach—if the coach is wrong or his philosophy is wrong, he must still go out and do it. At the same time, I have told him you can't believe

Courtesy Andrea Sankar, Mark Luborsky, and Robert Johnson

Anglers share fishing skills on the Detroit River.

I learned to fish from my father and uncle. When my cousins and I were kids, we would go out to fish together. The first fish I ever caught I caught just by dropping a line in the water. I tied a string around a beer can. I used an old spark plug as a sinker, and I found a hook. I dropped my line in, and I caught a sheepshead. When I got older, my father would have me sitting in the rain and thunder to fish with him. Fishing gives you something to pass down. You can take pride that you don't just take, take, take, take, but also . . . give.

everything everyone tells you in life. [My son] is real big on listening. He knows he doesn't know everything.

One group of anglers in particular takes seriously the multigenerational transference of life knowledge and skills that fishing offers beyond leisure and family time. For over twenty years, the River Rats Fishing Association (RRFA) has been offering grassroots fishing instructions to anyone who wants to learn how to fish along the Detroit River.

The RRFA began as a group of friends and extended family members who grew up fishing the shoreline and canals along the riverfront. "Pap," the fishing name of the lead organizer and founder of the association, explains why he started the RRFA:

Pap and his family and friends who continued to fish along the river into adulthood felt helpless against the disintegration of their neighborhoods during the 1970s, '80s, and '90s. Amid the traumatic events unfolding in the city, fishing provided peace of mind.

Nevertheless, the effects of Detroit's urban problems began to affect the fishing areas directly. As the city's budget began to wither, so too did the upkeep and maintenance of city parks, including the shoreline parks where the anglers gathered. The parks became open spaces where crime thrived as the city's budget forced cutbacks in law enforcement.

Many anglers realized that fishing could be used to make the fishing areas safer and cleaner. More importantly, their knowledge and skills in fishing could be used—"passed on"—to others who came to the river seeking peace of mind.

So, the first thing Pap and his friends did was to begin cleaning the park where they fished together most, Mariner

Park. "If the city won't do it, who will?" Pap and the others asked themselves. "We want to bring our families down here," Pap explains, "but who wants to step on broken glass?" Beginning in the 1990s, Pap and his angler network began bringing lawn mowers, rakes, and trash bags alongside their fishing poles and fishing gear.

Over time, other anglers and visitors to the shoreline began to hear how Mariner Park was being kept up and appeared to be a safer space to fish than other parks. As people new to Mariner Park began to arrive, Pap and the other Mariner Park anglers had opportunities to share and receive knowledge about fishing with other anglers. And they had opportunities to teach fishing to newcomers. The teaching began by simply giving people fish: "We always give people fish if they need it. However, we try to focus on teaching people how to fish. We teach everyone who wants to learn, even women and children. When we teach people how to fish, we are teaching the next generation." As the group became more organized around their fishing schedules and their focus on teaching fishing, they gave themselves a name: River Rats. Pap explains: "I don't really know how we came up with River Rats. I think it's because we just like spending all our time at the water." Nevertheless, within a couple of years, as the group expanded, Pap was given the title "mayor of the River Rats." They printed T-shirts and started organizing community picnics and fish fries at Mariner Park. As longtime anglers got older, the River Rats felt the need to honor them when they could not fish anymore or they died. Every year, the "Ceremony" is held, a picnic in which the anglers or family members who died in the previous year are remembered and honored.

The RRFA is a community that is organized around practice rather than a formalized hierarchy. Pap observes: "To be a River Rat, you just have to be willing to come down and teach people how to fish. Most people here don't even know they are River Rats. [One angler], he just came down here and learned how to fish. And then he started teaching other people how to fish. He's been teaching other people how to fish at Lakewood [Park]. If you respect what we are trying to do down here, then you are a River Rat."

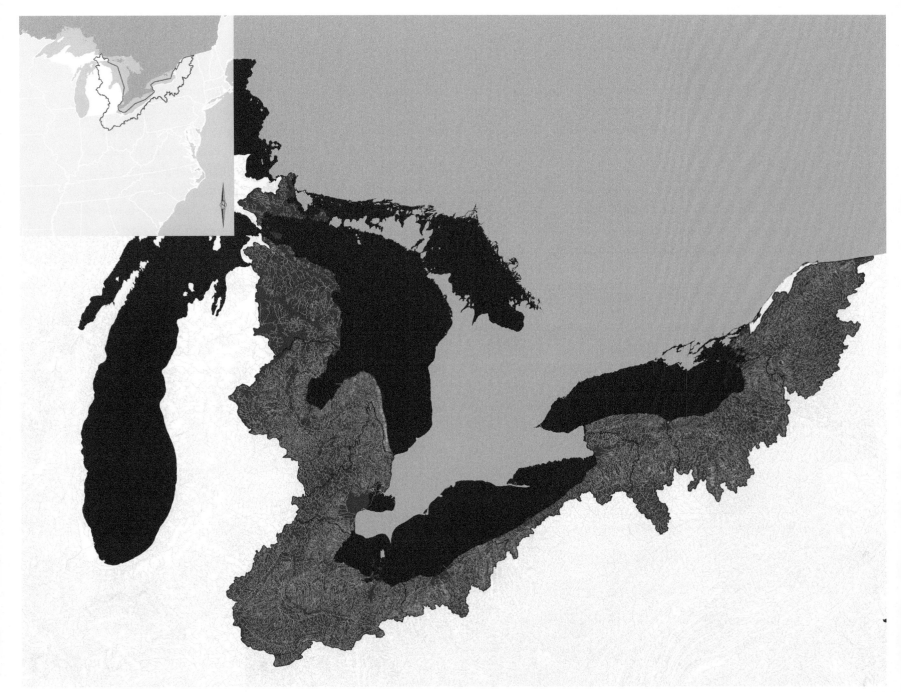

Great Lakes Watershed

Lauren Rosenthal's *Political/Hydrological* is an atlas that proposes dividing the United States into political units along watershed lines. This reproduction of her Great Lakes Watershed map visualizes a different geographical conception of the region hinted at by "The River Rats" (p. 101) and "Detroit/Windsor" (p. 106). Water, both in the Detroit River and Lake Michigan, provides a key site of commonality not only for Detroit residents but also for Detroiters and their neighbors in Windsor, Ontario—although, ironically, because of GIS data limitations Rosenthal's atlas does not include areas of Canada that share watersheds with the United States.

DETROIT/WINDSOR

Building a Cross-Border Commons

LEE RODNEY AND MICHAEL DARROCH

Detroit's activists have been working against the dividing power of race, gender, and class for decades, but often the international border that separates Detroit from Windsor is taken for granted. On any given day, one can view the dramatic display of border security on both sides of the river in the form of helicopters and patrol boats. But such shows of force also betray the resources deemed necessary by the US and Canadian governments to maintain the Detroit River as a zone of separation rather than one of connection and free movement. This enforced separation of land and peoples is belied by shared economic, social, and political histories that are far older than the governments that impose the border. In this piece, Lee Rodney and Michael Darroch describe how efforts to establish an urban commons that transcends the border. Rodney and Darroch are part of the IN/TERMINUS Research Group, an art research collective based in Windsor that has been active in documenting grassroots and artistic efforts to treat Detroit/Windsor as a unified city.

These twin cities occupy a unique position in North America. The Windsor-Detroit region is the largest metropolitan area that straddles the international boundary between Canada and the United States, measuring close to 4.5 million people in spite of out-migration associated with deindustrialization. The complications arising from the increasingly divided, postindustrial urban core has become the basis for social and relational art practices that seek to foster knowledge about the complex urban histories of the region and possible strategies for promoting alternative forms of ownership, agency, and exchange within the city.

The arts collective Broken City Lab (Justin Langlois, Hiba Abdallah, Josh Babcock, Michelle Soulliere, and Danielle Sabelli) was active in Windsor between 2010 and 2015. It hosted artist-led workshops that worked against the tide of the economic downturn in the city, boosting civic pride through a variety of activities that ranged from Windsor-branded tattoos to design workshops for transforming vacant lots. In the middle of the 2008–10 recession, they created a large-scale projection on the empty front side of the Chrysler Building. It was a direct message to Detroit that read: "We're in this together." Their work suggested an alternative communications strategy for the City of Windsor that wouldn't be dominated by advertisements for casinos and Chrysler, both of which flank the Detroit River on the Windsor side.

The vision of Windsor as a modern, international city—one strongly identified with Detroit—can be seen in nearly all photographs from the early part of the twentieth century. This is a far cry from the contemporary moment in which the two cities are becoming increasingly disconnected. Anecdotally, there is

Christina Naccarato

Since the time of the Underground Railroad, the international border has been an important if at times taken-for-granted presence in the history of the communities that bridge it. The message above was projected by the art collective Broken City Lab on the headquarters of the Windsor Chrysler Building, facing Detroit, in 2009.

now only one cab company in Detroit that will drive passengers across the border. In contrast, prior to 1942, there were several passenger ferries (in addition to the Detroit-Windsor Tunnel and the Ambassador Bridge) that once connected the two cities. Furthermore, in the early 1960s plans were in the works for a gondola crossing between the commercial centers of Windsor and Detroit. These were never realized, though they remained popular ideas for decades.[15] Now it is only possible to cross the river in a motor vehicle, and a passport is essential. This dwindling ease of access, coupled with the political and economic problems that emerged in Detroit and Windsor over the last fifty years, have dealt a blow to the transnational urban identity once fostered between the two cities. Similarly, until recently most Detroiters took the international border with Windsor for granted. Now it is clear that the internal class and racial divisions that carved up Detroit during the twentieth century have proved to be more significant, ongoing political issues.

However, part of Detroit's grassroots legacy, the sensibility toward thinking of urban issues in a cross-border fashion, still pervades Windsor. An example is the Citizens Environment Alliance (CEA), a nonprofit international education and research organization founded in Windsor in 1985. Concerned about the state of the Detroit River from chemical spills and its

effect on the drinking water for the region, the group maintains "an ecosystem approach to environmental planning and management."[16] Over the years the organization has branched off into other issues such as air quality, shore erosion, and other environmental concerns. The CEA holds an annual "State of the Detroit River" boat tour as an educational event to focus on cross-border environmental pollution, which has worked to improve water quality, air quality, and marine life.

This cross-border sensibility is also found around the Windsor Youth Centre (WYC), which was launched in 2011 by, among others, Tamara Kowalska and George Bozanich, both Windsorites; Bozanich later graduated from Detroit's Ecumenical Theological Seminary and has served as a pastor at Trinity-St. Mark's United Church of Christ in Delray, while Kowalska served until 2018 as the WYC's executive director. Located in a former storefront on Wyandotte Street East, one of Windsor's most diverse neighborhoods with strong connections to the Arabic-speaking communities of Dearborn, Michigan, the WYC was initiated by a small group of Windsor-Essex citizens (the Faith in Action committee of the United Church presbytery). The WYC is the only drop-in center in Windsor providing a safe and reliable place for homeless and at-risk youth between the ages of sixteen and twenty-four. Disheartened after visiting well-funded agencies in Toronto and other prosperous Canadian cities, they took inspiration from widespread grassroots initiatives in Detroit, including community-based urban farming projects. Opposed to a top-down model of charity support, the WYC adopted instead a Freirean model of affecting positive social change and personal liberation, emphasizing

The Ambassador Bridge connects Windsor, Ontario, with Southwest Detroit, literally bridging Lee Rodney's and Michael Darroch's neighborhood with that of Michelle Martinez, who (in an interview on p. 111) describes how her historical family land was seized for the construction of the bridge.

Bryan Day

individuals' capacity to make and remake themselves through constant dialogue and exchange. The WYC provides hot meals, toiletries, a food pantry, a teaching garden, computers coupled with help for homework and developing CVs, a relapse prevention program, support in finding safe and affordable housing, a parents' support program, education support, and referrals to other community agencies. Having first obtained funding from the United Church of Canada, the organization is made possible principally by the dozens of volunteers who regularly help prepare some one thousand meals per month and assist youth seeking apartments or employment. In 2018, the WYC merged with the Downtown Mission of Windsor.

"WE NEED TO PUT TOGETHER A PLAN THAT HONORS PEOPLE IN THIS PLACE, ON THIS LAND"

MICHELLE MARTINEZ

Michelle Martinez is an environmental justice activist from Southwest Detroit. Born in Detroit, she moved with her family to rural Michigan in 1986. In 2008, after graduating from the University of Michigan with a master's degree in environmental policy and a specialization in environmental justice, she returned to Detroit. Since then, Martinez has worked in the nonprofit sector and organized around various issues from farmworker rights to environmental justice.

In the following interview, Martinez, who is of Mexican, Colombian, and Native American heritage, reflects on her family's personal story of migration to Detroit, multigenerational histories of displacement that shape people's relationship to land, and alternative collective models of landownership that have emerged from resistance movements. Martinez also offers a critique of homeownership rooted in her perspective as a millennial. She argues that alternative models of collective landownership will succeed but only if structural racism can be undone. She suggests several examples for alternative models, including the heritage of *palenque* communities in Latin America, and closer to home, the work of the North End Community Garden in Detroit. Ayana Maria Rubio conducted this interview as part of the Uniting Detroiters project.

My heritage is both Mexican and Colombian. My mother's family came from the Mexican-American border in 1915. We have some documentation about my great-grandfather trying to find work in the coal mines and then coming to Detroit looking for a job in the rising automotive industry. He couldn't find a job in the automotive industry; he ended up shining shoes for some time. My mother's maternal side—they're Apache Indian. The US-Mexican border displaced them and the government tried to force them onto the reservation. They decided not to go to the reservation and were seeking opportunity so they came to Detroit. I think my great-grandfather was a rumrunner for a little while during Prohibition. My family on that side has been in Detroit for almost a hundred years. My dad is from Colombia. He came in the '70s, first to New York City and then to Detroit. His brother settled here, and my dad came here to help with his brother's business, which was wrought iron. Detroit was the place to come because of this idea that you could build a business; it was a place where you could find opportunity. My mother and father met at church and got married. That's the story.

Over many generations of my family being here in Southwest Detroit, we have owned land. Unfortunately, much of that land that was owned is now under the freeway, which made way for the Ambassador Bridge and the Gateway Project. My grandfather owned a store that no longer exists. My grandmother's house that she grew up in is the service drive. My great-grandfather's house in which he raised nine kids, that's now the service drive for the highway. So, we have had land and now it's gone because of that transportation infrastructure, like many in Detroit. We don't have a material history of what that multigenerational landownership looked like. I wish that we had that material history. I wish that I could still walk into my grandfather's house or my great-grandfather's house and see what that life was like.

What did homeownership mean to you growing up, and how has that changed?

I've always rented and I actually don't want to own a house. I think that it's an incredible amount of responsibility, but it's also an incredible amount of risk. I've seen people invest so much of their life and their energy, their time, and their spirit into a place, and then it's taken, either by a bank or by dispossession of one form or another by the state. I think that it has done more harm than it has good. For me, coming into adulthood in the 2000s and during the economic depression of 2008, I feel really detached from the process of homeownership. I don't understand homeownership. I have

seen families who have been in homes for many years and then leave the home. In a romantic sort of way, when I think of a home, it is a structure that has wood and brick and all these resources, and it could be something that was created for generations. It's a sad commentary. You look around at some of these houses that are foreclosed on and they're stripped down. They're just shells of what they were once. They get scooped up into a bulldozer and thrown away. I don't know. Homeownership seems like such a faraway idea of how we should understand property. Because of the finances, it doesn't work for my generation.

What kinds of stories about land and people's relationships to land do you think need to be told?

I really think we need to take a multigenerational look at what is happening here in Detroit and how we as people have come to Detroit. In my experience, thinking about the generations before me—my grandfather in Colombia was a coffee farmer, my great-grandparents along the US-Mexico border were displaced because of war by no fault of their own. They tried to create a life where they were and came to Detroit because they couldn't be there. I think a lot of people in Detroit have that same story. I think that story has been told over and over where people came from the South to the North to find opportunity because of displacement, because of war, because of slavery, because of the legacy of what happened in the South and American colonialism. That has a huge impact on why people move and the wars that were waged over land. We come as a generation or multiple generations to

Detroit, or to any place, cities, looking for an opportunity to work, and work becomes our home. We have less of an idea of how land is our home because we're displaced from that idea itself.

When we begin to talk about Detroit and how we can own the land, I think that brings up a whole lot of questions about what are the legal parameters of us owning land and what are the challenges of us owning land. That's where we come into problems because we've internalized so much of the idea of how we can't be a part of owning land. And I think it's relevant in the way that the city is being planned now. We're not solving the problems of foreclosure or displacement or dispossession. If we really asked ourselves the question of how to become a part of this land again, it requires a lot of uprooting of those ideas and building in skills of how we can learn to farm again, how we can learn to feed ourselves again, how we can learn to create a home in a place and a space that belongs to everybody in this place for multiple generations. I think that when we plan we need to put together a plan that honors people in this place on this land.

Are there any historical models of collective landownership that shape your relationship to land?

I think that's a really powerful question. When colonists brought people over from Africa and enslaved them, they made very specific designations for enslaved peoples, both indigenous and African American. They were pitting people against each other to keep them from rising up against the colonists. One of the interesting things is, no matter how people were segregated—so that they couldn't rise up against their slave masters—people came together in camaraderie. They came together in work and in after-work-hour activities. There were children between indigenous and Africans. A lot of things happened outside of the eyes of the colonial master.

One of the most amazing successes of that period was the way runaway slaves created entire societies of *palenques*—communities of resistance against the colonial master. Some of those in Central and South America grew to numbers of twenty thousand people and still have a legacy today of communal ownership of the land, communal growing of crops, and communal maintenance and governance of their own civil society. Those skills of resistance against this segregation of people were transferred to the children. Despite the colonial masters' paying off indigenous people to tell them where the runaway slaves were, or paying off enslaved Africans to find and kill runaway indigenous folks, people refused that financial incentive or incentive of "freedom" from slavery from their slave masters in favor of an alternative idea of their own control, their own autonomy.

How would you like to see land controlled and distributed in Detroit?

There's a lot of vacant property in the city. Vacant property is a very confusing and complicated issue. My experience organizing in the North End around vacant property is that there are a lot of people who want to see the land utilized in a way that provides a higher quality of life in the city. And I think to some extent there are a lot of people who want community gardens. There is an ability and a willingness for people to make these wonderful anchors inside of their neighborhood around this garden. Jerry Hebron, for example, in the North End Community Garden, started from absolutely nothing and now has a thirteen-lot garden, a house where she will be doing cooking classes. She has a hoop house that extends growing into a whole ten or eleven months into the year now. There's an enormous economic capability being able to do that. She also trains and hires people in the neighborhood who help her manage that garden, so there's a huge possibility for the folks who want to do food production. She takes that food and she delivers it to folks in elderly care homes. That's an amazing thing for people to have organic local fresh food that wouldn't be available at all to folks who can't leave to go find that somewhere else and who don't have the transportation to do that, the potential of having something like that, that belongs to everybody.

The challenges come when you have institutions that are unwilling to let go of that control. Part of the issue is that if you have an entire city block that was vacant you'd have ownership from thirty-five different people and nobody knows where those people are. Those people might not be alive, those people might not have the title anymore, those people might have inherited that property and don't know it. Some of the people live in Texas or somewhere else and have no idea what's happening to that lot. You have a lot of private owners all over the place who have no responsibility to the city and really haven't been contributing a huge amount. Maybe their small amount of taxes has been going [to fund the city], if they're paying taxes, but otherwise the blight to the city is more of a detriment than it is a contribution. I think people see land and they think because somebody else owns it or because it's been left behind, it has no value anymore. But when private landownership goes into productive use, productivity like in Jerry's case, you can

see all of the potential that would happen. So I'm really excited for the transference of what is blight into a community asset. When somebody wants to buy a lot, the city needs to be able to let that person buy that lot. If it's not being done by the city, then it needs to be locally controlled, but the city is not giving permission to the extent that people are willing to do that. If a group of people want to buy a lot, the city needs to create an ordinance that would allow that group of people to manage, lease, or purchase that space—give them the land title so it's managed properly.

The city, on the other hand, has been managing vacant lots with the taxpayers' dollars for decades. We pay taxes, we pay a high tax rate, to make sure that the city is mowing, that the city is picking up trash, that the city is plowing, and the things that are required to make sure the city can keep up with nature.

How do people in your neighborhood claim vacant land?

We take vacant land for sure. Like I said there's land here in Southwest Detroit, not as much as in other places, but certainly we've been hit by foreclosure and demolition in the same type of way. It's difficult to take land where there has been demolition because the quality is not good. It's construction debris, it's clay, it's the type of material that you would see being laid in a foundation rather than being put to some kind of productive use—for farming, for a play lot, for a school, for anything. And so when we find these vacant lots and we test the soil, we make sure that it doesn't have contaminants because we're growing food for people in the neighborhoods. I've seen people take vacant buildings for art, I think that's one of the best and most productive uses as well, that people can re-create and keep the identity and the history and the culture by putting graffiti up on certain areas so that they can put a stamp that identifies some kind of political or cultural identity for that neighborhood.

I would like there to be equity around land control and landownership. I would like to see the city give the same consideration and thought and infrastructure to the people of the city as they do to the corporations.

3

GROWING A REVOLUTION

f crumbling factories have been the popular icons of Detroit's collapse, gardens have just as often represented the city's rebirth. Over the past decade, Detroit's shift from Motown to "Growtown" has been widely heralded, attracting young migrants, tourists, investors, and journalists to the city. Today Detroit boasts more than fifteen hundred community, school, church, market, and backyard gardens.

While urban agriculture in Detroit is not new, the attention lavished on it is. The media tend to conjure an image of a postindustrial pastoral sublime in which horses and goats graze among deteriorated buildings, tractors inch down wide boulevards, and vegetables push through concrete rubble. These images can fetishize Detroit's agrarian landscape, particularly when they are divorced from contemporary debates over what form urban agriculture should take and who should benefit from it.

This chapter highlights why farming has emerged as a crucial racial and social justice issue in Detroit. It is structured around conversations with representatives of some of Detroit's leading food justice organizations, including D-Town Farm, Feedom Freedom Growers, Undoing Racism in Detroit's Food System, the Capuchin Soup Kitchen, Earthworks Urban Farm, and the Detroit Food Justice Task Force. Our contributors' analyses make it clear that Detroit's urban farms, gardens, and kitchens are themselves sites where struggle over the city's future plays out.

Many of the contributors to this chapter situate Detroit's agrarian landscape as an extension of a longer struggle for Black self-reliance and liberation. They point to how food is a historically important link between land control and self-determination and emphasize how community farming, in particular, can build solidarity, contribute to cooperative economics, and raise people's political consciousness.[1] In addition, the pieces also point to how gardening and food projects model new human-environmental relationships and foster a deeper understanding of the environment and the interconnectedness of life. Contributors also relate the importance of collective study to community garden projects, noting how they serve as a vehicle to bring people together to reflect on how the world is changing—politically, economically, socially, environmentally—and evaluate strategies of collective action in relationship to these changing conditions.

The chapter is threaded through with photographs of urban agriculture projects in Detroit by documentary photographer Amy Senese. A native Michigander, Senese lives in Detroit and has spent numerous hours volunteering in community gardens and taking photographs as she works. Her photos, taken in 2012, depict many of the projects mentioned in the chapter, including D-Town Farm, Feedom Freedom Growers, and the Georgia Street Harvest Festival.

While the organizations highlighted in this chapter approach their work in different ways, they are all focused on transforming power and feeding people in ways that go beyond food—from D-Town's emphasis on raising the consciousness of the Black community to Feedom Freedom's focus on creating a liberated territory where people can survive mentally, physically, and spiritually. Grassroots-led initiatives such as Undoing

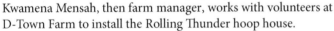

Kwamena Mensah, then farm manager, works with volunteers at D-Town Farm to install the Rolling Thunder hoop house.

Longtime beekeeper and founding member of the DBCFSN Aba Ifeoma monitors and prepares D-Town's bee hives for the winter months.

Racism in Detroit's Food System and the Detroit Food Justice Task Force have been instrumental in shifting the conversation about what it means to farm in Detroit by lifting up questions of race and encouraging white newcomers to confront histories of white supremacy in relationship to social service work and nonprofit funding. In an attempt to further this dialogue, the Detroit Food Justice Task Force launched the Cook Eat Talk program, premised on the idea that sitting down together to eat is a radical act and a way to build foundational relationships. It also inspired the Capuchin Soup Kitchen to shift its focus to an empowerment-based social service model. This approach is twofold: it includes building constituent power in their neighborhoods and organizing a volunteer program in which volunteers, who are often suburban whites, work alongside the formerly incarcerated, homeless, and people in treatment. In these ways, farming in Detroit is as much about bringing people together to build foundational relationships, develop a sense of common purpose, and grow other possible worlds as it is about transforming vacant lots into gardens.

This map highlights locations mentioned in the interviews and essays in this chapter.

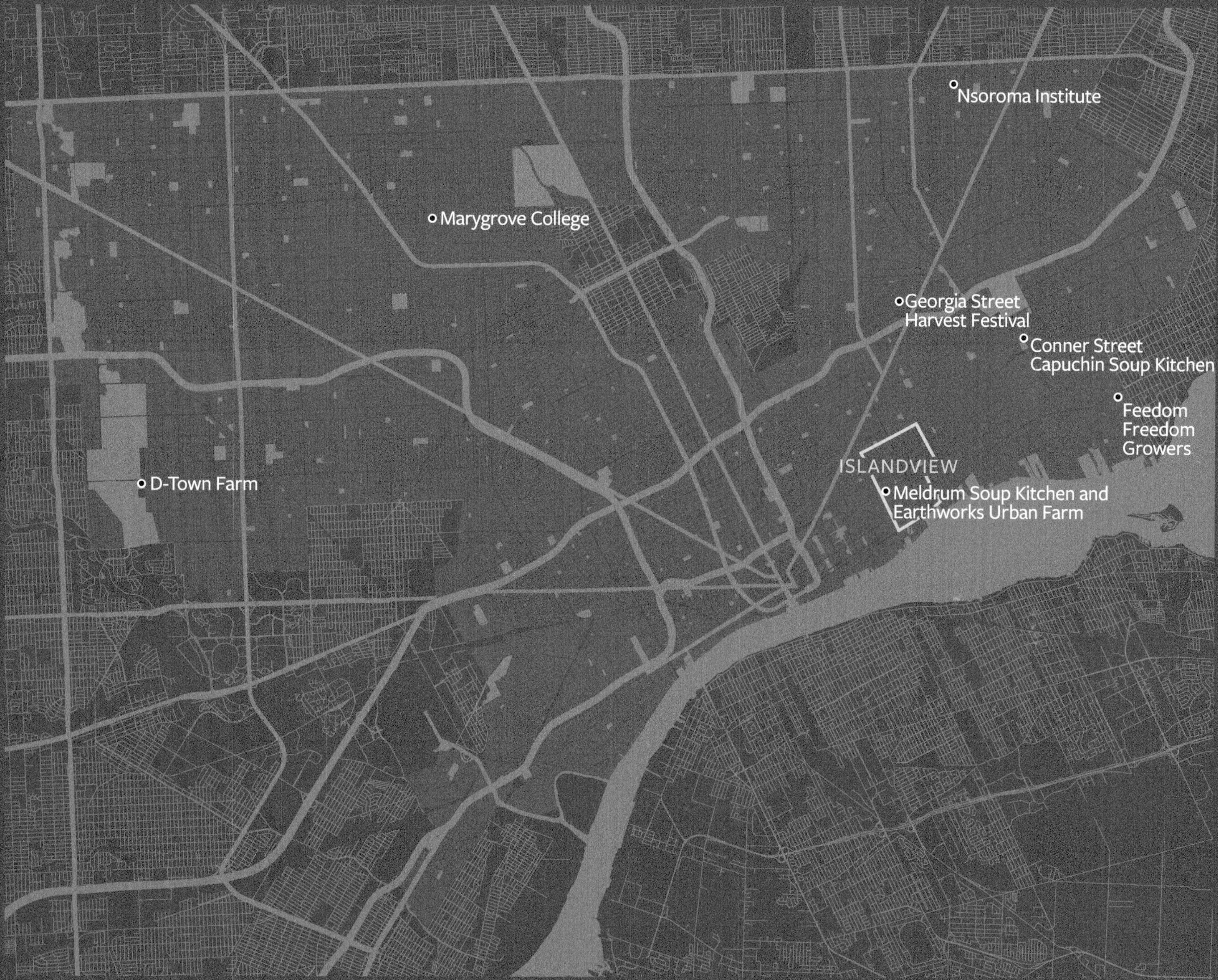

Nsoroma Institute

Marygrove College

Georgia Street
Harvest Festival

Conner Street
Capuchin Soup Kitchen

Feedom
Freedom
Growers

D-Town Farm

ISLANDVIEW

Meldrum Soup Kitchen and
Earthworks Urban Farm

URBAN AGRICULTURE
IN DETROIT

A Long Tradition

ALEX HILL

French Ribbon Farms

Detroit is a city built on agriculture. The indigenous Anishinaabeg utilized Detroit as a natural gathering place among Lake Huron, Lake Erie, and a handful of rivers and streams. The rich river soil made it easy to grow crops, hunt small-game animals, and conduct trade. The French settlers of the 1760s were lured to occupy the "new world" based on promises of free farmland. These so-called ribbon farms, divided into long narrow strips along the water, became some of the best known geographic landmarks in the city. In this early French map of Détroit, the ribbon farms are numbered by owner. Detroit's early settler families derived a great deal of wealth from farming stolen land, utilizing slaves, and eventually dividing and selling their large landholdings. Ribbon farms provided the template for Detroit's north-south streets—Cass, Beaubien, Brush, St. Antoine, and Rivard—and as such serve as a permanent memorial to the city's settler agrarian legacy hidden in plain sight.

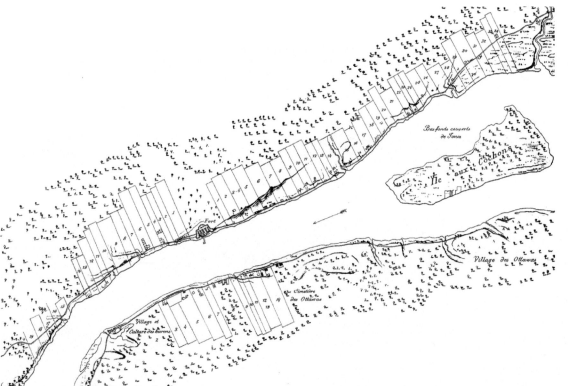

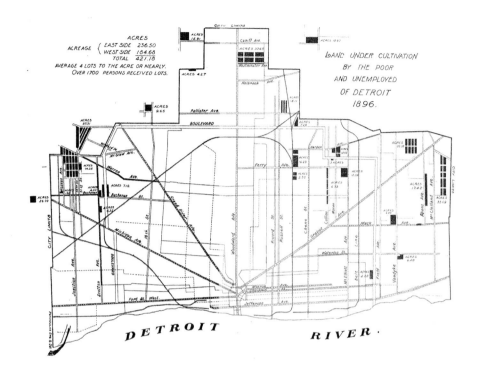

Pingree Potato Patches

After the economic collapse of 1893, Mayor Hazen Pingree launched Detroit's first citywide urban agriculture program with the aim of spurring self-reliance. By 1896, Pingree Potato Patches occupied two hundred acres in Detroit. The planning commission in 1896 noted that after the economic situation improved, the potato patches could be repurposed as city parks.

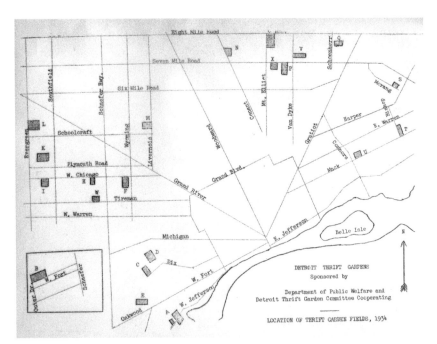

Detroit Thrift Gardens image and map used with permission of Detroit Historical Society.

Thrift Gardens in 1930s Detroit

Detroiters have often turned to urban agriculture in times of economic crises. During the Great Depression, Mayor Frank Murphy instituted a "thrift garden" program to allow the unemployed to provide for themselves and remain well fed. By 1934, there were sixty-six-hundred thrift gardens occupying four hundred acres of land. In a short time frame, the Great Migration began and Black people fleeing harsh treatment in southern states began setting up homes in the Eight Mile/Wyoming area, where there was ample space to build a house and farm the adjacent land.

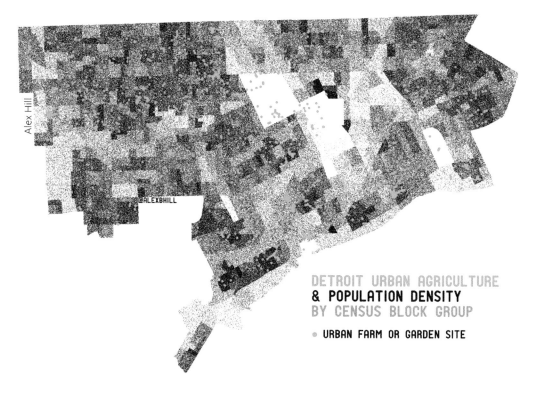

Alex Hill

@ALEXBHILL

DETROIT URBAN AGRICULTURE
& POPULATION DENSITY
BY CENSUS BLOCK GROUP

● URBAN FARM OR GARDEN SITE

An offshoot of the Gardening Angels program was the Detroit Agricultural Network, which launched in 2003 and supported seven hundred community gardens. The network continued to grow with support from Greening of Detroit, which also started up the Garden Resource Program and Grown in Detroit initiatives. The Garden Resource Program provided seed packets and workshops for gardeners. It has since turned into its own organization called Keep Growing Detroit, which is currently a network of over fifteen thousand gardeners working at almost fifteen hundred gardens. The organization continues to distribute seed packets, offer growing workshops, coordinate a cooperative of gardeners, and maintain its own market gardens.

This map, created by Alex Hill, shows the breadth of urban agriculture projects in Detroit. Because many urban farms and gardens are highly informal projects—and were illegal in Detroit until an urban farming ordinance was passed in 2013—it likely underreports urban agriculture projects in the city. Moreover, it only shows those gardens registered with

Detroit Urban Agriculture

After early urban agriculture efforts led by Mayor Hazen Pingree in the late 1800s and notable efforts with thrift gardens during the Great Depression, the city launched the Farm-A-Lot program during Mayor Coleman A. Young's tenure and amid the recession of 1973. The growing number of vacant lots in the city were to be repurposed for community urban agriculture projects. Young's program turned thirty-three hundred empty lots into urban gardens. Soon after, the US Department of Agriculture started up its own Urban Garden Program. In the 1980s, the Gardening Angels, a group of mainly African American southern-born elders, began planting flowers and gardens on vacant lots to combat crime and drugs. It was a way of caring for the community by caring for land and training young people in traditional agrarian practices and food preservation techniques.

Keep Growing Detroit in 2014. By overlaying population density with urban farms, Hill complicates the relationship between urban farming and depopulation. Given the degree to which depictions of urban farming in Detroit are linked to images of urban abandonment, one would expect that the most depopulated sections of the city would have the most farms. In contrast, agriculture projects tend to cluster near densely populated areas. The farms and community gardens appear quite evenly spread around the city (with the exceptions of some of the city's more sparsely populated areas in Southwest Detroit and near Coleman Young Airport). The geographic distribution of farms also punctures another stereotype: urban farming is not only associated with the gentrifying neighborhoods surrounding Downtown (though these areas certainly show large clusters of farms). Numerous farms also exist in outlying neighborhoods mostly populated by longtime residents.

"WE ACTUALLY HAVE THE CAPACITY TO DEFINE OUR OWN REALITY"

MALIK YAKINI

Malik Yakini is the director of the Detroit Black Community Food Security Network (DBCFSN) which was founded in 2006. The DBCFSN and its urban farming component, known as D-Town Farm, a seven-acre farm in Northwest Detroit, was shaped by experiences with urban agriculture at the Nsoroma Institute, an African-centered school founded in 1989, where Yakini served as a principal. In this interview, Yakini discusses how education and growing food go hand in hand. In recognition of the immense cultural importance of food, the network focuses on maintaining and reclaiming the traditions of enslaved African ancestors forcibly brought to the Americas. For example, the DBCFSN draws on concepts from traditional African cultures, from the idea of holism to *ujamaa*, or cooperative economics. They also emphasize consciousness raising and Black self-reliance as part of their efforts to provide healthier, more affordable food for Detroiters.

Malik Yakini, director of the Detroit Black Community Food Security Network (DBCFSN) with Hanifa Adjuman, DBCFSN's education and outreach coordinator.

This interview was conducted by Andrew Newman in 2012 as part of the Uniting Detroiters project.

What kind of work does the DBCFSN do?

We do several things, but all our work is focused around raising the consciousness of Detroit's Black community in regard to food-related issues, as well as building our capacity to provide food for ourselves.

The most labor-intensive project that we have is called D-Town Farm. It's a seven-acre organic farm in Rouge Park, which is the city's largest park. We grow about forty different crops at the farm. We have four hoop houses to extend the growing season. We raise bees for pollination and for honey. We have a large-scale composting operation that we're using to build the fertility of the soil. We do lots and lots of agritourism. In addition to being a production farm, it's also an educational facility. We're teaching people about the various techniques that can be used to ramp up urban agriculture and to model those techniques. We also model the human relationships that are necessary to make that happen, in hopes that other people will be inspired to do this work in their neighborhoods.

That's the most labor-intensive project. We also have a monthly food co-op called the Ujamaa Food Co-op. *Ujamaa* is a key Swahili word that means "cooperative economics," and at its root, the word *jamaa* means "family." The idea behind a co-op is that we're looking out for each other's needs collectively as if we were a biological family.

Presently, the co-op functions as a once-a-month buying club where members pool their money and buy from a major national distributor. The food is brought back to this building where our office is located. We divide the food up according to who ordered what, and people take their food home. In that way we're able to eliminate a lot of the middle layers that people end up paying for if they go to a grocery store—all the advertising, the people who bag the groceries, the cashier, the lighting, and all of that. We're able

to cut those costs and reduce people's food cost. We're working very hard now to morph the buying club into a brick-and-mortar retail cooperative store. We're expecting to open a store in about two years. It will be a fairly large retail store where people can get healthy food options for less than what they're used to paying at retail stores.

We also have a youth program called the Food Warriors Youth Development Program. We're currently servicing more than 150 children at about three different schools. We teach them about sustainable agriculture, nutrition, the importance of movement and exercise, and maintaining health. We also teach them about some of the dangers of the current industrial food system. We teach them about food security and give them some of the tools to assess what's going on in their own communities in terms of access to healthy food.

We also have a lecture series called "What's for Dinner," which we sponsor in conjunction with the Detroit Public Library. It runs once a month from April through October. We have various topics. For example, this month we'll be talking about breastfeeding and its importance in developing physically and emotionally healthy children.

I think those are our main projects at this point. We're also involved in some of the things that we don't sponsor. For example, we're involved in an initiative called Undoing Racism in the Detroit Food System, which seeks to make people aware of how race impacts food access and how race impacts the economics of food and—more importantly than just making us aware—begins to put in place some concrete steps to mitigate some of the impacts of that racism. And, finally, we're involved in policy work through the Detroit Food Policy Council, which we were the lead organization in starting. We also have a presence through our farm manager on the Michigan Food Policy Council. We're concerned about creating a healthy policy environment that can help some of the new food initiatives to thrive.

Why did you become interested in food and agriculture in particular?

For several years, I was principal of a school called Nsoroma Institute, which is an African-centered school. It started as a private school in 1989 and transformed into a charter school in 1997. The aim of the school is to instill within Black children a sense of their own heritage, a sense of their own history, a sense of their own culture to give them a grounding.

It's our analysis that one of the challenges facing African American people is that because we have in many ways been cut off from our traditional culture and the values that provide the undergirding for that culture, that we are kind of searching for an identity. Often what happens to people who have been cut off from their traditions, and who also are living under a group, is that the more powerful group retains most of the power. In this case, that would be white people, people from Europe, Western Europe primarily, both those who came and participated directly in the slave trade and the enslavement of Africans but also those whose ancestors maybe didn't participate directly.

Because of this paradigm we call white supremacy, those people benefit from having white skin in the society. And so it's our anal-ysis that in order to chart a healthy course for ourselves, and to not mock the culture and the norms and the values of the dominant society, then we have to have an understanding of our own traditions, and we should glean those aspects of our traditions that seem to make sense for our situation here.

Clearly we don't live in fourteenth-century Ghana or Sudan and so there are certain things that really wouldn't fit. But there are certain values, again, that provide the cultural undergirding, that we think are important and could help us in this situation. The school [Nsoroma Institute] is designed to instill those concepts in children. One of the important concepts that we have gleaned from traditional African culture is this idea that everything is inter-connected, that separation is an illusion. What tends to happen in Western society is that it tends to look very in depth at particular aspects of life. In fact, typically if a person studies for a PhD they'll drill very deep into a particular subject and have very in-depth knowledge about that subject. But oftentimes that knowledge is not connected to other things that have an impact on that and upon which that thing has an impact. This idea of holism is some-thing that is very much a part of traditional African cultures and the traditional African worldview.

As part of our understanding about this idea of interconnect-edness, we started doing gardening with the children in 2000 as a way of helping to connect them with nature and helping them to understand their relationship to the environment. The second reason that we started gardening is because we think it's important that Black people move toward being as self-reliant as possible. Growing our own food is one of the ways of building a sense of self-reliance. It's not that we think that by growing a few tomato plants that we're going to significantly reduce our dependence upon the major food system, but in a sense it's symbolic. What it does is it begins to build within people an understanding of their own capacity to care for their own needs. We wanted to plant those seeds in the children and the families at the school as we were at the same time, literally planting those seeds in the ground.

The work of the DBCFSN in many ways morphed out of the work that we were doing at Nsoroma Institute. We started in 2000 with an organic garden behind the school. A couple of years after that we enlarged the effort into something we call the Shamba Organic Garden Collective, which then included about twenty families of parents of students and staff members at the school. We would go to people's yards and till their gardens and help them plant gardens in yards around the city and vacant lots. We had about twenty gardens that were part of this collective. As the work continued to grow eventually we called a meeting and in 2006 formed the DBCFSN.

What are some examples of impacts that you've seen from your work?

At this point I think the major impact we're having is on people's consciousness, and we're certainly having an impact through the farm and through the modeling that I described earlier. There are many people who'll come out and see what we're doing at the farm and decide that they want to do gardens in their yards or in vacant lots next to their houses.

We're also impacting people's understanding of their relationship to the food system. One of the major messages we carry is that we have the capacity to produce our own food, to distribute our own food, to process our own food, that we're not just victims or pawns on the chessboard where these more powerful forces move us around; that is, we actually have the capacity to define our own reality.

And so that message is getting across to people as well. But you know this is an incremental process. It's very slow, and we're trying to impact consciousness that's really developed over hundreds of years for African people in this country. This kind of debilitating consciousness that we have is a result of enslavement and Jim Crow and all the things that came after that that suggest to us that we are less than other human beings and that we have less capacity than other people to define our reality.

We're clearly having an impact in the area of policy with the creation of the Detroit Food Policy Council and impacting the elected and appointed political leadership of the City of Detroit. Prior to 2006, when we began addressing the Detroit City Council, it was rare to hear political leaders in the city talk about the term *food security* and/or even to discuss urban agriculture. We can't solely take credit for that, but we have been one of the organizations that's participated in bringing this more to the forefront of the minds of those who are charged with running the City of Detroit. We've had impact on the children in our youth programs. We see that all the time with their desire to eat fresh fruits and vegetables, particularly if they participate in growing the vegetables. And we've seen some impact that those children have on their parents as a result of being exposed to gardening. So those are some of the impacts that I see that we've had.

RESURGET CINERIBUS

ISAAC GINSBERG MILLER

A fire in the middle of
the night, my head whipping
back to watch the embers
warp the black. A light,
neither epiphany nor end.

Fire, in its distance
watches, feral, eyes
shining keen then blinking
out, away from my life.

In childhood I'd don
a glossy helmet and climb
through splintering beams,
imagining a cape of smoke.

Now at the height of humid
summer I walk past elders
gardening the empty
plot next to their home.

Where the floorboards lay
they now tend heirlooms,
harvesting each bulb before
the stalks go to seed.

Alongside them, a basket
filled with cabbage and corn.
Twining the fence line:
marigolds, indigo bellflowers,
snapdragons.

The title of this poem is taken from Detroit's city motto "Speramus
Meliora; Resurget Cineribus," which translates as "We hope for better
things; it shall rise from the ashes."

Children run through the farm on a tour led by D-Town intern
Vaughn Johnson.

"LIBERATED TERRITORY IS A MEANS OF SURVIVAL"

WAYNE CURTIS

Wayne Curtis is an urban farmer and visual artist. He cofounded Feedom Freedom Growers with his spouse, Myrtle Thompson Curtis, on the far east side of Detroit in 2009. Feedom Freedom consists of about two dozen beds, a large hoop house, and an extensive composting station. It serves as a gathering spot for local youth and adults. A common space for collective study and intergenerational dialogue, the gardens offer "art in the garden" days, cooking classes, and workshops.

In 2012, Sara Safransky interviewed Curtis as part of the Uniting Detroiters project. In this excerpt from their conversation, Curtis explains Feedom Freedom as an extension of his past involvement in the Black Panther Party. Like the Black Panther Party survival programs, Feedom Freedom has a basic needs orientation and emphasizes self-determination that begins with creating a space con-

ducive to face-to-face relationships in the neighborhood. Curtis describes the work of Feedom Freedom through Huey P. Newton's concept of liberated territory: a strategy to secure control over the social and political mechanisms that organize human relationships from education to political organization.

Could you talk about your experience in the Black Panther Party?

My involvement in the party, I was basically a worker. I sold papers, which is important. I read, talked with people, creating an environment so that the survival programs could operate here in Detroit.* I went door-to-door Downtown, creating routes for people to contribute to the programs.

What did the party look like when you joined in 1970?

I had just returned from Vietnam. It looked like war because that was the frame of mind I was in, that's how I saw it. But as I became more involved, war took on a different concept—war of offense, war of defense, war of strategy. There was a whole infrastructure that I started to see. People were strategizing about how to protect

---

*In the 1960s and '70s, the Black Panther Party instituted survival programs that provided food, shoes, health care, and education, as well as legal, plumbing, and electrical services. At the organization's height, party chapters ran over sixty survival programs in different locations, nationally and internationally.

programs, how to protect people, how to protect the workers doing the work.

What we were doing and what the Vietnamese were doing was to me very similar. Then we started reading Mao Tse-tung.* Even though the [Chinese civil] war was in the '30s and '40s, the similarities were still the same.[2] It was a people's campaign to sustain themselves. These are the methods and strategies of what I call healing now, by which I mean the correct handling of contradictions among people who have lived it a thousand times.

Could you talk about how Feedom Freedom came about?

Before I met Myrtle, I was at Nsoroma.† They had a garden. There was always something conflicting in my mind about the philosophy of revolutionary intercommunalism and the philosophy of revolutionary Black cultural nationalism or Black nationalism.[3] I started realizing that the hairs are so thin—the hairs separating Black nationalism, or creating a space for Black people, in reference to revolutionary intercommunalism, which is still creating space in the Black community. I guess the only qualitative difference is that we're operating on a level of globalism. If you're really interested in the unity of opposites, it's jumped all the way to a global state, so that's how we have to face it. It affects almost everything that we do. I see people understanding naturally how reactionary globalization is. What is revolutionary globalization? We have the Zapatistas in Mexico, which remind me of the Black Panther Party.

So, at Nsoroma, they had farms. I kept going by there and I fell in love with the young people while they were falling in love with agriculture. And it was not just agriculture but the whole biological feedback of human existence took me, and how Black history or Black African history affects us. I started painting.

I realized when I started painting I was more attentive to understanding that the people weren't there any longer. The stores weren't there any longer. I mean there wasn't a store in Detroit that did not contribute to the Black Panther Party. We were everywhere in Detroit. We went to Hamtramck clothing stores. We had a free clothing program, and they donated clothing to us. All the meat markets gave chicken for our free food program and food giveaways. In Oakland, they gave out seventy-five thousand bags of groceries once a month. Here in Detroit, they gave out five thousand bags. We would go up to Chicago and help them bag food up there. They would come here and help us. I think point 3 [of the Black Panther Party's Ten Point Program], or one of the points, was we need to end the rivalry of capitalists in our Black community.

Oakland was the base of operations, which was liberated. They started moving up the ladder as far as business was concerned. We really started understanding the corporate control of communities because of the action of participating in electoral politics, which everybody, everybody, attacked us for doing. I couldn't understand it at the time. But we saw the whites of our leaders' eyes, what they wanted, and how they used politics to control people. Later

*Mao Tse-tung was a Chinese Communist revolutionary who founded the People's Republic of China and served as the Chairman of the Chinese Communist Party from 1949, when it was established, until his death in 1976.

†Nsoroma refers to the Nsoroma Institute, an African-centered private school that became a charter school in Detroit. The school closed in 2012.

I realized that they are the true constituents of the political base, of their own political base. They created that so they can function. Here we are, some crazy-ass motherfuckers from the street, sitting at the table with, I think, Kodak, one of the big companies in Oakland. I mean, they were really upset. But we had the power of the people. I mean literally we had that power.

But those circumstances, because of the drugs, because of globalization at its highest point, as far as these businesses moving out, that's why we were against capitalism in the first place, because there was this one nucleus. Emory Douglas* drew capitalism as this pig with everything and everyone sucking on it. With that gone, we had no means anymore because we totally depended upon that political and economic system—and that ideology—to survive. Now that it's not here, how do we get the resources that we need? How do we get the food that is needed? Now I understand the purpose of agriculture.

Like the Zapatistas, we're dealing with the same issues, but they're in Mexico. In Cuba, they're dealing with the same issues. I mean, how did that happen? The globalization of finance, of politics, of education—all of these have taken on a whole different facade that wasn't here before, and to me, it has to be studied because it's not the same. If you want to develop an ideology, you're going to have to understand all these particularities. We have to study.

The agricultural part of this is our way of organizing face-to-face relationships in the neighborhood, which is important, maybe not just around food, but around jobs, understanding there's a qualitative difference between work and job. You start understanding if work doesn't sustain you, then it's slavery. You start understanding that and actually create a situation where work does sustain you. Now you're getting into what revolution or societal transformation is all about.

What would good governance look like?

Like what's happening right here, right now. It's talking, getting information, discussing in relation to what we think we need to be doing: How do you sustain yourself? What's the infrastructure that would allow us to do that? How do we do that? What properties, resources, and relationships do we need to do that, to make that occur? It's the actual praxis and practice of having the concept or having a vision and then sitting down with the strategy. There may be several strategies before you come up with one that actually works. For us, that's what it is. It's not an absolute thing where it's like, okay, they're doing this and now it's cool. It's not like that. How we obtain power is an ongoing thing.

When Feedom Freedom first started, it was almost like I was in the [Black Panther] Party: "Okay, by next week we're going to do this and all of us are going to get together and this is what we're going to do." We didn't work like that. It's not working like that. People have their own ideas. That's been my revolution in understanding that and being able to have the sensitivity of understanding where people are at. But maybe from different levels or different spots or different spaces, I can help something that's going to help. Since everything is related and connected, what I

*Emory Douglas served as the minister of culture for the Black Panther Party from 1967 until it disbanded in the 1980s. He was the art director and main illustrator for the party's newspaper, *The Black Panther*.

do over there is going to affect what's done here. What you guys are doing is going to affect what's being done here. And this is our community. As ragtag as it is, this is our community. It's developing. This is not the absolute answer right here at Feedom Freedom, it's impossible—it's part of it.

You talk a lot about liberated territory and I'm wondering if you could speak a bit to the importance of that concept.

I guess liberated territory is something that can function under reactionary globalization. In wars, like in Vietnam, they had bases of liberated territory where they could conduct their affairs or war, but sometimes they would have to move them. I guess since Vietnam was occupied, they had these small bases of operation. Liberated territory is where our consciousness can come to the point for our survival. We've gained our political insight of what we're doing—understanding space; understanding territory; understanding development, the cognitive development of young people, structure, infrastructure, the organization; understanding how to have dialogue without slamming doors and walking out the front door.

That's hard.

It's very hard [*laughs*]. But if we lose this, what we've gained here, we can apply it someplace else. I think we're still learning the concept of liberated territory, the basis of operation, and maybe it's not the way to go now. I don't know. But right now, that's my premise. I saw it worked in Oakland. I saw that it's working in Mexico.

Damoni Carter harvests swiss chard at Feedom Freedom.

That's how I see liberated territory, where they're bringing in and centralizing resources so that they can survive mentally, physically, spiritually. Survive the onslaught from my enemies and survive until we can find out how to transform the situation. Like the survival program where you used to say: they're not revolutionary, because revolution is made out of sterner stuff.

This liberated territory is a means of survival until the time comes. It's liberated for a moment; it's liberated forever—we don't know. It's not even liberated yet because we don't determine our environmental destiny right now, but we're trying to get up to that. We have to understand all the things that are involved. But right now, I don't see any other way to define what we're doing other than creating a base of operations or a base of liberation.

Like you have food councils. These are political things that liberate, that are fighting for local politics. You may have to take that a step higher and control the executive or the legislative, community control of the executive, legislative, and judicial for the time being. I think that can be done. It might be harder now because of the state of our neighborhoods, the drugs, the hurt, the mental injuries, physical injuries. These injuries, this state of being wasn't by accident. And this has crippled our ability to define our future.

We have to do something now for the future. We have to make sure that the youth have an environment that's liberated. An environment where they can walk the street, an environment where the world is a classroom where they can learn, an environment—you have churches where people understand the concept of I'm thirsty and I've got some water. Maybe your role would be to keep that full, to find the resources to keep that full, so because of my consciousness I know I can come here and get some water, but to develop my consciousness more, I can create a situation where I can politically control that situation to make sure it helps you and make sure that it's always full.

You may need someone—like the young man coming down the street, who has no muffler—and the buildings, I mean everything shakes. Birds fly away. But what if there was a situation where we had the resources to pay somebody to fix his car? The lady down the street is complaining about this big tree over her house—we serve the people. And we're not giving away anything for free because it's going to take the power of the people to define a situation and make this continuum, this type of community to continue going on. I think the strategy now for us is to find the information and to understand that concept.

A young volunteer at D-Town Farm rakes between plants.

Amy Senese

"WE'RE JUST BEGINNING THE JOURNEY"

LILA CABBIL

In this interview, Lila Cabbil (1944–2019) discusses her involvement in a project called Undoing Racism in the Detroit Food System. Cabbil, who moved to Detroit from North Carolina as an infant, worked with the Rosa and Raymond Parks Institute for Self-Development and as a consultant in the area of race relations and youth development. She led trainings that strove to get participants to understand what it means to be anti-racist, focusing on concepts such as internalized privilege and internalized oppression. The Undoing Racism in the Detroit Food System project aimed to help individual growers learn to identify aspects of racism and white privilege in the city's food system and work toward a more just model. In this interview, Cabbil explains why rethinking the city's food system must begin with an analysis of racial inequality. She also emphasizes the need for more people to get involved in the work of undoing racism, beyond growers, from those who work in the restaurant industry to food processing to soup kitchens. This interview was conducted by Linda Campbell in 2012 as part of the Uniting Detroiters project.

How did Undoing Racism begin?

Undoing Racism in the Detroit Food System was a project that was initiated out of a collective of people at a [Great Lakes] Bioneers Conference who were interested in understanding more about racism.* Our main constituents are growers who have gardens. We also have a couple of large groups involved, like Earthworks and D-Town Farm, which are larger growers. We come together to have a dialogue around the kinds of impact that racism has had on the food system in terms of food security for people in the community. I think the challenge is bringing people out of their silos to enter into the dialogue but also getting people in a mind-set of understanding the power analysis that goes with racism and the difference between individual and structural racism, and, most importantly, their own role in participating in racism.

So it's really a process. While we have had Kellogg funding for the project, we are looking at how this work can continue and be sustained without having to depend on outside funding. In our community currently, I am concerned that funding has been influencing the work in a way that may not have the frame of self-determination. I also hope that we can look at ways to make our work more inclusive but also in way that really reflects people's lived experiences so that there is true community self-determination and empowerment.

*The Great Lakes Bioneers (glbd.org) is an environmental organization whose annual conference in Detroit is an important meeting place for environmental justice activists, urban farmers, gardeners, food justice activists, and others interested in thinking about solutions to environmental problems and social inequality in southeastern Michigan and the Great Lakes region. The neologism *bioneer* refers to biological pioneers.

What are some of the impacts of the work?

I can see some outcomes but I think the impact in terms of our large overwhelming title "Undoing Racism" is that we're just beginning the journey. What I will say is that there has been an increase in trainings and people understanding racism. There is an increased comfort level in terms of having the conversation. One of the things that we did was establish some ground rules for having a conversation where people could feel safe and be open and share opinions and experiences and perspectives. That has been helpful.

One of the things, again, that has been a shortcoming is that we really need to have a penetration of the food system so that we have more people coming to meetings than just those who are growing food. Ideally, we'd have more people representing the restaurant industry, people from food processing, even participation from our policy council. The other groups that I think we really want to do outreach to are the various soup kitchens and programs. There are many, many opportunities.

We were experiencing a lot of response from young white people in the city and even attracted people from as far as Flint and Ann Arbor for the dialogue sessions. We want to continue to have that interest. We also need to be more direct in guiding people into what kind of action steps they can take as a result of our discussions.

I think one of our recent impacting conversations has been understanding the commons. The dialogue was so rich in terms of people thinking about what we have in common. I think it's a beginning of pulling people out of that space of silo, in terms of looking at what are the commons and what are the things that we need to save in this city that have disappeared as commons.

Which undoing racism training model do you use?

We haven't actually stuck with one, but the one that has been the most impressive to the group has been the People's Institute for Survival and Beyond.* The reason why that one was particularly impacting was that several people in the group had not had an introduction to a power analysis and that was very, very helpful to them. The other thing that the People's Institute brought that was helpful was the history. The third thing that most people talked about was when they understood the actual impact of white supremacy and white privilege in terms of internalized racial superiority and internalized racial oppression. Those concepts were new and the idea that racism impacts everyone and is not just a white problem or is not just a problem of being a target was something that I think many people—I shouldn't say "I think," but from the evaluations—for many people, that was a first-time concept for them.

*The People's Institute of Survival and Beyond is a nationwide organization specializing in anti-racism and community-organizing training. The organization's 2010 workshop at Marygrove College was an influential session for Cabbil and other food justice activists in Detroit.

A young man participates in a sack race at the Georgia Street Harvest Festival.

Amy Senese

"POOR PEOPLE ARE NOT SOME EXOTIC BREED OF PEOPLE; THEY'RE OUR BROTHERS AND SISTERS"

BROTHER JERRY SMITH

Although urban farms garner a great deal of public attention, soup kitchens, which provide meals for hungry Detroiters are often overlooked. In 2012, as part of the Uniting Detroiters project, Linda Campbell and Sara Safransky interviewed Brother Jerry Smith, who was then the director of the Capuchin Soup Kitchen, affiliated with the Earthworks Urban Farm (see the interview with Patrick Crouch on p. 142). Originally from Minnesota, Smith is a member of the Capuchin Catholic religious order. After working for twenty years in Capuchin ministries in Milwaukee, he moved to Detroit in 2005 where he worked until February 2017, when he returned to Milwaukee. In this interview, he talks about how the soup kitchen shifted its focus from a "charity model" to one that helps the guests of the soup kitchen "discover the power that's within them." Smith's vision for the soup kitchen is not one defined by despair or as place of last resort. Rather, he views the organization as common ground where people from all walks of life, from guests in need to volunteers, build connections by working together. As a result, the soup kitchen has become an important site for community organizing and social change.

Could you talk about the history of the Soup Kitchen and its work today?

The soup kitchen began in 1929 during the Depression when people started lining up on the sidewalk asking for food to feed their families. At first, the brothers distributed food right from the doors of the monastery, but then the lines became so long and the need so overwhelming that a separate facility had to be constructed. That was the beginning of the soup kitchen. It's been serving people ever since. It was born out of a charity model, and for decades we were quite satisfied with that—"We take care of the poor."

In retrospect, it seems rather condescending. Now we have a whole different understanding. Besides providing for people's immediate physical needs, we can do so much more to discover the power that's within them. We can facilitate, or at least be partners with them, in their coming to have more control over their own lives. In order to do that, we also need to battle some forces that are mitigating against that, which is not always popular. It's easier to raise money to feed poor people than it is to raise money to help organize and help challenge the structures that conspire to keep people where they are.

Could you describe where we are right now?

Right now, we are at the Meldrum Soup Kitchen, which is on the near east side of Detroit, approximately two miles from Downtown. This is the site of the original soup kitchen. Although there is some business and industry in this neighborhood, the factories are pretty much gone. The neighborhood is hollowed-out, too. There are not many residences left in this immediate neighborhood.

Beyond the soup kitchen, what other kind of organizational activities are you all involved in?

We have two locations where we provide physical meals, and then we have another location where we distribute food packages for people to take home and prepare in their own homes, as well as clothing and appliances. We also have a twelve-bed residential treatment facility for men who are trying to recover their lives from addiction. We have a bakery that is staffed by men coming out of incarceration, homelessness, or treatment programs. At the Meldrum Soup Kitchen we host the Earthworks Urban Farm, which farms vacant lots. And at the Connor Kitchen, we have the children's program—it's a tutoring and art therapy program that seeks to help young people and their families have more control over what happens in their lives, in their schools, and in their neighborhoods.

We're feeding people in a lot of ways. I think the meals are what attract people to us initially. That provides us this wonderful pool of candidates for all these other things. People come for physical food, then they get hooked on all kinds of things that are happening here. I do a lot of public speaking. I always try to emphasize the other things we're doing so we're seen as bigger than this charity model thing. We're not here taking care of people. People are quite capable of taking care of themselves.

Could you give some examples of the impacts of your work?

The bakery, staffed by men coming out of incarceration or out of homelessness or treatment programs, is an example. In so many cases, volunteers are accustomed to coming to the soup kitchen and serving the poor, serving on a serving line. They're scooping mashed potatoes and passing out food. The bakery is very different. Volunteers come and actually work with the men. It's not that they're doing something for the bakers. They're doing it together. It's a real sense of mutuality. The volunteers talk about how this is a program that brought together people that would probably never come together under other circumstances.

Ex-convicts are teaching white suburban women how to make bread. This is wonderful. This is beautiful. So a lot of that happens here. Our work brings people together. People come to know other people and they realize we're all the same basically. Poor people are not some exotic breed of people; they're our brothers and sisters who have the same needs and wants and desires as we do. I think it can help. I think people then see the world differently. They're challenged to look at some things in our society that have affected people here in the city and they start thinking about those things.

D-Town intern Vaughn Johnson demonstrates the farm's method of sifting organic compost.

"THERE'S A NARRATIVE OF THE NEW DETROIT, BUT IT DOESN'T INCLUDE THE MAJORITY OF DETROIT"

PATRICK CROUCH

Patrick Crouch was born in Minneapolis, Minnesota, and grew up on the Eastern Shore of Maryland. After college, he started working on a farm and learned how to grow food. He moved to Detroit to work with Earthworks, the Capuchin Soup Kitchen's Earthworks Urban Farm, where he is now the farm manager. Earthworks was founded in 1997 and produces fourteen thousand pounds of produce, much of which is used for the Capuchin Soup Kitchen. They also grow transplants for urban gardens throughout Detroit. The garden plots at Earthworks are tended by interns, participants in a youth program, and, above all, volunteers from throughout metro Detroit.

In this interview, Crouch describes the challenges in working to align a nonprofit organization that is in a position of privilege vis-à-vis the community it serves with the goals of social justice as laid out by the Detroit Black Community Food Security Network. As Detroit increasingly becomes a city where needs are met by foundations and nonprofits that often come from outside the city, such reflections are instructive for how a balance of power between communities and funders might be achieved. This interview was conducted by Linda Campbell in 2012 as part of the Uniting Detroiters project.

Talk a little bit about the work that you do here at Earthworks.

We're called Earthworks Urban Farm. In some ways I think that misrepresents how much we do. We do a lot more than farming.

Earthworks really started out as being somewhat of a classic organization that was headed by a charismatic visionary. For the first seven years or so, Rick Samyn, who started the program, was the only employee. So it was his show. I was actually the first employee brought on. He did have some folks doing AmeriCorps, but I was the first employee.

We spent a long time thinking about what kind of an organization we wanted to be. Two things that really challenged us were the creation of the Detroit Black Community Food Security Network and their challenging of young whites who had leadership positions in the food system and questioning why that was. I think we had two options: one was to retreat and recoil. There was a little bit of that, like, you're calling us out, I don't like that. I don't like being called out. Very few of us do. And we could have stayed in that place, but instead we said, "Wow, this is an opportunity for us. This is an opportunity for us to face those challenges that have been made to us." I think one of the most painful things to realize when people make challenges to you is when they're right. So, in recognizing the truth that was in those challenges, I think that it really pushed us forward to ask questions about how our organization worked, what we prioritized, how we did our organizing work, how we created leadership.

I also think that working with you, Linda, and working with Building Movement Detroit really helped us ask questions about our assumptions about our work, about coming up with ideas about what we valued.* I think it really helped shift the way that we worked. We realized that slowing down and just creating community and creating space for healing was so important because how can we really expect to organize and create movement when we are so broken and so hurt? I think those are some things that changed the way that we've worked.

We're continuing to move forward, creating our own culture and pedagogy of how we do our work, constantly reevaluating and reflecting on our work. I think that we've institutionalized the idea that reflecting and evaluating and learning means that the organization will continue to grow and will not be the same in five years. I think that's a good thing.

*Building Movement Detroit has worked with a variety of direct service providers to help build the capacity of those organizations to work for systemic change through the voice and power of their service constituents. The Capuchin Soup Kitchen and Earthwork Farms were central in the formation of that work, focusing on building the capacity of residents to lead on important food security issues like urban agriculture in Detroit.

Talk to us a little bit about the day-to-day work of Earthworks, the geography of your work, and what kind of impact you think you're having in the city.

Some organizations work regionally or citywide. We contemplated that, and we looked at what other organizations were doing. We saw that there were organizations working specifically within the African American community. We saw there were organizations working on food security issues citywide. We felt like what we really wanted to do was set down some roots in our neighborhood and develop relationships with the people in our neighborhood. We've been pretty intentional about keeping our scope relatively close to the two-and-a-half-, three-, block radius that our gardens are in, and then within the broader, I would say mile-and-a-half, two-mile radius that encompasses the Islandview Village. That has formed how we do our day-to-day work, who we work with, but it's also allowed us to find partnerships with folks who are doing similar work in other parts of the city, so we can learn from them.

I sort of view it as being like an onion. There are different layers of how we work, but there's this nucleus-level layer where we focus most of our energy. That's right here in this neighborhood, that's right here with the people who come to the soup kitchen to eat, that's right here with the people who we are training right now.

Can you speak a little bit about the connection between Earthworks and the soup kitchen?

One of the ways that we relate to the kitchen is through the community garden spaces. We have spaces where folks can grow whatever they want as long as it's legal. A lot of people take home what they grow. They take it to a relative, or a lot of people donate it to the kitchen. But they do it on their own terms. I think that's a really important distinction to make, having a space where folks have control.

A lot of the folks we're working with have been told you need to stand in this line to get this, you need to provide this much information in order to get it. They've had so many hoops to jump through. I think it's really quite special to have a space where we can say, "any seeds that are in this box, they're yours to plant, whatever you want to do, whatever you want to do with this." I think it's been hugely transformative to see people growing their own food on their own terms and doing whatever they want with it. I think providing multiple channels where people can get involved is a really important part of our work.

Could you reflect a little on your work in light of the many changes happening in Detroit right now, particularly in relationship to who holds power?

I think we see corporations holding an increasing amount of power in their ability to influence who moves into the city, in particular with the incentives that are happening. We also see that nonprofits hold a huge amount of power through their ability to do development from smaller groups like community development corporations and larger groups like the Detroit Economic Growth Corporation. They have a huge amount of control over deciding what's happening in the city. And the foundations that are funding them have a huge amount of power. It's an especially impressive amount of power considering that they're able to provide money without any voter oversight of deciding what is being funded. In full disclosure, we are a beneficiary of that. So I'm not by any means suggesting that all foundations are bad. I don't think all foundations are good either. I think we all inhabit this gray area. But I do think that one of the things you find is that communities can feel powerless to those that have money, but they are actually doing the work of those foundations. Ultimately all that foundations do is dish out money and report on what they dished out money for. That's not bad, but ultimately it's the people on the ground who do the work. I really think that it's time for the foundations, and some do, but it's time for the foundations to recognize that this should be a very equal relationship, considering what you're getting out of the deal.

There have been a lot of articles about Detroit where people can go and experience this regenerative Detroit—this new birth—and not ever experience the Detroit that most people experience on a day-to-day basis. I mean, how many of these folks get on the bus and ride for forty-five minutes to get out to the Northeast Side to experience what residents in those neighborhoods are experiencing? How many of those folks have experienced what it's like to call the police and not have them show up for hours? How many folks have experienced what it's like to be the last house standing on a block and not be able to get any of the houses around demolished because they're unsafe and being squatted in? To me, that's the Detroit that's losing power. That's the Detroit that most people aren't aware even exists. There's a narrative of the new Detroit, but it doesn't include the majority of Detroit and, if anything, I would say, that it doesn't include folks who are originally Detroiters.

Patrick Geans-Ali and other volunteers from the East Michigan Environmental Action Council install a sunflower garden for Earth Day 2011 on Detroit's East Side.

"WE ARE TRYING TO BUILD FOUNDATIONAL RELATIONSHIPS THAT TRANSCEND ANY ISSUE"

LOTTIE SPADY

Lottie Spady is a poet, educator, herbalist, and activist who has worked on issues related to food, environmental, and media justice and education. She was a founding member of the Detroit Food Justice Task Force, which was launched to integrate food justice and food sovereignty principles into a discussion about urban agriculture. Thanks largely to her, the Detroit Food Justice Task Force developed a series of workshops called Cook Eat Talk, in which residents come together to cook and eat a local meal, which Spady describes as "in and of itself is a radical act." Cook Eat Talk provides residents, farmers, and food justice advocates with a common space to hold conversations about recipes for favorite dishes, experiment with new ideas about growing and distributing food in the city, and build foundational relationships. The model is increasingly being adopted elsewhere, making Detroit's approach to food justice one of the city's most important "export crops." This interview was conducted by Linda Campbell in 2012 as part of the Uniting Detroiters project.

What is the Detroit Food Justice Task Force?

The Detroit Food Justice Task Force came together as a response to a rush of interest around large-scale urban agriculture in the City of Detroit. There were some questions around the way decisions were being made as to who was receiving foundation support to start those kinds of endeavors. It generated a community conversation among urban agriculture groups, environmental justice groups, and other movement-building groups around the gaps that existed in our work that allowed such a thing to happen. Community education was identified as one gap, particularly the gap between the urban agriculture work going on and the folks who are most impacted by food injustices. We decided to come together with the goal of working within communities to identify their own solutions to filling that gap.

Can you give some examples of the impact that you have seen from food justice work happening in Detroit?

I think our Cook Eat Talk education model is going to have the most far-reaching impact because it is a grassroots educational model that meets people where they are. We don't come in as experts. We facilitate a conversation around challenges to food access in that particular area. We cook a healthy local meal together and eat together, which we believe in and of itself is a radical act because people aren't doing that anymore. We are trying to build foundational relationships that transcend any issue or action that the folks decide on. The relationships are the foundation.

And it's an easily replicated model. The next round, we're going to train community members to be facilitators of their own Cook Eat Talks. The model has reached all the way to Grand Rapids now. It has become a model for organizations such as Creative Community Pathways. They are using it now outside of food justice as a framework to discuss transportation justice. So it's really highly flexible and that's why I think it's going to be the most impactful thing that we've developed and done.

What are some of the ways that you believe the Food Justice Task Force can let those who hold power know about issues around food insecurity in the community and just overall the problems with the food system?

I think that the Detroit Food Justice Task Force can let folks know about these problems in at least two ways. One would be through the Cook Eat Talk sessions. We really have to work to develop an ongoing sustainable relationship with communities so people feel empowered to go to the food policy council meeting, go to the Whole Foods meeting, go to the Meijer's meeting, and begin to understand the food system.* How is Eastern Market set up? Who owns what? Is there a minority-owned trucking operation that's moving food around the city? Are there any Black-owned storage facilities? Does the current food system reflect the major populations that live in the city? I think our Cook Eat Talks can help that

process happen. On the other side is our communications and media strategy work—writing, writing, writing, blogging, tweeting, writing, blogging, tweeting. For example, making videos and trying to push back on the dominant narrative that supports all these other decisions that are being made that are not in our favor.

And we are looking at more sustainable models like membership, donations, and earned income strategies around food so that we are more self-sustaining. We are going to do this work with or without foundation funds because people are still hungry. That's not changing the fact that there are people who still aren't eating.

*Whole Foods Market opened a store in the Cass Corridor (now rebranded Midtown) neighborhood in 2013, and the Meijer grocery store chain also opened an outpost that year at the intersection of Eight Mile Road and Woodward Avenue. The store openings, that of Whole Foods in particular, became major touch points for debates in the city around food access, race, class, and gentrification.

"FOOD JUSTICE BEYOND URBAN AGRICULTURE"

LINDA CAMPBELL

Linda Campbell, one of the editors of this book, works with the Building Movement Project Detroit and is a founding member of the Detroit People's Platform as well as the Detroit Food Justice Task Force. Linda was born in St. Louis, but her work in Detroit goes back to 1970, when she arrived in the city as an employee with the Centers for Disease Control and Prevention and focused on organizing around public health. In this interview, she offers a holistic analysis of food, informed by her career in public health. Campbell cautions against an uncritical celebration of urban farming. While she supports many growers, she worries that predominately white newcomers are receiving access to land and support that has been long denied to African Americans in the city. She is also adamant that understandings of food justice must go far beyond urban agriculture to include the entirety of the city's food system, especially grocery stores and emergency food providers. This interview was conducted by Andrew Newman as part of the Uniting Detroiters project.

Aba Ifeoma walks visitors through the farm on a volunteer Sunday.

You've been working in Detroit since the early 1970s. Can you talk about what the environment was like at that time?

I was hired as a public health adviser. The federal government had just started hiring women for the position. The Public Health Service and Centers for Disease Control was a real old boys' network for many, many years, and they were just coming out of the Tuskegee syphilis scandal.[4] They teamed me up with some African American guys who lived and worked in Detroit. They taught me the city. It was basically public health outreach.

I was here to watch the transition from a white city—with a white police force, with whites in senior-level jobs in all of the agencies. When Coleman Young was elected, African Americans started making their way up in the civil services. I was part of an ushering in of Black leaders inside the city. There were some awfully smart African Americans that I worked for and who trained me. I didn't agree with everybody 100 percent; some of them were fairly conservative but they were highly trained and highly skilled. The continuous message was you have to do your very best. There was an ethic around excellence and delivery. People were mobilized and people had a vision. They saw themselves as part of a bigger movement for Black political empowerment. You had the rise of the Black political elite. The rise of the Black professional class. Not that there weren't Blacks in government before, but we weren't there in huge numbers. It was an incredible time to be in Detroit.

What was doing health outreach like, and how did it shape your future work?

Oftentimes I was in the field by myself. I remember this one young woman. It was a turning point for me. The hospital had been trying to contact this young woman for weeks. She had not kept her prenatal appointment. The nurse said, "This little girl is really in trouble. We need to get her back in. We really don't like the way her lab is looking." She said, "See if you can reach her. She is not responding to the public health nurse." So she gave me the referral. I saw why they weren't responding. When I got to the address, the place looked like it had been completely blown out. It was down on Cadillac Boulevard, way over on the East Side. I pulled up and looked up and I thought, "Nobody is living in there." The nurses had not been going up in there because from the outside you wouldn't think anyone was there.

I got back in my car. And then, something inside of me just said, "You should really go. You should really go and see what's going on." So there I am, in this abandoned building, walking up three flights of stairs, because she lived on the third floor. I go to the very back. I knocked on a door. And there she is, she and her boyfriend, and the baby. They couldn't have been more than sixteen years old, her boyfriend maybe seventeen. They were *young*. Very young. They were so gracious when they answered the door. I said, "The nurse wants you to come back." The first thing she said was, "Is there something wrong with my baby?" I'm not a medical person, so I just said, "They want you to come back." She said, "Can you take me?" I said, "If I take you now, will you go?" And she said, "Yeah, I'll go now." I said, "Okay." They called me "ma'am." Now I'm

twenty-two years old! It is unbelievable how gracious those kids were; they didn't know me from Adam. So they got all dressed, got the baby dressed, they got in the back of my car, and I drove them to Herman Kiefer.* That just moved me. It became who I was—connecting to people to who were in incredible need and figuring out a way to make shit work for them. I didn't know it was social justice or advocacy. I sat there and waited until they went through the clinic and then I took them back home. I wonder what happened to them. That put me on the path. So I have never been one to allow people to characterize folks as "the other."

How did you go from public health to food justice?

The thing about public health is that it is all encompassing. When I worked in the public health department my office was right around the corner from the nutrition department. I was there when they first began WIC.† If you are in public health you are going to be exposed to a whole variety of programs and services. Nutrition and health are pretty important parts of that, from infants on up. So, I always had an awareness about food and the role nutrition, awareness, and access to food played in the community.

I had been meeting and talking with folks about food-related changes that were taking place in the city, and this whole notion of

---

*Herman Kiefer was a city-owned hospital in Detroit, which was closed by the administration of Mayor David Bing in 2013.

†WIC refers to Women, Infants, and Children, a federal food assistance program serving low-income pregnant or nursing mothers and children younger than five years.

growing food and how it had taken on this kind of political connotation. Now, when I first came to Detroit in the early '70s, a lot of people grew food. My daughter's grandmother lived on the North End, and she was a Farm-A-Lot person. Coleman Young had started the Farm-A-Lot program. You got seeds, you could get a lot for fifty cents, and she had the lot next door to her. She grew food, and the family ate out of the garden. So there was that kind of thing in the back of my head, but it wasn't considered particularly political. I was like, "This is what we did in the South" and "I love to grow and I love good food, I love healthy food." You saw a lot of that kind of agriculture happening across the city.

But then those folks began to disappear. I remember one summer, her neighbors, who were growers, moved to Belleville. They bought some land and they began growing out there. A lot of the old-timers began leaving the neighborhood. You saw fewer and fewer of the old Farm-A-Lot folks. And then fast-forward, when people started talking about growing food and all of the political connotations around that, I was thinking, "Oh yeah, my daughter's grandmother used to be a farmer, but I don't know if she ever thought about herself that way!" People became much more aware of the division around who had access to healthy food and who did not.

I had conversations with people who wanted to ascribe growing food as an act of justice. I would push back on that. I would say, "No, it may be social entrepreneurship, and that's a good thing, but just because you grow food, it doesn't necessarily mean it is an act of justice." So I became one of the founding members of the Detroit Food Justice Task Force, and I've always brought that other lens to the work, you know, "What about these families that I see in the emergency food pantry who are not on the radar of the food growers or the food movement?"

You see an uncomfortable fit between the broader urban agriculture movement and food justice?

I do. I think there is more consciousness around articulating what food justice looks like *other* than growing your own food compared to, let's say, ten years ago. There were a lot of assumptions made. I mean don't get me wrong—growing food is great. I've grown. There are people who really do it and do it well. I have a really high level of respect for them. But there is a lot of mythmaking around the food movement in here in Detroit. When you look at who is characterized in the mythmaking, it is mostly young white folks. And they have been given liberties around land and access to resources that had not happened when my former mother-in-law was growing, as an older African American woman. I also didn't see the same kinds of liberties and access and support being given to the families in the emergency food pantries.

It's almost like there was a movement to take and occupy land as part of the movement and the mythmaking. It was almost like, "Yeah, why shouldn't we just take this land and grow on it. We are growing food!" It's like, "Do you own this land?" I remember asking that of a group of growers. I wasn't being that pointed. It was just a question that came up. They got so defensive with me. "No! We don't own it. It's just here. We came out here and we cleaned it up." "Wait a minute! You guys don't own this!?" I said. "And you are growing all of this stuff on it? What about taxes? Are you paying taxes?" [*laughs*] Oh my God!

I wasn't being a defender of the system as much as I was thinking historically, "Hmm… this is how people appropriate land and resources." That's where you begin to see the advantages and the wealth building, and where people begin to sort of, well, take control. So we pushed back.

I'm not fighting for cheap land for you to grow on. I'm fighting for land justice. I want to go from "I want to be able get cheap land like Hantz"* to thinking about land differently in Detroit. How are land-use decisions being made? Who is benefiting? Who is not benefiting? What does a land justice paradigm look like, as opposed to cheap land for individuals? So my work around food has evolved and gone in many different ways.

Can you talk a little more about food justice beyond urban agriculture?

Food justice beyond urban agriculture really focuses on the system. Who controls and defines what a local healthy food system looks like? Who identifies and controls the resources? How do you maximize equity for all in terms of access to food, including defining what is food and what food comes into their community. Who distributes the food? It is looking more broadly at the system and issues around equity, access, and fairness, and appropriateness. There is a relationship between food to things like land and development, and this notion of food sovereignty. You really began

*Hantz refers to Hantz Woodlands, a for-profit tree farm on Detroit's East Side, described in detail in chapter 5 (see p. 228).

to challenge the big corporate models of food control with controlling your food and controlling your land.

What are the different points of that system? Are there particular places that are important for making interventions?

Well, definitely retail. We lost our only Black grocery store owner in the state of Michigan. He left about a year and half ago. So who determines the ability to procure food in the community? We are completely locked out of that. That gets to finance. When it comes to financing and people of color, particularly African Americans, we need access to the financing that's needed to run a business and be successful. That's one place where there is a need to intervene. Again, there is land. How do you get control of land, not from the standpoint of an individual lens, but community decisions around land, so that land becomes a resource for the community whether it's to grow food or build houses. Land policy decision-making is another point of intervention. Schools are another because there are huge contracts, huge vendor opportunities for big food companies to make lots of money distributing what is essentially junk. They are tough to fight with one-on-one, but you can organize parents to have more say over what is fed to their children on a day-to-day basis. And then, at the household level, people have the food system that exists within their household: where people shop, how they prepare their food, what they buy; what is their purchasing power? It's important to help people reframe the way they see themselves as a legitimate consumer in making choices about their food and helping to create a local food—and health—system that works for them and their family.

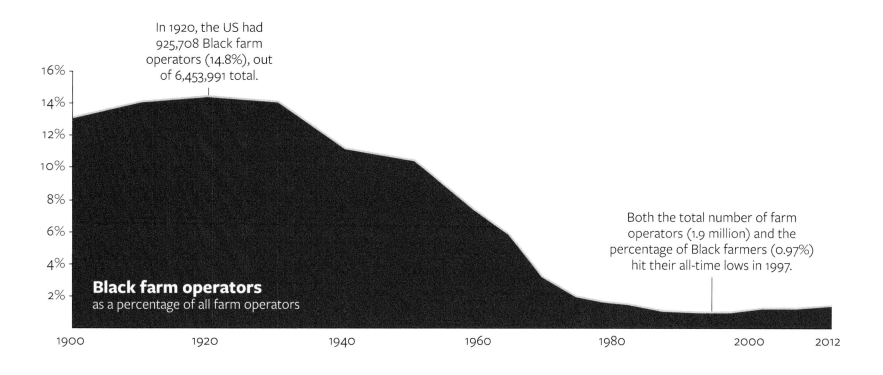

In 1920, the US had 925,708 Black farm operators (14.8%), out of 6,453,991 total.

Black farm operators
as a percentage of all farm operators

Both the total number of farm operators (1.9 million) and the percentage of Black farmers (0.97%) hit their all-time lows in 1997.

16%
14%
12%
10%
8%
6%
4%
2%

1900   1920   1940   1960   1980   2000   2012

Black Farm Operators in the United States, 1900–2012

The United States Census of Agriculture defines a farm operator as "a person who operates a farm, either doing the work or making day-to-day decisions about such things as planting, harvesting, feeding, and marketing." That category includes both farm owners as well as those who rent farms or land and, historically, sharecroppers. This chart shows the proportion of farm operators who were Black in the United States from 1900 to 2012. Wayne County, where Detroit is located, had 475 farm operators in 2012, of whom 20 (4.2 percent) were Black or African American. That number is above the state and national average, but is ten times lower than what would be expected if farm operators reflected Wayne County's overall demographics. Historical data on non-Black farm operators of color is not available for the same time range of this graph, but in 2012 out of 3,180,074 total farm operators the United Sates had 99,734 who were identified as Hispanic or Latina/o (3.1 percent), 71,947 identified as American Indian or Alaska Native (2.3 percent), and 24,067 identified as Asian (0.8 percent), in addition to 46,582 identified as Black or African American (1.5 percent).

In the time that you have been working on food-related issues, Detroit has undergone dramatic political and economic changes from emergency management and the bankruptcy to the foreclosure crisis and gentrification. How does all of that relate to food justice work?

I think those structural changes in the city have produced lots of contention around land. Five years ago, it was, "It's yours for the taking, too much land." Now it feels like there is land, but it has become less accessible. Land is being sectioned off and controlled in ways that don't benefit the average citizen. Does that have an impact on food justice work for small neighborhood growers? Yes. Whereas five years ago they might have been able to pay $100 and get a lot, or a couple of lots, that's becoming more difficult to do. I think the foreclosure crisis and the lack of homeownership limits the choices that people have. A lot of the backyard growers are gone. They have lost their homes in foreclosures or unjust evictions. A friend of mine once told me that they used to do an informal neighborhood CSA—community-supported agriculture—but that disappeared because people lost their homes.

And then there is the restaurant as the marker for economic success in the city. It's just crazy to me. Instead of opening up neighborhood-based markets, we are opening up restaurants that are expensive, that sell good food, but people in the neighborhood can't afford it. They become destination places. Again, there is a further divide between who has access to fresh affordable food and how restaurants and food are being used a class marker and a marker for gentrification.

Can you talk about the People's Platform and why food is one of the pillars?

The People's Platform is a reaction to the structural changes that you referenced earlier—the emergency manager, the consent decree, the collapse of local services, the takeover of our democracy. The People's Platform was formed as a strategy to build more neighborhood-based power, where folks could come together and organize and fight for the restoration of local services and their voice in local government, and build some kind of community power, and hold folks accountable. Food became one of our pillars because we focus on what we think of as a community safety net: food, land (which includes housing), transportation, jobs, and effective government representation.

4

SUSPENDING DEMOCRACY IS VIOLENCE

Revanchism is making a comeback in the United States. The term refers to a style of right-wing revenge politics, often with populist roots, that seeks to reverse the political gains made by people of color, women, LGBTQ people, immigrants, and other historically marginalized groups. The concept was popularized by the geographer Neil Smith, who defined it as "a revengeful and reactionary viciousness against various populations accused of stealing the city from the white upper classes."[1] This chapter historicizes and reveals the revanchist logic underlying the transformation of Detroit in the 2010s. We trace the process by which democracy was rolled back in Detroit and other majority Black cities in Michigan, leading to policies that have directly harmed residents. This systematic undoing of democracy in Michigan amounts to a form of violence directed primarily at people of color, immigrants, and the poor.

The following pages offer a chronology and analysis of the political battles that have taken place over development and governance in the city. Our chronology begins in 2011, with the Michigan legislature passing Public Act 4 (PA 4), which granted emergency managers, appointed at the behest of the governor, sweeping new powers to override local elected officials. It follows local struggles over the imposition of emergency management in Detroit and the city's eventual bankruptcy in 2013. It also examines how emergency managers were imposed on other majority Black cities in Michigan, particularly Flint, which suffered an unparalleled water crisis when the city's emergency manager switched its municipal water supply from the Detroit River to the Flint River in 2014, leading to extensive pipe corrosion that exposed residents to dangerous levels of lead. The chapter ends by considering how the revanchist aspects of urban governance in Michigan appear to anticipate President Donald Trump's agenda and the implications thereof for social movement organizing.

Revanchism describes both a style and substance of politics. It is often—but not always—marked by violent language stressing punitive reprisals and revenge, as well as fearmongering about being under siege by cultural others. At the same time, revanchism's rhetorical violence is accompanied with an increase in actual violence by state actors through militarized law enforcement and the redrawing of boundaries of who can be included and who should be excluded from the body politic. There is also a cross-pollination between revanchist regimes and more generalized "neoliberal" or pro-business policies such as privatization, austerity, union busting, gentrification, advancing entrepreneurial freedoms, and urban austerity. The racial violence that results from such policies is seen in the ways the poor, particularly poor people of color, increasingly face limited access to life essentials such as health care, shelter, proper food, and water.[2] The water shutoffs in Detroit and the water crisis in Flint illuminate this violence and its blatant devaluation and disregard for Black life.[3]

Revanchism has a long history in the United States, perhaps starting with the civic apartheid adopted by Southern states as a backlash to gains won by African Americans during the Reconstruction era.[4] It also has a locally specific history in Michigan politics since the 1960s, particularly regarding white responses to the election of former civil rights activist Coleman Young as Detroit's first Black mayor in 1973. Young served for twenty years. His trademark style was marked not only by an aggressive stance against racism but also a proud lack of deference toward whites in general. The revanchist response to Young and what he personified—a pro-union, African American political power base in Detroit—had a formative effect on Michigan's conservative establishment. It generated such strong counter-personas as L. Brooks Patterson, the six-term county executive of Oakland County, who in a 2014 interview with a staff writer at the *New Yorker* described Detroit as an "Indian reservation" that should be fenced off.[5]

During the late 2000s when a Tea Party–inspired wave swept Republicans into the majority in the Michigan legislature and led to the election of Republican Rick Snyder as governor in 2011, the stage was set for an urban versus suburban/rural political confrontation. In fact, the early establishment of emergency management provisions was already taking place under the administration of Democratic governor Jennifer Granholm (2003–10).

Since 1987 when the Mackinac Center for Public Policy was founded in Michigan, the state has been at the forefront of the national expansion of free-market and libertarian think tanks that draft market-centric policies for elected officials.[6] The political and economic restructuring of Detroit in the early 2010s must therefore be understood against the background of a long-running political battle between, on the one hand, an urban coalition of African Americans, white liberals, immigrant organizations, and some unions, and, on the other, rural- and suburban-based white conservative interests, which have typically been allied with corporate and financial interests (often tied to municipal creditors). Such interests have focused on limiting the expansion of the public domain, privatizing public property, and promoting policies that aim to discipline and punish underserved Michiganders by cutting social support.

While governor Rick Snyder (2011–18) often favored a more conciliatory tone than many revanchist politicians, this stylistic moderation was betrayed by the way state policy toward Detroit and other majority Black cities was formulated as well as by its despicable outcomes, most notably the Flint water crisis. Indeed, in several important respects, the revanchist aspects of urban restructuring in Michigan foreshadow Trump's approach toward policy making at a national level. Both approaches represent a turn away from governance centered around the creation of a broad, if still-contested policy consensus and instead approach policy as a Nietzschean imposition of will advanced by one interest alone, often using procedural rules to avoid compromise with competing stakeholders. Moreover, both approaches are marked by attempts to erode not just the opposing party—which is often the case in politics—but the very public institutions historically associated with democratic debate (as an example, the State of Michigan's temporary dissolution of the City of Detroit as an autonomous political entity under emergency management rule).

Such actions have deep symbolic meaning because Detroit and other Michigan cities, since the mid-twentieth century, have been culturally significant—and politically institutionalized—

This map highlights locations mentioned in the interviews and essays in this chapter.

BAGLEY

Marygrove College
(site of Detroit People's Platform Convention)

NORTH
END

JEFFERSON
CHALMERS

Wayne State University
Sugar Law Center (Cass Commons)

Detroit Institute of Art

OLYMPIA
DEVELOPMENT
AREA

BELLE ISLE

Detroit Water and Sewerage Department
Detroit City Hall

SOUTHWEST
DETROIT

Joe
Louis
Arena

Detroit-Windsor Tunnel

Cesar Chavez Middle School
(site of Hector Orozco's arrest)

bulwarks of African American and union power. The resonance of such "revenge" politics in Michigan helps explain why the historically Democratic-leaning state was a key—if tenuous— electoral college win for Trump in 2016, and it also explains why one of Trump's most visible and controversial cabinet members—Secretary of Education Betsy DeVos—is a long-established member of Michigan's conservative elite. If the struggles highlighted in this section appear local, these battles anticipate and epitomize contemporary struggles over American democracy at a national scale.

The following timeline historicizes the revanchist logic underlying the restructuring of Detroit. Just as important, it examines concrete actions toward rethinking governance and dispersing power that have emerged in response to emergency management and bankruptcy. The timeline is interspersed with interviews with Detroit activists who offer their own analyses about the state takeover and political moment. The analyses of Detroiters featured in this chapter place a historically minded understanding of the significance of Black home rule in Detroit in relationship to the anti-Blackness that drove the state takeover and underscore the importance of land and territory to self-determination. At the same time, they situate the questions of Black citizenship raised by the takeover in relationship to national and local struggles for immigrant rights and the rights of undocumented people.

This chapter highlights the extent to which residents have not only mobilized to protest policies but have also taken governance into their own hands—from the campaign to establish Community Benefits Agreements (CBAs), to Detroiters Resisting

MARCH JUNE DECEMBER

2011

PA 4 takes effect in Michigan, granting sweeping new powers to emergency managers, including the authority to negotiate, modify, or terminate labor contracts; impose pay cuts; hire and fire employees; sell, lease, or privatize assets; change budgets without legislative approval; and initiate municipal bankruptcy proceedings.

At this time, the cities of Benton Harbor, Ecorse, and Pontiac, as well as Detroit Public Schools, are already subject to various forms of outside management from Lansing, which are continued by PA 4. The passage of PA 4 is an important early political accomplishment for Republican governor Rick Snyder, who assumed office only three months before.

PA 4 is subject to a legal challenge led by the Detroit-based Sugar Law Center for Economic and Social Justice.

City of Flint enters emergency management.

Cities in Michigan Affected by Emergency Management	Population (2010)	Percentage Black (2010 US Census)
Allen Park	28,210	2.5
Benton Harbor (City and School District)	**10,038**	**91.4**
Detroit (City and School District)	**713,777**	**84.3**
Ecorse	9,512	48.6
Flint	**102,434**	**59.5**
Hamtramck	22,423	20.4
Highland Park (City and School District)	**11,176**	**95.6**
Inkster (Consent Agreement)	**25,369**	**76.2**
Lincoln Park	38.144	7.1
Muskegon Heights (School District only)	**10,856**	**81.3**
Pontiac (City and School District)	**59,515**	**55.3**

Cities in Michigan Affected by Emergency Management	Population (2010)	Percentage Black (2010 US Census)
River Rouge (Consent Agreement)	7,903	53.8
Royal Oak (Consent Agreement)	57,236	5.0
Wayne County (Consent Agreement)	1,820,573	39.0
Total	1,097,193	69.6

2012

In an attempt to avoid state-imposed emergency management, the Detroit City Council signs a Consent Agreement with the State of Michigan. The agreement creates a nine-member Financial Advisory Board, along with a corporate-style chief financial officer, and program management director. The board is charged with monitoring and evaluating the city's debts, expenditures, and payments in a wide variety of areas from the makeup of individual city departments, to contracts, to deals with creditors and bondholders. It is made up of a hodgepodge of partisan appointees consisting of three individuals appointed by the governor, one by the state treasurer, two by the mayor, and two by the city council. A ninth member (likely to be a tiebreaker in any deadlock) is appointed jointly by the governor and mayor and subject to confirmation by the city council.

While the mayor and city council still hold formal powers under the agreement, state oversight is widely viewed as an unwelcome concession that the City of Detroit is forced to make.

Emergency Management's development of an alternative to the bankruptcy restructuring plan, to the founding of the Detroit People's Platform in 2013. The harm done by revanchist policies is often great, but, as we show, it can also have the unintended consequence of galvanizing resistance. Grassroots politics in Detroit speak to the creativity of that resistance.

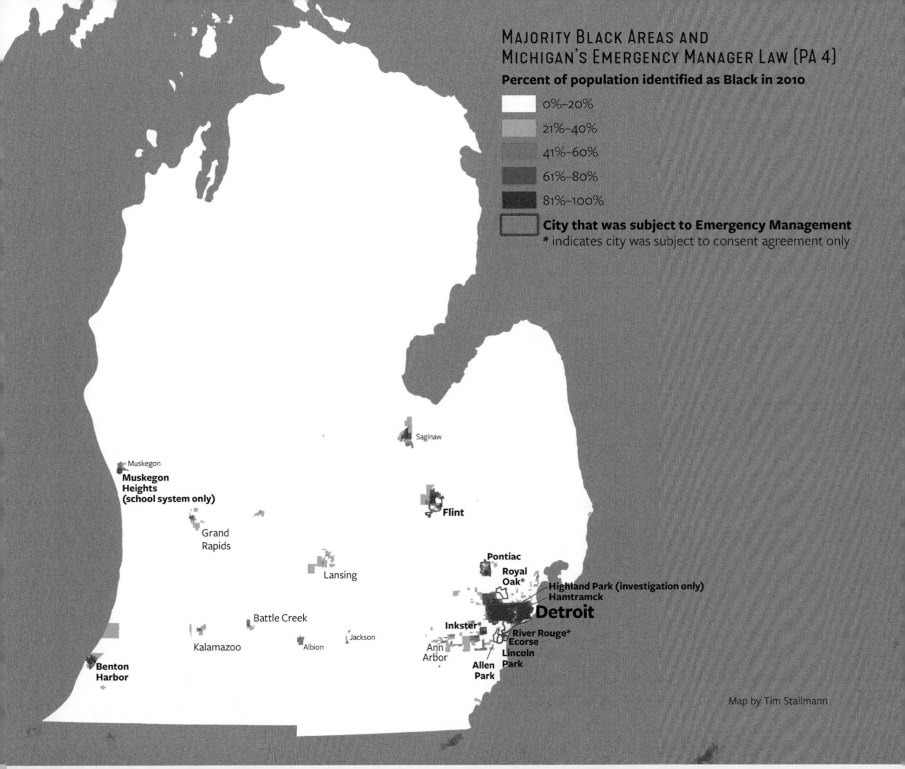

MAJORITY BLACK AREAS AND MICHIGAN'S EMERGENCY MANAGER LAW (PA 4)

Percent of population identified as Black in 2010

- 0%–20%
- 21%–40%
- 41%–60%
- 61%–80%
- 81%–100%

City that was subject to Emergency Management
* indicates city was subject to consent agreement only

Saginaw

Muskegon

Muskegon Heights (school system only)

Grand Rapids

Flint

Lansing

Pontiac

Royal Oak*

Highland Park (investigation only)
Hamtramck

Detroit

Battle Creek

Inkster*

River Rouge*
Ecorse

Kalamazoo

Albion

Jackson

Ann Arbor

Lincoln Park

Allen Park

Benton Harbor

Map by Tim Stallmann

"PUT YOUR BODY AND PUT YOUR VOICE INTO DEBATES"

TOVA PERLMUTTER

During the legal struggle over the constitutionality of PA 4, Tova Perlmutter was the executive director of the Sugar Law Center for Economic and Social Justice, the principal legal team opposing PA 4 in Michigan courts. Perlmutter sees legal cases as one of many tools to bring about social change. In this excerpt from an interview conducted by Danielle Atkinson, a collaborating partner in the Uniting Detroiters project, Perlmutter argues that legal cases such as Sugar Law's can also have a broader impact on public awareness and opinion that goes beyond what occurs in courts. Indeed, PA 4 would eventually be defeated by a grassroots petition rather than a court case.

Perlmutter is also adamant that place-based, district-oriented representation is critical to the democratic process. She is a proponent of district-based representation, which Detroit was in the process of adopting at the time of the interview. In 2012, the Detroit City Council approved boundaries

for seven new districts; one resident from each would be elected to serve on the city council. In addition, the council would have two at-large members. The Detroit City Council had not been governed by council districts since 1918. In addition to district representation, Perlmutter argues that physical presence—or place-based activism—is important for the success of creating more just forms of governance. For her, people must put their bodies, their voices, and their minds in service of a greater good.

The Sugar Law Center is the lead counsel and really brought together the team of lawyers who has worked for the last year—well, more than a year—on challenging the constitutionality of PA 4, the Michigan emergency manager law. We not only put together a lawsuit and challenged it in court and have done everything needed on the litigation side, but we've also put together a communication strategy to try to shift public opinion on this matter.

Now, again, we're small. We don't pay for television ads, but we have been consistently covered in the press, and we believe that it's making a difference in terms of the understanding of Michigan residents, Michigan citizens, and Michigan voters of why this law is such an affront to democracy in every way. The plaintiffs in our suit, they're twenty-eight wonderful people from around the state of Michigan, all of whom are using the lawsuit as a way to increase their impact on their neighbors and help them educate people about why this law is an affront and why people need to stand up and speak out.

We have a strong belief that the law is a tool, but not the only tool and frankly not the most important tool in making social change. We've only ever taken on legal battles where there are community actors, community activists, and leaders who have determined that this is a priority, that this is an issue, and that they need some level of technical legal assistance to make the change they want to see happen.

I never thought that particular patches of land mattered that much, because in my life I was very mobile. But I've come to understand that it matters tremendously where people are, and if you aren't in that space it can be very hard for you to understand it. So, I think that council by districts is important. Now part of the problem is that right now we have a situation where those elected to govern Detroit have essentially been pushed to the side through the imposition of an emergency manager. The say that citizens have in decision making is outrageously reduced.

One of the things that I keep relearning is how meaningful it is to put your body and put your voice into debates. Physically going to a place has impact, and speaking out changes the way people talk. Ultimately, the way people talk is the way they behave. I think we need to unite around, most fundamentally, having a voice and determining the fate of our own community and demanding that the state and the country help us recover, because it's not charity; it's payback.

2012

JUNE

President Barack Obama initiates the Deferred Action for Childhood Arrivals (DACA) program on June 15. DACA protects undocumented immigrants who entered the United States as minors from deportation. Activists continue to call for comprehensive immigration reform.

OCTOBER

Residents of Southwest Detroit protest after Immigration Control and Enforcement (ICE) agents detain Hector Orozco, an undocumented immigrant who was bringing his son to school. Southwest Detroit is home to the majority of Detroit's Latinx population.

NOVEMBER

Michigan voters repeal PA 4 in a ballot referendum. The defeat of PA 4 was a protracted struggle. A statewide campaign organized by Michigan Forward and Stand Up for Democracy collected 226,339 signed petitions in favor of putting the repeal on the ballot. Yet it was almost defeated by a court challenge led by a conservative group, Citizens for Fiscal Responsibility, which sought to throw out the petition on the basis of its font size.

DECEMBER

The Michigan state legislature passes Public Act 436 (PA 436), a repackaged version of PA 4. PA 436 is a direct rebuttal to the will of the voters as expressed in the referendum a month before. Given that the political mobilization behind the repeal was based in Michigan's predominately African American cities, and the power centers of the Michigan Republicans lay in mostly white suburbs and rural areas, the passing of PA 436 over the repeal showed the degree to which state politics magnified the political power of rural and suburban whites and diminished the voice of urban voters and African Americans in particular. In hindsight, the lightning pace at which the often-languid Michigan legislature developed and passed PA 436 serves as a vivid display of the urgency that Snyder and his allies attached to the emergency management policy, the full implications of which would become clear in the coming months.

Districts whose representatives voted **no** on PA 436
(46 districts, representing 4.1 million Michiganders, and nearly all of the impacted areas)

10%   20%   30%   40%   50%   60%   70%   80%   90%

Percentage of
people of color
in district (2010).

Gold highlight indicates
districts whose residents were
impacted by PA 436.

Districts whose representatives
voted **yes** on PA 436
(63 districts, representing 5.7 million
Michiganders but only one
impacted town, Benton Harbor)

Race and the PA 436 Vote in Michigan

This chart captures the sharp divide over the emergency management law (PA 436) in Michigan and highlights the extent to which representatives of the urban areas impacted by the law opposed it. In every case except for Benton Harbor, state House representatives from districts that were impacted by PA 436 opposed the bill. The districts supporting the bill, which ultimately passed, were also notably less racially diverse than those opposing it, as the figure shows.

ON CITYWIDE SUFFRAGE

"People who are undocumented are human. They have rights"

GABRIELA ALCAZAR

Gabriela Alcazar was born in Chicago and moved to the Detroit metropolitan area when she was ten years old. By her early twenties, Alcazar had become an important immigrant rights activist in Detroit's Latinx community. In this interview, conducted in 2012, she connects the issue of voters' rights and rights of undocumented people in Detroit to the importance of civil disobedience and activism. Her description of the impact of US Border Patrol and Immigration Customs Enforcement (ICE) raids in Southwest Detroit reveals the degree of surveillance and pressure Latinx people endured under the Obama Administration. With the election of Trump, the subsequent backlash against immigrants, and the rise of high-profile ICE roundups, her fundamental message about the political struggles and needs of undocumented people remains as prescient as ever. She also documents the political pressure already resonating from the State of Michigan against Detroit's immigrant community at this time. Ayana Rubio conducted this interview as part of the Uniting Detroiters project.

About two years ago, one of the schools in our neighborhood was raided by Immigration and Customs Enforcement (ICE). It wasn't actually the school, but all of the streets surrounding the school where parents park to drop off their kids at school. Parents were stopped when they were coming back to their cars. They were getting picked up by Immigration and Customs Enforcement. There were at least six ICE cars.

They were definitely targeting the school. They claimed that they initially had orders for certain people, which they may very well have, but by Homeland Security's own policy, they are not supposed to enforce at churches, schools, or hospitals. By their own provisions and their own standards, they were not supposed to be there that morning. A bunch of families were picked up and detained.

A lot of times people don't have lawyers. They don't speak the language. They're not provided with counsel in whatever language they speak. Sometimes they're signing papers—voluntary deportation. Voluntary deportation means you can't come back for ten years. Sometimes they'll let you get out of detention if you claim to be the only person who can take care of your kids, but a lot of times they won't.

There are so many kids that get caught up in the foster care system. Their parents get deported. They don't get picked up from school. The school calls whomever and if the kids don't have a lot of family or someone else to call, the kids may not know their parents got deported. Basically, the child ends up getting caught up in the system. By the time that you may be able to make it back here, you were charged with abandonment of your child. Your child got given to someone else. Maybe somebody adopted him and you have no rights to that child anymore.

People who are undocumented are human. They have rights. I think on a broader level we can identify and build relationships with other people and groups in the city, who are really disenfranchised on so many different levels. I think, as workers, capitalism affects us all equally and, if anything, pits us against each other. But the reality is that the reason why undocumented labor is wanted in this country is because they're able to strip not only undocumented workers of their rights, but make other people's power in their workplace significantly worse, so that would be a way to definitely build alliances with other people in the city.

Citywide suffrage is the idea that if you live in the city you should be allowed to vote for elected political representatives in the city. A lot of the people who live in the city who are undocumented are not allowed to have a driver's license, let alone voting rights. People always talk about how Southwest Detroit has one of the lowest voter turnout rates, a lot of its citizens are not civically engaged enough to go vote, they don't think it's important, whatever. A lot of the people who live here don't have citizenship. The idea of citywide suffrage is that people, for example, would be able to vote for elected school board members. People who are undocumented who have children, their children go to school. They should be allowed to have a say in the democratic process of their schools, which in and of itself is not a reality

for anyone in Detroit [in 2012] because we're under emergency financial management.

DACA—the "kind of dream" act—happened because of active civil disobedience across the country about undocumented youth. Even after DACA was signed, people were not very trusting, like, "Oh, okay, we occupy offices and then all of a sudden this happens. What's going to happen if Obama doesn't win and Republicans take over? What if we send in all these applications, which say, 'Hey we're here, we're undocumented,' and then all of a sudden, like Etch A Sketch, it never happened, now we're all deported." It was undocumented young people who put their livelihoods at risk; they participated in civil disobedience even though they had no legal status to be in this country. They are the ones that took that risk and got President Obama to instate the DACA program, which would protect, not just themselves, but thousands of other young people like themselves.

The secretary of state here in Michigan [Ruth Johnson] declared that she was not going to allow DACA immigrant youth to be able to get licenses because they were not legally present, which technically they're not. But that's the whole point of DACA, that you are allowed to do that. Obviously, people fought. They took it to court, and the secretary of state reversed her decision. We're one of the states where there was a fight to be able to even make that a reality. At that point, there had already been a lot more mobilizing going around the country, so it was just like, "Okay, if they retaliate in some way, we're just going to fight back." Folks from Grand Rapids, folks from Lansing, from Saginaw, came out. It was crazy how many young people came out, who beforehand, obviously, didn't feel like they could be a part of stuff. You could definitely see, especially in the state of Michigan, how many people came out to fight for what was already theirs.

2013

Detroiters from the North End Woodward Community Coalition (NEWCC) meet with Councilor Brenda Jones to develop a Community Benefits Agreement (CBA) ordinance. The measure would require real estate developers to reach a legally enforceable agreement with residents before breaking ground on projects that receive large public subsidies. NEWCC, along with the Detroit People's Platform, begins a multiyear campaign of research, negotiation trainings for residents, and meetings with business leaders and city officials to develop the ordinance.

After declaring Detroit to be in a "state of emergency," Governor Rick Snyder appoints Kevyn Orr, a bankruptcy lawyer, as emergency manager of Detroit. Orr's tenure becomes effective March 25, three days before PA 436 goes into power. As emergency manager, Orr governs by fiat: all policies now come in the form of "orders," which the emergency manager can "modify, rescind, or replace at any time." Order No. 1 "restores" Mayor David Bing's and council members' "salary, wages, compensation and other benefits . . . as if they had never been eliminated," making an unmistakable statement as to whom Detroit's elected officials now work for.[7] In seeking to preserve an appearance of normalcy, Order No. 1 actually betrays the degree to which a significant change of power and curtailment of democracy is occurring in Detroit.

Residents immediately begin a series of protests in downtown Detroit, including blocking traffic on freeways and roads. They decry emergency management as unconstitutional and argue that Orr has a conflict of interest because he was previously a partner in a law firm that represented some of Detroit's creditors. A number of groups mobilize in opposition to emergency management, including one calling itself D-REM, or Detroiters Resisting Emergency Management (an allusion to Detroit's historically significant DRUM—the Dodge Revolutionary Union Movement).

A group of lawyers, including representatives from Sugar Law Center for Economic and Social Justice, the Detroit and Michigan National Lawyers Guild, and the New York–based Center for Constitutional Rights file a federal civil rights and voting rights cause of action, contending that PA 436 effectively establishes a new form of government within the State of Michigan that violates due process rights, including collective bargaining, freedom of speech, the right to petition local government, and equal protection under the law.[8] A judge eventually allows the case to move forward around the equal protection clause.

In Flint, Michigan, Governor Rick Snyder, Treasurer Andy Dillon, and Chief of Staff Dennis Muchmore begin discussions with the Flint City Council about pursuing alternatives to Flint's use of the Detroit water supply. The Flint City Council votes in favor of adopting a new water system.

Detroit Water and Sewerage Department officials publicly criticize Flint's plan to withdraw from Detroit's water supply, saying it will lead to higher rates for all customers. Despite an offer by Detroit to lower its rates, Flint's emergency manager, Ed Kurtz, signals the city's departure from the Detroit system by signing a contract with the Karegnondi Water Authority.

THE DETROIT PEOPLE'S PLATFORM

On June 1, 2013, more than two hundred Detroit residents, activists, and community leaders gathered at Marygrove College for the first Detroit People's Platform Convention. Linda Campbell (of Building Movement Project Detroit and coeditor of this *Atlas*) took a lead role in organizing and facilitating the convention.

The People's Platform Convention followed from the work of the Uniting Detroiters project in which Building Movement Project Detroit spent a year meeting with residents and collecting oral histories in communities across the city. Based on those conversations, five platform issues arose: food justice, land justice, transportation justice, good government, and good jobs. At the convention, residents and activists from across the city ratified the five platform issues as essential to a sustainable, high quality of life for all Detroiters.

Since 2013, the Detroit People's Platform has evolved into a broad network of Detroit-based social justice organizations, activists, and residents committed to bringing about just transformation in economics and social dynamics through popular education, celebration, and organizing. They support and organize with district caucus leaders who live and work in each of the Detroit council districts. The People's Platform network comprises more than three thousand Detroiters and about twenty active caucus leaders. They use data, analysis, advocacy, media, and organizing to protect and increase participation in the democratic process and to demand that state and local decision makers consider racial equity and economic justice in their planning, funding, and policy-making decisions. They also publish the *People's Platform News*, an excerpt of which is shown on the opposite page.

WE SUPPORT THE COMMUNITY BENEFIT AGREEMENT ORDINANCE!

DETROIT People's PLATFORM NEWS

BUILDING MOVEMENT DETROIT

detroitpeoplesplatform.org

*"Economic growth and equity and inclusion can go hand in hand. With Detroit's proposed **Community Benefits Agreement Ordinance**, the city has the chance to join the ranks of other municipalities that have embraced this effective tool to improve the well-being of both its businesses and residents."*

Professor john powell and Julie Nelson
Haas Institute for a Fair and Inclusive Society

Vol. 05 January 2015

 @DetroitPeoples   DETPeoplesPlatform

INSIDE:

SPECIAL REPORT:
DEMOCRACY BY AUTHORITY
BIG CHANGES IN CITY GOVERNMENT
pg. 2
ANATOMY OF AN AUTHORITY
pg. 3
2014 REPORT-OUT
pg. 4
"A People's Story of Detroit"
DOCUMENTARY DEBUT!
pg. 4

SPECIAL REPORT
THE RESTRUCTURING OF DETROIT: DEMOCRACY BY AUTHORITY

REGIONAL TRANSIT AUTHORITY
GREAT LAKES WATER AUTHORITY
PUBLIC LIGHTING AUTHORITY OF DETROIT
DETROIT LAND BANK AUTHORITY

As Detroit comes out of Bankruptcy Court and Emergency Management many aspects of city government have been shifted to quasi-public/private authorities that have little or no accountability to citizens.
▶ pg. 2

UPDATE: CBA Ordinance

HB5977, an Anti-CBA bill died on the House floor at the close of the session last year. The bill was introduced by State Representative Earl Poleski (R) from Jackson County. A Detroit Regional Chamber representative traveled to Lansing to speak in support of the bill.

Equitable Detroit Coalition partners and Detroit People's Platform members engaged strategically to help stop the bill. By visiting Lansing to speak to lawmakers,

working closely with elected officials in both Detroit and Lansing, reaching out to statewide allies, contacting legislators and the governor's office we were able to stop the egregious assault on home rule that if was. **We continue to monitor Lansing.**

READ THE MOST RECENT DRAFT OF THE CBA ORDINANCE at equitabledetroit.org

CBA
STOP THE GIVE AWAYS!

WNUC 96.7 FM will be broadcasting and streaming from Detroit's North End. WNUC is licensed to the North End Woodward Community Coalition (NEWCC), a community-based coalition composed of organizations, businesses and residents concerned with the decisions that impact the transportation needs of thousands of residents in the North End of Detroit. NEWCC is a long standing partner of the Detroit People's Platform. More: northendwoodward.org

We Believe...

Detroit is not a blank slate. It is not abandoned. It is full of vibrant, resilient people who look out for each other and are committed to protecting the public assets and resources we share as a community. As neighbors and residents, both new and long-term, we know what our districts need and we are working together to ensure that all of us—regardless of race, class, or neighborhood—have a meaningful say in re-building our city.

We know that the city is changing quickly in the face of both challenges and opportunities. But if Detroiters don't get to the bottom of the real problems facing our communities, we will allow a false narrative of scarcity, right-sizing and incompetence to shift attention away from the powerful few who want to remake Detroit for their personal benefit. Supporters of the **People's Platform** promote a narrative of "People over profit and politics" and hold up quality of life as a basic right to all.

Detroiters have to raise the issues that matter to our neighborhoods and districts. And that is exactly what the People's Platform is doing. We are taking full advantage of the opportunity created by the new city charter to usher in a new kind of politics, returning us to the ideals of participatory democracy where Detroiters decide what's best for Detroit.

RIGHT TO THE CITY!

The Detroit People's Platform has joined as a member organization of the Right To The City Alliance. As part of our Land Justice work we will join RTTC on the national HOMES FOR ALL Campaign. RTTC is an alliance of racial, economic and environmental justice organizations that seeks to create regional and national impacts in the fields of housing, human rights, urban land, community development, civic engagement, criminal justice, environmental justice, and more. righttothecity.org

The *People's Platform News*, which has been published since 2013, documents the work of a coalition of activists engaged in urban development, transportation, housing, and food justice issues.

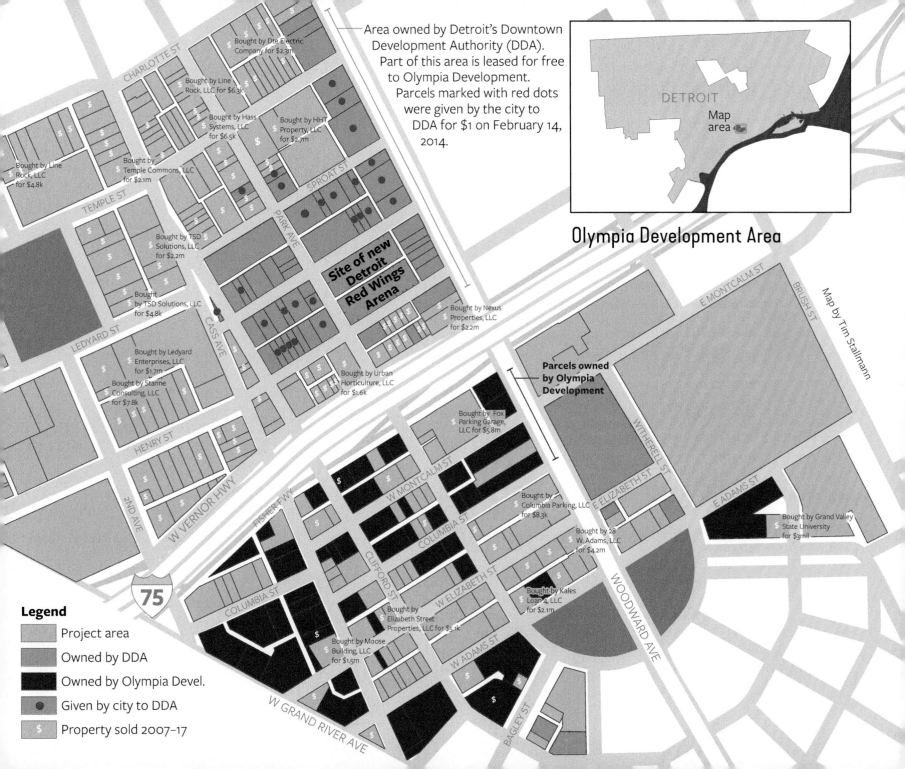

Area owned by Detroit's Downtown Development Authority (DDA). Part of this area is leased for free to Olympia Development. Parcels marked with red dots were given by the city to DDA for $1 on February 14, 2014.

DETROIT

Map area

Olympia Development Area

Bought by Dte Electric Company for $2.3m

Bought by Line Rock, LLC for $6.3k

Bought by Hass Systems, LLC for $6.5k

Bought by HHT Property, LLC for $2.7m

Bought by Line Rock, LLC for $4.8k

Bought by Temple Commons, LLC for $2.1m

Bought by TSD Solutions, LLC for $2.2m

Bought by TSD Solutions, LLC for $4.8k

Site of new Detroit Red Wings Arena

Bought by Nexus Properties, LLC for $2.2m

Bought by Ledyard Enterprises, LLC for $1.7m

Bought by Stanne Consulting, LLC for $7.8k

Bought by Urban Horticulture, LLC for $1.6k

Parcels owned by Olympia Development

Bought by Fox Parking Garage, LLC for $5.8m

Bought by Grand Valley State University for $3mil

Bought by Columbia Parking, LLC for $8.3k

Bought by 28 W. Adams, LLC for $4.2m

Bought by Kales Loan 4, LLC for $2.1m

Bought by Elizabeth Street Properties, LLC for $5.1k

Bought by Moose Building, LLC for $1.5m

Map by Tim Stallmann

CHARLOTTE ST
TEMPLE ST
LEDYARD ST
HENRY ST
PARK AVE
SPROAT ST
CASS AVE
2ND AVE
W VERNOR HWY
FISHER FWY
COLUMBIA ST
CLIFFORD ST
W MONTCALM ST
COLUMBIA ST
W ELIZABETH ST
W ADAMS ST
BAGLEY ST
W GRAND RIVER AVE
E MONTCALM ST
BRUSH ST
WITHERELL ST
E ELIZABETH ST
E ADAMS ST
WOODWARD AVE

75

Legend

- Project area
- Owned by DDA
- Owned by Olympia Devel.
- ● Given by city to DDA
- $ Property sold 2007–17

2013

Detroit becomes the largest municipality to enter bankruptcy, at a total value of $18.5 billion, according to Kevyn Orr. The Chapter 9 filing has the effect of suspending legal challenges to PA 436 until the city exits bankruptcy. Judge Steven Rhodes is assigned the case.

In the midst of the bankruptcy, the City of Detroit begins work on a deal to transfer a forty-five-block swath of land north of Downtown to Olympia Development (operated by the prominent Ilitch family) for the development of a new Red Wings hockey stadium to be called Little Caesars Arena (the hockey team and the national pizza chain are both owned by the Ilitch family). The city plans to sell the land for *one dollar*. Sixty percent of the stadium is to be paid for by public money. Specifically, the city will sell bonds (incur debt) for the project, which in turn will be paid off by local school and property taxes. In a break from the past thirty years, the Red Wings are no longer required to share revenue with the city, despite taxpayer investment in the arena. This misuse of public funds in the midst of a bankruptcy galvanizes support for a CBA ordinance in Detroit.

THE FIGHT FOR A COMMUNITY BENEFITS AGREEMENT ORDINANCE IN DETROIT

Adapted from *People's Platform News*, vol. 5, January 2014.

In 2013, a coalition of residents, including Rise Together Detroit, the Equitable Detroit Coalition, and the Detroit People's Platform, came together to organize for a Community Benefits Agreement (CBA) ordinance in Detroit. CBAs provide a tool to help ensure that public investments have a true community benefit rather than benefiting only powerful development interests. They are binding contracts negotiated between the host community and the project developer for the purposes of fulfilling specific and meaningful benefits to the community in exchange for the community's public support and approval of the project.

The fight for the CBA ordinance in Detroit illuminates the degree of indignation present in the city over ongoing displacement and the allotment of state funds to benefit large developers. At its core the CBA ordinance was envisioned as a way to give residents the power to negotiate with developers, or in short, let residents have a say in what kind of city Detroit is to become. According to the proposed ordinance, CBAs would be required for projects that used $300,000 or more of public funds, or had budgets in excess of $15 million. It called for standard minimum key provisions to be included in every CBA while allowing for such agreements to be tailored to the needs of particular communities and particular development projects. The proposed ordinance included provisions for:

- Priority employment for residents from the host community.
- Environmentally sound and sustainable construction practices throughout all phases of the project, as well as mitigation practices to reduce pollution, noise, and other environmental hazards and concerns.
- Proper advanced notice to homeowners, tenants, and businesses being displaced by development, as well as just compensation and/or relocation expenses where lawful and appropriate.
- A comprehensive safety and security plan, secondary policing, emergency call boxes, and enhanced lighting.
- A system where reporting and monitoring are required to ensure compliance with the CBA.

From the beginning, the proposed CBA ordinance was a fight. After community organizer Rev. Joan Ross and Councilor Brenda Jones introduced it into the Detroit City Council in 2013, it languished in the Planning and Development Committee with no effort to revive it. Then, in 2014, State Representative Earl Poleski (R) from rural Jackson County crafted an anti-CBA bill, HB5977, with the goal of killing the CBA ordinance while it was under study in Detroit. A Detroit Regional Chamber representative traveled to Lansing to speak in support of HB5977. However, the Equitable Detroit Coalition partners and Detroit People's Platform members managed to effectively defeat the bill by working closely with elected officials in both Detroit and Lansing and reaching out to statewide allies.

Soon after, knowing opposition to preempt a CBA ordinance would return in force, CBA supporters began a petition drive to put a CBA ordinance to a citywide voter referendum. When Councilor Scott Benson realized they had secured enough signatures to ensure its placement on the November 2016 ballot, he promptly crafted a competing watered-down CBA ordinance known as the "Benson Compromise." On the ballot, the original CBA ordinance was listed as "Proposal A" and Benson's Compromise as "Proposal B." In an unusual step for a voter referendum, voters would have to vote "yes" on one option *and* "no" on the other in order for their votes on either CBA ordinance to be considered valid. CBA supporters scrambled to create a voter education campaign to educate Detroiters about the difference between the two options. Meanwhile, Benson's well-financed opposition group, which included people like the mayor,

Gregg Newsom

demonstrates the power of community organization to ruffle the city (and the state's) power structure even when they fall just short of their started goals. Even though Prop A was defeated, the CBA movement continues to hold trainings to educate residents on tools they can use to negotiate with developers and influence the way the city is reinvented. They also continue to fight for a citywide CBA ordinance.

Even after the narrow defeat of Proposal A in 2016, the Detroit People's Platform has been holding training sessions for residents to learn how to access information on development in their neighborhoods, become informed of the nature of public subsidies, and build skills to negotiate with developers.

Michigan Republican lawmakers, and union workers (who lined up in solidarity with the construction workers' unions, which often side with real estate developers), organized a counter-advertising campaign in favor of Prop B.

In the end, the limited resourced community-run operation in support of Prop A came very close to winning. Proposal A secured 98,151 votes to Benson's 114,041. The amount of resources marshaled by the Benson group to hold off Prop A

NO ALTERNATIVE?

People's Plan for Restructuring

On February 24, 2014, at the Historic King Solomon Baptist Church, a coalition of community-based groups, including the National Action Network, Moratorium Now, and Detroiters Resisting Emergency Management (D-REM), released a "People's Plan for Restructuring toward a Sustainable Detroit" in response to Kevyn Orr's plan. The plan points the finger squarely at Wall Street investment banks and explicitly links the racist, predatory lending practices associated with the foreclosure crisis with the City of Detroit's indebtedness to these institutions. In a related vein, the plan focuses on the importance of land as the ultimate source of the city's wealth and seeks to ensure that Detroiters have the same access to landownership as banks and developers. Below we reprint the introduction to the People's Plan, which lays out their overall vision, as well as part 1, which delineates "people's alternatives" for financial security, community life, the restoration of democracy and self-government in Detroit, and youth development and welfare.[9]

INTRODUCTION

The restructuring and rebirth of Detroit will not be delivered by a state-imposed emergency manager, nor through Chapter 9 bankruptcy proceedings, foundation contributions, closed door deals, or other devious and misleading corporate schemes. Detroit's rebirth will be the result of the people's unrelenting demand for democratic self-governance, equal access to and management of the natural and economic resources of the city.

Currently, emergency managers in several Michigan cities have dictatorial powers to advance the interests of banks and private corporations over the public good. They have failed to bring about financial security. Rather, in one city and school district after another, they have dismantled the public school systems, sold off public resources, and eliminated essential civil services, while enriching a small group of cronies and contractors.

To secure the ends of our city charter and to ensure a vibrant, sustainable city reflecting the needs and the will of the people, we propose a set of alternatives. The people's alternatives are rooted in the certainty of our capacity to envision and create a city culture in which human rights are protected and citizens enjoy a higher quality of life.

FINANCIAL SECURITY

- The Michigan Legislature should immediately require automatic payroll deduction and mandatory withholding for all people working in the 22 cities where there is local income tax. Detroit currently loses between $40–50 million in revenue per year for lack of this elementary measure.
- The State must restore fully funded state revenue sharing to all cities, and act as an equitable and progressive

partner in a process of urban development that serves neighborhoods and human rights, rather than destroying democracy and civic capital. Since 1998, due to actions of the State Legislature, Detroit has lost $220 million in revenue sharing, as well as several hundred million dollars in foregone income taxes. Direct state cuts in revenue sharing accounted for nearly one third of the city's revenue losses between 2011 and 2013.

- Detroit requires an efficient, effective federal grants management officer to fully implement and take advantage of existing federal programs. Currently, Detroit returns millions of dollars to federal agencies that it has been unable to spend. Nearly $60 million dollars of accumulated or unspent federal dollars are included in the recent pledge by the Obama Administration to provide $300 million in targeted programs.

- Detroit must establish means to collect all outstanding property taxes. In 2011, Wayne County had to write off $170 million in uncollected taxes on Detroit properties. The highest priority should be to ensure that no current homeowners are foreclosed on or evicted in the effort to collect taxes. Over 50,000 homes are in tax foreclosure this year alone, according to the Wayne County Treasurer. In Detroit, when these homes are vacated because of foreclosure, they are stripped and add to the dynamic of neighborhood blight and diminished property tax revenue.

- All businesses operating within the City of Detroit, or providing services to it, must commit to hiring local people and using local goods and services. By 2020, 70 percent of goods and services should be secured from local sources.

- Bank of America, UBS, and any other Wall Street firms must immediately terminate the toxic interest rate swaps without penalties or further payment. Bank of America and UBS should repay Detroit the estimated $250 million they collected based on the illegal interest rate swaps, as well as the hundreds of millions of dollars paid by the Detroit Water and Sewerage Department in swaps termination fees.

- Detroit's predatory Wall Street-related financial expenses should be fully discharged in bankruptcy, without further cost to the city. The city budget reflects financial expenses that increased by $38.5 million between 2008 and 2013, accounting for 60 percent of the total increase in legacy costs. Legacy expenses are the cash flow consequences of "legacy liabilities." Unlike those underlying liabilities themselves, they are pertinent to remedying the cash flow crises. They include principal and interest payments on bonds issued by the city, payments in respect of derivatives, and future liabilities to pay pension and healthcare benefits for employees. In contrast with the city's operating expenses, which have been slashed by layoffs, cutbacks, and labor concessions/impositions, these amounts "owed" to the banks have increased rather than declined since the onset of the Great Recession. This is unsustainable, and only benefits Wall Street predators, not Detroiters.

- All vacant properties owned by banks should be assessed a $1,000 annual fee for maintenance and civil services.

- Budget concerns must emphasize eliminating the budget shortfall of $198 million rather than continually targeting the questionable figures relied on by the emergency manager to justify his actions based on inflated long-term debt.
- Pensioners should be held harmless, with no cuts at all, and medical benefits restored, as an act of faith toward citizens who deserve all of what little they are receiving, in equity.

COMMUNITY LIFE

The Detroit City Council must enact legislation to:

- Support urban homesteading, enabling people to legally move into abandoned structures and restore them. Utilization of the existing nuisance abatement act and other legislation, adequately staffed and properly implemented, would benefit Detroiters far more than throwing massive resources into blight removal, without adequate plans for community-based economic redevelopment.
- Restore the dollar-a-lot program, enabling home owners to purchase adjacent vacant lots.
- Establish rent control to protect current residents.
- Establish land trusts as equitable development alternatives for citizens, at comparable scale to public land given at bargain prices to ultra-high net worth individuals such as John Hantz, Dan Gilbert, and Mike Ilitch for private exploitation.

AUGUST   NOVEMBER   JANUARY   FEBRUARY

2013

As part of Detroit's bankruptcy proceedings, the city's premier cultural institutions become targets for economic restructuring. Emergency Manager Kevyn Orr announces a contract with Christie's Auction House to appraise the collection of the Detroit Institute of Art in preparation for a possible sale. The city also begins to look to other options for revenue, including leasing Belle Isle, the city's flagship public park, which is free and open to the public, to the State of Michigan, which would charge residents an entrance fee.

Mike Duggan is elected mayor of Detroit, receiving 55 percent of the vote. He is the first white mayor to be elected in the city since Coleman Young came to power in 1974. Duggan is the former president and CEO of the Detroit Medical Center (DMC). At the DMC, he was noted for his privatization efforts and oversaw a controversial merger in 2010 between the nonprofit DMC and Vanguard Health Systems, a for-profit corporation.

2014

Philanthropists and influential foundations work together to keep the Detroit Institute of Art from being forced to sell parts of its collection. Meanwhile, Detroit retirees take health care cuts for 2014 as part of the bankruptcy process.

Orr releases the first readjustment plan to take the city out of bankruptcy. Orr offers 26 percent cuts to general municipal workers and 14 percent cuts to firefighters and police. But in a classic "offer you can't refuse," Orr says that if the unions resist, then the cuts will be 34 percent to the general workforce and 10 percent to first responders, respectively. Cuts to retiree health care benefits would be 70–80 percent all around. Bondholders would be expected to take 80 percent cuts on their debts.

Under severe pressure from the emergency manager to cut costs, the Detroit Water and Sewerage Department announces it will shut off water to Detroiters who fall behind on water bills but not to any of its other two million customers, nor to local Detroit business customers. Shutoffs proceed at a rate of about one thousand households a week. A wide variety of groups respond to the water shutoffs by joining together in public protests and marches. Some residents engage in civil disobedience to halt the shutoffs (see the essay by James W. Perkinson, "Why I Choose to Block Water Shutoff Trucks," on p. 249).

Flint switches its water supply from the Detroit River to the Flint River. The Michigan Department of Environmental Quality announces that the water is "safe to drink." Water officials opt not to add corrosion-control treatment to the water, which prevents lead from leaching into tap water, even though providing the additive to an urban water supply is a standard safety practice around the United States. The omission is not brought to public attention by the media, nor is it publicly discussed or debated by Flint's elected officials or its emergency manager.

Detroit City Council president Brenda Jones introduces the proposed CBA ordinance to the city council. The ordinance is moved to the Planning and Development Committee, where it is held up for nearly two years.

Detroit settles with bondholders Ambac Assurance and Blackrock for 34 cents on each dollar of total debt and Governor Snyder signs what is referred to as the "Grand Bargain" legislation aimed at saving the collections of the Detroit Institute of Arts and the pensions of its workers.

Meanwhile, after making threats of deep pension cuts to public workers, Emergency Manager Orr negotiates separate settlements with retired police and firefighters, who accept a deal that leaves their pension fund untouched but drops cost of living increases to from 2.25 percent to 1 percent.[10] General municipal employees, on the other hand, have to stomach 4.5 percent cuts and an elimination of cost of living increases.

- Introduce place-based education for children, adults, and elders coming together to revitalize Detroit.
- Adopt community-based and transit-oriented economic development policies, projects, and criteria for public investment and improved quality of life in Detroit's neighborhoods.
- Increase quality and quantity of bus service.
- Stop and roll back privatization of essential government services that enrich corporate cronies without improving performance.

RESTORATION OF DEMOCRACY AND SELF-GOVERNMENT IN DETROIT

- Fulfill the obligation of the City Charter to establish Citizens Advisory Councils.
- Return the Detroit Public Schools and the seized EAA schools to the control of the democratically elected School Board.
- Guarantee transparent, public, and open decision-making.
- Require enforceable Community Benefit Agreements that are accountable to those most affected by all corporate economic development.
- Establish participatory budgeting within communities, neighborhoods, and block clubs.
- Establish a public interest bank to secure finances.
- Subject tax-free philanthropic special interests to democratic control and community accountability.

DEVELOPMENT AND WELFARE OF OUR YOUTH

- Restore art, music, and the full range of creative and recreational activities within our public schools.
- Open 24-hour recreation centers for youth.
- Enact legislation providing free access to Belle Isle for Detroit residents under 25.
- Ensure per pupil funding for Detroit students equal to that of the wealthier school districts.

2014

In an effort to motivate creditors to deal with the city, Emergency Manager Kevyn Orr's office uses rights to develop city property as a bargaining chip. Syncora, one of the city's principal creditors, reaches a deal in which the company receives a twenty-year-lease extension on the Detroit-Windsor Tunnel and options to purchase riverfront property for an equivalent of 26 cents on a dollar. Judge Steven Rhodes begins the planned confirmation trial to exit Detroit from bankruptcy. These efforts seem to confirm the fears expressed by activists and contributors in the preceding pages that emergency management and bankruptcy would be used to transfer publicly held land to private interests.

Shortly before leaving office, Orr signs EM 36, which abolishes citizens' district councils (CDCs) on the basis that they "no longer align with the City's urban renewal strategy, and, in some cases present a barrier to the effective and efficient development of blighted areas of the city."[11] CDCs were created in the mid-1940s in the state of Michigan to give residents a say in urban renewal projects from land-use decisions to the financing of proposed projects. They functioned as district-level planning advisory boards with elected members.

While Detroit had defunded CDCs over the years, a number of them remained active at the time Orr signed EM 26. The change is remarked on by several media outlets but then is quickly passed over in the news cycle. The removal of Detroit's CDCs represents a clear example of an emergency manager using unilateral power to overturn a democratic institution. It should be noted that the CDCs have no bearing whatsoever on the bankruptcy process that Orr was entrusted to oversee. In dissolving the CDCs, Orr removes an institution that had provided Detroiters with a voice of opposition against private developers (see the interview with Joselyn Fitzpatrick Harris, "We believe in people power," on p. 181).

Orr cedes control of the city to newly elected mayor Mike Duggan and the city council, but he remains in charge of the bankruptcy process.

"WE BELIEVE IN PEOPLE POWER"

JOSELYN FITZPATRICK HARRIS

Joselyn Fitzpatrick Harris is a lifelong resident of Detroit whose perspective is exemplary of many Detroiters in that she connects state-led efforts to impose political control over the city with other forms of dispossession. Harris's critique is rooted in her personal experience of having been raised in the once-vibrant African American neighborhood of Black Bottom, which was subsequently razed in the 1950s to make way for Lafayette Park.

Harris sees emergency management as part of a long pattern of race- and class-based contestation. For her, locally elected officials are losing power because they are an important political counterweight against the State of Michigan as well as the city's large land-holding institutions such as the Detroit Medical Center and Wayne State University. In addition to locally elected officials, Harris values citizens' district councils (CDCs) as an important tool for residents to shape development in their communities. She describes CDCs as functioning like the "city council in a local capacity." At the time of this interview in 2012, Harris was a member of the Jefferson-Chalmers CDC. In September 2014, after this interview with Linda Campbell took place, but in fulfillment of Harris's suspicions, Kevyn Orr's final emergency management order was to use his unchecked power to abolish Detroit's CDCs—even though the CDCs had no clear relationship to the bankruptcy proceedings, which were the focus of his task at the time.

As an individual, I'm opposed to the Consent Decree, and I'm opposed to an emergency manager. I've voiced my opinion and my frustration with that. But more importantly, the folks that we have elected to office, such as our mayor and our city council, are responsible for following the mandate of the jobs and the positions they've been put in. Of course, I understand that there's a hidden hand because Detroit is on very valuable property. We're situated in a very strategic location by a major waterway, and I know that there's more to it than our elected officials not being competent because many of them are. I know that strategically there is an element that wants to take the city back because they believe they own it.

And so what they do is that they make it appear that all of our elected officials are incompetent criminals, and they don't deserve to have their place in office. Therefore, because they're inept and incompetent, others have the right now to come in and take over. I disagree with that because I can see that hidden hand, it's just a matter of—we're in a capitalist society, this is very valuable land, we have a very valuable infrastructure, simple as that. If I want to play chess, I'm going to move you off the board. And to move you off the board, there are some things I have to do.

It's not only a breaking-down of the homes; it's also a breaking-down of the community. I saw that, of course, when I lived in Black Bottom. I saw how they strategically took everything apart and then built it back the way they wanted it to be.

I can't speak for everyone when we talk about who holds the power. We would say it's the people because we reside here and we pay taxes. But we also look at the corporations that have lots of power in the City of Detroit, especially in the downtown area, especially in what they're calling the Midtown area now. We're looking at the Detroit Medical Centers, the Wayne States, the Ilitches. We're looking at all these stakeholders as holding a little and a lot of power in our city. But we believe in people power and we believe in being organized and so we believe that we have power as well.

Our CDC—citizens' district council—it's composed of an elected body of residents who have a demonstrated interest in this community. There was an act passed that created citizens' district councils all around the city. It was a response to urban renewal.[12] This area was designated as an urban renewal area. As a result, a citizens' district council was established. The mission statement of our CDC is to support development and remove blight. We're the ones who are really connected to our city council.

We function like the city council in a local capacity, because whenever there is a developer that's seeking to do any kind of development in this community, that entity has to solicit the support of the CDC. When the developer goes before the city council, [the council will] ask them: "Have you communicated with the CDC? What is their stance on your development?" So we're a local entity that helps to represent the citizens. We represent the residents in this community so everything that comes to this community in the way of development has input from local residents and business owners.

UNITED NATIONS DEEMS WATER SHUTOFFS A HUMAN RIGHTS VIOLATION

n October 2014, a United Nations team visited Detroit to conduct an investigation of the water shutoffs. As a result, they issued a scathing report and deemed the shutoffs to be a human rights violation. The special rapporteur gave the following press statement:

Detroit is undergoing large-scale water disconnections . . . Without water, people cannot live a life with dignity—they have no water for drinking, cooking, bathing, flushing toilets, and keeping their clothes and houses clean. Despite the fact that water is essential for survival, the city has no data on how many people have been and are living without tap water, let alone information on age, disabilities, chronic illness, race or income level of the affected population. Denial of access to sufficient quantity of water threatens the rights to adequate housing, life, health, adequate food, integrity of the family. It exacerbates inequalities, stigmatizes people and renders the most vulnerable even more helpless. Lack of access to water and hygiene is also a real threat to public health as certain diseases could widely spread. In addition, thousands of households are living in fear that their water may be shut off at any time without due notice, that they may have to leave their homes and that children may be taken by child protection services as houses without water are deemed uninhabitable for children. In many cases, unpaid water bills are being attached to property taxes increasing the risk of foreclosure. . . .

We were deeply disturbed to observe the indignity people have faced and continue to live with in one of the wealthiest countries in the world and in a city that was a symbol of America's prosperity. We were also distressed to learn from the low-income African American residents of the impossible choices they are being compelled to make—to either pay their rent or their medical bill, or to pay their water bill.

It was touching to witness mothers' courage to strive to keep their children at home, and the support people were providing to each other to live in these unbearable circumstances. And it was heartbreaking to hear of the stigmatization associated with the shut-offs—in particular the public humiliation of having a blue mark imprinted on the sidewalk in front of homes when their water was shut off due to unpaid bills.

In line with the mandates entrusted to us by the Human Rights Council, we would like to underline that the

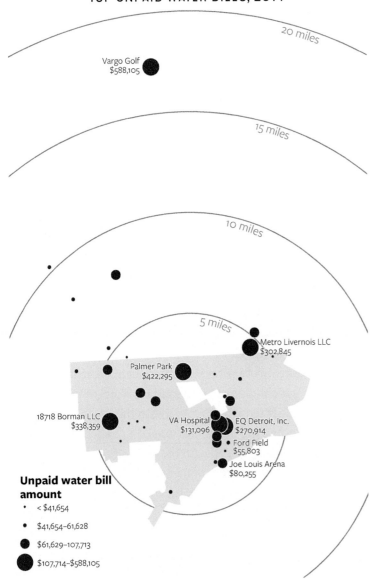

DETROIT WATER DEPARTMENT
TOP UNPAID WATER BILLS, 2014

20 miles

15 miles

10 miles

5 miles

Vargo Golf
$588,105

Metro Livernois LLC
$302,845

Palmer Park
$422,295

18718 Borman LLC
$338,359

VA Hospital
$131,096

EQ Detroit, Inc.
$270,914

Ford Field
$55,803

Joe Louis Arena
$80,255

Unpaid water bill amount

- · < $41,654
- • $41,654–61,628
- ● $61,629–107,713
- ⬤ $107,714–$588,105

In contrast to the underserved and African American residents most impacted by water shutoff policies, this map highlights that businesses across the Detroit metropolitan area collectively owe millions of dollars in unpaid water bills. In 2014, eleven thousand commercial and industrial accounts had a total of $37.5 million in past-due water or sewer bills, at an average of $3,127 owed per account, compared with $92.5 million in past-due residential bills across 143,467 accounts. Residential accounts, while accounting for a larger total amount of debt, had much lower average unpaid bills. The top unpaid account is a golf course in an affluent area of Oakland County. Others included the Ilitch-owned Joe Louis Arena, Ford Field, the State of Michigan, and a hospital. Yet many of these businesses did not face water shutoffs.

Map by Tim Stallmann, inspired by a concept from Alex B. Hill's *DETROITography* blog

2014

The final major creditor, bondholder Financial Guaranty Insurance Co., settles with the city for 13 cents on the dollar with rights to purchase and develop the Joe Louis Arena site into a hotel. The bankruptcy is now becoming a structure by which large amounts of public land can be transferred into private hands.

At least twenty-seven thousand households have now had their water turned off in Detroit. A United Nations (UN) team visits Detroit to conduct an investigation of the water shutoffs.

In Flint, General Motors announces it will stop using Flint water in its facilities because of corrosion noticed on production-line vehicles. There is little media attention given to GM's announcement despite the ongoing water issue in Detroit. Indeed, even after GM's concerns over the corrosive qualities of the water and a series of boil-water advisories earlier in the year linked to *E. coli*, the City of Flint maintains that its water is safe to drink. The episode will be a missed opportunity to correct problems with the Flint water supply, which will not be made public for another year.

Judge Steven Rhodes approves Detroit's exit from bankruptcy.

United States is bound by international human rights law and principles, including the right to life as well as the right to non-discrimination with respect to housing, water and sanitation, and the highest attainable standard of health. These obligations apply to all levels of Government—federal, state, and municipal. Moreover, they also extend to the various functions of State, including the judiciary. The rights to non-discrimination and equality are core principles of international human rights law. Governments are obliged not only to refrain from discrimination in the design and implementation of laws and policies, but must strive to ensure substantive equality for all. The United States has ratified the United Nations Convention on Elimination of Racial Discrimination which explicitly prohibits and calls for the elimination of racial discrimination in relation to several human rights directly affected by water disconnections, including the right to housing and the right to public health.[13]

"YOU HAVE TAXATION WITHOUT REPRESENTATION"

LEE GADDIES

Lee Gaddies, a longtime Detroiter and resident of the Bagley District, analyzes how current modes of governance facilitate an urban redevelopment strategy that is drawing a stark divide between Downtown and surrounding neighborhoods. Like Joselyn Fitzpatrick Harris, Gaddies considers governance in Detroit against the history of racist barriers to property ownership facing African Americans. For Gaddies, control of land, especially for African Americans, is linked to self-determination and citizenship. His analysis of injustice foregrounds the distinction between the rights and obligations of Detroit homeowners and Downtown real estate developers. Gaddies sees racism at work in the allegations of incompetence that are leveled at Detroit's municipal government, and he argues the resulting weakening of local governance has increased inequalities between Downtown and the neighborhoods. Linda Campbell conducted this interview as part of the Uniting Detroiters project in 2012.

Historically Blacks were isolated in certain neighborhoods. After the rebellion in '67, the housing market opened up to Black people. My parents' income—they were both factory workers—allowed them to move into Bagley because it's what they could afford. Two salaried autoworkers could afford quite a bit back then. That migration pattern echoes through my family who came off of land in the South and retired back to that land, never letting it go.

That has become indoctrinated in our family: that you are not owners of the land; you are stewards of that land for the next generation. I see that as part of my legacy and my heritage, that I am not an owner of, to dispense with as I see fit, but I am a caretaker for the next generation. . . . I think that we have allowed somebody else's vision of success to cloud that historic mandate to us. Once upon a time it was "Don't sell the farm," right? "Never sell the farm. Never ever ever ever!" I mean that was like a mantra because if you have land, you can grow food, you can feed yourself. If you have access to water you can irrigate your crops and feed yourself.

I think that we need to have that understanding of the relationship between being an independent people, ownership of land, and those rights that are associated with that here in America. When you have ownership of property and you're not going anywhere, and you're paying taxes and those tax dollars are being spent back in the community as a collective, I think that's an important asset.

What does governance mean? What does owning this house mean? What does your connection to this community mean? How are the taxes that are collected spent? That discussion is not happening in the mainstream media. Who is allowed to generate income and profit from your tax dollars?

You're allowed to pay taxes to support a stadium, but you're not allowed to generate any income by selling a hot dog or a slice of pizza at that stadium. Only certain people are allowed to make that money. The money is collected from the 139 square miles of Detroit, but that money that is collected is only spent in two square miles of Detroit, from the river to the Fox [Theatre], the casinos to Ford Field. That's where the money is being spent. Billions of dollars are being poured into an entertainment district for the suburbanites. It's not being put into my area, the Avenue of Fashion, or the Livernois shopping strip. It's not being put there. It's being collected there and then being moved and spent somewhere else. This issue is the misappropriation of funds—how those finances are being appropriated from us through taxation and then being spent in the private enterprises.

Through the dominant culture, they're telling us that you are too stupid to run a city, that you are too dumb to run Detroit, so therefore we need to put somebody in place because you can't elect people correctly, even though other cities around the country are going into default. They're not talking about the real issue—bonds being issued by banks and then the debt service to that bank. That's not on the table for discussion.

You have taxation without representation. You're taking people's money. We have a republican form of government here where you elect officials to go and represent you—that's city council, that's state reps, senators.

I think when you take people's money, but they have no say in how that money is spent or where it's being spent at, that's taxation without representation. I think it's unconstitutional. I think that the way emergency management has been applied has been absolutely racist. It's only been applied in cities that have predominately Black populations. Again, the dominant culture is stating that "you Black people cannot run your business; somebody else has to come in and run it for you." If that isn't the ultimate nanny state, I don't know what is.

ELECTION REFLECTION

SHEA HOWELL

Shea Howell is a longtime Detroit activist who works through the Boggs Center to Nurture Community Leadership. She is also a professor of communication at Oakland University. In 1997, Shea Howell started writing a weekly column called "Thinking for Ourselves" for the Detroit-based weekly *Michigan Citizen*, an important venue for Black thought and progressive activism. During the state takeover, Howell's weekly columns were important touchstones for dissent in the city. She diligently documented each week of the emergency management and bankruptcy process, titling her columns "Week 1 (Week 2, Week 3, and so on) of the Occupation." When the *Michigan Citizen* folded in December 2014 after thirty-six years of publication, Howell continued to publish her column through the blog of the James and Grace Lee Boggs Center to Nurture Community Leadership. In this piece, originally published on November 12, 2016, on *The Boggs' Blog,* Howell reflects on the election of Donald Trump as president of the United States. She argues that to counter the state violence that will be amplified by the Trump Administration, we must draw on love, courage, and hope to "create a world worth preserving."

SEPTEMBER OCTOBER DECEMBER JANUARY

2015

The Flint water crisis explodes when Dr. Mona Hannah-Attisha of Hurley Medical Center publicly releases her study that finds dangerously high lead levels in the blood of Flint children. A spokesperson for the Michigan Department of Environmental Quality rejects her report, calling it "near hysteria."

After more data on lead in Flint's water come to light, the director of Michigan Department of Environmental Quality publicly states: "I believe now we made a mistake" regarding the decision not to treat Flint water with anti-corrosive agents.

Flint reconnects to the Detroit Water and Sewerage system, but water quality will take an unspecified amount of time to improve.

Flint mayor Karen Weaver declares a state of emergency in the city due to lead-contaminated water.

As Detroit's Planning and Development Committee comes under pressure to allow the city council to vote on the CBA ordinance, state lawmakers in Lansing propose a bill to ban CBA ordinances from cities throughout the state. After vigorous protest by Detroiters—including at a city council special session where Rev. Joan C. Ross of the North End Woodward Community Coalition argues, "Don't let Lansing tell us what to do in our own neighborhoods!"[14]—the bill dies in committee.

2016

The National Guard is activated to assist in the distribution of water in Flint. Governor Snyder asks the federal government for financial help.

Multiple coalitions of allied community groups, including the Equitable Detroit Coalition and Rise Together Detroit solidify around the effort to pass the CBA ordinance. Though the ordinance has survived a Republican-led effort to kill it in Lansing, it is now opposed by Mayor Mike Duggan.

With the Planning and Development Committee still preventing the ordinance from going to vote, the coalition begins an effort to collect signatures to put CBAs directly on the November 2016 ballot.

In the wake of the Flint water crisis, Democrats in the US Congress introduce a bill that would hinder the ability of state governments to impose external control over cities, as was done in Detroit and Flint.

The Rise Together Detroit Coalition delivers over fifty-four hundred signatures in support of a voter referendum on the CBA. Bill Hickey of the Brightmoor Community Coalition states: "The City Council has had two years to vote on this ordinance without taking action. Today shows that the people of Detroit are ready to reclaim our democracy and have our voices heard. Now we have to get to work to convince the voters to vote yes. We will do that by pointing out that Detroit only truly rises when we all rise together."[15]

Detroit city councilor Scott Benson responds immediately by drafting a competing version of the CBA for the voter referendum, which is nearly identical to the first, except that it does not legally bind developers. It becomes known as the Benson Compromise, or Proposal B in the referendum.

As the election season heats up, the *Detroit Metro Times* publishes a report detailing a secretive so-called dark money fund known as Detroit Jobs First, established by a former appointee of Mayor Mike Duggan. The fund is dedicated to defeating the original CBA ordinance first proposed by Brenda Jones (now known as Proposal A) and funds TV advertisements against Proposal A. Its board of directors includes prominent representation by construction unions with stakes in urban megaprojects, including the Laborers' International Union of North America Local 1191 and Michigan Regional Council of Carpenters and Millwrights.[16]

The victory of Donald Trump has sent chills through many of us. Shock, grief, and fear are giving way to a deepening resolve to resist the onslaught of violence that is sure to come.

What America will become in the next fifty years depends on what we do now, individually and collectively. There are no simple answers, no quick solutions, and no going home again. We have to find new ways forward. This will require deeper thinking and more thoughtful actions than ever before. The stark choice between revolution and counter-revolution is here.

This choice has been evolving for a long time. In 1955 the Montgomery bus boycott broke the right-wing grip on America that controlled the life of most people. Following the Civil War, after a brief flowering of African American freedom, the forces of counter-revolution reasserted themselves. In the South, white supremacists used a combination of violence and legislation to restore their power.

In the rest of the country, whites did the same thing, often rioting and attacking vulnerable communities. From Maine to Oklahoma mobs drove African Americans out of their homes, creating thousands of "sundown towns" for "Whites Only." Immigration was tightly controlled, queers were killed for sport, people with disabilities were hidden in institutions, indigenous rights were violated, sexual exploitation was commonplace, and working conditions for most were often deadly. As we endured the World Wars, intellectual life was degraded by a virulent anti-communism, given voice by Joseph McCarthy whose campaign destroyed art, culture, and compassion. As Martin Luther

King observed, America was "the greatest purveyor of violence," and much of that violence was directed at one another.

All of that was shattered by the power of the liberation movements launched by ordinary people in Montgomery. Over the next two decades, America became a more human place. We became more aware of one another and our responsibilities for the sustainability of life on our fragile earth.

But the forces of white supremacy did not go away. They continued to organize, to evolve, and to challenge every hard-fought gain of the last fifty years. There is a long line from Ronald Reagan to Donald Trump. And Reagan and Trump embody the sensibilities of those who came before like Bull Connor, David Duke, George Lincoln Rockwell, Fred Phelps, Rush Limbaugh, Phyllis Schlafly, George Wallace, Huey Long, Father Coughlin, Orville Hubbard, Robert Welch, Lester "Ax Handle" Maddox, Coors and Koch, Andrew Jackson, and Nathan Forrest. Trump is no foreign fascist. He is part of a shameful American history of violence in support of power. It is a history we can no longer evade if we are to create a more human future.

The majority of us rejected Trump. But we must now face the forces he has unleashed. We know that they will try to take our homes, seize land, shut off water, pollute our air, close schools, lock up our children, defile our sacred places, bomb our homes, terrorize us in bedrooms and jail cells, ridicule our beliefs, risk our futures, incite riots, infiltrate our organizations, round us up, limit democracy, beat us, and kill us. We know this because this is what they have done. This is what they are doing. This is what they will do with renewed force.

2016

NOVEMBER

Donald Trump wins the US presidential election, carrying the battleground state of Michigan by approximately eleven thousand votes (a 0.25 percent margin of victory).

In Detroit, the CBA ordinance race is so close that the results are not called until the day after the election. Ultimately, the Benson Compromise narrowly beats the originally proposed CBA.

DECEMBER

In the immediate wake of Trump's electoral victory a spike in hate crimes occurs throughout Michigan, with many victims being people of color, especially Arab Americans. The Michigan Department of Civil Rights announces it has received approximately thirty reports of hate crimes since the November election, when it normally receives eight cases in an entire year. On Wayne State University's campus, many Muslim students—especially hijab-wearing women—organize to walk together in groups at night as fears of intimidation and attack prove to be well founded.

Generations of Wealth Extracted from Detroit, 1960–2010

Lee Gaddies's discussion of taxation without representation is one lens on the broader set of mechanisms by which wealth is transferred out of the pockets of inner-city Detroiters and into the suburbs. Taking inspiration from the Detroit Geographical Expedition and Institute's iconic "Direction of Money Transfers in Metropolitan Detroit" map,* we analyze the numerous vectors through which Detroit, often framed as a site of absence and impoverishment, is at the same time a key site of resource extraction for the entire metropolitan region.

Picturing Detroit as a landscape of vacancy, abandonment, loss, and ruin ignores the way that wealth has been systematically extracted from neighborhoods in the city. Over the past fifty years, money taken from the city and invested in the suburbs—over $70 billion from lost wages alone—has created deep disparities. Detroit's future has to include healing these wounds.

*See William Bunge, *Fitzgerald: Geography of a Revolution* (Athens: University of Georgia Press, 2011), 134.

PRISON INDUSTRY

Detroiters are over **three times more likely** to be incarcerated compared with Michigan residents as a whole. The state spends hundreds of millions of dollars on prisons that could go towards developing urban neighborhoods.

FORECLOSURES

Between 2005 and 2010, Detroit homeowners lost **over forty percent** of their home's market value because of the 2008 foreclosure crisis. Many tax foreclosures were based on unconstitutionally high tax assessments.

WAGE THEFT

From 1960–2010, Black workers in Detroit were cheated out of **over $70 billion** because of racism in hiring and pay, while white workers were paid more than the median. That's money that Black neighborhoods lost and white suburbs gained.

CHRONIC ILLNESS

Detroit children are **twice as likely** to be hospitalized with asthma as children in Michigan as a whole, and children are more than **fifty percent** more likely to die of heart disease. But residents of Detroit are more than **three times less likely** to be working as doctors than residents of the suburbs.

Tim Stallmann

Already the KKK is marching. Young men are shouting obscenities, high school students have erected walls against immigrant children, and countless acts of aggression are recorded daily.

After more than fifty years of political struggle for better lives, one thing should be clear. Only love can overcome this violence. As Dr. King said, "When I speak of love I am not speaking of some sentimental and weak response. . . . Love is somehow the key that unlocks the door which leads to ultimate reality. . . . Every nation must now develop an overriding loyalty to mankind as a whole in order to preserve the best in individual societies. We must find new ways to speak and act of peace and justice. . . . If we do not act we shall surely be dragged down the long, dark, and shameful corridors of time reserved for those who possess power without compassion, might without morality, and strength without sight. . . . Let us rededicate ourselves to the long and bitter—but beautiful—struggle for a new world."

We need to take the time to grieve together, for it is this grief that grounds us in our best hopes for the future. And then we must turn to one another to ask what now affirms life, what moves us toward ways of living that expand compassion and creativity? We are not alone in facing these questions. We have a collective memory of those who came before, struggling against racism, materialism, and militarism and for a vision of loving communities to enrich our thinking. Together we will find ways to open our hearts and imaginations.

Today, we welcome the resistance to this violence. But much more is required. We must draw upon our deepest spirits of love, honesty, courage, and hope if we are to create a world worth preserving.

2017

Michigan Republicans defeat an effort by Michigan Democrats to obtain a subpoena related to the Flint water crisis against Governor Rick Snyder. Democrats had hoped to compel the release of "key documents that he has been withholding from the committee for the past year, including evidence relating to his destruction of emails."[17]

The State of Michigan stops providing credit for Flint residents to pay their water bills, but residents continue to receive mixed messages on whether or not the water is safe to drink.

Acting on orders from President Trump, ICE agents greatly accelerate the level of deportation and roundups against immigrant communities throughout Michigan. In some cases, such as that of green card holder Yousef Ajin of Ann Arbor, community support in the form of letter writing, protests, coverage in local media, and pressure from elected officials proves effective in helping detainees win a stay from deportation.

Betsy DeVos, an important member of Michigan's conservative political establishment, who spearheaded disinvestment in public schools in favor of charters, is confirmed by the Senate as secretary of education for President Donald Trump.

The water crisis in Flint is still unresolved. Many residents do not feel safe drinking their tap water despite assurances from the state that it is no longer dangerous. Nevertheless, the city sends warning letters to over eight thousand residents, stating that if they do not pay overdue water bills they could lose their homes to foreclosure. Meanwhile, the Detroit Water and Sewerage Department begins a new round of shutoffs with nearly eighteen thousand households at risk for having their water turned off.[18]

DETROIT

TAWANA "HONEYCOMB" PETTY

We were supposed to turn our backs on you,
count down to your imminent demise,
dangle you by the limbs of misdeeds,
they wanted us to rate you inferior.
Plagued by deteriorating neighborhoods,
and a convoluted history,
you were never supposed to bloom from your ashes.
A lot like you have been discarded like debris,
deemed useless to naysayers and convictors,
yet you keep rising, clinging to vitality.
You refuse to allow statistics
to dictate your destiny,
and the media, will channel your journey.
And though some shall remain loyal,
others will mock your tribulations.
You were Coleman A. *Younged* into maturity,
both your gift and your curse.
Imported from adversity,
you've seen better decades,
yet you thrived during the worst of them.
Your best days have yet to arrive,
and though some won't stick around,
to witness your climb,

or rejoice in your restoration,
your destination is inevitable.
You've been on the bottom,
much longer than most.
And the bridges you'll journey,
won't be easy to coast.
But you'll make it,
and bring warriors with you.
Armed with devotion,
they will defend your dignity,
and honor your namesake.
You are Detroit,
the road to progression,
the mirror image of endurance,
and you hold the key,
to taking back our democracy!

5

GENTRIFICATION IS ONLY PART OF IT

Understanding Race and Displacement in Detroit

In the middle of the twentieth century, Detroit was synonymous with the American dream of homeownership. Despite the barriers presented by institutional racism, thousands of African Americans were able to purchase homes in the city. Detroiters' homes became a proud symbol of Black middle-class membership. Fifty years later, the fate of Detroit's neighborhoods has changed drastically. The 2008–9 foreclosure crisis hit Detroit particularly hard and redirected much of the wealth accumulated by middle-class families, especially Black and Brown households, back into the hands of financial institutions. As part of this process, entire neighborhoods in Detroit were emptied of people who often found themselves struggling to find affordable housing in the suburbs or having to move to different regions of the United States. Renters now outnumber homeowners in the city.

Urban displacement is on the rise globally, and Detroit is part of this trend. Residents in the city are threatened by well-known kinds of displacement, including foreclosures, gentrification, and evictions. Other forms of displacement, such as urban renewal, have been occurring for a long time. For example, as the map produced by the Detroit Geographical Expeditions and Institute shows, thousands of residents of the Trumbull area around Wayne State University were forced to relocate in the 1960s. In more recent years, new forms of displacement—including urban greening, nonprofit-driven development, and land contracts—have become common features of Detroit's landscape. While less frequently named, they are no less insidious.

Urban studies scholars have most often studied displacement by focusing on the myriad ways that people are pushed out of place, for example, by urban renewal, highway construction, and gentrification. In many cities, gentrification has become one of the key frameworks used to explain postindustrial urban change. It refers to the process whereby developers and speculators combine intentional neglect of their properties, increased rents, and direct personal threats to compel poor and working-class residents to move out of their neighborhoods, while at the same time reinvesting money in the properties and amenities in those neighborhoods to make them more attractive to wealthier residents.

Gentrification can often be driven by a search for lower-priced land for real estate investment, and conservative economists often describe rising rents as a natural market reaction to limited supply of either land or housing. While the vast supply of vacant land in Detroit might seem to make that impossible, our map of housing insecurity (see p. 212) points out that there are actually more people living in precarious housing conditions in the Motor City than in New York or San Francisco. Contrary to theories of supply and demand, the mere availability of undeveloped land in Detroit does not lessen the economic pressures on renters and homeowners, especially in areas such as Midtown and Woodbridge, where the branding of newly renamed neighborhoods creates artificial scarcity in the real estate market and drives up prices. Our essay on the campaign to prevent the displacement of senior citizens from the Griswold apartments and the letter UAW employee Betty Scruse penned to her Alden Park Towers landlord highlight the ethical depravity of developers and the legal system that allows tenants—not to mention elderly tenants in their nineties—to be evicted with a thirty-day notice so that their apartment can be renovated and rented to wealthier newcomers.

However, gentrification is *not* the only cause of displacement in Detroit, and it might not even be the most significant.[1] In addition to the pressures on renters in and around Midtown and Downtown, the use of land contracts by developers, redevelopment driven by nonprofits, public-private partnerships, and urban greening are driving dramatic waves of displacement throughout the Motor City. Tax foreclosures, which occur when homeowners can no longer afford to pay property taxes on their home, also account for a significant amount of displacement in Detroit. Research by Bernadette Atuahene and Tim Hodge demonstrates that the majority of tax foreclosures carried out in Detroit between 2009 and 2015 were based on unconstitutional tax assessments (see chart on p. 233).[2]

This confluence of profit-making strategies challenges scholars and activists to consider displacement beyond gentrification. In Detroit, where mass foreclosures coincide with municipal efforts to rethink public works and service delivery, entire neighborhoods and their inhabitants are being disconnected from the public infrastructures and amenities that have defined the modern city (something we discuss in more depth in chapter 6). This combination of displacement and disconnection has come about as part of a new vision of urban development, epitomized by the Detroit Future City Strategic Framework, a citywide plan released by a public-private consortium in 2013. As we discuss in this chapter, this version of the city's future reimagines depopulated neighborhoods as green landscapes, which find new value as environmentally friendly forms of urban infrastructure rather than as places that might be called home by Detroiters. Examples of green landscapes that will replace disconnected and depopulated neighborhoods include "carbon forests" as well as urban farms on a massive scale, such as the new for-profit Hantz Woodlands shown in Gregg Newsom's haunting photographs (pp. 229-30).

If the green urbanism ideal is laudable for promoting environmentally sustainable urban forms, little attention has been paid to the people who live in "depopulated" neighborhoods that green urbanists want to set aside for ecological uses. Indeed, as our analysis of the Detroit Future City plan shows, *depopulated* is not the same as *empty*. Under the plan more than 137,000 people will be faced with public works and service delivery cutbacks. In many cases, entire neighborhoods (and their inhabitants) deemed not to carry the promise of future profits are slated for disconnection from the infrastructures and services needed to thrive. This displacement process is one of being left behind rather than pushed out.

Our contributors in this chapter highlight several different ways Detroiters are resisting displacement and working to confront what Aaron Handelsman describes at the end of the chapter as "spatial racism." They include efforts to get a moratorium on tax foreclosures, as described by Gloria House, the founding of community land trusts, discussed by Aaron Handelsman, and the establishment of a community-controlled radio station, addressed by Rev. Joan Ross. These projects demonstrate the importance of self-determination as a critical counterstrategy to the urban displacement and "government and corporate racist lawlessness" upon which the revitalization of Detroit is predicated, to quote contributor House. In these times, House argues, engaging in resistance is not enough. We must "build new forms of community," she writes, and work together to "envision and construct an altogether new society."

This map highlights locations mentioned in the interviews and essays in this chapter.

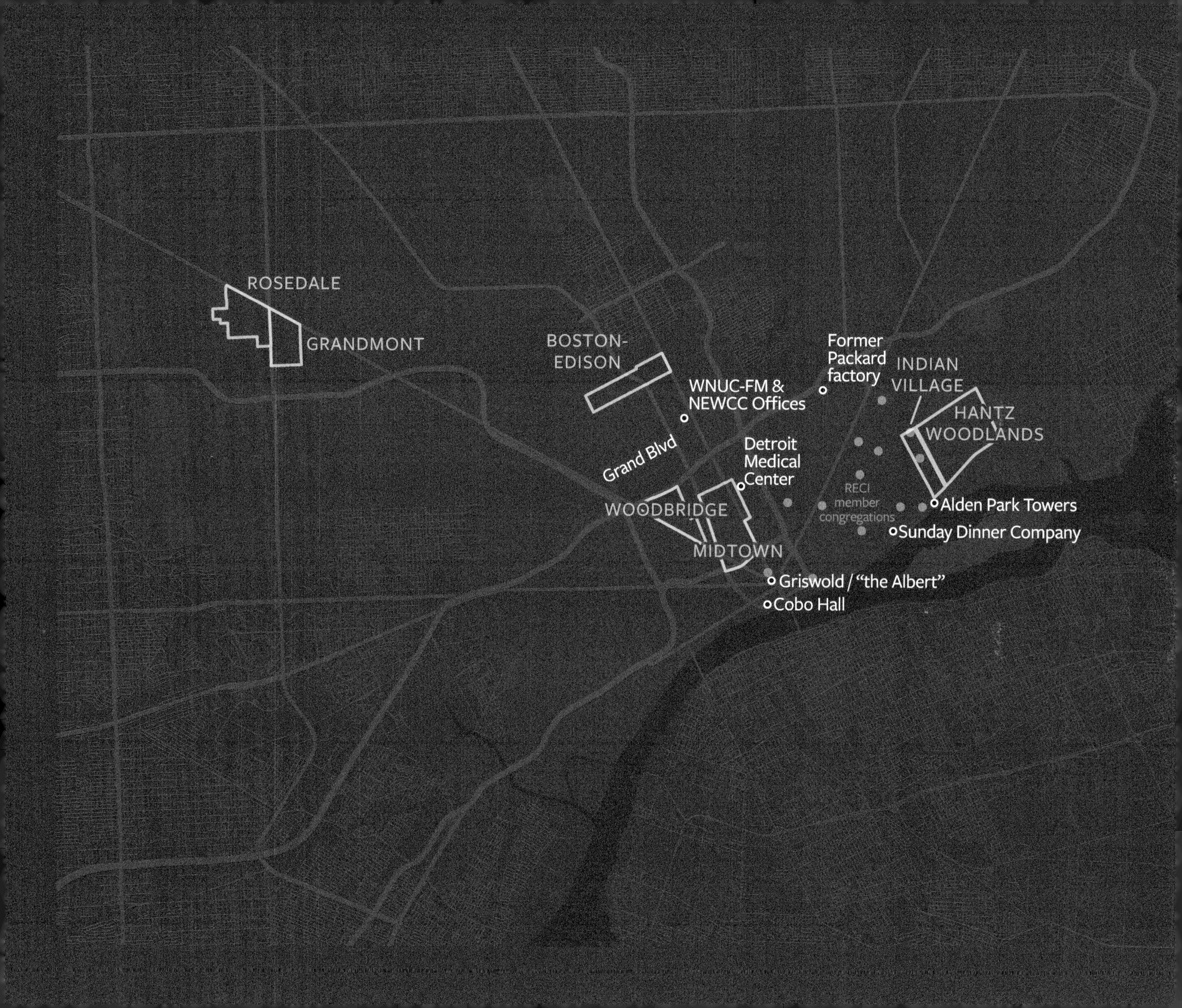

ROSEDALE

GRANDMONT

BOSTON-
EDISON

WNUC-FM &
NEWCC Offices

Former
Packard
factory

INDIAN
VILLAGE

HANTZ
WOODLANDS

Grand Blvd

Detroit
Medical
Center

RECI
member
congregations

Alden Park Towers

Sunday Dinner Company

WOODBRIDGE

MIDTOWN

Griswold / "the Albert"

Cobo Hall

BLACK HOMEOWNERSHIP IN DETROIT

LINDA CAMPBELL, ANDREW NEWMAN, SARA SAFRANSKY, AND TIM STALLMANN

The rise of Detroit's African American middle class is one of the most important stories in the city's modern history, even if it is frequently overshadowed by the rise and fall of automotive manufacturing. The series of maps (to the right) of rates of Black homeownership around the city over half a century might also be read as a reflection of the dreams, hopes, and disappointments of the tens of thousands of African American Detroiters who sought to make the city their home. While barred from homeownership in communities across the United States (including many of Detroit's suburbs and white enclaves within the city), African Americans were able find property within reach in parts of Detroit in the 1960s. This was due to an open-housing movement, combined with stable employment in the automotive industry and professional fields such as law, medicine, and teaching. For many African Americans, some of whom had been living in poverty in the rural South just before coming to Detroit, homeownership in the Motor City represented a long-sought, hard-won fulfillment of the American dream.

Between 1970 and 1980, however, two contradictory factors began to emerge that signaled a future homeownership crisis. Black home buyers continued to purchase property in desirable neighborhoods away from the downtown area, such as Seven Mile/Wyoming and other northwestern sections of the city (often on the heels of white homeowners fleeing for the suburbs). At the same time, the disappearance of African American homeowners in the North End, along West Grand Boulevard, and especially in the East Side, accompanied a series of devastating factory closings, some of which, in the case of the famous Packard plant, closed in 1958, and others even earlier. Many of these central neighborhoods have never recovered from this loss.

Throughout the 1980s and 1990s, some African American families were able to relocate to relatively affluent nearby northwestern suburbs, notably Southfield, Michigan. Only a few wealthy enclaves, such as Boston-Edison in the central part of the city and Indian Village on the East Side bucked this trend.

The 2000s began optimistically in Detroit. Some homeowners began to move back to certain neighborhoods in the Northwest side, with the leafy Grandmont-Rosedale neighborhood in particular seeing an influx of buyers. The transition to 2010, however, shows the tragic impact of the foreclosure crisis, as predatory lenders—many of whom targeted aspiring African American homeowners—not only snuffed out the dreams of families but also curbed the growth of whole neighborhoods. The 2010 map also demonstrates that the neighborhoods where African American homeowners hold the most equity are decidedly farther away from the areas that are the center of urban

Map by Tim Stallmann

Black Homeownership in Detroit, 1960–2010

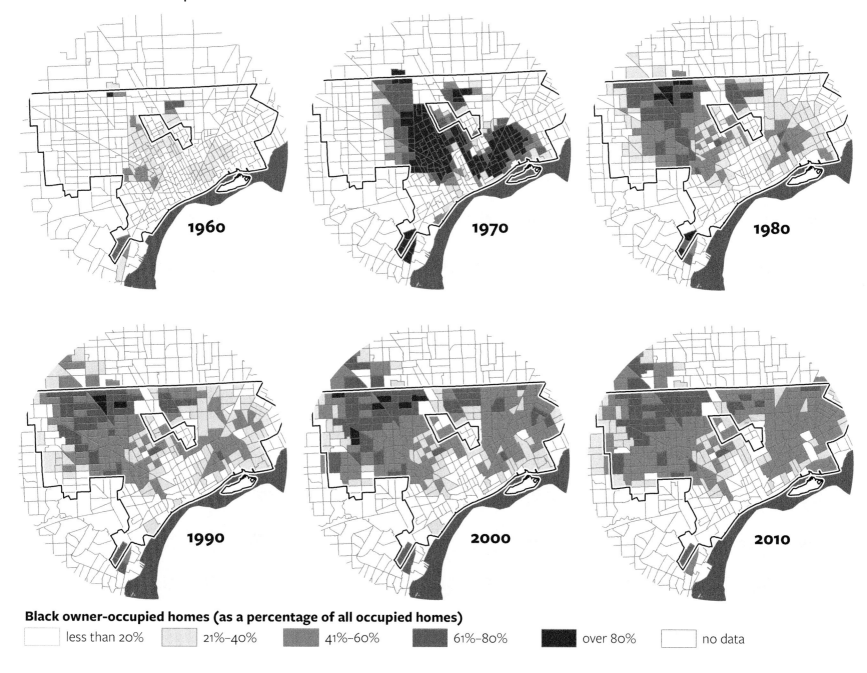

Black owner-occupied homes (as a percentage of all occupied homes)

less than 20%   21%–40%   41%–60%   61%–80%   over 80%   no data

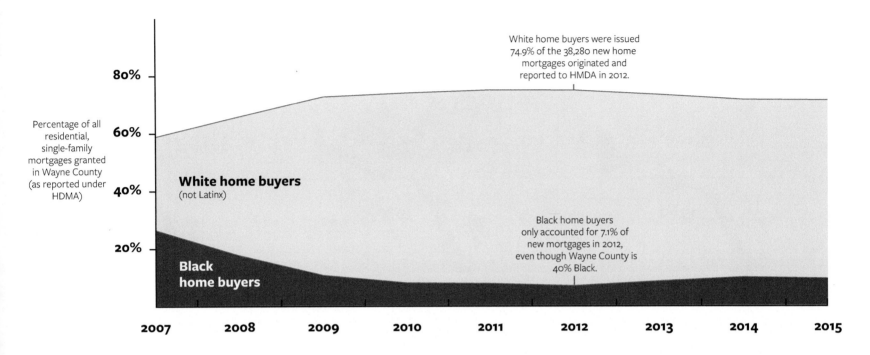

Percentage of all residential, single-family mortgages granted in Wayne County (as reported under HDMA)

White home buyers were issued 74.9% of the 38,280 new home mortgages originated and reported to HMDA in 2012.

White home buyers
(not Latinx)

Black home buyers only accounted for 7.1% of new mortgages in 2012, even though Wayne County is 40% Black.

Black home buyers

80%
60%
40%
20%

2007   2008   2009   2010   2011   2012   2013   2014   2015

revitalization efforts in the city, such as Downtown, Midtown, Corktown, and Southwest Detroit. This discrepancy highlights the racial inequities of the current revitalization effort: African American renters in the center of the city will have to pay higher rents, while African American homeowners in the outlying neighborhoods are positioned too far away from the center to benefit from increased property values.

The Home Mortgage Disclosure Act data provide another lens into racial disparities in home buying in Detroit, in particular the disparate impact of new restrictions on mortgage lending after the market crash of 2006–8. African Americans make up 40

percent of Wayne County's population, which includes Detroit. However, even around the peak of the early 2000s housing bubble, African American home buyers never accounted for more than 30 percent of mortgages granted in Wayne County. Nearly 60 percent of the mortgages were granted to white home buyers (who make up about 55 percent of the county's population) during the same period. The subsequent years reveal a growing racial divide in terms of home mortgages. From 2007–11, the number of mortgages granted to African Americans declined sharply, dropping to less than 10 percent by 2012. In contrast, the percentage of whites approved for mortgages during the same period climbed rapidly to nearly 80 percent. While this chart focuses in on the particular dynamics of shifts in access to credit for Black Detroiters, in 2012, Latinx home buyers were approved for 1,435 mortgages (2.0 percent of the total, down slightly from 2007), Asian home buyers for 2,615 (3.6 percent, more than double the 2007 share), and Native American home buyers for 260 (0.3 percent, about the same as 2007).

These statistics suggest that race impacts home buying in more than one way. White home buyers in Wayne County enjoyed a degree of access to capital that was vastly disproportionate to their demographic representation, while African Americans were generally underfinanced. At the same time, from a mortgage perspective, the Great Recession had strong negative impacts on the number of African Americans that obtained mortgages, while the share of white home buyers grew. Since real estate values generally drop during recessions, this meant that white home buyers were better leveraged to take advantage of the "buyer's market" during the downturn. Ironically, African Americans came the closest to equitable levels of financing during the boom period, which witnessed a higher-priced "seller's market" in most areas.

Asian American Homeownership in Detroit, 1990–2010

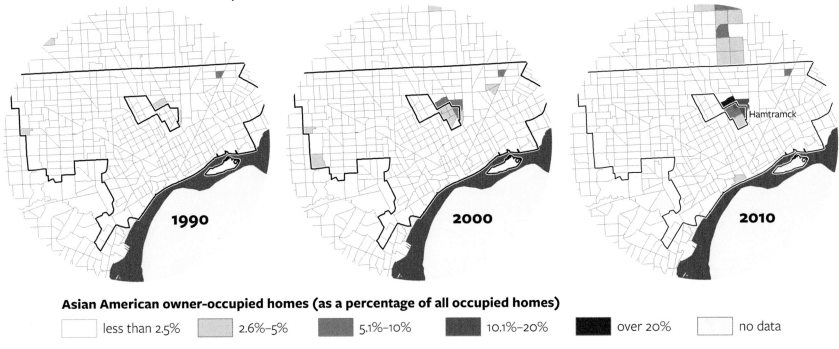

1990

2000

2010

Hamtramck

Asian American owner-occupied homes (as a percentage of all occupied homes)

less than 2.5%   2.6%–5%   5.1%–10%   10.1%–20%   over 20%   no data

Asian American Homeownership

This map, generated from census data on Asian American home-ownership in Detroit captures several dynamics at once, given the number of ethnicities subsumed underneath this label. Many of metro Detroit's South Asian and East Asian communities have been historically concentrated in the suburbs, as indicated here. A notable exception is the Bangladeshi community, which this map shows growing dramatically in and around Hamtramck, a city once synonymous with Polish immigration. Detroit's Chinatown, the history of which predates the 1990 start date of this map series is not visible here (see the section on the Detroit Asian Youth Project in chapter 6 for more information on this aspect of the city's history).

Map by Tim Stallmann

Latinx Homeownership in Detroit, 1990–2010

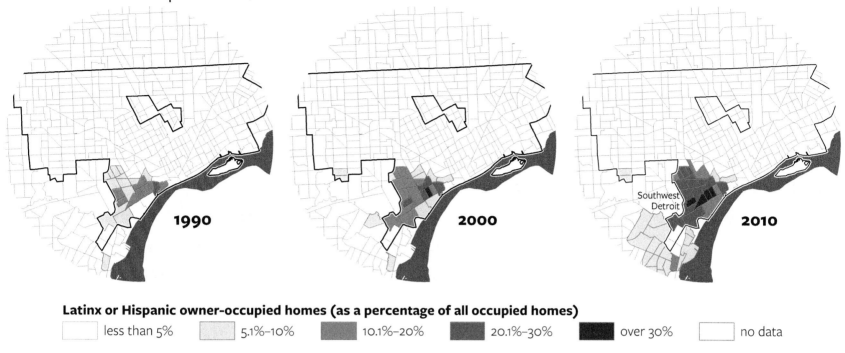

Latinx or Hispanic owner-occupied homes (as a percentage of all occupied homes)

less than 5%	5.1%–10%	10.1%–20%	20.1%–30%	over 30%	no data

Latinx Homeownership

Detroit has been home to a Latinx community of significant size
since the 1920s. In contrast to the shifting settlement patterns of
Black homeowners and whites over time, the core area of Latinx
homeownership, often known as Mexicantown, has been firmly
ensconced in Southwest Detroit, growing outward from a center
along Bagley Street and Vernor Highway.

Map by Tim Stallmann

CORPORATE POWER AND THE REINVENTION OF DETROIT

Address Given to the Women's International League for Peace and Freedom Congress at Wayne State University, 2014

GLORIA HOUSE

Gloria House, a longtime civil rights activist and professor at University of Michigan–Dearborn and Wayne State University, originally delivered this speech to the Congress of the Women's International League for Peace and Freedom. She argues that current efforts to redevelop Detroit are reproducing racist patterns of urban development instead of overturning them. House argues that the exacerbation of racial inequalities underlying the so-called revitalization of Detroit must be understood against Michigan's history of political contestation. She does not specifically use the term *revanchism*, but she contextualizes the redevelopment of Detroit against a backdrop of revenge politics undertaken by members of the state's conservative elite who have wanted to "take the city back"

since the 1967 uprising and the mayorship of Coleman Young. Young, the first Black mayor of Detroit, was elected in 1973 and served for twenty years, until 1994. House asserts that the "bashing" of Black political leadership since the era of Coleman Young helped pave the way for emergency management, leading to political disempowerment of African Americans at the same moment the city was changing its direction from an urban redevelopment point of view. Given these power dynamics, House concludes that Detroiters must resist oppressive forces and, at the same time, work to "envision and construct an altogether new society."

In our city there are approximately forty square miles of abandoned land. Thousands of homes have been lost to foreclosures, thousands have collapsed in ruins, while more than seventy-eight thousand vacant houses remain standing, like relics of a forgotten era. This is a city of loss of population; loss of tax base; deficient city services in lighting, transportation, repair of infrastructure; this is a city where the public school system has been dismantled and looted; this is a space of hunger (with children hardest hit); this is a place of homelessness and outrageous and persistent police brutality against people of color and their children; this is the space of closed parks, loss of medical services, unemployment, and theft of pensions. This is a space of profound suffering and dispossession while millions of dollars are appropriated for demolition of homes, and hundreds of millions are paid to lawyers and other consultants to "manage" our city affairs.

The political policies and strategies leading to this place have been in effect for many years. Practices of capitalist exploitation in Detroit are rooted in a stubborn, unrelenting racism that has fractured city life since the nineteenth century. Racism flared in violence from the period of the Civil War through the First and Second World Wars, exploded in the riot of 1943, and shocked the nation in the rebellion of 1967. And during all those years, whites were moving away from the city, steadily seeking to establish neighborhoods from which they could exclude African Americans—often resorting to violent assaults in order to preserve segregation. The shift of the auto companies to the suburbs and the South further exacerbated unemployment problems for African Americans in the inner city, while discriminatory federal housing policies facilitated the exodus of whites to the suburbs.

Excluded from new suburban housing developments, and segregated in the city core, African Americans faced additional problems. From the 1950s, when the power structure spoke of urban renewal in the city, this meant Black removal, uprooting of Black communities and businesses from the city core. This is the legacy of racist spatial politics in Detroit and its suburbs, and this legacy influences the current political dynamics of the city, where a US version of ethnic cleansing is now in process against African Americans and other poor communities. If the intent of ethnic cleansing was not clear before the water shutoffs, it must certainly be obvious to everyone at this point.

Though the 1967 rebellion expressed African Americans' frustration with long-standing socioeconomic disadvantages and injustice, the power elite responded as if they were the victims. An intense anger accompanied their abandonment of the city, and they watched scornfully as it deteriorated in population and tax base, necessary services, and overall quality of life. This resentment was represented in ongoing media bashing of the city and its African American leadership, a bashing that became increasingly hostile during the mayoral tenure of Coleman Young. The effect of this pervasive media attack was to infer that African Americans are not capable of governing ourselves, whether in the mayor's office, as members of the city council, or on an elected school board. The racist propaganda was generated not only in the popular media but also in the elite publications of white intellectuals and cultural leaders. We can see the success of this propaganda offensive in the recent mayoral campaign and election of Mike Duggan.*

By the mid-1970s, however, the corporate elite recognized its enormous mistake in abandoning Detroit, with its vital infrastructure of communications and finance connecting Michigan, Ohio, Illinois, and Canada, and its location on the Detroit River with links to the lake waterways that provide freshwater security in a time when scarcity is imminent and also ensure easy access to international transportation and trade. And so the reclamation began.

Corporate reclaiming of the city has meant the design of two Detroits, one flourishing, affluent, inviting, meant to serve the corporate agenda; the other, a neglected, abandoned wasteland. In fact, with the addition of the newly announced hockey arena

*Mike Duggan was elected mayor of Detroit in 2013. He was the first white mayor to serve the majority Black city since before Coleman Young was elected in the early 1970s.

plans,* we can see how from Grand Boulevard right down the center of the old city core to the riverfront, a new city is evolving, a consolidation of privately owned spaces: Midtown, Ilitchville, Gilbertville, and the riverfront.

The attractive, redesigned city core is successfully enticing individuals and families of the managerial class back into the city. This "whiter" upwardly mobile population will provide an anchor for dominant corporate interests, managing the corporate offices, overseeing the technology, and supervising the manual laborers who clean and maintain the exclusive offices and amenities of a corporate command city. This is not the city of a massive working class that we once knew. In this city, which functions as a command city for powerful multinationals in a global economy, there is no need for a massive working class or a city that would accommodate them. With the creation of this corporate-owned city, with its symphony, its DIA [Detroit Institute of Arts], its opera house, its posh restaurants, bars, ballparks, and other entertainment centers, has come the increased militarization of the city police force and its integration into a network of law enforcement agencies, including Homeland Security and Border Patrol.

Simultaneously, the corporate elite has launched a determined campaign to plunder the city's assets—to seize, control, reconfigure, and/or privatize major city assets and institutions such as Recorder's Court,† Detroit Medical Center, Cobo Hall, Belle Isle and other parks, the public schools—and now to take another step toward control and privatization of the Department of Water and Sewerage. Such objectives have been facilitated by the illegal imposition of emergency managers and the circum-

vention of duly elected public officials by foundations and other private agencies in the processes of city policy and development. Through such strategies, the majority Black populations in several Michigan cities have been disenfranchised.

In pockets throughout the city, individuals and groups are resisting this takeover in every way we know how. Moratorium NOW! is continuing its struggle against foreclosures; others are working toward food security through farming; still others are creating artist co-ops, small businesses, forums for resolving conflict, and educational and cultural programs and activities. And most recently we are working to provide emergency water relief.

Detroit has a national reputation for its spunky organizers, innovators, ingenious leaders, and problem solvers. But these innovators have not been included in planning Detroit's future. In fact, the resources and energy of many such organizers are being exhausted in the daily work of resistance.

One of the problems we are facing as organizers is the difficulty of coming to terms with the inhumanity, savagery, and barbarism of corporate emergency management strategies and the fact that these strategies involve simultaneous assaults on multiple arenas of our lives. Moreover, with the media at their command, the corporations have successfully popularized narratives that mask or disguise their objectives.

*For more on the Ilitch hockey arena plans, see the map on p. 172.

†The Recorder's Court was a state court in which the judges were elected from Detroit. As a result, it was presided over by a greater number of African American judges than the Circuit Court. It was effectively abolished when it merged with the Wayne County Circuit Court in 1997.

In the face of this kind of domination, those of us who insist on self-determination, who insist on discovering alternative means to sustain our lives, must begin to envision and construct an altogether new society. The methods of securing social order and justice that we have fashioned in the past do not apply now because we do not have a scaffolding of law to which we can appeal and on which to rely, as this is a time of government and corporate racist lawlessness. Though we have to continue the forms of resistance with which we are familiar to hold back the assault against our humanity, it is important to recognize that there is an additional, essential arena of work. That work is the conceiving or imagining and building of new forms of community that our children and grandchildren will continue to develop. That is our calling in this time and this place: resistance to oppressive forces, on the one hand; conceiving and building of a new society on the other.

Manuel "Matty" Moroun
owns 599 total properties here and
in Corktown (southwest of downtown)

Michael Kelly
owns 693 total properties scattered around the city,
with a concentration here

Highland
Park

Hamtramck

Grand River Avenue

Woodward Avenue

I-94

Gratiot Avenue

I-75

West Fort Street

Michigan Avenue

Melvin Washington
owns 799 total
properties

PROPERTY SPECULATION IN DETROIT, 2016

Property Speculation Rate, 2016
Percentage of property owned by speculators
(those who own at least 3 other properties)

- less than 5%
- 5%–10%
- 11%–15%
- 16%–20%
- over 20%

parcel owned by a major speculator,
as defined by Property Praxis

Property Speculation in Detroit

Single-family homeownership has significantly shaped the material and cultural history of Detroit. Today, in contrast, a significant number of lots in the city, especially those with abandoned and deteriorating homes, are owned by a relatively small number of people. As this map, based on the work of the Property Praxis project (primarily Alex Hill, Josh Akers, and Aaron Petcoff), shows, three landowners—Manuel "Matty" Moroun, Michael Kelly, and Melvin Washington—own approximately two thousand parcels in the city, the majority of which contain vacant, abandoned, and deteriorated properties.

While large landowners are not automatically speculators by definition,* this pattern of ownership offers a window on how speculation and displacement operate in Detroit: speculators make fortunes while residents get none of the associated benefits of urban development. The approach favored by these owners can be contrasted to developers such Dan Gilbert, who often embrace publicity as a business strategy by undertaking high-profile megaprojects downtown and cultivating an image of themselves as "rescuing" the city. Away from the limelight, Moroun, Kelly, and Washington have quietly amassed large numbers of properties by purchasing bank and tax foreclosures. Whether scatter-shot holdings like Kelly or in strategic locations like Moroun, a vast number of these properties are left undeveloped or in states of extreme deterioration. In some cases, large portions of neighborhoods are being left "fallow" in expectation of rising prices in the future, often after another investor assumes the risks of undertaking development.

At times, these fallow properties are monetized in the interim through predatory land contracts only to be repossessed through foreclosure later. The use of land contracts as a predatory lending tool dates back to the early twentieth century, when they were frequently used in African American neighborhoods where residents were otherwise unable to access credit. Today land contracts are again an increasingly common way that real estate investors profit off the backs of those residents in nongentrifying neighborhoods with less access to wealth, many of whom are people of color. In a land contract, residents sign a contract to purchase a home, with the seller providing financing rather than a bank. "Buyers" are required to make monthly payments as they would for a mortgage, but the seller continues to hold the legal title until the full home price is paid off. Buyers do not build any intermediate equity in their home, and if they fail to make payments (or don't have the funds to make the required balloon payment at the end of the loan), they lose their entire investment. Meanwhile, sellers are not responsible for repairs or upkeep in the way that they would be if they were renting the property. Land contracts bring profits for owners without any semblance of development for the city.[†]

This fits a broader pattern of global "land grabs" as a strategy to accumulate wealth, particularly in an era of unstable stock markets. Activists and scholars have used the term *land grabbing* in recent years to draw attention to the global spate of large-scale land acquisitions by corporate or state entities, particularly in rural areas in the global South. Detroit fits the global profile of land grabbing in that large-scale purchases of land deemed as marginal, empty, and available are driven by shifts in the global economy as opposed to purely local dynamics.[‡] Indeed, the *Economist*, one of the most popular outlets in the international finance media, argued in 2011 that despite all the gloom in Detroit, it's "so cheap, there's hope," as evidenced by the return of "pioneering types" to the city.[§] This and similar press have created a land rush whereby a range of investors and speculators have snapped up large quantities of land in the late 2000s and early 2010s.

---

*The definition of *speculation* used in this map is (1) ownership of three or more parcels in an area in which the owner does not have a taxable address; (2) ownership of a large number of parcels in varying conditions and disuse; (3) single vacant or abandoned property held by an owner with an out-of-state or international address; or (4) residential property that serves as a taxable address for multiple owners with three or more holdings in the city.

†See Joshua Akers, "The Actually Existing Markets of Shrinking Cities," Metropolitics, April 18, 2017, www.metropolitiques.eu/IMG/pdf/met-akers2.pdf.

‡ See Ben White, Saturnino M. Borras Jr., Ruth Hall, Ian Scoones, and Wendy Wolford, "The New Enclosures: Critical Perspectives on Corporate Land Deals," *Journal of Peasant Studies* 39, nos. 3–4 (2012): 619–47.

§"So Cheap, There's Hope," *Economist*, October 22, 2011, www.economist.com/united-states/2011/10/22/so-cheap-theres-hope.

Map by Tim Stallmann, with thanks to Alex B. Hill for sharing data and insight from the Property Praxis project

LETTER TO ALDEN PARK TOWERS MANAGEMENT

In recent years, Detroit has often been described as having a "surplus land" problem. This, combined with the number of vacant buildings in the city, has led to a perception that redevelopment in Detroit is simply a matter of filling up empty spaces. But housing markets do not operate in such simple ways. This letter of protest to a landlord, written by Betty Scruse, a UAW employee residing at Alden Park Towers, with the help of Jaqueline Lacey, a student at Wayne State University, offers a view of current redevelopment in Detroit from an angle not normally captured in the dominant "comeback" narrative.* For Scruse and many other residents, Detroit's urban revitalization has arrived at their doorstep in the form of an eviction notice slid under the door. Scruse holds a stable job at the UAW and resides in a middle-class community. However, because of a lack of concrete tenants' protections in Detroit (caused in part by a preemptive ban on rent control passed in the Michigan legislature in 1988, Public Act 226), any renter in Detroit, regardless of their income, can be pushed out at the whim of landlords.

* In 2013, the Detroit Metro Convention and Visitors Bureau launched a campaign to market Detroit as "America's Great Comeback City."

March 20, 2013

New Management
Alden Towers Apartment
8100 E Jefferson Ave
Detroit, MI 48214

Dear New Management:

On March 1, 2013, I received an eviction notice to vacate my beautiful water view apartment by March 31, 2013. I was very disappointed to receive a notice, which didn't result from my non-payment of rent. Although I am gainfully employed, and my rent is current, I began to feel like a homeless person. I cried tears to learn I must continue working daily, find a new place, which was not a part of my agenda this month, and pack to move from a 3-bedroom, 1,300 square foot apartment. I had planned on living at Alden Towers until I retired because I am employed by the International Union, UAW directly next door. Unfortunately, those plans will never be realized because I have received an eviction notice from the new management company.

You have residents who have resided at Alden Towers for more than fifteen years along with several senior citizens who also plan to probably die there, but you showed them no respect either. Good-paying, loyal tenants endured so much ugliness while living there and never once did we place our rents in escrow or wanted it pro-rated because we didn't get what we deserve as tenants. Tenants endured no heat during cold winter nights, no hot water, elevators not working, and outside doors not working properly and never once did you compensate us for all of the sub-standard, deplorable inconveniences. Some of us moved to Alden Towers because public transportation is easily accessible, [because of] school districts and, like myself, [to be] near places of employment.

Ironically, you hired Detroit police officers for protection when we are the victims, but you chose to use the bully tactics. You didn't represent yourself in "good faith"—that's why you hired police officers. If your company had good intentions and wanted to be fair to us you wouldn't have needed police protection.

Now, I have experienced living while Black, and the word to describe our situation is called gentrification. This generally results in displacement of poorer pre-gentrification residents, who are economically disadvantaged and unable to pay increased rents, and property taxes, or afford to invest in real estate.

Sincerely,
Betty A. Scruse
Resident

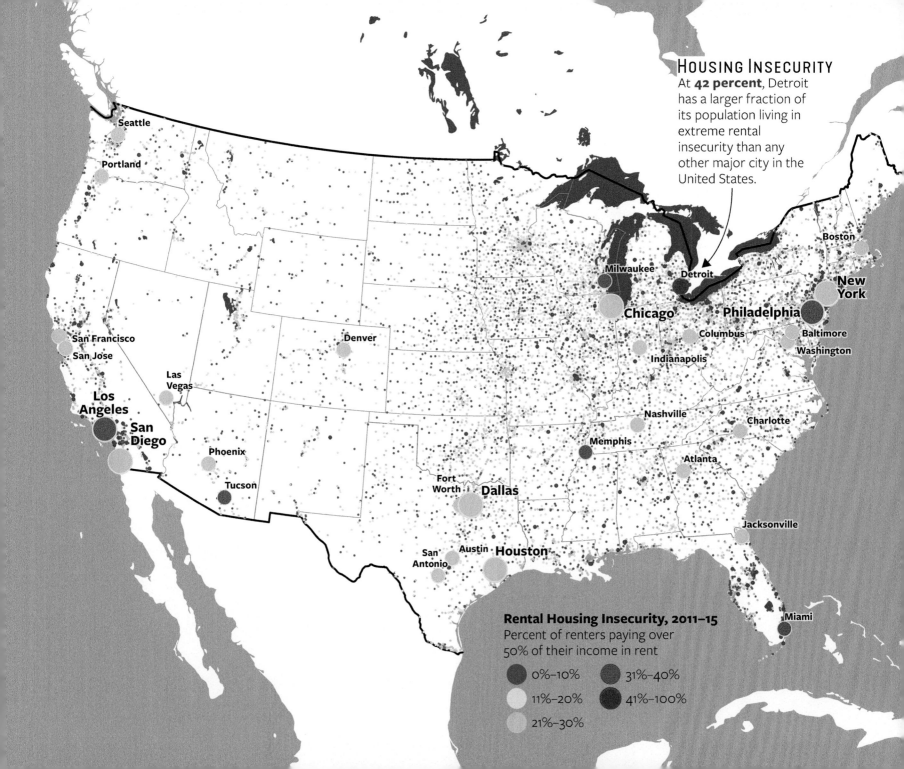

HOUSING INSECURITY

At **42 percent**, Detroit has a larger fraction of its population living in extreme rental insecurity than any other major city in the United States.

Rental Housing Insecurity, 2011–15

Percent of renters paying over 50% of their income in rent

- 0%–10%
- 11%–20%
- 21%–30%
- 31%–40%
- 41%–100%

Seattle
Portland
San Francisco
San Jose
Los Angeles
San Diego
Las Vegas
Phoenix
Tucson
Denver
San Antonio
Austin
Houston
Fort Worth
Dallas
Milwaukee
Chicago
Memphis
Nashville
Indianapolis
Columbus
Atlanta
Charlotte
Detroit
Philadelphia
Baltimore
Washington
New York
Boston
Jacksonville
Miami

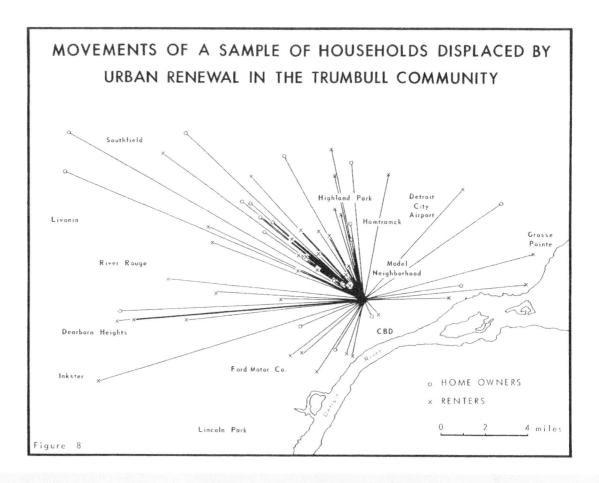

MOVEMENTS OF A SAMPLE OF HOUSEHOLDS DISPLACED BY URBAN RENEWAL IN THE TRUMBULL COMMUNITY

Southfield

Livonia

River Rouge

Dearborn Heights

Inkster

Highland Park

Hamtramck

Detroit City Airport

Grosse Pointe

Model Neighborhood

CBD

Ford Motor Co.

Lincoln Park

o HOME OWNERS

x RENTERS

0   2   4 miles

Figure 8

Housing Insecurity in Detroit

Real estate prices in Detroit may be much lower than cities like New York, Chicago, and San Francisco, but a glut of often uninhabitable homes for sale at bargain-basement prices has done little to guarantee housing security in the poorest of the nation's major cities. In fact, the ease by which property can be bought, amassed, and flipped in Detroit seems to have increased the likelihood that tenants will be subjected to rent gouging. This map shows how Detroit compares to other cities in America in terms of the proportion of the population spending more than half their income on housing. Even when compared to cities reputed to be expensive for renters, such New York and San Francisco, Detroit is in a class by itself.

Map by Tim Stallmann

DGEI Map of Displacement from the Trumbull Community

This map, produced by the Detroit Geographical Expedition and Institute in the late 1960s, shows that Detroit has a long legacy of displacing residents as part of urban redevelopment. Despite winning a court injunction against the city's urban clearance programs in 1970, residents of the Trumbull neighborhood were eventually pushed out. As this map shows they largely chose to locate farther away from the central city. These same dynamics continue today, as evidenced by the cases of Alden Park Towers and the Griswold apartments, described in this chapter.

THE CAMPAIGN FOR THE GRISWOLD SENIORS

"If I had the money, I wouldn't move"

LINDA CAMPBELL, ANDREW NEWMAN, SARA SAFRANSKY, AND TIM STALLMANN

n 2014, as real estate development picked up pace in Detroit, housing rights advocates worked to counter the growing issue of displacement, especially for the most economically vulnerable Detroiters. The risk of eviction and displacement was particularly acute for senior citizens who were faced with the financial impact of expiring housing vouchers. The Hannan Center, a nonprofit organization with a ninety-year history of working with elderly residents in Detroit, created a committee—Senior Housing Preservation—and one of its participants was Linda Campbell of the Detroit People's Platform. Through her work with the committee and her acquaintance with Gloria Rivera (founder of the Great Lakes Bioneers and member of the Parish of St. Aloysius in Detroit), Campbell and the Senior Housing Preservation coalition learned about seniors facing displacement from the Griswold, an apartment building in Downtown.

For thirty years, the Griswold had been home to over a hundred senior citizens whose rent was subsidized by federal Section 8 housing vouchers. In 2014, the development group Broder & Sachse announced a plan to renovate the building as market-rate apartments and rebrand it as the Albert. The residents received notices that they had to vacate the premises and were offered Section 8 vouchers for new apartments. In response, the residents began to organize. Campbell and advocates with Senior Housing Preservation visited the building and learned that many of the seniors could not afford to move and often did not want to move.

The Griswold was a small, close-knit community and many residents had been neighbors for decades. Linda and other advocates for the preservation of senior housing collected testimony from the residents about conditions in the building and their forced relocation. One man declared, "If I had the money, I wouldn't move." He described learning that he had to leave as "traumatic," and for others, the very thought of forced relocation created tremendous stress. One woman said to Linda, "I think, oh my God, how can I stand this? I've been reading my Bible more and more and this has given me solace. . . . You get nervous and you get excited and you can't sleep, and I can't sleep." A ninety-two-year-old woman cried with the advocates at the thought of merely having to relocate. Several residents were particularly distressed about having to relocate away from the St. Aloysius Church, their primary social and psychological anchor.

The seniors reported that developers had quietly slipped letters under their doors requiring they "vacate the premises" in short notice. The developers then began renovation and with

Kate Levy

These images are taken from "Holding Down the Fort," a film created by Kate Levy and commissioned by the Senior Housing Preservation Coalition, which shows senior citizens from Downtown and Midtown Detroit facing displacement.

many seniors still in the building; the construction dust triggered respiratory difficulties for several of the elderly residents, resulting in hospitalizations.

Linda found that many seniors felt this disturbing cruelty was part of a general pattern that characterized Downtown redevelopment. One man described the story of a homeless woman he knew who had "died right in a doorway" in the shadow of new luxury developments. He saw the tragedy as the sign of change in Downtown where people were no longer "warm and caring," where the new outlook was an "I got a piece of bread—I don't care if you starve." Another woman described her feelings about neighborhood change to the advocates in the following terms: "They don't want to see no old people in Downtown Detroit and they don't want to see any homeless people either. They took away all the benches. Now that's a sin against God!"

The People's Platform and Senior Housing Preservation sought to raise awareness about the dislocation of the seniors from the Griswold and the potential for further displacement in Midtown and Downtown. Several news outlets produced reports on the events, and multiple protests were held. A videographer, Kate Levy, produced a guerrilla film in which she reappropriated a promotional video about the redevelopment and interlaced it with interviews conducted with many of the seniors who lived in the Griswold.[3] The Levy film offered a devastating critique of the Albert simply by using the rhetoric of real estate marketing against itself. The promotional film begins with an excited young white woman proclaiming, "Detroit is my generation's city." Levy then inserts an interview with an elderly African American woman in a wheelchair, a resident of the Griswold, who says, "I had planned to be here until I died!" In another instance in the promotional video, a white voice states, "We took ownership." As those words flash, Levy then inserts a clip from an interview with an elderly woman in a wheelchair who holds a notice to vacate the premises and says, "All these fumes [from construction] are making us sick—many of us are going to the hospital." According to housing advocates, the stress caused by the dislocation contributed to deaths among the seniors; the Levy film claims that seven people passed away shortly after having been forced to move.

Unfortunately, stories like those of the Griswold seniors have become increasingly common in urban America.[4] When real estate development is permitted to occur without regard for the rights of even the most vulnerable residents, the results have a catastrophic and tragic impact on the lives of those who are evicted and pushed out. Often mainstream policy makers and commentators in the media treat displacement of this kind as an inevitable outcome of market logic. Such a perspective turns a blind eye to the preventable decisions that were made by Detroit's developers and elected officials that resulted in the suffering experienced by the seniors who lived at the Griswold.

DETROIT FUTURE CITY

Urban Sustainability as a Force of Displacement

LINDA CAMPBELL, ANDREW NEWMAN, SARA SAFRANSKY, AND TIM STALLMANN

n 2013, a public-private consortium released one of the boldest efforts to reimagine an American city to date—the Detroit Future City (DFC) Strategic Framework. The citywide plan emerged from the Detroit Works Project, a contentious planning process launched in 2010 by Mayor David Bing that aimed to "right size" the city and has been strongly supported by successive mayoral administrations as well as the major philanthropic foundations that fund the majority of the area's community organizations. The DFC plan seeks to mitigate urban shrinkage and the harms that cities have historically done to the global environment. It envisions new urban forms such as carbon forests, wetlands optimized for stormwater management, and areas given over for wind and solar power generation.

At its core, however, the logic that governs this reorganization of the city is less innovative: it is based on a proprietary Market Value Analysis (MVA) that carves the city's neighborhoods into zones based on their level of real estate market activity (see p. 218). Adapting the logic of investment banking to the planning of communities, the MVA suggests "leveraging" strong neighborhoods—as if they were just another part of an investment portfolio—by increasing infrastructure provisions to those parts of the city projected to grow over time. Meanwhile, vast swaths of the city that do not appear to be favored by market forces are given over to "strategic renewal," which includes a combination of infrastructure cutbacks and implementation of the urban greening projects described above.

Ultimately, the DFC divides Detroit into sections, prioritizing some for traditional urban revitalization and setting aside others for experiments in urban depopulation. Modern urban planning has long been criticized for promising a better standard of living for all while failing to live up these ideals for some. But rarely have urbanists—who have historically been chided as overly utopian—sought from the start to disconnect a large group of people and hence create a situation in which spatial inequality is a starting point for urbanization rather than an undesired by-product of it.

The estimated 137,000 Detroiters who reside in "repurpose" and "reuse" areas now find themselves subjected to a new form of displacement: rather than being forced to move, their neighborhoods are essentially shifted away from them. Mayor Bing's controversial warning at the launch of the Detroit Works Project seems to be coming to fruition: Those residents who remain in certain areas, he said, "need to understand that they're not going to get the kind of services they require." They would be better off, he concluded, in parts of the city where they'd receive "water, sewer, lighting, public safety—all of that."[5] In a novel form of

Strategic Renewal Is Right-Sizing

Detroit Future City uses the phrase "**strategic renewal**" to mean dismantling and removing infrastructure from some areas of the city while spending more money on infrastructure in others.

Infrastructure means roads, water and sewer pipes, powerlines and substations, street lights, and bus service.

In parts of the city planned for "Replace, Repurpose or Decommission," strategic renewal will mean the end of scheduled bus service, less frequent trash collection, bulldozing some roads into rubble, and cutting off water, power, and gas to vacant blocks.

Only 47,600 people live in areas targeted for upgraded services.

These zones mostly follow existing business districts, and are the only parts of the city that will see service upgrades.

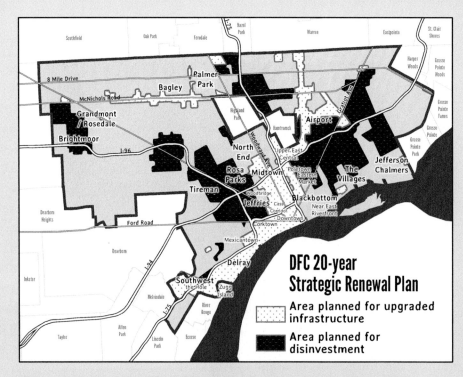

DFC 20-year Strategic Renewal Plan

- ⬚ Area planned for upgraded infrastructure
- ■ Area planned for disinvestment

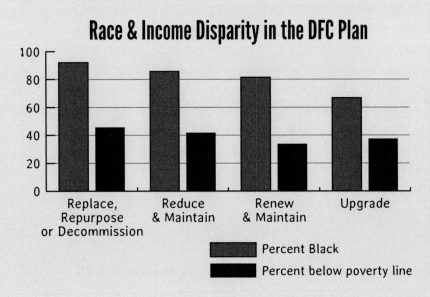

Race & Income Disparity in the DFC Plan

Bar chart axis: 0, 20, 40, 60, 80, 100

Categories: Replace, Repurpose or Decommission; Reduce & Maintain; Renew & Maintain; Upgrade

Legend:
- ▨ Percent Black
- ■ Percent below poverty line

One out of every five Black Detroiters lives in an area planned for disinvestment.

That's compared to just 12% of the white population. The "Replace, Repurpose or Decommission" area is 92% Black, while the "Upgrade" area is only 67%.

137,300 people live in areas targeted for disinvestment and removal of infrastructure.

22% of Detroit's land and 19% of Detroit's population lives in areas labeled for "Replace, Repurpose or Decommission" of infrastructure in the DFC plan.

Neighborhoods that will be targeted include: Brightmoor, Chandler Park, Condon, Davison, East Riverside, Finney, Foch, Jefferson/Mack, Jeffries, Nolan, Rosa Parks, Tireman, and Kettering.

racialized citizenship, many Detroiters, unlike their suburban neighbors, must now accept that access to municipal services and infrastructure—water, power, garbage collection—is viewed from the start as an "entitlement" that cannot be taken for granted as a basic amenity of modern existence.

"We don't have no fire station. We don't have no police station. You don't have a bunch of things. It just no longer exists. I said when I was a little girl one day I would like to own my own shop up on Woodward because I watched this Black woman have an alteration shop, and I look back now and there's so many abandoned buildings and so many burned-up houses, I was like, 'How do you just . . . how does the economy allow a live community like this to die?'" —TANESHA FLOWERS

Tanesha Flowers is a Detroit resident and member of the Detroit Action Commonwealth, a nonprofit membership organization that works to develop individual and collective power to challenge the root causes of poverty and homelessness and advance social justice.

The flyer shown at left was created by Tim Stallmann for the Detroit People's Platform in an early phase of the *Atlas* process. It shows that under the Detroit Future City (DFC) Strategic Framework approximately 137,000 Detroiters live in areas of the city slated for cutbacks in basic services ranging from utilities to transit and basic maintenance. The DFC plan itself contains dozens of maps drawn from an impressive array of data, but not one conveys details about the differential impact of the plan across geography and race.

Land Use

Commercial

Governmental / Institutional

Industrial

Market Type

< 5 sales 2009-10

A

B

C

D

E

F

G

H

I

Reinvestment Partners

Reinvestment Fund Detroit
Market Value Analysis

This map is part of a Market Value Analysis (MVA) of Detroit created by Reinvestment Fund, a community development financial institution in Philadelphia, in coordination with the City of Detroit and Detroit Future City (DFC). Reinvestment Fund has made MVA maps for over thirty US cities including New Orleans, San Antonio, Camden, Newark, Pittsburgh, Philadelphia, Baltimore, St. Louis, Milwaukee, Houston, and Dallas.

The organization markets the MVA as a data-driven, user-friendly, apolitical, and objective representation of market value that will guide city officials on where and how to direct "scarce" public resources and leverage private investment. The MVA clusters census blockgroups based on a set of factors which relate to their real estate market performance. On this map, purple and blue areas (clusters "A" and "B") have the highest median sales prices and are identified as "steady" markets in the accompanying analysis. Red areas (clusters "H" and "I") have the lowest median sales prices and are identified as "distressed," and the remaining areas fall into some mix of "transitional" and "distressed."

According to the DFC plan, high-vacancy neighborhoods, or distressed markets, in MVA parlance, are being targeted for a particular type of greening (see the Hantz Woodlands example on p. 227). Over time, they are to be repurposed with the landscape features we more often associate with the countryside than the city, such as forests, ponds, and farms. Meanwhile, traditional public services (water, streetlights, garbage pickup) and the engineered infrastructures that deliver services will be reduced and then eventually withdrawn.

As the case of Detroit demonstrates, the MVA is far from an apolitical map of market viability. Rather, it is a new spatial technology of urban governance that echoes the HOLC redlining map shown in chapter 1, and works to reconfigure the function of city government by respatializing the state's role as a distributor of resources and the meaning of "public" in public services through the intermediation of the private sector in ways that are highly racialized.

THE RIVERFRONT EAST CONGREGATION INITIATIVE

"Do they have our community's
best interests at heart?"

KATHLEEN FOSTER, JEANETTE MARBLE, AND DEBORAH WILLIAMSON

Kathleen Foster, Jeanette Marble, and Deborah Williamson are Detroit residents and members of the Riverfront East Congregation Initiative (RECI), a collaboration of seventeen diverse faith-based communities with twenty-six thousand congregants that seeks to shape the future of Detroit's East Side, an area of the city with some of the highest foreclosure rates. The efforts of RECI are a powerful example of how neighborhood groups are developing responses to problems associated with foreclosures, speculation, and land use. While many block clubs and neighborhood associations in Detroit self-organize to care for the urban landscape, RECI stands out for its mission to build more participatory and empowered communities through "asset-based organizing" and "place-based min-istry" in the neighborhoods surrounding their collective congregations.

RECI has sought to support what it calls the "economy of the community" by building social relationships. For example, when the state made welfare cuts, RECI members made a resource guide map (see p. 225)—"a list of folks who were providing resources to the community"—and encouraged congregation members to make use of their services and also support them. RECI aims to empower the community. Its members reject the idea that there is only one way to do development in the city, namely with developers coming in from the outside without the consent of the community. Instead, RECI advocates practicing a form of common governance and collective decision-making that is about developing a shared under-standing of "who we are and what we want for ourselves." This interview was conducted by Andrew Newman and Sara Safransky.

We're interested in how Detroit's neighborhoods have changed over time. Could you talk about where you live?

Kathleen: I live on Farnsworth, right off Mt. Elliot, East Grand Boulevard area, right around the corner from the old Packard factory. I live a block away from where I visited my great-grandmother as a child. The thing I remember most coming up through there is how full the neighborhood was, how there were houses on every lot, how there were corner stores, mom-and-pop stores, how a train ran right down the tracks over there that went across the boulevard, and there were warehouses where it brought goods and unloaded them.

Now I live a block away. When I moved there, it was a very full neighborhood. I was like the third Black family to move onto the block. Today there are vacant lots and vacant houses. However, nobody is burning anything down in my neighborhood. The neighbors cut the grass of vacant houses. They board up different properties. For all intents and purposes, they keep the fronts looking like people still frequent them. There is urban farming in my neighborhood, and they share vegetables.

It is still such a vibrant neighborhood for being in the inner city. You almost have to see it to believe it. Although the neighborhood has changed in the way of the population, the life is not gone out of the neighborhood. It's just so lively—not that we don't have situations that cause alarm or whatever, but I feel safe. I'm out in my yard at five-thirty or six o'clock in the morning and I'm out in my yard at two or three o'clock until night. I just love it there. We don't even have a fence between my yard and my neighbor's yard. We cut each other's grass. I have a deck, and we share that.

How have foreclosures impacted the community and what are people doing to address these issues?

Jeanette: I think that it's given people the sense that they're not as safe because there are so many vacant houses. Some people like you say, [Kathleen], go out, and they'll still take care of the property, mow the lawn, but it has affected our area a lot. You have people that squat. Then the mortgage company comes and sends them out. Then they'll come back and squat some more. As long as they take care of it, I don't care.

Kathleen: I have a totally different view of the foreclosure epidemic because of my profession. I am a HUD [Housing and Urban Development] housing counselor. Because of my profession, when I talk about the spirit of Detroit and the hope that a lot of people have, there is a lot of hopelessness when you go into foreclosure. What I've found out is people don't know their rights. They don't know their options. They get engulfed by the fear of the process—the fact that they no longer have the amount of employment they had at one time when they bought this particular property. They don't see an avenue to be okay in this situation. I get an immense amount of pleasure in educating my clients about the foreclosure process and giving them some other choices. You're going to have some place to live. You still have money. Maybe when you leave the place, pack up your memories, along with your other goods and things, you'll be able to move forward because where this house is foreclosing in this neighborhood for $30,000, that's the low end—how about they just sold one right around the corner from you with the same amenities for $3,000? You could go through foreclosure and then go over here and buy a house and own it free and clear.

You mentioned that residents take care of vacant houses. How do they organize that?

Kathleen: On my block there are three or four lots that are just vacant; it's the flip side of foreclosure. This gentleman just bought a house right across the street from me for $500. A whole house, three bedrooms, one and a half bathrooms, and it has a lot attached to it. Even before he moved in, the gentleman that lived on the far end of the lot was mowing half of it. The guy that lives on my side of the street was mowing the other half. So it always stayed cut. It's not like they said, "This is the second Saturday of the month and we're going to go out here and cut this grass." When they're doing their own, they just do the one next door. They just keep it going like that. They don't organize to do it. They just do it. Because you know everything did not disappear at once. So little by degree when things became vacant, they just took over responsibility of the next one and the next and the next one and the next one.

You've mentioned gardens a couple of times as being an important part of the community. Could you talk a little more about why they are important?

Kathleen: They provide relationships. The gentleman that bought the house for $500, he has a garden and he's always welcoming us to come over and have some of whatever. The gardens are conversation pieces. Anytime I have ever gotten out of my car to go talk to anybody that's in a garden, I am never met with resistance. They always welcome conversation with open arms. I've never met anybody who was standoffish. They're always like, "Come on in." It's nice to know people. Gardens provide relationships.

You've talked about RECI's work on land-use issues and mapping community assets. They say there are roughly one hundred thousand residential "vacant" parcels in the city and approximately half of these are what we've started referring to as "de facto public." How would you like to see that land controlled and distributed?

Deborah: One of the issues that RECI is working on now is Hantz Farms, which wants to buy up a big chunk of land from the city to put up Christmas trees. We spoke with Mike Score, the president of the project. He came to RECI and we asked him a lot of questions. He didn't have a lot of answers for us. RECI is really interested in making sure the land is not just given away to someone who after four years, if they don't profit from Christmas trees, can just do whatever he wants with it. The area of the land sale would be like three Chrysler plants. That's how much land he wants to buy. My thought was, "That's going to be Hantz country." One of the issues RECI is looking into is exactly what he's planning to do with the land and if he's planning on helping the city out in any way.

Jeanette: I would like to see the land be made more accessible to the people in the community at a reasonable rate. At one time, the lots were like $300 and you could buy the lot right next door to your house. Well, if you didn't live next door to it and you lived across the street, because you were in the community, you still had first recourse. That changed. Now it goes through the auction, and a lot of land developers or corporations came in and started gobbling up different lots without the community having the access or the benefit of being able to purchase it at a price that would have been reasonable. Even if they just got it and put a fence around it and cut the grass, it still would have been a vested interest in the

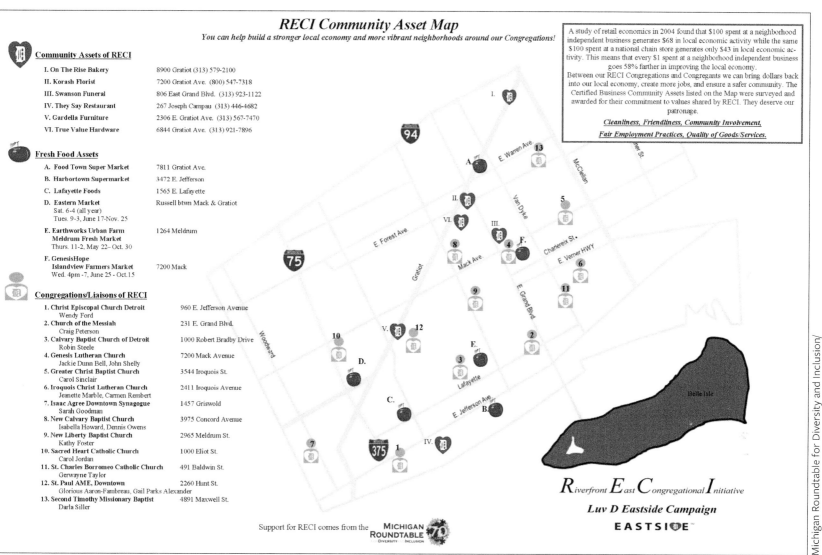

RECI Community Asset Map

You can help build a stronger local economy and more vibrant neighborhoods around our Congregations!

Community Assets of RECI

I. On The Rise Bakery	8900 Gratiot (313) 579-2100	
II. Korash Florist	7200 Gratiot Ave. (800) 547-7318	
III. Swanson Funeral	806 East Grand Blvd. (313) 923-1122	
IV. They Say Restaurant	267 Joseph Campau (313) 446-4682	
V. Gardella Furniture	2306 E. Gratiot Ave. (313) 567-7470	
VI. True Value Hardware	6844 Gratiot Ave. (313) 921-7896	

Fresh Food Assets

A. Food Town Super Market	7811 Gratiot Ave.
B. Harbortown Supermarket	3472 E. Jefferson
C. Lafayette Foods	1565 E. Lafayette
D. Eastern Market	Russell btwn Mack & Gratiot
Sat. 6-4 (all year) Tues. 9-3, June 17-Nov. 25	
E. Earthworks Urban Farm Meldrum Fresh Market	1264 Meldrum
Thurs. 11-2, May 22– Oct. 30	
F. GenesisHope Islandview Farmers Market	7200 Mack
Wed. 4pm -7, June 25 - Oct.15	

Congregations/Liaisons of RECI

1. Christ Episcopal Church Detroit	960 E. Jefferson Avenue
Wendy Ford	
2. Church of the Messiah	231 E. Grand Blvd.
Craig Peterson	
3. Calvary Baptist Church of Detroit	1000 Robert Bradby Drive
Robin Steele	
4. Genesis Lutheran Church	7200 Mack Avenue
Jackie Dunn Bell, John Shelly	
5. Greater Christ Baptist Church	3544 Iroquois St.
Carol Sinclair	
6. Iroquois Christ Lutheran Church	2411 Iroquois Avenue
Jeanette Marble, Carmen Rembert	
7. Isaac Agree Downtown Synagogue	1457 Griswold
Sarah Goodman	
8. New Calvary Baptist Church	3975 Concord Avenue
Isabella Howard, Dennis Owens	
9. New Liberty Baptist Church	2965 Meldrum St.
Kathy Foster	
10. Sacred Heart Catholic Church	1000 Eliot St.
Carol Jordan	
11. St. Charles Borromeo Catholic Church	491 Baldwin St.
Gerwayne Taylor	
12. St. Paul AME, Downtown	2260 Hunt St.
Glorious Aaron-Fambreau, Gail Parks Alexander	
13. Second Timothy Missionary Baptist	4891 Maxwell St.
Darla Siller	

A study of retail economics in 2004 found that $100 spent at a neighborhood independent business generates $68 in local economic activity while the same $100 spent at a national chain store generates only $43 in local economic activity. This means that every $1 spent at a neighborhood independent business goes 58% farther in improving the local economy.

Between our RECI Congregations and Congregants we can bring dollars back into our local economy, create more jobs, and ensure a safer community. The Certified Business Community Assets listed on the Map were surveyed and awarded for their commitment to values shared by RECI. They deserve our patronage.

Cleanliness, Friendliness, Community Involvement, Fair Employment Practices, Quality of Goods/Services.

Riverfront East Congregational Initiative

Luv D Eastside Campaign

EASTSIDE™

Support for RECI comes from the **MICHIGAN ROUNDTABLE** DIVERSITY · INCLUSION

RECI Map of Community Assets

community. As it is now, the people who have bought the land are not even maintaining it. They're not being held accountable. They own it and they're invisible. We have to live with that.

These are men who lived outside the City of Detroit. They have hundreds, and some of them have thousands, of lots that they have bought from the city. Even if they are fined, they don't pay. They're not maintaining the houses, the vacant lots, or anything. It's a big issue.

Kathleen: That's one of my greatest areas of grief, too, along with the foreclosure epidemic. You have, like you said, corporations, the businesses owning land, not paying taxes, not maintaining, but here you have somebody in a house that's struggling to pay and they just can't, but they're doing the best they can and they get thrown out only for that land or that house to become accessible again to another corporation or another business to ignore until things get better and they can make a huge profit off it.

Has RECI been working on any strategies to deal with these issues?

Deborah: Actually tonight we have one of the working groups—it's Education Social Action—and we're organizing an educational forum to help congregants understand the policies and practices that the city has around land use and to hear from folks who have been affected by the different ways land can and cannot be acquired. It's also a forum to educate about some of the development proposals beginning to pop up in our community. We come together and we talk about these things, and we talk about the effect that it will have on our community and is this something that we really want in our community? Do they have our community's best interest at heart?

There's so much that we don't know about these proposals and even after we've invited someone, like Hantz, I know that was frustrating for many of us in the RECI group because we felt there were far more unanswered questions. There is currently no tool of accountability in place to hold these people's feet to the fire about what they say they're going to do.

Jeanette: Another example is our academy-learning days. Every Saturday we learned about another asset. We learned about the Sunday Dinner Company and the great things they were doing for the community.* We learned about folks that were at risk and coming back. We learned about Yusef Shakur and everything he stands for [see interview with Shakur on p. 293]. We went back to our congregations and lifted up these businesses to let them know that if you want the city to come back we have to support these businesses that are giving back to the city. They give back every day, and they do it so humbly—that was one of the things that affected me to keep going with all the things I was going through.

*The Sunday Dinner Company is a family-owned soul food restaurant on Detroit's East Side.

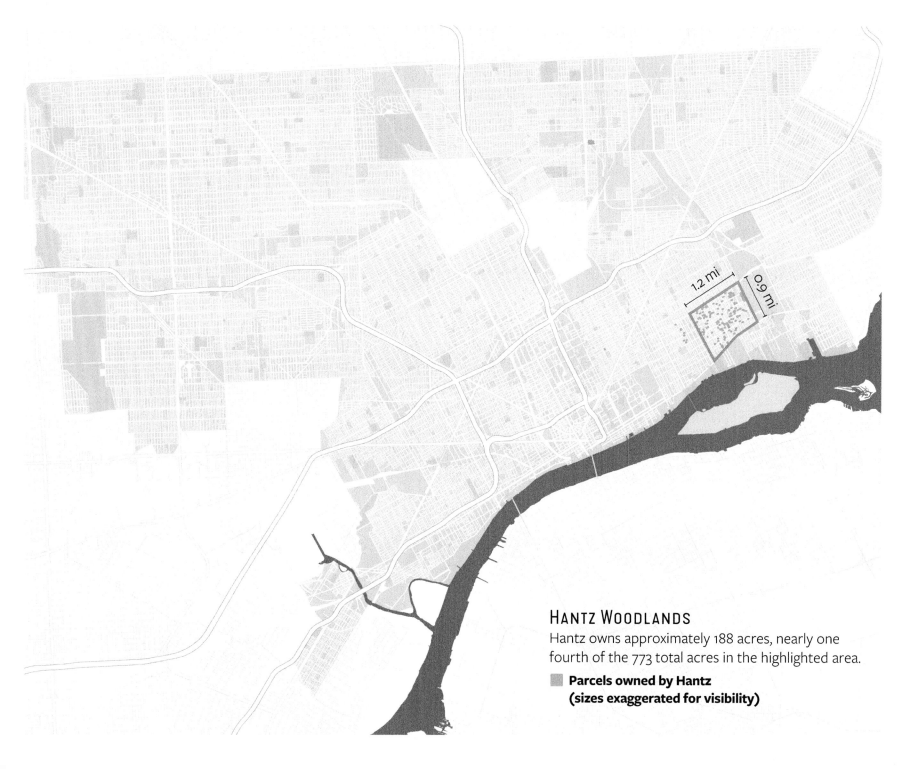

1.2 mi

0.9 mi

Hantz Woodlands

Hantz owns approximately 188 acres, nearly one fourth of the 773 total acres in the highlighted area.

 Parcels owned by Hantz (sizes exaggerated for visibility)

Hantz Woodlands Project

In the twenty-first century, land grabs, or the accumulation of enormous tracts of farmland by large commercial enterprises, are a global issue. Detroiters are now experiencing an urban version of this phenomenon. In 2012, the City of Detroit approved a massive land sale to businessman John Hantz for the construction of a hardwood tree farm after a protracted battle with residents and community activists opposed to the sale, particularly the city's well-organized food justice movement. According to the deal, the city would sell Hantz Woodlands approximately fifteen hundred parcels, or 140 acres, for only $520,000 in an area near the waterfront deemed by the MVA to be a "distressed" market and slated for innovative green production under the DFC plan. In turn, Hantz Woodlands would agree to plant at least fifteen thousand hardwood trees and maintain the landscape on the property. If John Hantz followed the agreement, in four years he would be given right of first refusal to buy all city-owned lots in a one-mile radius of the site. As one city planner put it after the deal was struck, "Hantz could potentially own one-fourteenth of Detroit." Moreover, after four years expired, he would not be bound to tree farming or agrarian production but rather could use the land for any purpose. Hantz Woodlands is an example of the private management of city land that is imagined as both green and good for redevelopment in a city where the government is rolling back services. The map on p. 227 depicts the Hantz Woodlands footprint. The accompanying photos by Gregg Newsom document the surreal experience of having a commercial tree farm on his city block.

Gregg Newsom

Gregg Newsom

TOWARD LAND JUSTICE

"When we stop dreaming, we have no hope but to remain stuck in a nightmare. Dreaming . . . we remember the taste of freedom"

AARON HANDELSMAN

In the fall of 2015 the Detroit People's Platform and the Greater Woodward Community Development Corporation embarked on a bold course of action to establish a community land trust (CLT) in Detroit. As Aaron Handelsman explains below, a CLT is a model based on the cooperative ownership of land, which can allow residents to retain control of their homes despite the threat of displacement.

In this interview, conducted by Sara Safransky, Handelsman, who was then the policy director for the Detroit People's Platform, elaborates on how the model was developed in Detroit and how it fits into a land justice framework. His interview shows the importance of coordinating with translocal organizations, specifically the Right to the City Alliance (RTC),* as well as global activist networks in developing critiques and alternative frameworks for addressing land and housing injustice.

Handelsman also provides a frank assessment of the difficulties of realizing a radical vision based on land justice. He describes working against the "ingrained" importance of individual homeownership in American society and the difficulties of actually forming a CLT, particularly in occupied homes that were assembled from the Wayne County Tax Foreclosure Auction.

What is a community land trust?

A CLT is a legal tool that creates shared ownership of space according to the mission defined in a nonprofit's bylaws. By definition, a CLT is a nonprofit organization (or a program of a nonprofit organization) that is set up to use, hold, develop, and maintain land for some purpose. Often, that purpose is to keep housing permanently affordable by putting limits on resale value. What makes a CLT unique are the particular restraints on how land will be developed, sold, or transferred, and to whom. The way that it looks in practice is varied.

The CLT model invites community members to develop new kinds of relationships between themselves and their land to accomplish shared goals. At the same time, it's high-capacity work that's only as good as the relationships it's built on, and it takes a lot of resources and commitment.

*The Right to the City Alliance is a national alliance of racial, economic, and environmental justice organizations that work in the areas of housing, human rights, urban land, community development, civic engagement, criminal justice, environmental justice, and more.

I understand a CLT recently formed in Detroit. How did you become involved in this work?

The People's Platform began promoting CLTs because we realized that the government, especially under emergency management, was not working for existing residents but planning for their displacement. At the same time, it was incentivizing development and amenities for new residents who were wealthier and whiter. We realized it was not just a matter of organizing to educate decision makers about the needs and aspirations of community; it was that organizing no longer worked in the way that it used to, because the people who are supposed to care about us don't. We wanted a visionary organizing strategy for people who are deeply invested in their communities to mobilize around acquiring and developing land, before it got taken away from them and thus permanently removed from the commons.

The enclosure of the commons is accelerating. We thought CLTs could be a buffer, a way to promote stewardship, permanent affordability, and public access to land that was being taken out of the commons, again not merely as a defensive tool but as a visionary one. We understood that if we could get land now, then we'd have time to decide what it should look like, but if we were spending the majority of our time fighting the profit-driven developments, we would certainly not also be able to plan or implement an alternative vision. At the same time, if we were only planning what we want to do ourselves but not getting any land, then by the time we had our plans drawn up it was going to be too late. The idea was to move on all of these things at the same time. Really modest proposal [*laughs*].

That sounds like an important realization, if a challenging one. How did you go about organizing?

The working group around CLTs started out by doing research. There was a regular group of about fifteen folks who met, and we taught ourselves about CLTs and how they worked. We quickly realized we needed an easy-to-understand explanation of CLTs and examples of how they've been used to accomplish various goals. That would allow folks who were part of the coalition to go out and organize their communities and build momentum around the idea. Over time, the group continued to work on education, think about policy issues, and develop more tools. We also ended up connecting with the Homes for All (HFA) campaign of the Right to the City Alliance (RTC), which asserts that housing is a human right and that we have a right to remain, reclaim, and rebuild the communities we call home. Our connections with HFA and RTC helped provide more of a translocal and international frame on the work and connected us with a lot of other resources and valuable perspectives and partners.

I didn't know what this term *translocal* meant before I joined RTC and HFA. You might understand *trans* and *local*, but what does that mean in this context? I think of it as an evolution of the "national" organizing model that is instead decentralized where there are self-governing local chapters and affiliated organizations all tackling a shared issue (housing/community control of land) with shared goals. The local groups are self-governing, though, and independent, and maintain their own specific local goals and organizing strategies that are tailored to their local context, but we come together to share what we learn across our unique experiences to

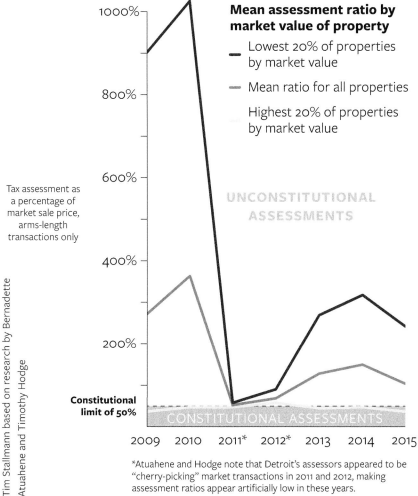

Mean assessment ratio by market value of property

— Lowest 20% of properties by market value

— Mean ratio for all properties

Highest 20% of properties by market value

UNCONSTITUTIONAL ASSESSMENTS

Tax assessment as a percentage of market sale price, arms-length transactions only

Constitutional limit of 50%

CONSTITUTIONAL ASSESSMENTS

2009 2010 2011* 2012* 2013 2014 2015

*Atuahene and Hodge note that Detroit's assessors appeared to be "cherry-picking" market transactions in 2011 and 2012, making assessment ratios appear artificially low in these years.

Tim Stallmann based on research by Bernadette Atuahene and Timothy Hodge

Wayne County Tax Assessments as a Percentage of Market Value, 2008–15

According to researchers Bernadette Atuahene and Timothy Hodge, a shocking number of tax foreclosures in Detroit are illegal. The Michigan state constitution specifies that tax assessments must be less than 50 percent of a property's market value. Atuahene and Hodge found that Detroit's tax assessments routinely violated that rule. The lowest market-valued properties were taxed at assessments higher than their market value (in some years up to 9 times higher), whereas the highest-valued properties were consistently assessed at 40 to 50 percent of their market value. This disparity meant that some of Detroit's lowest-income residents were facing property tax bills that were many times larger than the constitutional limit. As Atuahene and Hodge write, "Detroit residents are being hit twice: not only are their assessed values illegally high, they are then multiplied by one of the nation's highest [tax] rates." Because of these artificially inflated tax bills, scores of Detroiters are losing their homes through tax foreclosure, a process Atuahene and Hodge call stategraft. The illegality of the tax assessment process, combined with the fact that Wayne County foreclosed on approximately one in four Detroit properties for tax reasons, resulted in a staggering scale of displacement.

see what's useful to the whole. We can also support one another's campaigns from afar.

In 2015, after two years of organizing around land justice and CLTs, the Wayne County tax foreclosure crisis began to unfold in a more visible and violent way.* Due to changes in enforcement and several other factors, one hundred thousand residents were suddenly faced with imminent displacement. That crisis put everything in a really different light and created a sense of urgency around taking tangible action. That October, I went to Berlin with a coalition of folks from Right to the City to participate in a convening called Alternative Housing, Alternative Future: A Transatlantic Roundtable, hosted by Rosa Luxemburg Stiftung–New York Office and the RTC. The event brought together people from New York City; Oakland, California; Jackson, Mississippi; and Montreal, as well as European activists from Athens, Barcelona, Berlin, Hamburg, Leeds, Lisbon, and London to talk about best practices for alternative housing and building the commons.

I presented on Detroit. Afterwards, a woman from Greece came up to me and said, "I thought things were bad in Greece with austerity, and it just doesn't even hold a candle to what you're talking about and facing in Detroit." This was right at the time when Greece was all over the international news for the crazy onslaught of austerity. It was really eye-opening for me to have that kind of commentary made.

At the conference, I also became aware of an organizing model from Spain created by the PAH in response to the 2008 recession to mobilize residents. PAH stands for Plataforma de Afectados por la Hipoteca (or Platform for People Affected by Mortgages, in English). I also learned about a co-op/CLT hybrid in Montreal called Milton Parc. Something clicked in my brain and I thought, "Holy cow, if we did all those things in Detroit right now.… It's the moment. We have to act, we have to stop talking about CLTs and we have to make one happen."

This was right in the midst of the annual foreclosure auction. It was midnight in Berlin, but it was only 6 p.m. in the States, so I jumped on the phone and started making calls. Over the course of the next twenty-four hours we basically got everyone to agree to this vision of crowd funding to buy foreclosed, occupied homes at the auction and place them into a land trust. Over the next eight days, we exceeded our goal, raised $108,000, and bought fifteen occupied homes that are now owned by the Storehouse for Hope, which is a 501(c)(3) nonprofit in the process of building out a new set of bylaws for the CLT project.

I followed the campaign from afar. It was amazing how quickly you were able to raise funds.

It was amazing, but in retrospect, this was far from an ideal way to seed a land trust. One, it is a scattered site: the homes are all over the city, which makes organizing and having neighborhood-wide impact more challenging. Second, the process was rushed and contradictions abounded. You want people to have the right to self-determine, but then I'm meeting with folks everywhere who are homeless and/or squatting, or living in homes without water and gas. They are freezing to death in winter. They are having their

---

*Each October, Wayne County, which encompasses Detroit, holds the country's largest tax foreclosure auction. Houses can be sold for as little as $500.

water shut off. You want to build capacity and leadership, but the people who you would ideally do that with—those who are most directly affected—are literally trying to survive the day and might not if something doesn't change immediately. Right now, we are organizing more, but it's slow and it never feels like enough, which is hard.

When we approached people about buying their homes at auction, we were meeting them at a time of emergency without having years to develop trusting relationships, which naturally takes a long time to do given the history of speculators and investors coming in and making promises they don't keep. We only bid on houses whose homeowners went through a process and said yes, but it would be dishonest to say that people had a full understanding of what was going on. The hope is that over time people will be able to buy back their homes for the purchase price, except in cases where they say, "Renting is all I can manage."

Traditionally, we would have just bought the homes and given them back to folks, but the state legislature had just passed a law that made it illegal for any third party to buy the home of a tax-foreclosed person and give it back to them. So any nonprofit that did that risked losing their 501(c)(3) status, which seemed like a high cost.

My ideal vision was that the tenants would become organized and be part of a new model combining aspects of CLTs with aspects of the PAH, where residents would have the support of a collective and pay it forward by becoming leaders for housing justice in their communities. Some are participating in meetings, but some are not responding to the letters or phone calls from Storehouse of Hope. It is going to be a really interesting thing to work out because there is a need to come to an agreement at some point with the tenants about what the future looks like.

Can you talk about what land justice means to you?

Land justice means that existing communities get to decide what development looks like for themselves and their communities. Residents have ownership of community assets and have the final say in deciding what the future of the neighborhood looks like. We believe that land should be decommodified and removed from the speculative market, which would help prevent things like displacement and speculative investment. We think of CLTs or cooperatives as tools to better manage the realities of limited quantity with the inherent value of land as a resource. When we talk about community control, we mean balancing the needs of the individual with the needs of the collective through shared ownership and accountability, shared vision setting and decision-making, not just a seat at the table. Land justice also implies no displacement. We are living in a time when people being displaced to make way for profit is often talked about as a given, and we think that that is insane and unacceptable. If we settle for incremental, status quo changes within systems that were never designed for us to thrive in, who does that serve? When we stop dreaming, we have no hope but to remain stuck in a nightmare. If we won't dream something like the possibility of no displacement (or no white supremacy, patriarchy, etc.), we foreclose on the possibility of real transformation. Having the courage to think beyond what we're told is reasonable. Dreaming beyond a stifling status quo, we remember the taste of freedom.

Can you talk about some of the challenges that stand in the way of realizing this vision of land justice?

One challenge in general is mythological. There is this American myth that landownership is the key to security. When people rely on this "right" to individual landownership, they can never be secure because they will remain unorganized. And yet we're living in a context, and in Detroit in particular, where that myth is really strong because Detroit has such a strong history of single-family homeownership. It was the birthplace of the Black middle class and the middle class in the United States in general. The city never built up, but built out horizontally, so everyone had their own home. That physical and historical reality strengthens the mythology, and it's very difficult to counteract it because it is such an ingrained ideal and value.

But what our recent and not-so-recent history shows us is that there is no such thing as security through individual ownership. It doesn't matter if you own or rent or squat—you can be removed if somebody wants to remove you. Whether it is through predatory lending, redlining, block busting, government malfeasance in assessing and collecting taxes, or just being Black in an area where the city government decides you don't belong anymore and decides to exercise the rights of eminent domain—you can be removed. When communities aren't organized to understand and lean on their interdependence, all members are more vulnerable.

On an educational and ideological level, a second challenge is helping people to see the differences between what they believe to be true and what they might have actually experienced. Right to the City has a really helpful frame. They refer to pretty much everyone as a tenant, including people who "own" their homes. If you own your home and you have a mortgage, then you're just a bank tenant. If you lose your job, then you are likely going to lose your house in three to six months.

A third challenge in terms of achieving land justice is the regional context of spatial racism. Detroit as an entity is seen in a regional context as a toxic and corrupt place that is full of toxic and corrupt people. "If Detroiters are suffering, it's because they deserve it." A lot of that ties in with historical racism and segregation and the fact that Detroit is a majority African American city surrounded by really affluent and really white suburbs. You have this major metropolitan area, which is the heart of the region, but the region hates its heart. It strips it of resources. The state does the same thing, so there is this constant extraction, which creates major structural problems. For example, Wayne County continues to be solvent by cannibalizing Detroit through the property tax foreclosure and auction! If you want to look at why policy and financing and bonding matter so much, there is your answer. You literally have a county destroying its major city because it gets kickbacks when taxes go uncollected.

Fourth, we have neoliberalism and this existential crisis that many places face today. It's nowhere more apparent than in Detroit, where we have these questions, like, "What is a city? What is government? What is development? Whom is it for?" You have this whole entrepreneurial organization of government such that providing basic services is no longer seen as what government is there to do. The role of government has been relegated to using public resources to create opportunities for private profit.

Finally, it's important to acknowledge that nobody has all of the answers right now, but we know the answers will not come by doing business as usual. We need strategic partnerships, alliances, and information sharing to create and implement new visions. We also need to accept that our commitment to our own personal transformation and bold imagination has to be as strong as our analysis of the broken systems and organizations we seek to replace.

"MOST OF THE WORK WE DO IS SYSTEMS CHANGE WORK"

REV. JOAN ROSS

In this interview by Andrew Newman and Sara Safransky, Rev. Joan Ross offers an analysis of development and strategic disinvestment in Detroit, as well as an all-encompassing vision of sustainable community from transit justice to digital justice. Reverend Ross has been a leader in several of Detroit's most important grassroots initiatives, including the movement for a Community Benefits Agreement ordinance in Detroit (see chapter 4) and the Storehouse for Hope Community Land Trust (see the interview with Aaron Handelsman, "Toward Land Justice" on p. 231). Her work with North End Woodward Community Coalition (NEWCC) has been vital for Detroit's transit justice movement (see "The Right to Mobility" on p. 269).

In conjunction with NEWCC, Reverend Ross helped establish a community radio station WNUC 96.7 FM, which "promotes social justice, solidarity, and visionary activism."[6] An important tool for establishing a sense of neighborhood coherence, WNUC broadcasts in Downtown, Midtown, Highland Park, Hamtramck, New Center, and the North End as well as online. The volunteer-run station features local and nationally syndicated content. In addition, NEWCC has joined other communities to provide residents with affordable internet access and implement community ownership of the physical infrastructure of the network itself. Reverend Ross stresses linkages and connections as the basis for systems change and for creating sustainable communities.

Could you describe the North End, the area where you are doing your work?

The North End at one point was the "gravy area" for Detroit. It includes Boston Edison, Arden Park, some of the larger historic kinds of homes. Our strategy aims to sustain families in these beautiful old traditional kinds of homes so that they will be able to afford to stay there.

You could build new homes all you want, but if people can't pay the utilities to stay in those homes, within a couple of years you're going to cycle them into vacant property again.

The North End had a great decline that started happening when the two freeways, the M-10 and I-75, came in on both sides of the community. The people moved to the suburbs. Then these larger homes gave way to becoming group homes or shelter kinds of homes. There was very little regulation on them so the neighborhood began to deteriorate at that point. It became a heavy rental community.

There was also deliberate disinvestment from the North End because it was the next frontier. It has been a strategy to allow certain decay to happen so that it could be called blight. Then they could tear down homes and buy the lots for a dollar, which is very much what has happened over the last few years.

In 2010, we could enter the Wayne County Tax Foreclosure Auction and purchase property in the North End for $300 or $500. Now we can't purchase property in the North End. We have houses now that are listed for $175,000.[7] This is because of the proximity of the North End to Midtown and Downtown.

Back in 2012 and 2013, we tried to buy fifteen lots in the North End. We actually owned the property next to these lots. The city always talked about the Side Lot Program* they had, but they wouldn't sell us the lots. They kept losing the papers, and losing this and that, and saying, "Reapply"—and these are big packages, not simple application forms. So, you wonder: why wouldn't they, when they had this Side Lot Program, why wouldn't they sell me the side lot next to our property? I believe they hold property like that for when they can remove the rest of the houses on the block that are blighted. Then they call it a redevelopment package. You saw the same thing happen in the Cass Corridor. For many years the Ilitch family owned lots of land that was blighted; then all of sudden there was the plan that emerged. [Ilitch's redevelopment plan to build a stadium complex in the Cass Corridor area is illustrated in the Olympia development area map on p. 172.] So I think there is a strategy.

It that why residents formed the NEWCC?

NEWCC originally started off as a transit justice group. We were very concerned about the issues related to what was called the M-1 at the time [now the QLine], the light rail project coming into Detroit and coming into our community. It comes in our neighborhood, but it does not pick up in our neighborhood. NEWCC dared to ask the question of why community isn't involved in development in their neighborhoods. You have to walk out of our neighborhood to board this thing. So we dared to ask, "What color is money? Is it Black and white, or is it green? And why wouldn't you pick up in our neighborhood if the idea is to get passenger ridership on that streetcar project?"

The work of NEWCC began to take on a lot of different forms by necessity. Everything on the planet impacts transit. When they turned the lights off in Detroit, we had people that couldn't get to bus stops in the morning because it was dark, we had kids standing on corners in the dark, so we began to look at how to take charge of some things in our community. We put in our own lights at the time, and we had to put them on private property so they would not belong to the city but would belong to community. We put in solar lights in the various places in our community to aid our children, really, who were standing on dark corners waiting for school buses in the morning.

*This program allows property owners to buy vacant, city-owned lots adjacent to their property for $100.

In addressing transit, you ended up focusing on other issues related to community development. Can you give us another example of the work you've been doing?

NEWCC is part of a group of three neighborhoods that has started our own internet. We are part creating what's called the Equitable Internet Initiative. NEWCC is not really an internet service provider. We purchase access from a local provider who has a gigabit network that we then redistribute. We employ five people from the community who have had extensive training not just in the technology but also in community organizing. This team engages community, handles the installation, and maintains the system. In addition, NEWCC established a community advisory council made up of folks who are on the network as well as other community folks who assist with other aspects of maintaining a community network.

During this past year while we have been installing the network, families have had the service at no cost, but in order to keep the network going and to enable us to expand it, we will have to charge a small fee. We can tier that fee so, for example, businesses might pay slightly more. We also have a system where you can pay $5 more to help somebody who can't afford it. If you can donate this month but not next month or not next year, that's okay. We are asking the community to support its own network. Right now, we have about fifty households in the North End who are receiving the internet through us, and we hope to expand that. With the capability we have we could do up to two thousand households in the North End.

In Detroit, 40 percent of the residents don't have access to the internet. Some of us take it for granted, but today the internet is no longer a luxury but a necessity. Today you can't apply for jobs, you can't apply for benefits, you can't check on anything if you don't have internet access! So I think that's extremely important work that needs to go on because it changes systems, it changes the whole picture. This is part of digital justice. For one community to have access to gigabit technology while other communities have no access to the internet at all is digital injustice.

Most of the work we do is systems change work. We need to create totally sustainable community, not just a piece of work here and a piece of work there.

Could you talk a little bit about your work around community land control and how that's related to systems change and creating sustainable community?

Another side of what we do is the Storehouse of Hope, which operates the only community land trust in the City of Detroit.[8] Community land trusts are operated throughout the country and the world to keep community ownership and to stem gentrification but, more importantly, to provide permanently affordable housing, not just for this generation but the next generation. This land will always belong to community. The house will belong to the person who buys it, but the land belongs to community.

We formed it in 2015 in response to tremendous and unconstitutional tax foreclosures that went on that year, when over forty thousand residents were evicted through tax foreclosure. Our target market is folks who have incomes that are at or below 50 percent of the area median income. Right now, our residents are 30 percent and below area median income. These are folks who are really being priced and pushed out of Detroit. The City of Detroit's view of affordable housing is really folks who are 60 to 80 percent of the area median income. So they really don't have a permanently affordable low-income housing plan at all. If it were not for the land trust and programs like that, folks would be pushed out of Detroit. We created a GoFundMe campaign, and with the help of partners like Building Movement, raised over $108,000 in seven days with the hope of helping some of the families save their homes.

We were successful in purchasing fifteen homes; nine of those families are still in those homes. We are trying to stabilize them. Right now they are under a lease agreement. At the end of four years, they can purchase their homes back; in the meantime we pay the water bill and the taxes and they pay 30 percent of what they can pay from their income. The community land trust is still the only land trust in Detroit. We get no help and no benefits from any foundations or anyone to run any of the programs that we are sustaining, with the exception of our mobile food pantry operations.

NEWCC's commitment to community ownership extends from the land to the airwaves. Can you tell us a little bit about the community radio station?

Through our work over the years, we've found that community does have a voice, but nobody is listening, especially the media. In 2014, we applied to the FCC [Federal Communications Commission] to create and operate our own community radio station. We actually started the first and the only community radio station in Detroit with a full terrestrial signal, 96.7 FM WNUC, which stands for North End Uniting Communities. That station is a completely volunteer platform that operates twenty-four hours a day, seven days a week. We have volunteers that come in and create their own shows. We also pick up a lot of very important nationally syndicated shows on the station.

The station empowers the community with changing the narrative: we create our own narrative. A lot of time reporters come in and write stories about Detroiters, but they themselves are not of Detroit. Through the radio station we create a platform upon which we tell our story. We share the station with communities all over the city. If they are not in our signal area, we are also available online through streaming. We have people from as far away as Colorado, Texas, and Washington, who are listening to the content coming out of Detroit. One of our programs has already been picked up by four other cities in community radio, so we feel we are making a positive contribution to other cities who may be facing some of the same things we go through by sharing our stories of how we overcome things and deal with struggles, and I think that is powerful.

6

THE RIGHT TO THE CITY

The phrase "the right to the city," coined by the philosopher Henri Lefebvre, has become a broad rallying cry for social movements around the world.[1] From Cape Town, South Africa, to Hamburg, Germany, citizens use "the right to the city" to oppose the privatization and enclosure of public spaces, housing, and infrastructures. Right-to-the-city activists use it to fight against gentrification in Montreal and slum clearance in Chennai. In Athens and Madrid, residents call for a right to the city to resist austerity and marshal support for alternative, noncapitalist economic spaces. The number of groups calling for a right to the city underlines important links among many of today's urban movements, but at the same time it suggests a need to specify the usefulness of the concept.

This chapter examines how Detroiters are demanding a right to the city and working to realize a more just society. We begin by asking an important question: What exactly does the right to the city mean? For Lefebvre and those who have subsequently interpreted his work, the right to the city means the right to collectively shape the city and communities in which we live—physically, socially, and politically.[2] Lefebvre developed the concept because he recognized that under capitalism, cities effectively became moneymaking engines that benefited a small elite of developers, financiers, and other private-sector stakeholders while providing no benefit to, or excluding the majority of residents altogether. Geographer Kafui Attoh has clarified the right to the city further by suggesting that it can refer to the right of residents to be included in the "democratic management" of the city in which they live as well as to the moral right to protest and resist laws that exclude residents from this process. As such, the right to the city is about the possibilities of a self-determined urban society free from capitalism, racism, and patriarchy and working to collectively bring about that vision.[3]

This chapter foregrounds the importance of Detroit's long history of Black politics in shaping the right to the city as both a protest demand and a vision for the future. It also underscores how racism is often an underlying force that denies residents their right to the city in the first place. The chapter is organized around five sections that examine everyday acts of resistance and visions for the future according to the following themes:

- the right to water
- the right to environmental justice
- the right to mobility
- the right to education
- the right to live free from crime and police harassment

These themes include far more perspectives than a single chapter can contain. However, by considering them side by side, we hope to convey the all-encompassing ways that Detroiters are reimagining urban activism, and the urgency to do so.

From acts of civil disobedience to the development of community oversight boards, this chapter illuminates the diverse kinds of analysis, strategies, and tactics that residents are using to fight for the right to the city. At the same time, our contributors emphasize how Detroiters' conceptualizations of the right to the city are not simply defensive but rather proactive and visionary. They are engaged in deep thinking about difficult questions: How should water be governed? Who is accountable for clean air and soil? How do we stay safe from crime and police harassment? How do we undo racism? How do we unite around dignity?

We offer contributors' engagements with these questions as an invitation to readers to reflect with us on what it means to develop what Lefebvre called an urban strategy, or a way to rethink and plan what a city can be. As geographer Mark Purcell writes of Lefebvre's vision of urban strategy, "The urban constitutes a revolution, but one that requires millions of everyday acts of resistance and creation."[4] While Detroiters are engaged in urban strategies that vary widely in scale, this chapter highlights the critical importance of neighborhood-based efforts that might seem small scale or fledgling at first glance. We argue that these function as bright spots of political creativity. Combined in the aggregate, they might be read as constellations signaling possible routes for cultural change and social transformation.

This map highlights locations mentioned in the interviews and essays in this chapter.

Renaissance High School

FITZGERALD

Conner Street
Capuchin Soup Kitchen
(DAC meets here)

QLine
Route

Greater Detroit
Resource Recovery Facility (Incinerator)

Urban Network
Cyber Cafe

EMEAC Office
(Cass Commons)

Meldrum Soup Kitchen
(DAC meets here)

St. Leo's Soup Kitchen
(DAC meets here)

Former Site of DAY Project mural
Ford Field

The NOAH Project
(DAC meets here)

Detroit Water and Sewerage Department office

Homrich Wrecking
site of Homrich 9 protest

Joe Louis Arena

OAKWOOD
HEIGHTS

Marathon Petroleum

Air Products

48217

THE RIGHT TO WATER

LINDA CAMPBELL, ANDREW NEWMAN,
SARA SAFRANSKY, AND TIM STALLMANN

Water—and the right to access it—is one of the defining urban issues of the twenty-first century. The fact that Detroit and other Michigan cities (notably Flint) are located so near the Great Lakes while experiencing water crises testifies to these difficulties as politically produced. Activists in Detroit have contested water shutoffs with great effectiveness, often mobilizing around the theme that "water is a commons," to quote contributor James W. Perkinson. Perkinson's essay is a vivid explanation for why he chose civil disobedience as a form of protest. In pointing out that Michigan law "names denial of water to dogs and cats a crime, but codifies no such protection for humans," he provides the moral case for direct action.

When the City of Detroit shuts off water, it creates an immediate threat to the survival of individuals as well as a denial of the right to the city for low-income residents as a group. In this section, two maps illustrate the way race and class profoundly shape who has access to vital water infrastructure. The map produced by We the People of Detroit highlights the disparate impact of water shutoff policy on African Americans; it draws a sharp contrast with Alex Hill's map, which shows the white-owned corporations that have the highest unpaid water bills but that are not faced with shutoffs. To resist water shutoffs is therefore to take a stand against racism and class inequality in one of its most dire forms.

Another contributor, the late Charity Hicks (1967–2014) began organizing Detroiters around the right to water in the 2000s, long before Detroit's water shutoffs received public attention during the bankruptcy. Hicks's analysis of the underlying causes of the water crisis focuses on the racism that has defined African Americans as "expendable" in the eyes of political leaders. In response to this ideology, she offers a political strategy that goes far beyond merely granting Detroiters access to water. In Hicks's vision, water is a site of political convergence. She connects the fight for access to this vital resource with environmental struggles, labor struggles for public sector workers, and social and economic justice in the city more broadly. Additionally, she offers a vision for the city that draws on the "profound resiliency" and "informal networks" of the Black community; she foresees neighborhoods in which people are "rich in relationships." Both Hicks's and Perkinson's visions capture the spirit of the right-to-the-city approach in that they both begin with an apparently singular issue—the right to water—and build a new vision of urban community that asserts the importance of racial justice and the promise of political solutions that have their roots in the experiences and traditions of Black communities.

Race and Water Shutoffs

The Detroit Water and Sewerage Department (DWSD) serves most of the broader Detroit–Wayne metropolitan area, but actual water shutoff policies vary widely depending on municipality. Detroit itself has among the strictest water shutoff policies despite the fact that it is one of the poorest municipalities in which residents struggle to pay their bills. This means that low-income African Americans are punished for not paying water bills while wealthier, predominately white communities in the suburbs experience lenient policies, even though all citizens are connected to the same system.

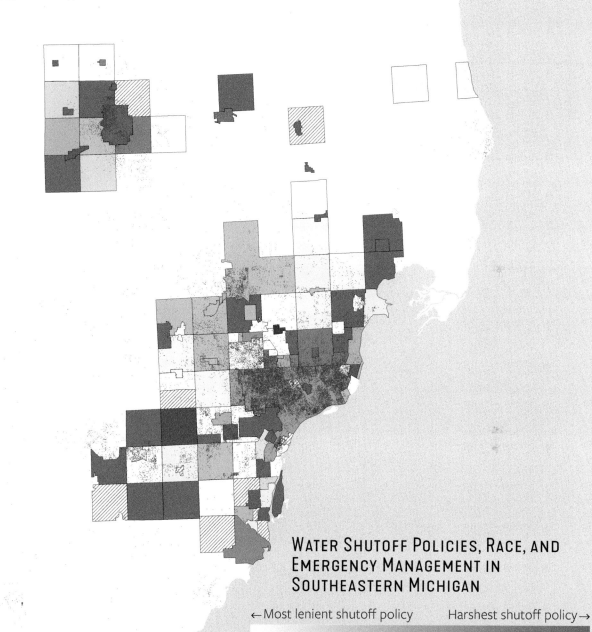

WATER SHUTOFF POLICIES, RACE, AND EMERGENCY MANAGEMENT IN SOUTHEASTERN MICHIGAN

←Most lenient shutoff policy   Harshest shutoff policy→

• Each dot represents the location of 25 Black people

Map by Emily Kutil, We the People of Detroit Research Collective

In response to the mass water shutoffs of 2014, residents held protests
and engaged in civil disobedience.

WHY I CHOOSE TO BLOCK WATER SHUTOFF TRUCKS

JAMES W. PERKINSON

James W. Perkinson is a longtime Detroiter, activist, and scholar of theology. In July 2014, he and eight other protesters were arrested for blocking the trucks of Homrich Wrecking Inc., a private contractor hired to shut off water access to thousands of Detroit residents, earning them the moniker the "Homrich 9." In this op-ed (previously published in 2014 in *Sojourners: Faith in Action for Social Justice*), Perkinson reflects on his decision to engage in civil disobedience, calling attention to the status of water as a "commons," the racist double standards that mark the justification for water shutoffs, the blaming of victims that occurred in media discussions, and the injustice behind the fact that corporate entities were not required to pay delinquent accounts at the same time that low-income Detroiters faced shutoffs.

Water was created by none of us—just like air and earth and fire. It was not made to be enslaved in a market price or bottled into a good yielding ownership and power. Water is a commons, a precious gift given by the creator. But today, water is becoming the subject of war.

Here in the city of "the strait" (*le détroit*) linking two of the Great Lakes that together contain one fifth of the world's fresh water, we now face a cruel irony. By summer's end, half of Detroit's residents may be without access. And most of those are the most vulnerable among us. As the Detroit Water and Sewerage Department (DWSD) initiates a draconian campaign of intensified shutoffs, the anguish mounts. A sudden move to clear the books of ninety million dollars of "bad debt" has resulted in a lucrative deal for Homrich Wrecking Inc., whose trucks roll out of their East Side lot daily to close the taps.

Promised $5.6 million for two years' effort, Homrich aims to cut off water to as many as 150,000 residences by this summer's end alone. Two-thirds of those are households with children, facing family breakup once the flow stops because Michigan law mandates that no child shall be raised in a house without water. Amazingly, Michigan law also names denial of water to dogs and cats a crime, but codifies no such protection for humans. So we now have homes with kids who can't drink, homes with elders who can't bathe, homes with patients unable to change wound dressings. Some of them have been without access for as long as a year now.

But the trucks continue to roll, the water keys turn on the front lawn, the taps run dry. So some of us have resorted to putting our bodies in the way of those trucks. Because news articles and weekly demonstrations in front of the Water Board downtown, letters to authorities and debates on TV, and even a UN complaint, naming the shutoffs a human rights violation, have not succeeded—we have turned to direct action.

SUPPORT THE HOMRICH 9

They took a stand against the inhumane water shut-offs in Detroit by blocking the trucks of the private contractor being paid millions of dollars to torture low-income people. Now they are being prosecuted for "disorderly conduct."

<u>Join them as they tell the court and the world:</u>

WATER IS A HUMAN RIGHT
Monday, December 8, 2014

11:30 Press Conference, Central United Methodist Church, Adams and Woodward
12:30 March to 36th District Court
1:00 Rally at 36th District Court, 421 Madison Ave.
1:30 Pre-trial hearing at 36th District Court

For more information: Detroiters Resisting Emergency Management: d-rem.org

D-REM

Flyer for rally in support of the Homrich 9, a group of protesters who were arrested for blocking the trucks of Homrich Wrecking, the company contracted by DWSD to turn off Detroiters' water mains.

On July 10, 2014, a new front of resistance to this water takeover was opened. The driveway in front of Homrich Inc. became the site of arrests. Ten concerned citizens were doing what they might to increase the decibel level of the demand: *Halt the shutoffs! Restore the service! Engage the Water Affordability Plan long-ago developed to deal with nonpayment and arrearage!*

Much of the vitriol galvanized in reaction to our outcry against the shutoff policy has taken the form of "If you can't pay, you can't play." "Water purification, delivery, and disposal are not free. Period." On a recent national newscast, MSNBC commentator Hank Winchester gave voice to the sentiment so readily evident in mainstream talk about the shutoffs: "Some of these people have a desperate need [for help]," he said. "But there are other people—and this is where it gets controversial—who simply don't want to pay the water bill, who'd rather spend money on cable."

Controversial indeed! But perhaps not the way Winchester intended. The comment carries layers of assumptions. Did Winchester have a single factual story at hand to back up his claim? What we do know is that there *are* corporations that would rather *make* money on cable broadcasts of their events than pay their water bills—such as Joe Louis Arena (home of the Red Wings) or Ford Field (home of the Lions), which owe, respectively, $80,000 and $55,000 to DWSD and which at the time of the national broadcast were not facing shutoffs. When white-owned corporations don't pay, there is no mention of the fact and no rebuke, but if poor people of color struggle with bills, then all manner of stereotype and indignant excoriation come rolling to the surface. The racist disparagement could not be more evident.

But the situation is much more complex than mainstream media typically discusses. Why might a city whose unemployment is near 50 percent, whose history is one of de facto plundering as white populations and corporations took jobs, assets, and taxes to suburbs, whose newspapers were taken over by outside interests in the 1990s, whose houses were subjected to subprime swindles and foreclosures throughout the new millennium, whose banks negotiated fraudulent swaps to transfer public assets and monies to private coffers, whose compromised officials and emergency managers are collaborating with privatizers and lawyers to further jack the city jewels into state and corporate control—why indeed would such a city house so many ordinary folk who struggle to pay bills?

Water is a gift given by the creator. All living beings are its beneficiaries. None of us created it. None of us can produce it in a factory. The fact that it so often now needs cleansing is not primarily because ordinary people have polluted it. The fact that the average Detroit bill is nearly twice the national average is not the fault of neighborhood folk who remain in the city. The fact that its assessment has been increased 119 percent over the last decade and 8.7 percent over recent months is not due to mismanagement in the average household. The fact that over $500 million in bonds raised for infrastructure improvements have been siphoned off to banks making record profits over recent years is not due to decisions made by citizens. The fact that Detroit Future City articulates a plan, long in the making, to triage some city neighborhoods for redesign in the image of the suburb, and that a decade of foreclosures and now "ethnic cleansing by water shutoff" may well serve such plans rather

nicely, is not a vision hatched on inner-city porches. The fact that Emergency Manager Kevyn Orr and the governor are likely eager to clear bad debt from the DWSD books to entice a private investor to buy the system to turn a profit—likely to increase rates threefold—is not a motive much explored in media coverage of the moment. But none of this comes up for discussion when DWSD announces the increased shutoffs and Homrich begins turning the keys.

So, in addition to monitoring a water crisis hotline, canvassing neighborhoods for needs, and then delivering water, some of us have taken to the streets and put our bodies in the way of trucks. Not because we think that alone changes anything. But to give punctuation to the communication: Don't throw brothers and sisters under the bus (or rather, truck)! Given a job loss or other personal financial emergency, the next shutoff could be your own. And then—who would speak for *you*?

Water Shutoffs Timeline

In 2008, Chris Griffith, Aurora Harris, Monica Lewis-Patrick, Cecily McClellan, and Debra Taylor cofounded We the People of Detroit in response to the imposition of emergency management over Detroit Public Schools. The community-based grassroots organization works to educate and empower Detroit residents on issues related to civil rights, land, water, education, and the democratic process.
One of their initiatives has been the We the People of Detroit Research Collective. The collaboration, among activists, researchers, and designers, seeks to produce research with and for Detroit residents. In 2014, the group began generating important maps and graphics related to the water shutoffs in Detroit and emergency management across Michigan. The following two pages feature an excerpt from their report, Mapping the Water Crisis, designed by Emily Kutil and used with permission.

Water Shutoffs, Emergency Management, and Community Resistance: January 2010–October 2015

Since 2013, the City of Detroit has shut off water to tens of thousands of its residents. The following graph places the mass water shutoffs in context with Emergency Management, Detroit's bankruptcy, the removal of the City of Flint from Detroit's water system, and the creation of the Great Lakes Water Authority. The graph also indicates periods during which city water shutoffs declined, possibly in response to widescale popular resistance in the forms of civil disobedience, demonstrations, and media protests, or the interventions of powerful organizations such as the United Nations.

Resistance to the mass water shutoffs has also taken the form of legal and legislative action. The *Lyda et al. v. City of Detroit* lawsuit was brought in July 2014 by ten Detroit families experiencing water shutoffs; with legal claims based on constitutional due process, equal protection, health and safety, public trust, and the human right to water. The parties also requested a temporary restraining order against water shutoffs. While all lawsuits against the City of Detroit were stayed for the duration of the bankruptcy proceedings, Judge Stephen Rhodes allowed the lawsuit to go through.

Hearings were held in front of Judge Rhodes in bankruptcy court. After two days of testimony, Judge Rhodes determined that, despite irreparable harm caused to families by water shutoffs, he would not issue an order to permanently halt the shutoffs. Rhodes cited the revenue losses the city might incur, which would in turn hinder the pending regionalization deal. Rhodes concluded that access to water is not a right.

In December 2015, the Michigan Water as a Human Right Bill Package was introduced in the Michigan House. Representatives Chang, Garrett, Neeley, and the late Plawecki collaborated with a national team of lawyers and water rights advocates, including Alice Jennings, a lead counsel on the Lyda et al. case. The bills proposed include a water affordability measure that bases water bills on household incomes, and includes shutoff protections for seniors, children, and people with disabilities.

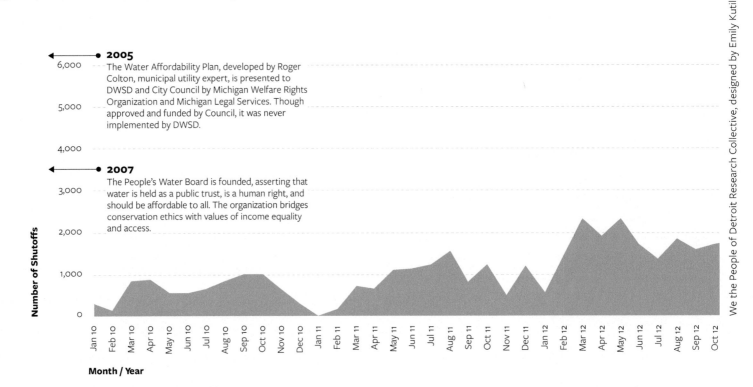

2005
The Water Affordability Plan, developed by Roger Colton, municipal utility expert, is presented to DWSD and City Council by Michigan Welfare Rights Organization and Michigan Legal Services. Though approved and funded by Council, it was never implemented by DWSD.

2007
The People's Water Board is founded, asserting that water is held as a public trust, is a human right, and should be affordable to all. The organization bridges conservation ethics with values of income equality and access.

Number of Shutoffs

Month / Year

We the People of Detroit Research Collective, designed by Emily Kutil

March 2013
The City of Detroit is placed under the control of Kevyn Orr, a state-appointed Emergency Manager.

July 2013
Kevyn Orr declares bankruptcy on behalf of the City of Detroit.

Detroiters Resisting Emergency Management joins with People's Platform in a forum on Emergency Management. Undertaking a variety of resistance actions and conferences, D-REM advances the water struggle though media work, providing statements, analyses, accessible documents, and popular editorials.

May 15, 2014
Charity Hicks, food, water, and environmental activist, is arrested for resisting the shutoff of her neighbors' water.

April 2014
Detroit enters into a two-year, $5.6 million contract with Homrich, Inc., a demolition company, to shut off water from citizens who are either 45 days late or over $150 delinquent on their water bills.

The City of Flint is removed from DWSD's system and begins drawing water from the Flint River. The loss of Flint as a customer contributes to DWSD's financial precarity and to the replacement of DWSD with the Great Lakes Water Authority.

July 2014
We the People begins Water Hotline and water deliveries, becoming a primary organizing force.

Activists block water shutoff trucks at the Homrich contractor's facility for seven hours as police and media look on. Nine people are arrested, though Baxter Jones, wheelchaired disability activist, is never charged.

The Netroots Nation conference in downtown Detroit occasions a mass march for water affordability and to stop the shutoffs.

The *Lyda et al v. City of Detroit* lawsuit is brought by ten Detroit families experiencing water shutoffs.

July 21–August 25, 2014
The City of Detroit institutes a temporary moratorium on water shutoffs after activists draw national media attention.

September 2014
The Great Lakes Water Authority is formed.

October 17–20, 2014
United Nations Special Rapporteurs for Water and Housing visit Detroit and accuse the city of human rights violations.

July 3–10, 2015
Activists walk 70 miles from Detroit to Flint, connecting Detroit shutoffs to the poisoning of Flint water.

Nov 12 | Dec 12 | Jan 13 | Feb 13 | Mar 13 | Apr 13 | May 13 | Jun 13 | Jul 13 | Aug 13 | Sep 13 | Oct 13 | Nov 13 | Dec 13 | Jan 14 | Feb 14 | Mar 14 | Apr 14 | May 14 | Jun 14 | Jul 14 | Aug 14 | Sep 14 | Oct 14 | Nov 14 | Dec 14 | Jan 15 | Feb 15 | Mar 15 | Apr 15 | May 15 | Jun 15 | Jul 15 | Aug 15 | Sep 15 | Oct 15

EMERGENCY MANAGEMENT

"HOW DO WE UNITE AROUND DIGNITY?"

CHARITY HICKS

Charity Hicks (1967–2014) was a lifelong Detroiter and a leader of the People's Water Board. Hicks worked tirelessly for the rights of Detroiters to access affordable water for years before the issue entered the global spotlight in 2014. This interview, which was conducted in 2012 before the mass water shutoffs, shows how Hicks's framing of the issue went far beyond access to water alone. She connects water to environmental justice, governance, and the sustenance of healthy, civic-minded communities centered on the principles of the commons. In March 2014, Hicks was arrested and detained overnight for speaking out against the Detroit Water and Sewerage Department shutting off her neighbors' water access because they couldn't afford their bills. Just four months later, during the peak of Detroit's mass water shutoffs, she tragically lost her life. Charity Hicks was forty-seven years old. This interview was conducted by Linda Campbell and Isra El-beshir as part of the Uniting Detroiters project.

I know that some of your public work has very much focused on one of the most valuable resources we have here in Detroit—water. Can you talk about the People's Water Board and your involvement?

The board started in 2008, but ideas about it were swirling from 2003 to 2004. For the past decade [prior to 2012], there has been an overwhelming amount of water meter shutoffs. And in Detroit, actually throughout the region, there were profound issues of pollution. Every time it rained or we had a wet weather event, the wastewater treatment plant and the whole system would dump partially treated, or even raw sewage, into the Rouge River and the Detroit River.

The People's Water Board was crafted to shadow the municipal water board [the Detroit Water and Sewerage Department's Board of Water Commissioners], which served at the pleasure of the mayor. It emerged from the conversion of a number of things. One, Michigan Welfare Rights was fighting for a water access plan called the Detroit Water Affordability Plan. They were protesting the unbelievable amount that water costs—it is a human rights issue to not be able to wash clothes, brush your teeth, cook, flush your toilet. They were fighting for everybody to pay something for the public water system and for affordability. Two, the unions that work for the water department were fighting for their jobs. They were like, "We are civil servants. We are skilled. The people pay us to maintain the infrastructure and to deliver water and treat water and we have a right to that under the city charter and under this municipal enterprise." And three, the environmentalist community, which was led by the Sierra Club, was livid at the pollution and the raw sewage that was going into the lakes and streams.

Water became a common ground. Labor jumped in it, social justice and economic justice jumped in it, and ecological and environmental justice jumped in it. It was a realization that water was important.

Can you talk about what impact the People's Water Board has had in and around Detroit?

We do have some wins. We got the municipal water board to start publishing their minutes on the website. We are still working on providing video of the meetings for public access. For the past three years, we have shadowed every municipal water board meeting. We protest or we call awareness to shutoffs. We have stenciled storm drains [as a public reminder that litter and pollutants that enter storm drains end up in the waterway]. We have held a water film series in public libraries, showing, for example, *Blue Gold, Water Wars, A Flow*, and *A World without Water*.

We do a lot of education. We talk about water. We talk about invasive species. We talk about the combined sewer system and the need for improvements in the infrastructure. Detroit's water system is over a hundred years old. You can imagine the type of fittings and upgrades needed. The need for investment in that infrastructure is now. Every time I pass a water main break, I cringe. The first thing I think about is the people who do not have water. The system is so old that it does break and you have to build regular maintenance and repair into your cost. But I also think about

the water that is lost from the break, particularly in relationship to people who have had their water shut off.

I think what we see in Detroit is some profound level of benign and even malicious neglect by those with power. And if you really wanted to affirm a community, you will see people as assets to be invested in and to be strengthened. You cannot see people as a determent. You cannot see people as "those people," "other people," "poor people," because the question is, particularly from my anti-racism training, Why are people poor? That is the question we need to ask ourselves: Why are people poor? Nobody wakes up and says, "I will not have anything to eat. I won't have shelter. I think I will be homeless." You gotta know that somebody wants something better for themselves, and so my question is, Why are people poor? Why are they? Why are people poor?

In thinking about Detroit and the conditions that we see in our city, how would you describe your vision?

On one level, I relish the Black community because I think there is a profound resiliency that is operating here that is kind of reminiscent of plantation life. The economic order just marginalizes you. On the plantation, we were property and we were worth something. As long as we were making money for somebody—an industrialist, a capitalist—we were skilled labor, or just labor, we were worth something. But now it is like we are not worth anything, we are expendable. I don't think we really see the beauty in ourselves because we don't see that resiliency—that in the face of all odds, having a job or not having a job, in the face of this racialized region, it is like we are still here and some of us are even thriving, but I think the majority of us are in survival mode. We are paycheck to paycheck, hand to mouth. We rob Peter to pay Paul, all the chatter. And it builds a sense of anxiety, high blood pressure, frustration, and still we move through.

If we were to look at creating new community, what would the work look like moving forward? What would our neighborhoods look like?

We definitely should be able to borrow sugar from each other and a few eggs. Somebody will be cooking and take some meals up the road. We definitely would have relationships. I go straight to the lived experience because we oftentimes speak in flowery words and we go too academic, but we need to go kitchen table. We need to go bread and butter, to the lived experience of Detroiters. In a new framework, we would be rich in relationships. One of the most profound things about the Black community is our informal networks. We live literally in overlapping relationships. We would be in these networks. They would be elastic and we would be wealthy.

Let's expand a little bit on your notion of civic mindedness. As you know, very recently, the Michigan legislature passed an unprecedented law, Public Act 4. How do you think a consent decree or emergency management would impact your work, particularly with the People's Water Board?

I think it is going to further increase shutoffs. I think that it is going to make it harder for us to engage people in a dialogue. The con-

sent decree would actually destroy our ability to have that dialogue on the commons, which is our water. There will be resistance and pushback. We are promoting ecological citizenship. We can continue, but the leverage point has been that we own this system, it is ours, so let us be skillful in the operation and dialogue of it.

Do you think opportunities exist to create a good governance structure in Detroit?

Yes, I really do. I am an optimist. I really believe we can bring the "we" space back. We can re-create civic mindedness. We really can take the opportunity to ask questions about how we want to live and begin to create the kind of awareness of how we govern, how we hold our public institutions and the people that are inside of them—whether they are elected, appointed, or civil servants—accountable to operating in our interests.

I think Detroiters really should unite around the restoration of dignity. We have destroyed dignity by impoverishing people and shaming them at the same time. It is like blaming the victim. We've got thousands of families that have been taken off cash assistance. The whole safety net is unraveled. How do we unite around dignity? What is the moral imperative around how we unite around each other? Where is our dignity?

CHARITY HICKS: IN MEMORIAM

LINDA CAMPBELL, ANDREW NEWMAN, SARA SAFRANSKY, AND TIM STALLMANN

n July 2014, at the height of the water crisis in Detroit, Charity Hicks traveled to New York City where she was scheduled to speak on a panel titled "Land and Ocean Grabs: The Need for Solidarity across Geography and with Academia" at the Left Forum. While waiting for a bus near Penn Station to travel to the conference, she became the victim of a hit-and-run. After lying in a coma for three months, she made her transition. Hicks was known for her energy, humor, strength, and commitment to struggles for a better world. Earlier in 2014, she traveled to Brazil as part of a delegation of fifteen representatives from US social and political organizations. They attended the MST (Movimento dos Trabalhadores Rurais Sem Terra; Landless Workers Movement) Congress to learn about the movement in Brazil, with the aim of strengthening domestic social justice movements. Upon learning of Hicks's death, the MST issued a moving statement that we quote in part here:

> Charity left us the seeds of her dreams and ideals. The seeds of the struggle for a better world, where the land is in the hands of the people who live and work it; where water and all natural resources are a heritage of peoples;

ACCESS TO WATER IS A HUMAN RIGHT

Charity Hicks 1967-2014

WAGE LOVE

Juan Martinez

This memorial image was created by Juan Martinez in memory of Charity Hicks, who issued a call to "wage love" in response to the mass water shutoffs in 2014, before her tragic death.

> where there is healthy food for all people; where there are no exploiters or exploited.
>
> We now have the duty of watering that seed of struggle. Grow it, care for it. In each mobilization; in each march; in each land occupation; in every struggle; the seed and the presence of Charity will be with us.[5]

THE RIGHT TO ENVIRONMENTAL JUSTICE

LINDA CAMPBELL, ANDREW NEWMAN,
SARA SAFRANSKY, AND TIM STALLMANN

n Detroit, as in many other American cities, the final decades of the twentieth century saw the rise of the environmental justice movement, which sought to address the ways that environmental contamination disproportionately impacted communities of color. This section includes interviews with Rhonda Anderson and Vincent Martin, who have organized some of Detroit's most visible and successful environmental justice campaigns. They have long represented communities that live in the shadow of the Marathon Oil refinery and other industries in Southwest Detroit and adjoining communities. As a result of their work, the 48217 zip code has become synonymous with grassroots-led organizing against polluters. But as Anderson and Martin make clear, environmental justice is about more than combating environmental racism. It requires that we "reimagine ourselves" at a broad level, through self-education, telling our own stories, and reorganizing the economic realm by replacing polluting industries and creating new kinds of work.

This all-encompassing vision also characterizes the thinking of William Copeland, climate justice director of East Michigan Environmental Action Council. Copeland discusses the importance of education and youth organizing—"planting seeds," as he puts it, for environmental justice in the decades that lie ahead. For Copeland, education involves a focus on environmental issues, making sure young people develop an awareness of the history and politics that have shaped Detroit, and, of course, skills for jobs.

An essay by environmental historian Josiah Rector, which probes the underlying causes of environmental racism, follows the interviews. He examines how the construction of the Greater Detroit Resource Recovery facility just east of Midtown Detroit, which was the world's largest garbage incinerator when it was built, is closely intertwined with the city's dire fiscal situation since the 1970s. The facility is responsible for the discharge of lead and mercury into the air, as well as the discharge of a hundred thousand automobiles' worth of carbon dioxide emissions each year. In addition to being a source of local and global climate damage, the incinerator was financed by municipal bonds that would ultimately saddle Detroiters with $1.2 billion in debt. In his account of the movements that have arisen to contest the incinerator, Rector, like all the contributors, makes it clear that the path to environmental justice is closely tied to the capacity to economically and socially reimagine what a city is and for whom it is ultimately built to serve.

"WE MUST BE THE VOICE THAT SAYS WHAT THE CHANGE IS GOING TO BE IN OUR OWN COMMUNITIES"

RHONDA ANDERSON AND VINCENT MARTIN

Located near heavy industry and, in particular, the Marathon Oil refinery, residents of the 48217 zip code in Southwest Detroit have been at the front lines of environmental justice struggles in Michigan. Thanks in no small part to years of effort by Rhonda Anderson and Vincent Martin, these are among the city's most politically well-organized communities. Martin, who lives in Southwest Detroit and works for Human Synergy Works, has been organizing around environmental justice issues for decades. Rhonda Anderson is a Sierra Club organizer and community advocate. She is a recipient of the Virginia Ferguson Award

(presented for exemplary service with the Sierra Club) and was named by the *Michigan Chronicle* as "One of the 10 Voices of Change for 2007." In this interview, Anderson and Martin discuss the relationship between segregation and environmental racism, and their visions for more environmentally and socially just futures. This interview was conducted by Linda Campbell as part of the Uniting Detroiters project. Bolded locations are shown in the accompanying map.

VINCENT: Out of the twenty-seven industrial entities in Detroit proper, the 48217 zip code is home to thirteen of them. We have a situation out there because of the EPA [Environmental Protection Agency] regulations. Companies can pollute a certain amount. That means we've got thirteen different agencies polluting a certain amount, which is overburdening the community.

There's one major project that's going on—**Marathon Oil**. In 2007, Marathon announced that they were going to do a $2.2 billion expansion of the only oil refinery in all of the state of Michigan. It happens to be in 48217.

Oakwood Heights bordered the expansion area. It is a historically Italian community, but in more recent years a number of Latino families have moved into the area as older Italians have moved out. A study just came out that we have the highest rate of cancer—bronchial lung cancer—in Michigan. One of the worst effects of pollution is on cognitive learning for kids under six years old.

When Marathon was going to help build a play-scape on the old **Jeffries School** site, they went in and dug it up. The dirt was red. It was contaminated with arsenic. This is dirt on which we played football, baseball, went to school on, ate lunches on. The sad part about the area is it is still like that. They didn't come and mitigate after they found it. They just covered it up and put a fence around it with a sign that says, "You can use this no longer. It's contaminated."

We've been going to the city trying to get support, but we don't see the political will from the City of Detroit. They're putting us up against a wall where we may want to secede from the city and go back to what we were before we became Detroit. We were called the Ecorse Township, River Rouge. Ecorse was all one township. That way, the tax base that's around here would stop going downtown and go to our community. Then we could start building our community. I think you'd see a major difference.

RHONDA: The Sierra Club has a major campaign to close down existing coal-powered plants. There are four coal-powered plants along the Detroit River. One is in River Rouge. There's another one—a municipal coal-powered plant—in Wyandotte. There's one in Trenton and then there's one in Monroe. From our involvement we've heard from DTE itself that they're seriously looking at closing down one of these power plants, or they could transfer from coal, which is the dirtiest form, to natural gas, which is another risky situation. But in our campaign to close these coal-power plants, one of the things that we've had to admit to ourselves is, okay, you erase that tax base from that community, then what do you put in its place? That's where the whole reimagining comes in place. How can you assist a community in reimagining themselves? What do they see there?

VINCENT: It's kind of hard to reimagine ourselves at the same time we're having more pollution. They're going to start processing heavy tar-sand oil. We don't know how that's going to affect our community over time for the next ten, fifteen, twenty years.

We also got another nemesis in our area—a new hydrogen plant called **Air Products** that came in under the Marathon permit. One of the issues is that we've got so many underground pipelines going through Southwest Detroit, Ecorse, River Rouge. There is so much interstate commerce that I'm afraid it's getting to the point where it could be a very volatile situation. A hydrogen explosion would have devastating effects. It would wipe out Southeast Michigan, period, because our pipeline goes all the way through Wayne County.

Again and again, they use our properties to do interstate commerce. Why are the people being taxed if the city is already getting tax dollars from the commerce? It's exploitation of poor people.

I think we need to move toward a process where we have empowered communities. The community needs to be put in the forefront with the decision-making process. Right now, the money is going backward. It's going to these agencies and they've got the community hostage after they get the dollars. I think if we did it the other way around, it would bring more accountability and more transparency.

RHONDA: I think the answer lies with us—that is, for us to learn and educate ourselves, to speak out for ourselves, and not think always that someone is going to come in and save us. We can only save ourselves. That means that we have to self-educate. Projects like you're doing right now—to help people to tell their own stories

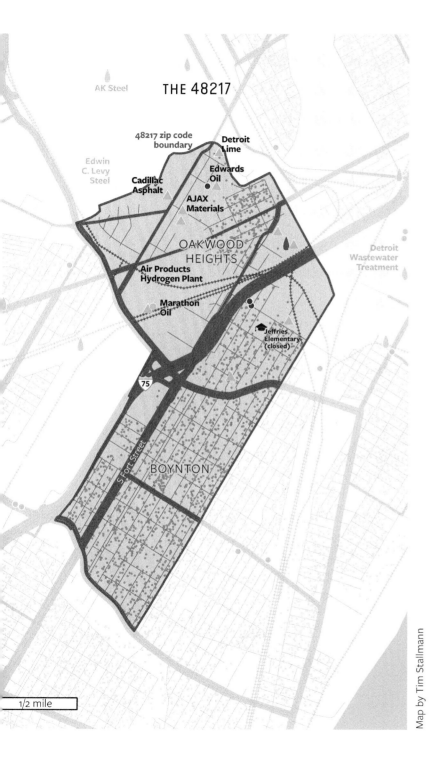

THE 48217

AK Steel

48217 zip code boundary

Detroit Lime

Edwin C. Levy Steel

Edwards Oil

Cadillac Asphalt

AJAX Materials

OAKWOOD HEIGHTS

Detroit Wastewater Treatment

Air Products Hydrogen Plant

Marathon Oil

Jeffries Elementary (closed)

[75]

S Fort Street

BOYNTON

1/2 mile

so that people can see that the answer lies within themselves. It's not coming from the city administration, the city council, or any of those guys. They're not here to do it. They can help us, but they are not here to do it. We must be the voice that says what the change is going to be in our own communities.

Pollution Sites

▲ Air pollution site

● Hazardous waste site

● Brownfield or superfund site

🜄 Water pollution site

Average Daily Traffic

—— < 3,000 vehicles

━━ 3,001–6,000 vehicles

━━ 6,001–12,000 vehicles

━━ 12,001–24,000 vehicles

━━ 24,001–118,965 vehicles

Population

⠿ Each dot represents 5 people

"FROM THE ORGANIZATION OF YOUTH, WE ARE TRYING TO LAY A FOUNDATION"

WILLIAM COPELAND

William Copeland is an artist and organizer from Detroit. At the time of this interview in 2012, Copeland served as the Youth Coordinator for the East Michigan Environmental Action Council (EMEAC). He is now EMEAC's climate justice director. EMEAC was founded in 1972 in response to a number of environmental concerns that were plaguing Southeast Michigan, including algae blooms in the Great Lakes and inland water, household and industrial waste, and air pollution. As Copeland shares below, when EMEAC moved from the suburbs to the city, it also shifted its focus to fighting for the right of Detroiters to live in a city free of contaminated air, water, and soil. In this interview, Copeland talks about the importance of engaging young people in political education to ground them in a sense of the world and also to lay the foundation for the future development of the environmental justice movement. For Copeland, addressing environmental racism means drawing a connection between pollution in Detroit and the extrajudicial killings of Black and Brown people in order to show the broad-based need for social justice movements. Isra El-beshir conducted this interview as part of the Uniting Detroiters project.

What kind of work does EMEAC do?

EMEAC is an environmental justice organization. It does a variety of work in the city to fight against pollution and environmental degradation. If you look statistically and geographically, you will see that those issues are more concentrated in communities of color than in white communities, even keeping income and other factors the same.

How has EMEAC changed over time?

There have been three major changes. EMEAC used to be more of an environmental organization. The office was in the suburbs. The organization did a lot with sprawl and wetlands, traditional types of environmental issues. When Diana Copeland became the director, she moved the office into Detroit, and EMEAC began working on environmental justice. It is a forty-five-year-old organization, and those changes took place in the last six or seven years. More recently, EMEAC was an anchor organization during the 2010 US Social Forum that was held in Detroit, and took a big leadership position then that we are continuing still.* The third change is the formation of the Young Educators Alliance, which is our youth group. A lot of young people are now involved in EMEAC.

I started working with EMEAC after the US Social Forum, which took place in summer 2010. The event brought twenty thousand to twenty-five thousand people to Detroit. EMEAC was one of the four local host organizations. I was one of the local coordinators. One of the aspects that I worked with was the youth. There were a couple of youth organizers who were working nationwide to gather youth and let them know about the Social Forum. When it came to getting the word out in Detroit, there were a number of challenges that we faced. Youth organizing was at a very low level in the City of Detroit.

By contrast, the City of Boston brought two hundred young people to the US Social Forum. Just youth. They had buses—they did a whole youth caravan with two hundred young people. Those were just the ones that could make the trip! If they had two hundred that could make the trip, how many more couldn't make the trip? That just goes to show how established youth organizing is in other cities.

Learning about these things, I started talking to my wife and other people in EMEAC about how we could contribute to youth organizing in Detroit. One of the things that I noticed was that in Detroit you have a lot of youth programs, but in many cases the adults are speaking for the youth. In many cases, there will be a presentation and the adults will say, "Well, this is our youth, this is

this person, this is that person, this is why we were founded, this is this and this is that," and maybe the youth will sing or do one small part of the action, but the adults are the conduits. They are the go-between. The adults are in many ways the activists and the organizers. And so, we saw that as an obstacle. We wanted to bring a different approach that would allow the youth to develop and speak for themselves, represent themselves, and make their own decisions.

What are some of the impacts of your work?

From the organization of youth, we are trying to lay a foundation. We are trying to think about it ten years down the line—that there are going to be more organizers. Many will be here, but some might move to other places. As the elders get older and older, we need to make sure that there continues to be people to take over the organization. We are planting the seeds so that a few years from now there are more fifteen-, sixteen-, eighteen-year-olds who are in the media, who are at the protests, who are organizing the protests, who are working with adults, who are working side by side. There will be sixteen-, eighteen-, twenty-, twenty-three-, twenty-five-year-olds. If you look at history, for example, if you look at the Black Panthers, it was founded by very young people. Young people have a certain energy. Young people, especially when they understand the situation is messed up, they'll take it to a whole 'nother level. They will do things that parents would be too scared to do. They'll really elevate those situations. I think that that's the hope.

We hope that any listeners [or readers] who are teenagers or have teenage children go to our website [www.emeac.org] and

*In 2001, tens of thousands of activists gathered for the first World Social Forum in Porto Alegre, Brazil, to protest the kinds of globalization promoted by the World Economic Forum. The forum's slogan is "Another World Is Possible." The first US Social Forum was held in Atlanta, Georgia, in 2007. The second took place in Detroit in 2010.

check us out. They should join our work because right now... look at the killing of Trayvon Martin.* For every young person, young person of color, you need to have social awareness. We don't have the luxury of being in this society and not having awareness.

For instance, with the younger people, we've had discussions: "Are people in Detroit lazy? Does Detroit have abandoned buildings and buildings that are falling apart because Black people and Detroiters are lazy?" Some people have that perception. You know, they don't know the social history. They don't know the economic history. They are young. Maybe their parents said, "Oh, their house looks like that because they are too lazy to upkeep it." You hear different things like that—and so we are raising young people and empowering young people who can speak, who can represent their own views, who can form their own opinions, who can work with each other, stand up for themselves. On a practical level, those are skills that will help for jobs. They will help for college. They will help for things like that, but really they will also help young people make sense of the world and be empowered to make changes in the world.

*Trayvon Martin, an African American teenager, was walking back to a family member's house in a suburban, gated community in Sanford, Florida, on February 26, 2012, after buying Skittles at a convenience store, when he was shot and killed by a Neighborhood Watch member who claimed Martin looked suspicious. Martin's murder, and the subsequent trial at which the Neighborhood Watch member was acquitted, was one of several extrajudicial killings of Black people in the mid-2010s that sparked youth outrage and galvanized the Black Lives Matter movement.

TOXIC DEBT

The Detroit Incinerator, Municipal Bonds, and Environmental Racism

JOSIAH RECTOR

In the mid-1970s, Detroit was running out of landfills for trash, and the energy crisis was pushing up the costs of disposing of trash elsewhere. Mayor Coleman Young and officials in his Department of Public Works bought the sales pitch of the incinerator industry, which presented local governments with "waste-to-energy" incineration technology as a solution to the energy crisis. Despite the space-age name, the technology was simple: trash burners that produced electricity with steam. Despite widespread protest, city officials made plans to build what would be, when it opened in 1989, the world's largest trash incinerator, the Greater Detroit Resource Recovery facility.[6] In this short essay, Josiah Rector, a US and environmental historian, shares an untold story about the incinerator that is critical to understanding Detroit's economic crisis: he exposes the close link among air pollution, Wall Street bond traders, and mounting debt that paved the way for bankruptcy.

In 1991, the City of Detroit faced an $88 million budget short-fall. To fill the gap, Mayor Coleman Young and the Detroit City Council announced plans to sell the Greater Detroit Resource Recovery facility to Philip Morris, USA, and General Electric for $54 million. The facility, located at the intersection of Russell and Ferry Streets, was the world's largest municipal trash incinerator at the time; it had started burning two years earlier despite relentless protests and lawsuits by a coalition of environmental activists called the Evergreen Alliance. Under the deal, which lasted from 1991 to 2008, Philip Morris owned 70 percent of the facility; General Electric owned 30 percent. In addition, Philip Morris received $200 million in federal tax breaks for buying the facility, under an obscure loophole for "waste-to-energy" facilities in the Reagan Administration's 1986 Tax Reform Act. At the time, Philip Morris was the world's largest cigarette company, with a market capitalization of $68 billion. The deal benefited the firm's shareholders, including Bloomfield Hills billionaire Roger Penske, who sat on the boards of both Philip Morris and General Electric while they owned the incinerator.[7]

Perhaps it was fitting that a corporation known for cancer-causing products owned the Detroit incinerator for seventeen years. In 1986—the year that construction began on the incinerator—the Michigan Department of Natural Resources announced that the incinerator's release of dioxin could cause up to thirty-six cancer deaths for every one million metro Detroiters. Dioxins are highly toxic cancer-causing chemicals that damage the immune system and disrupt hormones. In 1990, after tests found its dioxin levels were one thousand times the legal Environmental

Kate Levy

Asthma Hospitalization Rates per 10,000 people (by zip code)

fewer than 15 cases

———————— *Michigan state-wide avg.*

16 - 25 cases

26 - 50 cases

51 - 60 cases

over 60 cases

Map by Tim Stallmann

The Detroit incinerator was a significant source of air pollution located in the heart of the city. The finances surrounding it also contributed to the city's municipal bankruptcy.

Asthma Rates and Polluters

This map shows the wide distribution of air pollution sources throughout the metropolitan region. Hospitalization rates due to asthma are markedly higher in central Detroit than in the rest of the area, underlying varying degrees of environmental suffering that exist between the city and the suburbs.

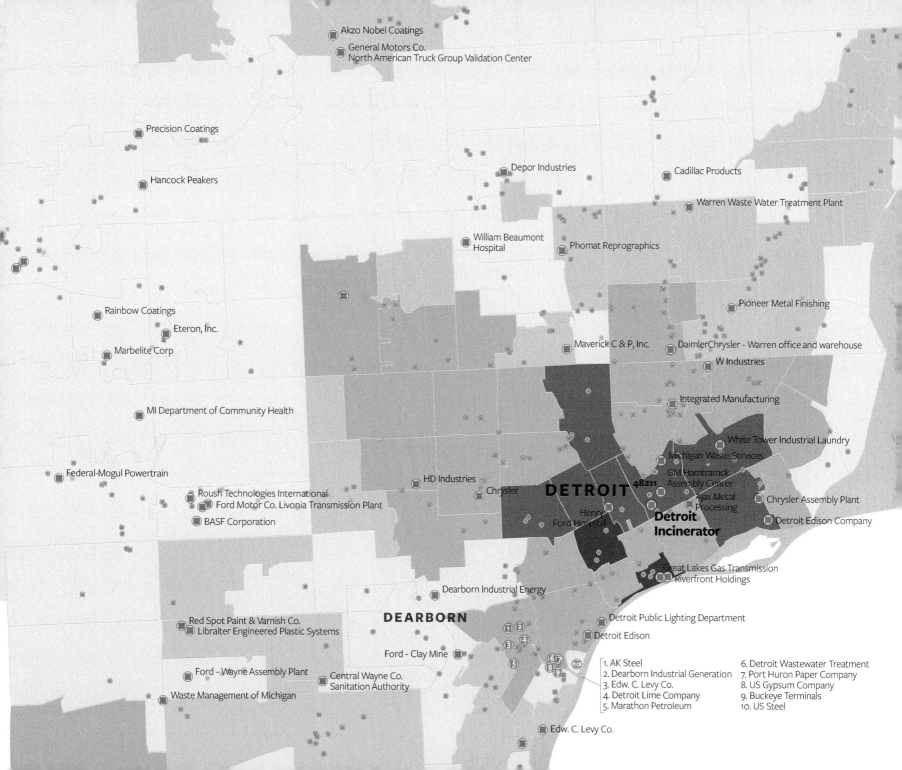

Akzo Nobel Coatings

General Motors Co.
North American Truck Group Validation Center

Precision Coatings

Hancock Peakers

Depor Industries

Cadillac Products

Warren Waste Water Treatment Plant

William Beaumont
Hospital

Phomat Reprographics

Rainbow Coatings

Pioneer Metal Finishing

Eteron, Inc.

Marbelite Corp

Maverick C & P, Inc.

DaimlerChrysler - Warren office and warehouse

W Industries

MI Department of Community Health

Integrated Manufacturing

White Tower Industrial Laundry

Michigan Waste Services

Federal-Mogul Powertrain

HD Industries

GM Hamtramck
Assembly Center

Roush Technologies International

Chrysler

DETROIT 48211

Ford Motor Co. Livonia Transmission Plant

Ajax Metal
Processing

Chrysler Assembly Plant

BASF Corporation

Henry
Ford Hospital

**Detroit
Incinerator**

Detroit Edison Company

Great Lakes Gas Transmission

Riverfront Holdings

Dearborn Industrial Energy

Detroit Public Lighting Department

DEARBORN

Red Spot Paint & Varnish Co.

Detroit Edison

Libralter Engineered Plastic Systems

Ford - Clay Mine

Ford - Wayne Assembly Plant

Central Wayne Co.
Sanitation Authority

Waste Management of Michigan

1. AK Steel	6. Detroit Wastewater Treatment
2. Dearborn Industrial Generation	7. Port Huron Paper Company
3. Edw. C. Levy Co.	8. US Gypsum Company
4. Detroit Lime Company	9. Buckeye Terminals
5. Marathon Petroleum	10. US Steel

Edw. C. Levy Co.

Protection Agency (EPA) limit, the Michigan Air Pollution Control Commission (MAPCC) ordered the city to install pollution controls on the incinerator.[8] However, the MAPCC gave the city seven years to install the pollution controls. Detroit Renewable Energy, which purchased the facility in 2010, has tried to rebrand it as "green," even while continuing the tradition of air pollution law violations. Between 2013 and 2018 alone, the incinerator violated emissions standards 750 times.[9]

According to EPA data, the people living in the half-mile radius around the incinerator in 2016 were 79 percent people of color and 74 percent low income.[10] Yet the trash the incinerator burned came from across the region, including from affluent, mostly white suburbs that paid lower trash disposal costs than Detroit. While the suburbs enjoy cleaner air, Detroiters breathe chemicals released from burning the region's trash.

Between 1998 and 2001, the incinerator emitted 396 pounds of lead and in 1999 alone, it emitted 320 pounds of mercury. Both lead and mercury are neurotoxins that cause brain damage. A 2001 study by the Harvard School of Public Health found that the zip code around the incinerator (48211) had the highest rate of childhood lead poisoning and asthma-related hospitalizations in the city.[11] In 2010, the incinerator was annually emitting more than twelve tons of fine particulate matter, which scores of studies have linked to lung cancer and asthma.[12] It was also emitting more than forty-one tons of hydrogen chloride, which the Centers for Disease Control and Prevention calls "irritating and corrosive to any tissue it contacts."[13]

For decades, the Detroit incinerator increased the risk of lead poisoning, asthma, and cancer among Detroiters, especially low-income African Americans. These health problems are a particularly heavy burden in families that are already medically underserved.

At the same time, the incinerator enriched wealthy investors while impoverishing Detroit taxpayers. The city initially financed the incinerator by selling $486 million in municipal bonds to Citigroup, Merrill Lynch, and other Wall Street banks. However, as operating costs went far over budget, the city sold more bonds to the banks, increasing Detroit's incinerator debt to $1.4 billion. According to *Bond Buyer* magazine, by 1999 the incinerator was the largest single source of Detroit's municipal debt.[14] (That record would be broken a few years later by even riskier deals with several of the same banks.[15]) Without Detroit's debt service payments on the incinerator, the city's waste disposal costs would have been $46 per ton in the 1990s and 2000s. With the debt service, they averaged $150 per ton, over three times the national average.[16]

On March 27, 2019, thirty years after the incinerator started burning, Detroit Renewable Power announced it was permanently shutting down the facility.[17] Leaders of the Breathe Free Detroit campaign (which collected 15,000 signatures calling for Mayor Duggan to close the incinerator in 2018) praised the decision, while demanding jobs with "comparable wages and benefits" for the 150 laid-off incinerator workers and protections for residents who could be "priced out or pushed out of one of Detroit's most rapidly gentrifying neighborhoods."[18] Detroiters can finally breathe easier, but the struggle for environmental justice is far from over.

THE RIGHT TO MOBILITY

LINDA CAMPBELL, ANDREW NEWMAN, SARA SAFRANSKY, AND TIM STALLMANN

n February 2015, the *Detroit Free Press* profiled the "incredible commute" of James Robertson, a fifty-six-year-old factory worker who, lacking an automobile, endured an *eight-hour* daily sojourn by foot and bus to travel twenty-three miles between his home in Detroit's North End and his workplace in suburban Bloomfield Hills.[19] Robertson's story highlights an acute problem facing many Detroiters: not only is public transit poorly funded in the metropolitan region, but the network itself is splintered because the suburbs have been unwilling to provide comprehensive connectivity with Detroit proper. In addition, automotive insurance companies impose the nation's most expensive rates in the country on Detroiters, leaving one in four households in the city that put America on wheels without a car.[20] The result of these insurance practices is a transit version of redlining: Detroiters have to pay more money to insure their vehicles, meaning they have less ability to move through an increasingly sprawling metropolis. This lack of mobility affects residents' ability to access jobs, education, and even affordable, healthy food.

Syri Simpson's "Jericho Speech" lays out the stakes that underlie effective transit infrastructure for Detroiters. In the speech, she decries the fact that a single light rail line along Woodward Avenue in Midtown and Downtown (now known as the QLine) was given priority over the development of a regionally scaled bus rapid transit system, pointing out that the QLine is "is neither rapid nor a system." For Simpson, the problems with the QLine are twofold: first, the relatively affluent residents and workers of the small area that it serves tend to already have access to means of mobility, which makes them less needy for transit, while those in outlying areas (which tend to be communities of color) do not benefit from it, despite their dire need for mobility. Second, she sees the project itself, which was largely funded by corporations and private-sector entities (Quicken Loans ultimately purchased the rights to name the QLine after itself) as "taking the historic Woodward Avenue, a public road symbolic of our region's history" and "privatizing it and all it represents for the benefit of the few." In other words, Simpson sees the QLine project as an attempt to remake the identity of one of Detroit's most symbolic roads, signaling how the struggle for transit justice is part of a broader attempt by Detroiters to reclaim their right to the city in the face of corporate-driven urban revitalization.

M-1 Streetcar: redevelopment without transit justice

> The 3.3-mile M-1 Streetcar invests **$25 million in public federal money** into a project that will increase property values for a small number of private investors but will not contribute to transit justice in Detroit.

> Almost 74,000 Detroiters live more than a quarter mile from a transit stop. The M-1 Streetcar does **nothing** to change this. In the North End alone since 2009, DDOT routes 8, 20, and 24 have been eliminated. While the current streetcar proposal includes a maintenance facility in the North End, riders will not be able to board at it.

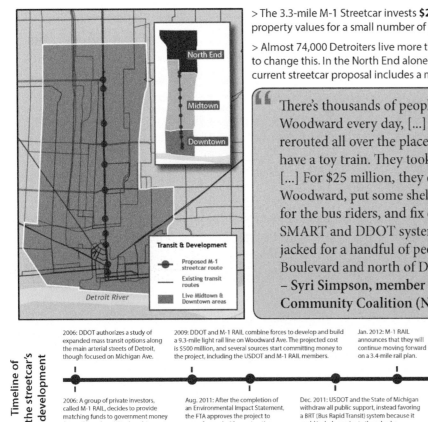

Transit & Development

● — ● Proposed M-1 streetcar route

— Existing transit routes

▮ Live Midtown & Downtown areas

Detroit River

North End

Midtown

Downtown

" There's thousands of people that ride up and down Woodward every day, [...] but they're going to be rerouted all over the place for a handful of people to have a toy train. They took $25 million of public money. [...] For $25 million, they couldn't fix the potholes on Woodward, put some shelters and benches down there for the bus riders, and fix every doggone bus in the SMART and DDOT system? [...] Everybody is being jacked for a handful of people that live south of the Boulevard and north of Downtown.

– Syri Simpson, member of North End Woodward Community Coalition (NEWCC)

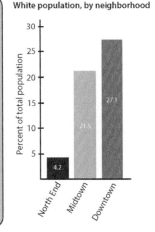

White population, by neighborhood

Percent of total population

North End — 4.2
Midtown — 21.5
Downtown — 27.1

Timeline of the streetcar's development

2006: DDOT authorizes a study of expanded mass transit options along the main arterial streets of Detroit, though focused on Michigan Ave.

2009: DDOT and M-1 RAIL combine forces to develop and build a 9.3-mile light rail line on Woodward Ave. The projected cost is $500 million, and several sources start committing money to the project, including the USDOT and M-1 RAIL members.

Jan. 2012: M-1 RAIL announces that they will continue moving forward on a 3.4-mile rail plan.

Jan. 2013: M-1 RAIL announces that USDOT has committed $25 million to the M-1 Rail Line, now a redesigned as a streetcar.

Apr. 2013: M-1 RAIL receives final environmental clearance to begin work on the project. Ground to be broken Fall 2013.

2006: A group of private investors, called M-1 RAIL, decides to provide matching funds to government money for a rail line along Woodward Ave.

Aug. 2011: After the completion of an Environmental Impact Statement, the FTA approves the project to move forward with construction.

Dec. 2011: USDOT and the State of Michigan withdraw all public support, instead favoring a BRT (Bus Rapid Transit) system because it could include service to the suburbs.

Nov. 2012: A SEMCOG study, the Woodward Avenue Rapid Transit Alternatives Analysis, praised Bus Rapid Transit over rail, stating, "[BRT] in a fixed guideway mimics rail while offering more flexibility to serve destinations."

Key Players:
- M-1 RAIL (a nonprofit entity composed of local business leaders)
- SEMCOG Southeast Michigan Council of Governments
- FTA Federal Transit Administration
- DDOT Detroit Dept. of Transportation
- MDOT Michigan Dept. of Transportation
- USDOT U.S. Dept. of Transportation

Data sources: U.S. Census Bureau, Data Driven Detroit, MDOT, Live Midtown, Live Downtown, M-1 RAIL, Detroit Free Press, Crain's Business Weekly.

Shown above is an original flyer from the M-1 Transit Justice Campaign, one of the groups opposing the M-1 (later QLine) streetcar. One of the great ironies of the QLine, as the flyer points out, is that in a majority African American city that has one of the country's highest urban poverty rates, the light rail line serves one of the whitest, most affluent parts of the city. Ultimately the problem lies not with mass transit, or even the light rail itself, but with a development strategy that channels private capital and government funds to a very limited part of the city.

Infographic by Olivia Dobbs and Emma Slager

JERICHO SPEECH

SYRI SIMPSON

Syri Simpson, a Detroit resident, made the following speech as part of a seven-day march—the Jericho Journey—organized by Rev. Joan Ross and the North End Woodward Community Coalition to protest a planned light rail and the lack of adequate transit for Detroiters. In her speech, delivered at a site that later became the Penske Station on the QLine (or M-1 Streetcar, as it was then called), Simpson talks about the difficulties of getting around in Detroit for those who are car-less. She argues that the working poor have a right to stay in the city and a right to accessible public transportation.

Gregg Newsom

In 2013, a group of Detroiters led by the North End Woodward Community Coalition held a seven-day protest march to call attention to the lack of adequate transit for Detroiters—and the fact that the planned light rail (later called the QLine) did not address these inequities.

am a Detroiter and I am a bus rider. I stand here today with other bus riders, other Detroiters.

I think about justice, about basic respect, and I ask that the needs of one hundred thousand transit passengers, your fellow Detroiters, be balanced against the wants of an affluent few.

We are old and we are young. We are parents and students. We are disabled. We are healthy. We are employees and job seekers. We are retirees. We are going to school, to the doctor, to our places of worship. Our day-to-day lives depend on access to public transportation.

Two years ago, we looked forward to a rapid transit system. We were told it would provide permanent, reliable transportation across our region. We awoke from that dream to find outsiders dismantling our once reliable bus system, leaving hundreds of riders standing in the elements while overcrowded, haphazardly scheduled buses roll past us.

Instead of a rapid transit system linking our community to the rest of our region, benefiting all, we are presented with a project benefiting only those whose transportation needs are already met—a project that is neither rapid nor a system.

How disrespectful of our community it is to build a maintenance and trash station in our neighborhood but not pick up a single rider!* This project neither benefits nor serves our community—it abuses us. In fact, it abuses everyone by taking historic Woodward Avenue, a public road symbolic of our region's history and development, and privatizing it and all it represents for the benefit of a few who've come here for profit, not progress.

Development in Detroit should not be at the expense of Detroiters. The working poor are often told to pull themselves up by their bootstraps. Can we pull ourselves up when our feet are nailed down, when our boots are weighted?

Public transit is not a free ride, nor is it beneficial only to the poor. It is beneficial to the southeastern Michigan community. It is essential to the Detroit community.

With the M-1 Streetcar, the wealthy are riding on the shoulders of the working poor. We all lose when others are forced to suffer needlessly.

If it is not in your heart to be concerned for bus riders as people, consider how our being able to get to our jobs may impact you and your job or business. Consider who will clean your streets and homes, who will serve your food, wait on your customers, wash your car, and care for your young and elderly. The people who do these jobs are your brothers, your sisters, your fellow Detroiters, and many of them are bus riders.

Bus riders live and work here, and we want to continue to be productive, contributing citizens of Detroit.

We were Detroiters before the developers came, and we will be here when they've gone. We are the builders of our city; we will stay to maintain it.

Belle Isle, the Detroit Water System, and Woodward Avenue are part of the heritage Detroiters have earned. Detroit is our children's irreplaceable birthright. Famished and desperate as we may appear to our more favored brethren, we will not sell our birthright for a pot of red lentils—a mess of pottage—or lose our blessing because our city's fathers are too blind to recognize us.[†]

We are the children and heirs of Detroit; the hands that built it, the wheels that keep it going. We are not interlopers. We are the heart and the spirit of this city, and we will not be moved or shaken by anybody's toy train. In the face of the worst abuses, we stand for justice and respect, and we won't stop till we get it.

*Simpson is referring to the Greater Detroit Resource Recovery facility (the Detroit incinerator) and a Detroit Department of Transportation maintenance facility, both located on E. Ferry Street.

†Simpson's words echo the biblical story of Jacob and Esau in Genesis 25: 29–34.

THE RIGHT TO EDUCATION

LINDA CAMPBELL, ANDREW NEWMAN,
SARA SAFRANSKY, AND TIM STALLMANN

t is a telling indicator of our times that education is often left out from discussions of urban revitalization, which usually refer just to restaurant openings, entertainment, and housing developments. From this narrow perspective that focuses on the city's role as a center of consumerism, if not tourism, the revitalization of Detroit is often claimed to be in full swing. The role of public education, which lies at the heart of the city's capacity to produce and sustain its own middle class—as opposed to attracting middle-class spenders, workers, and home buyers from elsewhere—is notably absent from the dominant narrative of urban revitalization.

Public school enrollment in Detroit peaked in 1966. Since then it has steadily declined. The reasons for the school crisis are complicated, but chief among them is the history of court-mandated busing, which led white parents to withdraw their children from public schools, and the *Milliken v. Bradley* ruling in 1974, which essentially reversed mandated busing by allowing the segregation of schools if the segregation was considered to be de facto rather than de jure. More recently, Detroit has been a key site of school choice experimentation—with students com-

ing out on the losing end. Detroit is second only to New Orleans in the share of students in charter schools, many of which perform worse than the city's public schools.[21]

The issues surrounding education in Detroit are too vast to fully explain in the following pages. Instead, in this section, we highlight some of the voices of students and educators who have addressed education and youth activism in the past and present. We have included a reprinted map created by the Detroit Geographical Expedition and Institute (DGEI) in the late 1960s. The DGEI project was a collaborative effort that included a partnership between William Bunge, a professor of geography at Wayne State University, and Gwendolyn Warren, a high school student. Warren, who had organized for change within her school before joining the DGEI, helped push Bunge and the other participants to adopt a more education-based model in its relationship to the community.[22] The map asks the reader to see urban space from the vantage point of children.

Detroit students continue to play an important role in speaking out about social and physical conditions in schools and the need for education reform, though these perspectives tend to be overlooked in the adult-dominated mainstream media. Imani Harris, a Detroit Public Schools (DPS) student, expressed this sense of invisibility in a letter she authored for a class assignment: "I'm sure that none of you even know what our schools like look, let alone what we look like." Harris wrote her letter in support of her teachers who held "sickouts" in response to the policies of the state-imposed emergency manager, Darnell Earley (the same emergency manager who had previously been in control of Flint during the contamination of its water supply). During this protest, teachers and students

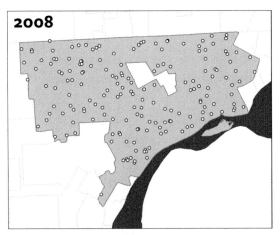

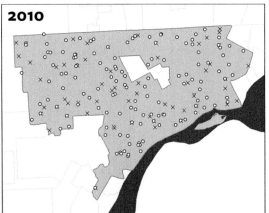

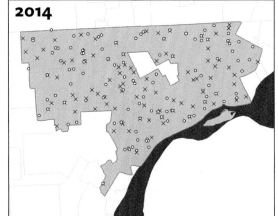

Legend

O Schools that were open in the given year

X Schools that closed between 2008 and the given year

School Closures

Between 2008 and 2014, the DPS administration closed 188 schools across the city, arguing that the closures were a necessary response to the declining school-age population and a decrease in public school "market share" as compared to charter and private schools. By 2013, charter schools in Detroit claimed more students than public schools. Little thought appears to have been given to the impact that a landscape of shuttered schools has on a community at an emotional and economic level. Kate Levy's photo collage highlights the loss neighborhoods face when their schools are closed.

Map by Tim Stallmann

also took to Twitter to post images of the atrocious physical conditions in schools that have proliferated under emergency manager control.

In response to these conditions and in pursuit of more child-centered and social justice–oriented approaches to education, local residents organized the Detroit Independent Freedom Schools Movement. This later generation of freedom schools is based on the freedom schools that were organized by African Americans as part of the civil rights movement in the 1960s and is meant to supplement but not replace education in traditional schools.[23] The Freedom Schools Movement reflects intergenerational organizing and youth-led movements as discussed by William Copeland in the previous section. Two other examples include the Detroit Asian Youth Project, which focuses on cultivating leadership in Detroit's Asian American community, and

the Detroit Future Youth Network (these networks created the Detroit Chinatown mural featured on p. 286).

Jenny Lee, director of Allied Media Projects describes the importance of her own participation in one youth program, Detroit Summer, established by Grace Lee Boggs and Jimmy Boggs, and its influence on her later efforts to establish programs such as Detroit Future Schools (rebranded in 2017 as People in Education). People in Education seeks to challenge

Kate Levy

DGEI Map of Spaces for Adults and Youth in Fitzgerald, 1969

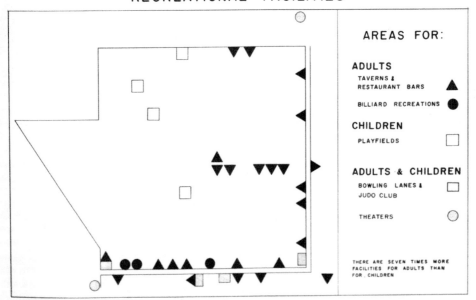

RECREATIONAL FACILITIES

AREAS FOR:

ADULTS
TAVERNS & RESTAURANT BARS ▲
BILLIARD RECREATIONS ●

CHILDREN
PLAYFIELDS ☐

ADULTS & CHILDREN
BOWLING LANES & JUDO CLUB ☐
THEATERS ◯

THERE ARE SEVEN TIMES MORE FACILITIES FOR ADULTS THAN FOR CHILDREN

What does a child's view of a city say about our urban priorities? The map (opposite page) is our updated version of the above map produced by the Detroit Geographical Expedition and Institute (DGEI), a community research project centered in the Fitzgerald neighborhood, for its 1971 atlas, *Fitzgerald: Geography of a Revolution*.

A large part of the DGEI's work centered on the geography of children and childhood in the city. Its maps promoted a vision of a more child-centered city and highlighted the importance of play space, good schools, and safe streets. The DGEI called attention to the fact that Black children did not often have the same access to these amenities as white children, and it documented the degree to which Black children in the city were being hit by white commuters who were speeding to work from the suburbs. In 1966, the DGEI studied the lack of availability of recreational facilities for adults and children in the Fitzgerald neighborhood of Detroit. It found:

> A good neighborhood is a neighborhood with abundant opportunities for play. . . . But to these inadequacies neither Parks and Recreation nor the schools are responding with

intellectual or emotional understanding. They view the flood of children as a nefarious scheme on the part of Fitzgerald residents to curry special concessions. The callousness of Parks and Recreation, which suggested racial bias, led to an investigation of the Department by the Commission on Community Relations during the fall of 1966.*

In 2014, the neighborhood (census tracts 5361 and 5363) had an estimated 730 children and 367 teenagers. Today there is more of a numerical balance between play spaces for children and spaces for adults, but the nature of recreational spaces have changed for all ages. The taverns and billiard halls of 1960s Fitzgerald have been supplanted by a small number of liquor stores serving the area. The parks still exist, but the bowling lanes, judo club, and theaters documented on the DGEI map no longer do. Today children's spaces are primarily represented by day care and child care businesses.

* William Bunge, *Fitzgerald: Geography of a Revolution* (Athens: University of Georgia Press, 2011 [1971]), 153–55.

Spaces for Adults and Youth in Fitzgerald, 2014

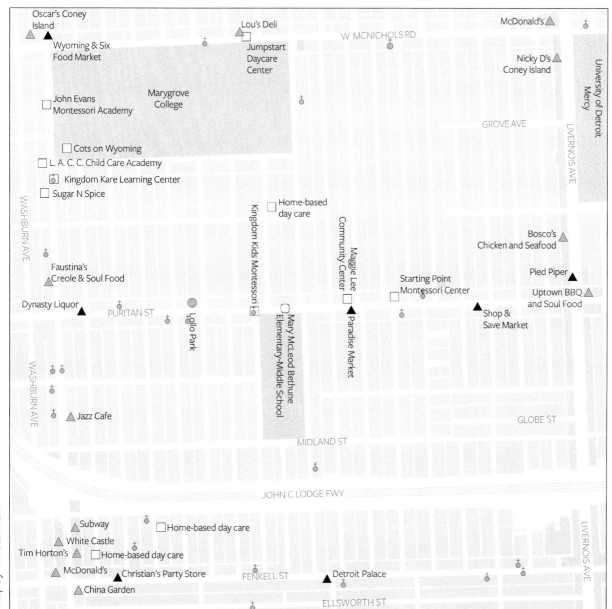

Oscar's Coney Island

Lou's Deli

McDonald's

W MCNICHOLS RD

Wyoming & Six Food Market

Jumpstart Daycare Center

Nicky D's Coney Island

University of Detroit Mercy

John Evans Montessori Academy

Marygrove College

GROVE AVE

LIVERNOIS AVE

Cots on Wyoming

L. A. C. C. Child Care Academy

Kingdom Kare Learning Center

Sugar N Spice

Home-based day care

WASHBURN AVE

Kingdom Kids Montessori

Maggie Lee Community Center

Bosco's Chicken and Seafood

Faustina's Creole & Soul Food

Pied Piper

Starting Point Montessori Center

Uptown BBQ and Soul Food

Dynasty Liquor

PURITAN ST

Lollo Park

Mary McLeod Bethune Elementary-Middle School

Paradise Market

Shop & Save Market

WASHBURN AVE

Jazz Cafe

GLOBE ST

MIDLAND ST

JOHN C LODGE FWY

Subway

Home-based day care

White Castle

Tim Horton's

Home-based day care

LIVERNOIS AVE

McDonald's

Christian's Party Store

FENKELL ST

Detroit Palace

China Garden

ELLSWORTH ST

Spaces for Adults
▲ Liquor stores

Spaces for Children
☐ Child care centers

○ Schools

Spaces for Adults and children
● Parks

▲ Restaurants and food stores

⚲ Churches

Zoning
Commercial

Mixed commercial and residential

Residential

Map by Tim Stallmann

the dominant paradigms of education, which they see as curtailing the ability of young people to become "self-actualizing people." As part of the Allied Media Projects and the Digital Justice Coalition, Lee and other activists and educators have sought to reimagine education in a manner that goes far beyond the boundaries of a conventional school.

Taking a different angle, the late Janice Hale (1948–2017), a former professor in Wayne State University's College of Education, contributes an essay that returns the focus of a justice-based approach to the craft of teaching itself. "Children in African American schools are taught to pass tests," writes Hale, whereas "[c]hildren in white middle-class schools are taught the curriculum in an engaging fashion." Hale's teaching philosophy, which resonates with Lee's vision of "revaluing young people's brilliance," amounts to a dramatic transformation of public schools from the inside out, beginning in the classroom.

These diverse perspectives offer a critical new perspective on the meaning of the right to the city from the standpoint of youth, teachers, and youth organizers. Moreover, youth and education remind us of the importance of taking a long-term view of the city as a form of social infrastructure that nurtures and shapes future generations of leaders.

DETROIT STUDENTS WILL FIGHT BACK

IMANI HARRIS

In January 2016, while under the control of Emergency Manager Darnell Earley, teachers and students in Detroit schools began a series of protests and "sickouts." For months, teachers staged the sickouts to draw attention to the fiscal crisis, the poor state of DPS, and their opposition to Governor Rick Snyder's education policies. As with many recent protest movements, Twitter and other forms of social media played an important role.

When Imani Harris, a sophomore at Renaissance High School, wrote the following "open letter" of protest as part of a class assignment about the conditions in Detroit schools, her mother, Wytrice Harris, shared it on Facebook using the hashtag #dpsstudentfightsback. It was quickly reproduced across a number of news outlets as an example of solidarity between students and teachers in the teacher sickouts. By February 2016, organizing efforts led to Earley's resignation and the governor's appointment of Judge Steven Rhodes (the bankruptcy judge who presided over Detroit's process) as the DPS transition manager, which involved guiding school reform bills through the state legislature, implementing them in the city, and managing the district's finances.

Since she wrote this open letter, Harris, who is now a graduate of Renaissance High and a student at the Medill School of Journalism at Northwestern University, has published a number of editorial pieces about Detroit politics from a young person's perspective.

My name is Imani Harris and I am a student at Renaissance High School. I am a sophomore and have spent both of my high school years at Renaissance. Throughout my time at this school I have experienced good and bad things. As this year has gone by I have noticed many of the teacher sickouts and protests. As I looked into them I have learned that I agree with everything these teachers stand for and I stand with them. Class sizes are too large, teaching conditions are horrible in some schools, and we barely have any resources. Things need to change, and we won't stop until they do.

Teachers who have participated in this sickout should not have their teaching certification taken away. First and foremost, there are already enough vacancies without you taking away twenty-three more teachers. The teachers are standing up for what they believe in, and are doing so peacefully. Trying to silence teachers by threatening to take away their jobs is childish and unfair to my education. When you have lost these teachers, how will you replace them? Who wants to work in a school district where ceilings fall on student's heads, and mushrooms grow in the hallways? I did not have an English teacher for the first four months of school, and last year I did not have a French teacher the whole first semester. With a history of all these vacancies, how will firing twenty-three teachers help your case at all?

I have a teacher named Zachary Sweet. He is one of the twenty-three teachers who may lose their job. Mr. Sweet is honestly the best teacher I've ever had. He is very dedicated to his job, he comes early in the morning to school to tutor, and stays after school for hours just to make sure that we understand. If there's anything we don't understand, he alters and tries again the next day. Mr. Sweet is my Honors Algebra 2 and Honors Geometry teacher, but he also teaches a German 1 class. Where would you find a teacher that can teach all three of those classes effectively? When would you be able to find a teacher to do so? Would this teacher be here before the end of the school year, or will I just have to figure it out myself while DPS continues to pick on teachers who just want better for us?

Legislators, the emergency manager, and others have said that teachers are hindering our education by doing these sick-outs, but the reality is that none of you live in Detroit, and none of you have children who go to a DPS school. None of you have to come to school every day and share books (if we even have books), or be in the middle of doing work and the lights cut off. None of you have to worry about your safety every day of your life, or walk past mushrooms growing in the hallway. None of

you have to skip lunch every day because the food is moldy, and the milk is old. None of you experience what we experience, and until you have, you have no right to speak on anything happening in our district. Our teachers are doing what is best for us, and my education is not being hindered any more than it was when I went a whole semester without a French/English teacher.

I was always taught to stand up for what I believe in, and never back down. We have come too far, and opened too many doors to stop now. Things finally have a chance to turn around, and not only for my school, but for all of the other DPS schools. We deserve better. DPS students are treated as dollar signs, and/or just a number on a slate. I'm sure that none of you even know what our schools look like, let alone what we look like. How can you all take away our teachers and tell us that's what's best for us, when you don't even know us? It's totally unfair to even threaten to do this, and scare off our teachers while also impairing my education. If you want to do what's best for us, make a change. Students support this cause just as much as teachers do. We deserve so much more. What the District is doing in DPS is criminal, and wrong.

Sincerely,
Imani Harris
Renaissance sophomore

HUMANIZING SCHOOLING IN DETROIT

JENNY LEE

Youth programs are vital pathways for young people to become engaged citizens. They are particularly important when school systems are under strain. Jenny Lee, Executive Director of Allied Media Projects, has been active and influential in Detroit through her work with several programs related to youth and media. In this interview, Lee discusses her involvement in a youth program called Detroit Summer and the impact it had on her when she was nineteen years old. She also talks about her role in helping to develop Detroit Future Schools, which is part of Allied Media Projects, a nonprofit organization that uses media strategies to advance social justice. Detroit Future Schools (rebranded in 2017 as People in Education) seeks to transform schools from within by pairing artists and teachers who implement digital media arts curricula aimed at teaching students about engaging in creative problem solving in their communities.

Lee also discusses the relationship between youth programs and the Allied Media Conference, which has made Detroit the site of yearly gatherings where social justice ac-

tivists from around the United States exchange ideas about how to use media to create a more just world. She raises the critical question of what it would mean to "humanize schooling" in Detroit. Sara Safransky conducted this interview as part of the Uniting Detroiters project.

Let's start with Detroit Summer. What is it?

Detroit Summer is a youth leadership organization that's been around since 1992. It was started by a coalition of activists, including Grace Lee Boggs and the late Jimmy Boggs, Shea Howell, and a number of other people who worked with different major twentieth-century social movements—anti-poverty, civil rights, Black power—within Detroit.

What was the impetus for Detroit Summer?

At the time Detroit Summer was founded, a lot of adults had been targeting young people as the source of a lot of problems in the city. Detroit Summer was about considering what options young people really had in the context of Detroit's deindustrializing economy, the disinvestment of capital in humans and resources from Detroit into the suburbs. It engaged the questions of what people in the city are going to do, not just do for work but for salvaging an identity and a sense of place and hope in the context of social and economic injustice.

Detroit Summer was about revaluing young people's brilliance, creative energy, and vision and saying we can create a structure in which that energy is channeled into the work of restoring community, building new types of relationships, and healing ourselves and our communities.

How has Detroit Summer evolved over the years?

This year is the twentieth anniversary of Detroit Summer. It has evolved a lot over twenty years. Starting in 2006–7, we began doing more media arts–based youth leadership work with the Live Arts Media Project. It was the same process and the same principles that we would use when starting community gardens, working with the people in a particular neighborhood to ask what was needed and then providing that. For example, we worked with the Gardening Angels, which was a group of seniors who had their own gardens and/or farms of various scales. Detroit Summer brought young people to support them.

Our turn to media-based work was a response to heightened national attention around Detroit's dropout rate. A lot of the young people in Detroit Summer had dropped out or were considering dropping out. Detroit Summer was invited to different forums to talk about how to respond to the crisis. In the vast majority of those forums, it was adults talking about the problem. Young people weren't really engaged in solving the problem. Their experiences were probably the most important missing piece from that process.

How did this realization shape Detroit Summer's programming?

In response, we created a hip-hop audio documentary, which was a yearlong process. A lot of activists were used to thinking about media as a megaphone: if you had the right idea and right media, people could be convinced that global justice was necessary and corporations were evil or whatever. Detroit Summer, along with a lot of people, was coming into awareness that it was not enough to just have the ideas and use media to blast them out. We realized this with the Live Arts Media Project, while we were making media together as a community.

A group of ten Detroit Summer youth interviewed their teachers, their peers, community activists, artists, and anybody with a relationship to the issue of youth dropping out. The documentary synthesized a lot of different experiences and ideas. It became a jumping-off point for much broader conversations about the education crisis in Detroit.

How is Detroit Summer connected to the Allied Media Conference?

Detroit Summer's media arts programming was inspired by our participation in the Allied Media Conference (AMC), which at that point was held in Bowling Green, Ohio. The AMC is a national gathering of independent media activists, social justice community organizers, technologists, educators, artists, and youth. The conference has been around for fourteen years. Since 2007, it's been held in Detroit. This year (2012) we expect about two thousand people to come to the conference where they will develop and share media strategies aimed at building a more just and creative world.

Allied Media Projects (AMP) is a nonprofit that formed in 2002. Until 2008, the conference was the entirety of AMP's programming, but more and more organizations were approaching AMP after the conference, wanting further training. They wanted to know how to expand on what they learned at the conference, but we could only provide so much. There was a dearth of people locally who had the combined skills—the technical skills associated with being a digital media producer, an ability to teach people from different experiences and levels, a social justice framework for why we make media, and, finally, accountability and availability. We started to think about how we could grow our capacity locally to integrate media into social justice work.

How has this work expanded over the years?

We had a huge opportunity to expand our work in 2009 with the Broadband Technologies Opportunities Program, which was a component of the Stimulus Act. At a 2009 AMC session, we talked about how we could apply for these funds, which were targeted at getting people to adopt the internet. We were part of a national effort to redefine broadband adoption, for example, in terms of people making their own media, using storytelling for organizing, running online businesses, and thinking about the role of the internet in strengthening community-organizing infrastructure. The Detroit Digital Justice Coalition was born out of these discussions and spent a year thinking deeply about how we could apply for these funds, not just in terms of what would be a successful grant application but, first and foremost, what our vision was for what we were calling a "healthy digital ecology" for Detroit.

What does "healthy digital ecology" mean?

We didn't agree with the framework of the "digital divide," where you have a digitally connected paradise over here and a digitally disconnected wilderness over here. We were thinking critically about the role of digital technology and its possibilities and the principles that needed to ground a healthy digital ecology. For us, these principles were access, participation, common ownership, and healthy communities, and our ideas for programming emerged from there. We formed a partnership with Michigan State that helped this sort of ragtag grassroots coalition of organizers be successful in securing this massive federal grant, which was awarded to us in 2010. Since then, we have been implementing those programs, which we envisioned through the Digital Justice Coalition. Those are Detroit Future Media, Detroit Future Schools, and Detroit Future Youth.

Tell us about the Detroit Future Schools program.

The basic outline of Detroit Future Schools is that we select teachers who are committed to transforming the purpose and practice of education in their classrooms. We recognize that the established, dominant definition of what school is for is really outdated and at this point harmful to young people's ability to come away from education as self-actualizing people. We also recognize that the practice of education within that dominant system reinforces inequity, alienation, and is generally harming young people's ability to become who they need to become.

We identify teachers who share a commitment to transforming the purpose and practice of education and partner them with digital media artists who come out of our Detroit Future Media program, in which we teach them how to use digital media to facilitate creative problem-solving within communities. We offer a yearlong professional development program for teachers and artists in which they collaboratively build a digital media arts–integrated curriculum and implement it in their classroom.[24]

Could you talk about the impacts of the Detroit Future Schools program?

We're doing near constant evaluation and documentation of these programs. What we've seen as far as impact is that students will say in interviews that on the days that they have a Detroit Future Schools artist in the classroom, they feel more human. In terms of the teachers, Detroit teachers are dealing with one of the most volatile school systems in the country. They are incredibly underresourced, overburdened, and stretched thin, but they commit to the Detroit Future Schools program. They consistently come to these bimonthly meet-ups that we have on a volunteer basis. I think they come not only for the technical support they're receiving from Detroit Future Schools, which is a big deal, but also for the emotional support of belonging to a network of other teachers who are trying to make the shifts and interventions within the school system as they are.

Finally, I think the artists are being transformed by the students with whom they're working. On a daily basis, they're seeing people's ability to innovate and be resilient in the face of all these life-threatening circumstances, and the potential that exists for our city to be transformed through the imaginations of young people.

CREATIVE TEACHING

Key to Detroit School Reform

JANICE HALE

Approaches offered by the Detroit Geographical Expedition Institute (p. 276) and Detroit Future Schools/People in Education (pp. 283–84) offer a radical reimagining of what school ought to be. In this piece, Janice Hale (1948–2017) argues for a reimagination of the classroom, specifically for the importance of developing culturally appropriate pedagogies and curricula. A professor of early childhood education and founding director of the Institute for the Study of the African American Child at Wayne State University, Hale's work had a major influence on teaching strategies that are focused on the experiences and lives of African American children in inner-city communities. She was the author of numerous books and articles, including *Learning while Black: Creating Educational Excellence for African American Children* (Baltimore: Johns Hopkins University Press, 2011).

The focus of the conversation about education reform in Detroit is perennially on money. We need more money for teacher salaries and benefits; more money to repair dilapidated buildings; more money for books and materials;

and variations along those lines. These are important concerns. However, an equally important pathway that must be developed is the cultivation of a vision for how to achieve educational excellence for African American children until that equity of resources can be achieved.

The model of school reform outlined in my book *Learning while Black* has three components. The foundational component is classroom instruction; the other two components—cultural enrichment and the instructional accountability infrastructure—support instruction in the classroom.[25] There are three generally recognized purposes for educating children: (1) imparting skills, such as the ability to read, write, spell, and calculate; (2) creating information growth—a cadre of knowledge about the world that most educated people know; and (3) providing children with the opportunity to develop talents and interests that can lead to fulfilling leisure time pursuits, the identification of careers, and an opportunity to make a creative contribution to the world. It is the perspective of this model that the way in which these purposes are achieved (educational strategies) is just as important as what is taught (educational content).

Children in African American schools are taught to pass tests. Children in white middle-class schools are taught the curriculum in an engaging fashion. A process of education must be crafted that motivates African American children to regard academic activities as interesting and fun. They must be guided on a journey to a lifelong love of learning.

Soh Suzuki

Detroit Summer and founding members of the Detroit Asian Youth Project (started in the summer of 2004) created the Detroit China-town Mural in 2003 as a way to commemorate the historical impor-tance of Chinatown and the Asian American community in Detroit. The mural connects the Civil Rights Movement and Asian American struggles for inclusion in metro Detroit in later years. It features a particularly poignant image on the bottom left corner: the grieving mother of Vincent Chin. Chin was a Chinese American engineer who was murdered by recently laid-off autoworkers in Detroit in 1982, during the height of anti-Japan sentiment rooted in automo-bile factory closures. Chin's murderers only received three years of probation for the crime, and the outrage caused by the verdict was an important factor in the expansion of political organizing among Asian Americans in the United States as a whole.

Describing the Detroit Asian Youth Project, Soh Suzuki says, "On the one hand, I think of the success in our program in terms of when the youth who have participated go on to college and what not, but more importantly it's when they come back to Detroit eventually and want to take leadership roles."

In November 2016, the Detroit Asian Youth project removed the mural as a statement of resistance to the Cass Corridor gentrification that led to the building on which the mural was installed being sold and redeveloped into a high-end restaurant.

THE RIGHT TO LIVE FREE FROM CRIME AND POLICE HARASSMENT

LINDA CAMPBELL, ANDREW NEWMAN, SARA SAFRANSKY, AND TIM STALLMANN

For years, emergency medical service response times in Detroit were far below the national average. This disparity persisted until 2017, when the number of working ambulances in the city climbed from six to thirty-seven.[26] The issue of policing has been more complex, however. Detroit's police department has been nearly paralyzed from cutbacks in certain periods. For example, in 2013, it dropped "homicide report" from inclusion as a "priority one call," meaning that even some reports of murder were not guaranteed priority police responses.[27] At the same time, however, there is a long history in Detroit of high-visibility, politically driven, violent, and often unaccountable police campaigns, such as the "Big Four" (a.k.a. "Tac Squads") in the 1960s, Stop the Robberies, Enjoy Safe Streets (STRESS) in the early 1970s, and Operation Restore Order in the mid-2010s, all of which were designed to make a statement in the form of high numbers of arrests, high-profile operations,

and drug seizures.[28] Such operations, rather than increasing the safety of Detroiters, have instead resulted in racist police harassment and unjust killings and beatings of African Americans. The 1967 uprising, after all, was sparked by police harassment at a raid on a returning Vietnam veteran's homecoming party in the Big Four era.

The criminal justice system thus fails Detroiters in two ways: the city suffers from a grievously high-crime rate while at the same time Detroiters are victims of police harassment. Like many other Black communities around the country, Detroiters have been subjected to extremely high rates of incarceration and imprisonment, as the map on p. 289 shows. Redevelopment and gentrification have intensified this process. One incarcerated Detroiter, Lacino Hamilton, reports: "I was either stopped, arrested, and/or conveyed to the police station once or twice a month for the entire ten years I lived in and frequented the Cass Corridor, supposedly for 'identification purposes,' by regular beat police."[29] Such harassment of African Americans in public space is a regular feature of many cities undergoing gentrification and redevelopment.

Detroiters have responded to this contradictory situation in a number of ways. For example, in their interview Tanesha Flowers and Herbert Jones discuss how Detroiters have developed "street courts," which allow residents, especially the homeless, to receive officially recognized due process in an environment free of fear. Meanwhile, Yusef "Bunchy" Shakur speaks about his work with the Urban Network, which is an example of the social infrastructure created by Detroiters to preempt youth from becoming involved in gangs. In another case not

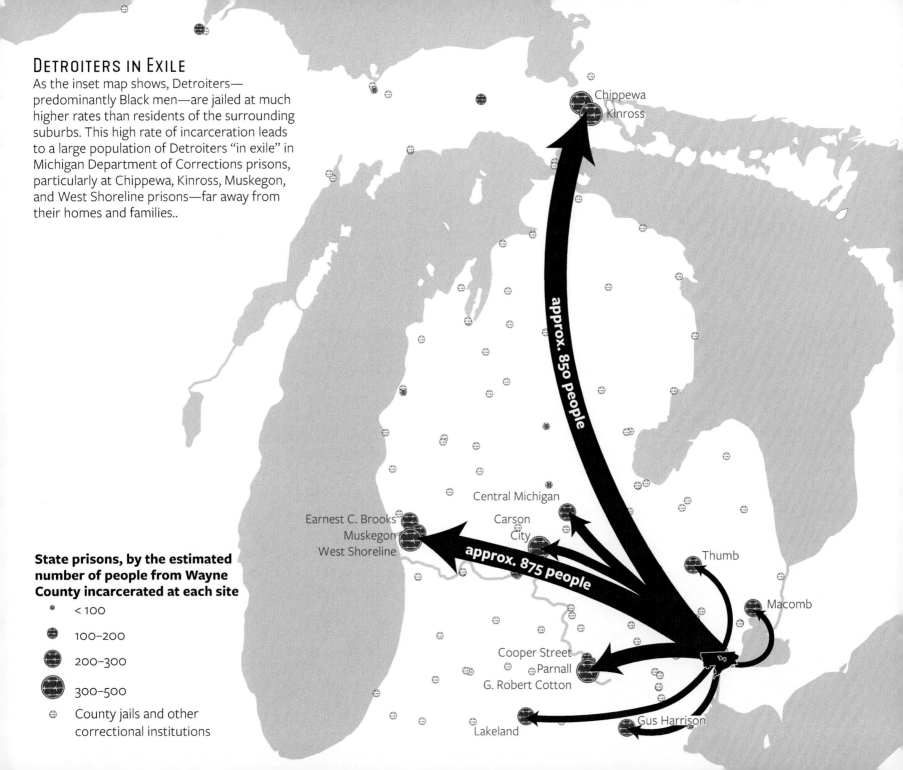

Detroiters in Exile

As the inset map shows, Detroiters—predominantly Black men—are jailed at much higher rates than residents of the surrounding suburbs. This high rate of incarceration leads to a large population of Detroiters "in exile" in Michigan Department of Corrections prisons, particularly at Chippewa, Kinross, Muskegon, and West Shoreline prisons—far away from their homes and families..

Chippewa
Kinross

approx. 850 people

Central Michigan

Carson
City

Earnest C. Brooks
Muskegon
West Shoreline

approx. 875 people

Thumb

Macomb

State prisons, by the estimated number of people from Wayne County incarcerated at each site

·   < 100

●   100–200

⬤   200–300

⬤   300–500

⊕   County jails and other correctional institutions

Cooper Street
Parnall
G. Robert Cotton

Lakeland

Gus Harrison

INCARCERATION RATES IN DETROIT

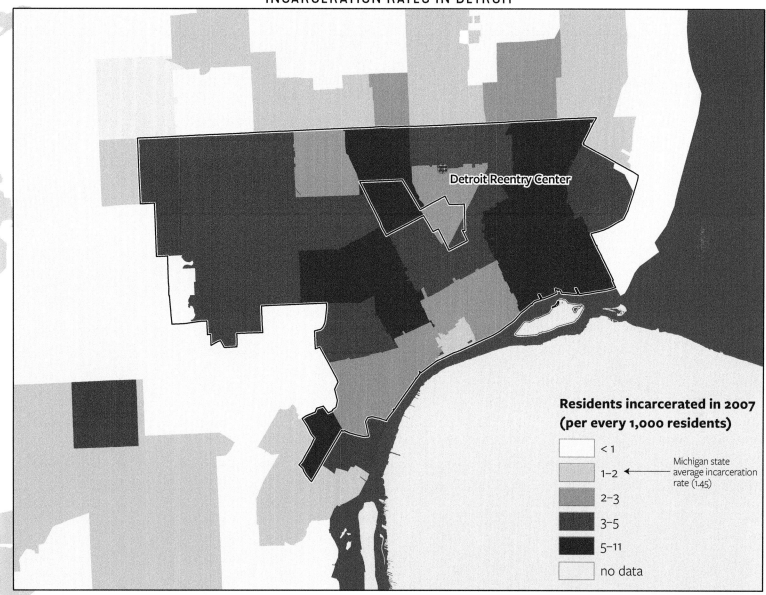

Detroit Reentry Center

**Residents incarcerated in 2007
(per every 1,000 residents)**

	< 1
	1–2
	2–3
	3–5
	5–11
	no data

Michigan state
average incarceration
rate (1.45)

Maps by Tim Stallmann

featured in the *Atlas*, Bill Wiley-Kellerman, among other residents, has worked to establish a restorative justice center after a brutal act of violence against a homeless man by a homeowner in the gentrified neighborhood of Corktown. It is also common for residents to resort to policing communities themselves through self-organized community watches.[30] One important community endeavor, led by the late Ron Scott, has been the Detroit Coalition against Police Brutality and their initiative called Peace Zones for Life, which teaches conflict resolution in neighborhoods to reduce crime and improve police-community relations.

"PEOPLE HOLD POWER. ORGANIZED PEOPLE HOLD POWER."

Detroit Action Commonwealth

TANESHA FLOWERS AND HERBERT JONES

Tanesha Flowers and Herbert Jones are members of Detroit Action Commonwealth (DAC). DAC was founded at a Detroit soup kitchen in 2008 and exemplifies the ways Detroiters are organizing for their right to due process and fair legal representation as part of a broader struggle for the right to the city. DAC won an important victory for the citizenship rights of poor Detroiters to be recognized by successfully suing the State of Michigan to waive fees for ID cards for certain groups of lower income people. The organization has also helped to develop a "street court" that allows poor people and people of color, who have been traditionally subjected to unjust treatment and abuse by courts, to interact with the legal system without prohibitive fees or fears of arrest and incarceration. The street court offers homeless individuals and those at risk of homelessness the "opportunity to resolve certain types of civil infractions and misdemeanors, including warrants, by crediting their personal ameliorative efforts to address the causes of their offending behaviors (such as job training, education, and alcohol and drug rehabilitation) toward their outstanding fines, costs, and/or jail time." DAC has more than thirty-two hundred members across three chapters, all located at soup kitchens in Detroit. This interview with Flowers and Jones, which Linda Campbell conducted as part of the Uniting Detroiters project, illustrates that local-level efforts to create a justice infrastructure can be effective, especially with the help of an independent judiciary—even if change remains elusive at the national scale.

Tell me about DAC and the role that DAC plays in this changed city.

Herbert: DAC is people helping other people or empowering other people. We're a mecca for information, for instance, voting. People think if you don't have an ID, you can't vote. People think if you're a felon, you can't vote. We educate people on how to vote, on where to vote. We educate people on the candidates. We are a community resource. That's what we do. We help people help themselves.

What is a "street court"?

Tanesha: The street court is a community court, where if warrants are out for you or you owe tickets you can come to one of the three locations and you can see an agent. They'll take you to whatever the contingency plan is and then you will go in front of a judge in the community. They'll help you get rid of your warrants and your tickets…. Then the community court system doesn't have to keep doing all that paperwork and building up unnecessary fees. When people were scared to go to court, it was a blessing for the court to come to the community because it took the afraid-ness out of the process, with people saying, "Well, I don't wanna go to this court, I'm gonna get arrested." When the street court came, it was a way to address the issues that the people had in the community without them fearing that "if I go to 36th District, I'm gonna be incarcerated."

What other projects are important to DAC?

Herbert: We have voter registration. We want to empower people. We don't tell them who to vote for, but we encourage them to vote. We have a series of candidates all over the city coming in to speak to the community. We bring the candidates to the community and they have a chance to get to know these people. They have a chance for questions and answers. They have a chance to really express their vote. And we get rid of the disclaimers of "If you have a felony, no ID." All those little things that people hear about, most of it is not true. We want to educate people on where to vote, how to vote, and when to vote. We don't care who you vote for as long as you do vote.

Tanesha: Blacks are basically known as people who don't vote. So what we do is that every single DAC meeting we say to our community that in order to change our circumstances we have to first stand up for our circumstances. We exist in a time when the legis-

lature is trying to cut all community programs from food stamps to medical to whatever. At some point, you have to stand up and represent yourself. We sued the State of Michigan so everybody could have an ID because if you say this ID is required for us to have and you got homeless people who can't afford the ID, okay, duh! They're homeless!

You won your lawsuit?

Tanesha: Yes, we did. Yes, we did.

As a result, people who are homeless who don't have IDs, they can get IDs now?

Tanesha: Yes, it means that whoever is a resident of the City of Detroit who cannot afford an ID or birth certificate can come to DAC on a Friday. We can take you down and you can get your birth certificate and your ID. That's what that means.

So let me ask you this: Who do you think has power? Who holds power in Detroit right now?

Herbert: People. People hold power. Organized people hold power. The better you're informed, the more you know, the better you are, and then you can make a smart decision, a wise decision. If you're informed, you can also hold people accountable because they can't just tell you anything. If you hold people accountable, they'll do a better job. They'll have an interest in your interests.

RECLAIMING OUR SOULS

YUSEF "BUNCHY" SHAKUR

Yusef "Bunchy" Shakur is an author, educator, organizer, Detroit resident, and formerly incarcerated gang member. Since 2008, he has run a bookstore and cafe called the Urban Network Cyber Cafe on the West Side in the Zone 8 neighborhood. As the name suggests, the Urban Network is more than a bookstore—it serves as a social infrastructure that supports the community. The Urban Network is a community space that offers a public computer station, features local art, hosts poetry readings, and organizes an annual back-to-school backpack drive, which is featured on the cover of this book. As Shakur describes in this interview conducted by Andrew Newman and Linda Campbell, the Urban Network is his response to combating the social dynamics that lead to the breakdown of many Black families, including political corruption in the neighborhood and lack of resources, strong education, and job opportunities.

Those same dynamics ultimately led Shakur to join the notorious Zone 8 gang, become what he calls a "streetholic," and be imprisoned at the age of nineteen. In prison, where he met his father for the first time, Shakur had a political awakening. During his nine years behind bars, he studied the history of Black struggle, discovering the likes of Huey P. Newton and Fred Hampton, who became his examples rather than the dope seller. Books, as he put it, resurrected him. The Urban Network emerged from the political consciousness that Shakur gained in prison, namely that he had an obligation to those who had struggled and sacrificed to make the world a better place and improve his community. Out of prison, Shakur has worked relentlessly to build community in Detroit—"restoring the neighborhood back in the hood."

How do you describe your work?

It varies, but more importantly it comes out of my own experience. It comes out of the Black experience. By that I mean the Black family, the Black community, the extension of Black folks being snatched from Africa and being brought into America and that continuation of coming out of slavery, civil rights, the Black power movement, the crack era, mass incarceration—so all those dynamics have impacted and shaped Black folks. And when we get down to the bottom, in particular to Black families, where it has emerged that Black mothers are raising Black kids by themselves in the absence of Black fathers. This whole social dynamic of guys seeing street life as a form of occupation has crippled the Black family.

What is the history of your organization in terms of who is involved and its geographical reach?

First of all, it's my neighborhood—feeding the people I've engaged with, the people that's selling dope, the people that's prostituting.

All those people are part of my neighborhood. You may not agree with what they are doing, but they are struggling. And I'm part of that and I'm fortunate enough to understand why they do what they do. I have the obligation to help educate them, to help empower them, not chastise them, not condemn them.

How would you define your neighborhood?

I would define it as a Third World neighborhood, as many urban communities across the country are Third World neighborhoods. But within those conditions you have hope, you have people who have a desire to be loved and to love others, to experience peace, to be hopeful, to raise their kids, to be great. Unfortunately, the resources are not there.

What are some of the impacts you have seen of your work?

There's so many to name. Before we expanded, the Urban Network was just the bookstore. Before the bookstore, I was in the neighborhood doing work, just walking, engaging folks, developing building blocks so people can see this is another option in our community. One day one of the guys was like, "I haven't eaten in a day and a half and I'm hungry and I'm thinking about lopping someone upside the head." So I went to the register and I gave him ten dollars. The point is, he intervened, he stopped what he was doing, and came in. I didn't have to chase him down. I wouldn't have even known what he was going to do. He didn't want to do that. There's a lot of cats out here who don't necessarily want to do what they end up doing, but there is no one they can turn to. Him coming in

and asking for help, that's based upon a relationship we've been able to build.

Who's in power in Detroit?

That's an interesting question [*laughs*]. Who's in power in Detroit? I think the spirit of the people is in power in Detroit. I always emphasize on the neighborhoods; the heart of any city is the neighborhoods. Unfortunately, when I hear that question, I hear it more from a hierarchical way, from the top. With any building, you start from the bottom; the foundation has to be strong for the top to look pretty.

You have Corktown. You have Midtown. You have Downtown. What about the neighborhoods? What about around town? We have to cultivate those relationships. We have rough times, we keep hearing about shootings and murders, but at the same time you have the old-timers, the grandmothers, the grandfathers, the people on the block, in the community who are keeping everything together, folks like myself who are just figuring it out, stepping it up to what we should have been doing. It's the spirit that is greater than anything that man or woman can comprehend: to be a human being, to live in peace—that's the power in the city.

What's your ideal vision for your community and for Detroit?

My ideal vision for Detroit is first and foremost having a safe neighborhood, having families who can have struggles but have the ability to love each other in spite of all those struggles, being able to break bread with each other, and not getting caught up on fantasy that there aren't enough jobs in America. If I hire the guy in the neighborhood to start cutting my grass, that's a job for him. That's neighborhood building. This is how we have to connect. We have to start thinking outside the box, reclaiming our souls, reclaiming that connection to each other, developing trust within each other, looking at the whole political and religious structure of our community and redefining that from a human standpoint. We have to fix our problems and challenge the folks at these large institutions to give a damn.

ANOTHER CITY IS POSSIBLE

LINDA CAMPBELL, ANDREW NEWMAN, SARA SAFRANSKY, AND TIM STALLMANN

t is only by confronting racial injustice and inequality head-on that social justice movements, scholars, and communities can stand up against the tide of revenge-based politics sweeping America and the globe. The conversations that gave rise to this book took place as Detroiters analyzed and reacted to a rising tide of revanchism in Michigan, which targeted the gains of historically oppressed peoples, including Black radicals, labor unionists, LGBTQ organizers, and immigrants' rights groups. Now that revenge politics have swept far beyond Michigan (and, for that matter, the United States), the experiences and stories of struggle shared in these pages are no longer simply Detroit or American stories. Rather, the analyses and visions of our contributors speak to the importance of transforming the city as central to forging more just and equitable global societies.

In the seven years this book was being developed, between 2012 and 2019, a great deal of change swept Detroit, from the initial forays of Mayor David Bing into the Detroit Works Project to Detroit's growing cultural profile as a center of innovative urban revitalization, the onset of emergency management and bankruptcy, the election of Mayor Mike Duggan, and the rash of water shutoffs that garnered international condemnation. Over that same period, the lives of many involved in this book changed greatly, too. Five of the people whose words and thoughts are featured here—Grace Lee Boggs, Lila Cabbil, Janice Hale, Kaleema Hasan, and Charity Hicks—passed away before they could see this project completed. Several babies were born to this book's contributors and editors, and many of us have participated in grassroots campaigns that emerged during this time. Such change is the problem of attempting to set down in print an atlas that charts the dynamic lives and work of people in a city. Life in Detroit continues to grow and change, but for all the transformation that occurs, there is something distinct that continues to give this city a unique form. We hope that this book conveys that distinctiveness in a way that does justice to the voices of Detroiters.

Just as important, we hope that Detroiters' vision, intelligence, and creativity will resonate far and wide, and that the knowledge that Detroiters have gained through these years of struggle will spur conversations in many other places and times. From the outset of the *Atlas*, we've been guided by the belief that a critical evaluation of Detroit's past and present can help not only clarify the depths of crisis we face as a global society but also point toward hopeful ways forward. The *Atlas* has been premised on the contention that something broadly applicable is to be gained from attending to the historical specificity of social movement organizing in Detroit, from how the city has historically served as a key site of Black radicalism and radical labor politics, to grassroots responses to the current political conjuncture.

Our approach has been shaped by coeditor Linda Campbell's interest in the potential for the project to serve movement-building processes and contribute to an infrastructure for grassroots organizing adequate to our times. In one of our early meetings, amid the state takeover by emergency management, Linda reflected on the labor landscape in Detroit in the early 1970s: "Everybody had an uncle, a cousin, or someone who was either a committee man in the labor movement inside a factory or they were active in their churches. There was a give and take. There were strikes. There was agitation. There was tension." She described how the labor movement put pressure on management, which both led to gains for factory workers and public-sector employees and benefited those who lived in the community by generally raising the standards of living and quality of life.

In Linda's analysis, the structure of work in the factories created an infrastructure for political organizing as well as local leadership at the grassroots level. The decline of manufacturing in Detroit and other industrial cities in the global North, combined with the militant repression of Black and labor radicals, created not only a challenge of how to think about the question of industrialism and the future of work but also a problem of how to think about resistance and the organizational capacity of social movements.

Detroit is often upheld as an extreme manifestation of the postindustrial labor crisis, with approximately half of its working-age residents officially unemployed. Yet in the twenty-first century, this level of unemployment is increasingly normal. This *Atlas* archives the ways that, in the early 2010s, some Detroiters responded to a new economic and political climate by working to build more adequate infrastructures for survival, care, and political organizing.

Capitalism sustains itself through continually creating new frontiers and relations of inequality among human groups. Saskia Sassen, an urban sociologist and scholar of globalization, suggests that global capitalism has entered a new stage of predatory formation that requires increasingly complex maneuvers to exploit new frontiers or reconstitute old ones. Detroit exemplifies Sassen's assertion that inequality no longer captures what is happening. She argues that the current moment is better understood as one of *expulsion*—in particular, the expulsion of poor people, specifically, poor communities of color, from "life space."[1]

This new geography of abandonment is produced through market-based policies and a neoliberal ethos that renders poor people invisible and disposable. Detroit reveals that this geography of abandonment is inextricably linked to racial capitalism and anti-Blackness. Racial hierarchies are being made and remade through supposedly neutral market appraisals that render Black spaces as lacking value and wasted. The *Atlas* analyzes how such spaces are being reincorporated by capital through debt, deregulation, and redevelopment.[2] The city provides a window onto the current terrain of urban struggle that includes contestations over real estate speculation, gentrification, and philanthropy-driven development, the privatization of infrastructure and the withdrawal of public works, and rising nationalism, xenophobia, and extrajudicial police killings. In particular, it illuminates how these struggles play out in a majority-Black American metropolis and how people organize in response.

On the face of it, many struggles in Detroit appear to be about the equitable distribution of services. As the *Atlas* shows, however, many of those involved in resistance are often, at the core, working to undo and repair the legacies of colonialism, slavery, and racial capitalism by organizing life differently in their neighborhoods. From land trusts to community gardens to soup kitchens, Detroiters are reclaiming land from capitalist interests, practicing collective self-reliance and self-determination, fostering new environmental relationships, building economic cooperatives, and engaging in political education and consciousness raising. The *Atlas* points to the ways that these efforts are fundamentally rooted in place.

It highlights the importance of *land, agriculture, infrastructure*, and *governance* as key sites of resistance and organization in the twenty-first-century city. In each of these arenas, Detroit has important lessons for cities globally. As chapter 1 highlights, people have struggled over Detroit's *land* since before the city's existence. Yet today the ethereal nature of global financial markets have made amassing and commodifying land far easier than before. The extent of land dispossession in Detroit today illuminates an urgent need voiced by urban social movements to decommodify land and housing, and fundamentally rethink market-driven, individual-centered ideals of private property and personhood.

In the area of *agriculture*, the *Atlas* emphasizes a crucial point: any vision of a future food system that is not explicitly anti-racist will fall into perpetuating systematic racism. This perspective is very much a product of Detroit's history, and it offers a corrective to dominant white-led alternative food movements, which remain generally unconcerned with problems of racial inequality in the same way that the mainstream environmental movement was before the rise of environmental justice.[3]

The experiences Detroiters have faced with water shutoffs and planned deprovisioning of *infrastructure* highlight the fact that transit, streetlights, water pipes, and schools do not merely provide services, but also help give the city unity and connectivity in a cultural and political sense. These infrastructural systems and public institutions were often established on the hard-won principle that all residents possessed the right to the city. In the twenty-first century, maintaining that principle with regard to infrastructure, in the face of revanchism and the new geography of abandonment, has become a key site of struggle.

Finally, Detroiters' experiences of *governance* by foundations, the struggle over a Community Benefits Agreement ordinance, and efforts toward self-governance and management of community resources at the neighborhood level (for example, the Riverfront East Congregational Initiative or Feedom Freedom Growers) highlight how both contemporary power grabs and grassroots struggles for democracy are taking place outside the traditional realm of public institutions. They also illustrate a dual strategy that entails engaging grassroots power to make demands on the state and working collectively to build more just worlds anew.

In the mid-twentieth century, as Linda pointed out, the urban factory was a primary location of struggle. By contrast, the *Atlas* contributors suggest that in the twenty-first century the struggle is over the city itself.[4] Given this shift, they emphasize the potential power of place-based political organizing. And they suggest the importance of face-to-face neighborhood interactions to cultivating community and nurturing a new grassroots social infrastructure.

In 2012, the filmmakers Heidi Ewing and Rachel Grady released *Detropia*, a documentary that won acclaim from the Sundance Film Festival and the National Board of Review of Motion Pictures. Much of the film's cinematic impact is drawn from juxtaposing images of dramatic urban abandonment with music from the Detroit Opera, notably Verdi's *Nabucco*. In a telling demonstration of the power of documentary filmmaking to blur the lines between life and art, the city's landscape functions much like the romantic ruins that stereotypically adorn the backdrop of an opera set, and the city's history is presented as a tragedy worthy of Verdi or Puccini. Across many genres—film, image, and text—in both fiction and nonfiction, there is a tendency to view Detroit in terms of extremes of human experience. The individual stories may differ as to whether Detroit is a place of suffering, resilience, abandonment, or vibrancy, but across the vast majority of accounts by both those inside and outside the city, Detroit—and the lives of Detroiters—are understood as an exception to the norm.

Ironically, Detroit's last decade of water shutoffs, emergency management, and land grabs clearly demonstrates that there are important and damaging implications when a place—and the people in it—are viewed as exceptions. If, on the contrary, we are willing to entertain the idea that Detroit is not so exceptional—if what happens in Detroit is in fact common in many places—then what people in Detroit say and do has direct importance globally for both cities and citizens.

Forgoing the melodrama and arguing against Detroit's exceptionality does not mean minimizing the injustice experienced by its residents, nor does it mean downplaying the proven capacity of Detroiters to envision social alternatives in the face of that oppression. Rather, we write against these extreme representations because the idea of the city as an exceptional space has provided the rationale for depriving residents of rights in a systematic way. It was, in fact, the officially declared "state of emergency" in 2012 that was used to install an emergency manager, thus depriving citizens of local democratic representation and creating the conditions, as we showed in chapter 4, that led to water shutoffs in Detroit (as well as a water crisis in Flint). The accepted state of abnormality that supposedly defines Detroit has also provided the moral and political justification for the extreme cutbacks in life-supporting infrastructure that are at the heart of the Detroit Future City framework. It has also justified a disruptive reorganization of the Detroit Public School system that has not only closed and defunded schools but also left children and parents lost in the system. By characterizing Detroit as an extreme and exotic space, our political leaders and our society as whole have been permitted to create and maintain the city as a unique kind of space where rampantly unequal treatment is both tolerated and perpetuated.

We write against Detroit's exceptionality in order to make the apparently radical claim that Detroiters deserve the same rights and standards as other citizens and also as a way to highlight the importance that Detroit holds for understanding other cities around the world. All too often Detroit is claimed to be significant simply because it is said to be *extreme*—but just naming a harsh example does little to change our understanding of cities, social movements, or racism. What if Detroit's importance is not due to the ways that it is different but instead due to its capacity to reveal processes that are also occurring in so many cities in America and around the world? What if Detroit—and the stories of Detroiters—are captivating not because they are so different but rather because they have so much in common with such a wide variety of people and places?

The *Atlas* has been an attempt to argue precisely that point. But, in keeping with the spirit of the project, we'll give the last word to some of our contributors, who share their visions for the future of Detroit:

It's interesting. You know my vision for Detroit's future is not that different from what we already have. I don't like to travel and I always say to my kids, "Why would we leave paradise? We are already here." To me paradise is the place where you know everyone . . . so your depth and your roots and all that's around you are here. As long as we have each other to share ideas with, to share meals with, it's ideal.

—Elena Herrada

I would like to live in a community where everybody has the means to live a dignified life. I was with a man not long ago who is very active here at the soup kitchen. He is just a really good guy, and he didn't have money for a bus fare. I felt just absolutely terrible—somebody without money for bus fare. That's unspeakable in this society. In this world, people who have to come here to eat, who would be hungry if they weren't here, it's unacceptable. So, my ideal world is where people have what they need to live a dignified decent life and they have some control over what happens to them, that they have choices. I think right now so many of the people we serve basically don't have much control at all over their lives because their poverty has decided so much for them.

—Brother Jerry Smith

I see a system where class is no longer a problem and everybody has equal economic opportunity. I see tool shares and skill trades and time banking and ways of exchanging information and education with each other and other members of the community, without there having to be financial individuality.

—Curtis McGuire

My vision for Detroit is that there would be the restoration of the participation of everyday people and that everyday people would feel valued, they would feel that their voice counts, that their needs are of concern to the larger community, and that there is hope for our collective survival.

—Lila Cabbil

It's really simple: people being able to have dialogue and discussion about what they need to do. Community would be able to recognize and deal with the fact that this is not happening and ask, "What else can we do?" We can still educate ourselves. We can still do whatever we need to do to sustain ourselves. We can create institutions that serve us. Like we used to say, "The Black Panther Party is the ox of people." Now I say, "The community is our ox that we have to formulate and feed so it will serve us."

—Wayne Curtis

My ideal vision for Detroit is that we have all our basic needs met to a point where we can focus on being proactive and imaginative instead of always getting in this quagmire of the lights aren't on, the trash is not picked up, I can't go outside at night because it's dangerous and the fire, EMS, or police are probably not coming when I need them. My vision is to have all that stuff taken care of so that we can be creative together, building a community that not just works for everyone but in which everyone is thriving.

—Dessa Cosma

We need to reconnect ourselves to our place in the spectrum. Humans think they're the end of evolution—that universe created the universe to bring us forth, which is a pretty egotistical notion. We need to check ourselves

and get back into the ecosystem, and look at our neighborhoods as ecosystems that require all these different aspects to work.

—Lottie Spady

I believe in community self-determination. I think communities should be able to define for themselves what they want and what is in their best interest. I wouldn't try to impose on communities what they should have. I have some personal ideas of what would be good, but I think what's needed is for people to begin to think deeply and to engage themselves in what benefits their community and then begin to engage in the process of bringing those things about.

—Malik Yakini

I think that if there were ways that people who aren't in government could make their own decisions together—in communities or collectively or in councils—that would be more effective. . . . From my experience in different organizing projects, it has been really important to look at how we fulfill our immediate everyday needs—to be in a place where we feel stable, energized, and healthy to be able to organize because there's so much burnout that happens and so much stress. Part of trying to be healthy and feel empowered, or have power, is to be able to do something with other people. So if we see organizing as helping each other more communally and as living our lives and addressing immediate needs and working on ourselves, then we would have more energy to trust in each other and experience with each other; to be able to take on larger projects outside of our houses, our neighborhoods, our blocks, or our personal relationships.

—Carmen Malis King

One of the challenges of grassroots power is it takes more work. If you just let the politicians do everything, then you can just sit and watch the news and say, "That's good or that's bad." Grassroots power depends on . . . You gotta come to meetings. You gotta know what's happening. So I would like to see that as a change, where more and more people are involved.

—William Copeland

The greatest thing is once the people get a voice, you can't stop them. Once they have their voice, they start putting on their own meetings. In 48217 they had, I don't know how many, meetings that they planned themselves without any assistance from anyone. They brought the mayor out there. They brought the city council out to their community.

What I've seen is tremendous, tremendous acknowledgment of people's power. It's not like they didn't have any power. They had the power. It was just realizing it and then using it.

—Rhonda Anderson

NOTES

INTRODUCTION

1 As of 2016, Detroit's population was recorded as 672,795 by the US Census. A number of authors have written about the relationship between depopulation and mythmaking in Detroit. See, for example, Rebecca J. Kinney, *Beautiful Wasteland: The Rise of Detroit as America's Postindustrial Frontier* (Minneapolis: University of Minnesota Press, 2016); and Sara Safransky, "Greening the Urban Frontier: Race, Property, and Resettlement in Detroit," *Geoforum* 56 (2014): 237–48. On the "ungeography" of Black lives, see Katherine McKittrick, "On Plantations, Prisons, and a Black Sense of Place," *Social & Cultural Geography* 12, no. 8 (2011): 947–63.

2 The editors have made an intentional choice to capitalize *Black* as a noun and adjective referring to race in this book instead of using the more common lowercase rendering of *black*. While we recognize that not all people racially marked as black in the United States identify first and foremost as Black in a cultural sense, and that there many types of blackness,—we adopt this orthography to push back against a pervasive anti-Blackness that persists within language. Indeed, this book is written against the impact that such ideologies have had on redevelopment and democracy in Detroit. We do not capitalize *white* because the term more clearly references skin color rather than a historically developed cultural identity. In this sense, and in following a long tradition of thinking stretching back to W. E. B. Dubois, we capitalize *Brown* as well as *Black*, as in "Black and Brown communities," according to the logic that one would capitalize "Italian communities," "Polish communities," or "Jewish communities."

3 See Counter Cartographies Collective, Craig Dalton, and Liz Mason-Deese, "Counter (Mapping) Actions: Mapping as Militant Research," *ACME: An International Journal for Critical Geographies* 11, no. 3 (2012): 439–66, www.acme-journal.org/index.php/acme/article/view/941.

4 The editorial collective for the *Atlas* was born out of the Uniting Detroiters project. Coeditor Linda Campbell is the director of Building Movement Project Detroit. Coeditors Andrew Newman and Sara Safransky joined the project as academic "learning partners" and helped facilitate the research. Tim Stallmann joined the team initially to help with the mapmaking component and then became fully ensconced as a coeditor.

5 The *Atlas* and documentary have been completed with additional assistance from Heidi Bisson, Olivia Dobbs, Isra El-beshir, Ayana Maria Rubio, Jimmy Johnson, Gregg Newsom, Emma Slager, Denis Sloan, Justin Thompson, and Jeremy Whiting. In addition, the Uniting Detroiters advisory board also provided input on our process and included Shane Bernardo, Shea Howell, Gregg Newsom, and Lottie Spady.

6 As Gary Wilder writes, "Thinking *with* . . . entailed a deliberate strategy of generous reading. . . . To read generously is not to suspend critical evaluation but sometimes to extend the logic of their propositions far beyond where they may have stopped." See Gary Wilder, *Freedom Time: Negritude, Decolonization, and the Future of the World* (Durham, NC: Duke University Press, 2014).

7 Fifty percent of the proceeds from the sale of the *Atlas* will go to the Transforming Power Fund, and the other half will purchase copies of the book for community organizations and those who cannot afford it.

8 Neil Smith, *The New Urban Frontier: Gentrification and the Revanchist City* (New York: Routledge, 1996), xvii.

9   Quoted in Quinn Klinefelter, "It's City vs. Creditors in Detroit Bankruptcy Trial," *Morning Edition*, National Public Radio, October 23, 2013, www.npr.org/2013/10/23/239681817/its-city-vs-creditors-in-detroit-bankruptcy-trial.

10 Building on Elinor Ostrom's *Governing the Commons* (Cambridge: Cambridge University Press, 2015) and Michael Hardt and Antonio Negri's *Commonwealth* (Cambridge, MA: Belknap Press, 2009), scholars have developed the concept of "urban" commons. See Paul Chatterton, "Seeking the Urban Common: Furthering the Debate on Spatial Justice," *City* 14, no. 6 (2010): 625–28; Andrew Newman, "Gatekeepers of the Urban Commons? Vigilant Citizenship and Neoliberal Space in Multiethnic Paris," *Antipode* 45, no. 4 (2013): 947–64; Amanda Huron, "Working with Strangers in Saturated Space: Reclaiming and Maintaining the Urban Commons," *Antipode* 47, no. 4 (2015): 963–79; and Ash Amin and Philip Howell, eds., *Releasing the Commons: Rethinking the Futures of the Commons* (New York: Routledge, 2016).

11 See Henri Lefebvre, *Writing on Cities*, trans. and ed. Eleonore Kofman and Elizabeth Lebas (Oxford: Blackwell, 1996), 158. For other analysis of Lefebvre, see Mark Purcell, "Excavating Lefebvre: The Right to the City and Its Urban Politics of the Inhabitant," *GeoJournal* 58, nos. 2–3 (2002): 99–108; Don Mitchell, *The Right to the City: Social Justice and the Fight for Public Space* (New York: Guilford Press, 2003); David Harvey, *Rebel Cities: From the Right to the City to the Urban Revolution* (London: Verso Books, 2012); and James Holston, "Come to the Street: Urban Protest, Brazil 2013," *Anthropological Quarterly* 87, no. 3 (2014): 887–900.

12 Prominent exceptions include Gareth Millington, *"Race," Culture and the Right to the City: Centres, Peripheries, Margins* (London: Springer, 2011); Keisha-Khan Y. Perry, *Black Women against the Land Grab: The Fight for Racial Justice in Brazil* (Minneapolis: University of Minnesota Press, 2013); and AbdouMaliq Simone, "It's Just the City after All!" *International Journal of Urban and Regional Research* 40, no. 1 (2016): 210–18. See, especially, Stefano Harney and Fred Moten, *The Undercommons: Fugitive Planning and Black Study* (New York: Minor Compositions, 2013).

13 Anna Tsing, *Friction: An Ethnography of Global Connection* (Princeton, NJ: Princeton University Press, 2005), 68.

14 Our workshop conversations were wide ranging. We discussed residents' visions for Detroit's future, the challenges associated with realizing those futures, and opportunities for strengthening and expanding an infrastructure to support movement building in the city. Many of the interviews appear in excerpted form in this book. The editors have done their best to frame these stories alongside maps in ways that give the reader a sense of the breadth and depth of Detroit's political, cultural, and emotional landscape.

15 See Cedric Robinson, *Black Marxism: The Making of the Black Radical Tradition* (Durham: University of North Carolina Press, 1983); and Jodi Melamed, "Racial Capitalism," *Critical Ethnic Studies* 1, no. 1 (2015): 76–85.

16 Settler colonies are places where settlers come to stay, displacing previous inhabitants and establishing their own governments. Examples include the United States, South Africa, Canada, Australia, and Israel. For an introduction see Lorenzo Veracini, *Settler Colonialism: A Theoretical Overview* (New York: Palgrave Macmillan, 2010); Patrick Wolfe, "The Settler Complex : An Introduction," *American Indian Culture and Research Journal* 37, no. 2 (2013): 1–22; Patrick Wolfe, "Land, Labor, and Difference: Elementary Structures of Race," *American Historical Review* 106, no. 3 (2001): 866–905; and Patrick Wolfe, *Settler Colonialism and the Transformation of Anthropology* (New York: Cassell, 1999). We

build on a growing body of scholarship that draws attention to how settler colonialism also shapes anti-Black racism and Black displacement. For example, see Frank Wilderson's use of the category "settler-master," arguing that the master and settler were the same person, in his *Red, White, & Black: Cinema and the Structure of U.S. Antagonisms* (Durham, NC: Duke University Press, 2010).

17 See E. P. Thompson, "History from Below," *Times Literary Supplement*, April 7, 1966, reprinted in Dorothy Thompson, ed., *The Essential E. P. Thompson* (New York: New Press, 2001), 481–89; and Howard Zinn, *A People's History of the United States: 1492–Present* (New York: Routledge, 2015).

18 The groundbreaking work of the Detroit Digital Justice Coalition to reenvision what democratic and accountable spatial data look like in the city is documented in their zines *Opening Data* (Detroit: Allied Media Projects, 2015) and *Opening Data 2* (Detroit: Allied Media Projects, 2018).

19 Examples of charting space through images, stories, and songs outside or alongside the Western cartographic tradition are numerous as well; one particularly resonant current effort is Maylei Blackwell and Mishuana Goeman's Mapping Indigenous L.A. project at UCLA (mila.ucla.edu). For a more thorough treatise on the power of cartography and its historical relationship to the rise of states and empires, see Denis Wood, *Rethinking the Power of Maps* (New York: Guilford Press, 2010).

20 The maps and reports created by the DGEI are now viewed as a trailblazing example of geography oriented toward social justice. We view the workshops as an underappreciated influence of the DGEI. For examples of this work, see William Bunge, *Fitzgerald: Geography of a Revolution* (Athens: University of Georgia Press, 2011); and the 2017 Antipode Symposium on DGEI Then and Now, https://antipodefoundation.org/2017/02/23/dgei-field-notes/. See also Snow F. Grigsby's *An X-Ray Picture of Detroit* (Detroit: S. F. Grigsby, 1933), which used a detailed reading of the city's budget to calculate financially what the impact of true racial equality in employment would be for the Black community.

CHAPTER 1

1 For more on the term *commons* as it relates to urban social movements, see David Harvey, *Rebel Cities: From the Right to the City to the Urban Revolution* (New York: Verso, 2013).

2 Katherine McKittrick, *Demonic Grounds: Black Women and the Cartographies of Struggle* (Minneapolis: University of Minnesota Press, 2006), 146.

3 James Boggs and Grace Lee Boggs, *Revolution and Evolution in the Twentieth Century* (New York: Monthly Review Press, 1974), 170. They describe the clock metaphor as coming originally from Neil Postman and Charles Weingartner's *Teaching as a Subversive Activity: A No-Holds-Barred Assault on Outdated Teaching Methods—with Dramatic and Practical Proposals on How Education Can Be Made Relevant to Today's World* (New York: Delacorte Press, 1969).

4 Gregory Wigmore, "Before the Railroad: From Slavery to Freedom in the Canadian-American Borderland," *Journal of American History* 98, no. 2 (2011): 437–54.

5 For more on the development of this faculty-student research project, see the Mapping Slavery in Detroit project website, www.mappingdetroitslavery.com.

6 Tiya Miles, "Slavery in Early Detroit," *Michigan History* (May–June 2013): 33–37; Jorge Castellanos, "Black Slavery in Detroit," in *Detroit Perspectives: Crossroads and Turning Points*, ed. Wilma Wood Henrickson (Detroit: Wayne State University Press, 1991), 85–93; and Brett Rushforth, *Bonds of Alliance: Indigenous & Atlantic*

Slaveries in New France (Chapel Hill: University of North Carolina Press, 2012), 209, 253–55.

7   Roy Finkenbine, "A Community Militant and Organized: The Colored Vigilant Committee of Detroit," in *A Fluid Frontier: Slavery, Resistance, and the Underground Railroad in the Detroit River Borderland*, ed. Karolyn Smardz Frost and Veta Smith Tucker (Detroit: Wayne State University Press, 2016), 158.

8   Our account of the harrowing story of the Blackburns, as well as the Underground Railroad in general, owes a great debt to Frost and Tucker's outstanding history, *A Fluid Frontier*. See, in particular, Karolyn Smardz Frost, "Forging Transnational Networks for Freedom: From the War of 1812 to the Blackburn Riots of 1833," in Frost and Tucker, *A Fluid Frontier*, 43–66.

9   For more on Unemployed Councils, see James J. Lorence, *Organizing the Unemployed: Community and Union Activists in the Industrial Heartland* (Albany, NY: SUNY Press, 1996).

10 Nicola Pizzolato, "The American Worker and the Forze Nuove: Turin and Detroit at the Twilight of Fordism," *Viewpoint Magazine* 3 (September 25, 2013), www.viewpointmag.com/2013/09/25/the-american-worker-and-the-forze-nuove-turin-and-detroit-at-the-twilight-of-fordism/.

11 Ernie Allen, "Dying from the Inside: The Decline of the League of Revolutionary Black Workers," in *They Should Have Served that Cup of Coffee: Seven Radicals Remember the '60s*, ed. Dick Cluster (Cambridge, MA: South End Press, 1999), 71–110; Nicola Pizzolato, "Transnational Radicals: Labour Dissent and Political Activism in Detroit and Turin (1950–1970)," *IRSH* 56 (2011): 1–30; James A. Geschwender, *Class, Race, and Worker Insurgency* (New York: Cambridge University Press, 1977); and Dan Georgakas and Marvin Surkin, *Detroit: I Do Mind Dying* (Cambridge, MA: South End Press, 1977).

12 Heather Ann Thompson, *Whose Detroit: Politics, Labor, and Race in a Modern American City* (Ithaca, NY: Cornell University Press, 2001).

13 Figures are from Kris Warner, *Protecting Fundamental Labor Rights* (Center for Economic and Policy Research report, Washington, DC, 2012), www.cepr.net/documents/publications/canada-2012–08.pdf; and Mahmud Tayyab, "Debt and Discipline: Neoliberal Political Economy and the Working Classes," *Kentucky Law Journal* 101, no. 1 (2013): 18–19n117. In the private sector, the decline in unionization rates has been even more dramatic, falling from 25 percent in 1975 to 6.9 percent in 2010.

14 David Freund, *Colored Property: State Policy and White Racial Politics in Suburban America* (Chicago: University of Chicago Press, 2007), 16.

15 Freund, *Colored Property*.

16 Freund, *Colored Property*.

17 Beth Tompkins Bates, *The Making of Black Detroit in the Age of Henry Ford* (Chapel Hill: University of North Carolina Press, 2012), 108.

18 The Black Legion was active in Ohio, Michigan, Indiana, and Kentucky. In the mid-1930s, the organization claimed sixty thousand to one hundred thousand members. See Peter Amann, "Vigilante Fascism: The Black Legion as an American Hybrid," *Comparative Studies in Society and History* 25, no. 3 (1983): 490–524.

19 Freund, *Colored Property*.

20 Figure is from George Lipsitz, *The Possessive Investment in Whiteness: How White People Profit from Identity Politics* (Philadelphia: Temple University Press, 2006), 6. Lipsitz is citing Harvard Sitkoff, *The Struggle for Black Equality* (New York: Hill and Wang, 1981), 176.

21 Freund, *Colored Property*, 36.

22 Thomas Sugrue, *The Origins of the Urban Crisis* (Princeton, NJ:

Princeton University Press, 2014).

23 Freund, *Colored Property*, 5–6.

24 MLKJP, GAMK, Martin Luther King Jr. Papers (series I–IV), Martin Luther King, Jr. Center for Nonviolent Social Change, Atlanta, GA, T-26, Stanford University's Martin Luther King, Jr. Research and Education Institute, kinginstitute.stanford.edu/king-papers/documents/address-freedom-rally-cobo-hall.

25 In their usage of the term *uprising* or *rebellion*, many in Detroit echo the views of British historian Edward P. Thompson, who once described *riot* as a "four-letter word" because it transforms people from politically motivated, rational-thinking actors into an irrational mob. See Edward P. Thompson, "The Moral Economy of the English Crowd in the Eighteenth Century," *Past & Present* 50 (1971): 76–136. The title of this section is taken from a quote in Thompson's article, 76.

26 Sidney Fine, *Violence in the Model City: The Cavanagh Administration, Race Relations, and the Detroit Riot of 1967* (East Lansing: Michigan State University Press, 1989), 163.

27 Max Herman, *Fighting in the Streets: Ethnic Succession and Urban Unrest in Twentieth Century America* (New York: Peter Lang, 2005), 76.

28 "Jesse Davis, 11/29/2016," Detroit '67 Audio Oral History, interviewed by Celeste Goedert, Detroit '67: Looking Back to Move Forward, Detroit Historical Society, January 27, 2017, detroit1967.detroithistorical.org/items/show/479.

29 "Jesse Davis, 11/29/2016." In addition to Jesse Davis's interview, the oral histories of others who witnessed the '67 rebellion are also archived and available on Detroit '67: Looking Back to Move Forward, Detroit Historical Society, detroit1967.detroithistorical.org.

30 According to Fine in *Violence in the Model City*, this included 611 supermarkets, food, and grocery stores; 537 cleaners and laundries; 326 clothing and department stores; 285 liquor stores, bars, and lounges; 240 drug stores; and 198 furniture stores.

31 Sugrue, *Origins of Urban Crisis*, 143.

32 We thank Kaleema Hasan for providing us with a copy of a 2013 speech made by Susana Adame at the First Unitarian Universalist Church of Detroit, which contained this quote from the church bulletin.

33 Fine, *Violence in the Model City*, 387.

34 Boggs and Boggs, *Revolution and Evolution in the Twentieth Century*, 264.

35 Boggs and Boggs, *Revolution and Evolution in the Twentieth Century*, 19.

36 Boggs and Boggs, *Revolution and Evolution in the Twentieth Century*, xx.

37 Some of these titles include Boggs and Boggs, *Revolution and Evolution in the Twentieth Century*; James Boggs, Grace Lee Boggs, Freddy Paine, and Lyman Paine, *Conversations in Maine: Exploring Our Nation's Future* (Minneapolis: University of Minnesota Press, 2018 [1978]); Grace Lee Boggs, *Living for Change: An Autobiography* (Minneapolis: University of Minnesota Press, 1998); Grace Lee Boggs (with Scott Kurashige), *The Next American Revolution: Sustainable Activism for the Twenty-First Century* (Berkeley: University of California Press, 2011).

38 Grace Lee Boggs, *Living for Change*, 36.

39 Grace Lee Boggs, *Living for Change*, 79.

40 Zak Rosen and Neil Greenberg (with Jay Allison), "Fake City, Real Dreams," *Transom*, August 27, 2008, transom.org/2008/fake-city-real-dreams/.

CHAPTER 2

1 On the "land question," see Henry Bernstein, *Class Dynamics of Agrarian Change*, vol. 1, Agrarian Change & Peasant Studies (West Hartford, CT: Kumarian Press, 2010); Nancy Lee Peluso and Christian Lund, "New Frontiers of Land Control: Introduction," *Journal of Peasant Studies* 38, no. 4 (2011): 667–81. On land politics in Detroit, see Sara Safransky, "Rethinking Land Struggle in the Postindustrial City," *Antipode* 49, no. 4 (2017): 1079–1100; and Sara Safransky, "Land Justice as a Historical Diagnostic: Thinking with Detroit," *Annals of the American Association of Geographers* 108, no. 2 (2018): 499–512.

2 It should be noted that Detroit's ecological landscape never fit the frontier-sounding description of "prairie" in the first place; rather, the area is a patchwork of oak openings and mixed deciduous woodlands. For more on the representation—and production—of "nature" in Detroit, see Nate Millington, "Post-Industrial Imaginaries: Nature, Representation, and Ruin in Detroit, Michigan," *International Journal of Urban and Regional Research* 37, no. 1 (2013): 279–96; and Sara Safransky, "Greening the Urban Frontier: Race, Property, and Resettlement in Detroit," *Geoforum* 56 (2014): 237–48.

3 Keith Basso, *Wisdom Sits in Places: Landscape and Language among the Western Apache* (Albuquerque: University of New Mexico Press, 1996).

4 On "racial regimes of ownership," see Brenna Bhandar, *Colonial Lives of Property: Law, Land, and Racial Regimes of Ownership* (Durham, NC: Duke University Press, 2018).

5 See, for instance, Jennifer Conlin, "Detroit Pushes Back with Young Muscles," *New York Times*, July 3, 2011; Matt Haber, "Remaking Detroit: Can Creative Companies Save an American City on the Brink?" *Fast Company*, February 13, 2013, www.fastcompany.com/1682409/remaking-detroit-can-creative-companies-save-an-american-city-on-the-brink; and Edward Helmore, "'Detroit Will Rise Again': Glimmers of Defiance after City's Bankruptcy," *Guardian*, July 20, 2013.

6 Keith B. Richburg, "Detroit's Demise Was Decades in the Making," *Washington Post*, July 9, 2013.

7 Sean Hemmerle, "The Remains of Detroit," *Time*, October 5, 2009; Yves Marchand and Romaine Meffre, "Detroit's Beautiful, Horrible Decline," *Time*, October 5, 2009.

8 "Manuel Moroun and Family," *Forbes*, January 14, 2015.

9 M. D. Harmon, "Who to Blame for the Death of Detroit?" *Maine Wire*, July 25, 2013.

10 Christine MacDonald, "Private Landowners Complicate Reshaping of Detroit," *Detroit News*, February 3, 2011.

11 Christine MacDonald, "Pot Bust Tied to Land Speculator," *Detroit News*, August 26, 2011.

12 Detroit news outlets periodically run stories about dumping in the city. See, for example, Kenneth J. Coleman, "And Still They're Dumping on Detroit," *Michigan Chronicle*, February 9, 1994; Charles Ramirez, "Detroit's Property Has Become Dumping Ground," *Detroit News*, May 2, 2006; and Ronnie Dahl, "Abandoned Boats Shipwrecked on the Streets of Detroit," WXYZ Detroit, October 30, 2014, www.wxyz.com/news/region/detroit/photos-the-abandoned-boats-of-detroit.

13 See, for example, Ian Austen, "A Black Mound of Canadian Oil Waste Is Rising over Detroit," *New York Times*, May 18, 2013.

14 Then-governor Rick Snyder officially signed off on the purchase agreement between John Hantz and Emergency Manager Kevyn Orr on October 18, 2013. Ironically, the purchase had been approved by the Detroit City Council in 2012—before its legal power was taken away by emergency management.

15 Andrew Foot, *Windsor Modern: A Guidebook to Modern Architecture 1940–1970 in Windsor, Ontario Canada* (self-pub., 2007).

16 "Who Is the CEA?," Citizens Environment Alliance, www.citizensenvironmentalliance.org/about_cea.html.

CHAPTER 3

1 See for example, Kameshwari Pothukuchi, "Five Decades of Community Food Planning in Detroit: City and Grassroots, Growth and Equity," *Journal of Planning Education and Research* 35, no. 4 (2015): 419–34; Jessi Quizar, "Who Cares for Detroit? Urban Agriculture, Black Self-Determination, and Struggles over Urban Space" (PhD diss., University of Southern California, 2014); Monica M. White, "Sisters of the Soil: Urban Gardening as Resistance in Detroit," *Race/Ethnicity: Multidisciplinary Global Contexts* 5, no. 1 (2011): 13–28.

2 For a discussion of the relationship between Maoism and Black radicalism, see Robin D. G. Kelley and Betsy Esch, "Black Like Mao," *Souls* 1, no. 4 (1999): 6–41; also see Mao Tse-tung, "Statement Supporting the American Negroes in Their Just Struggle against Racial Discrimination by U.S. Imperialism," *Peking Review* 9, no. 33 (1966): 24–27. The Chinese Civil War took place between 1927 and 1949 when the Chinese Communist Party overthrew the Kuomintang-led government.

3 For more on the importance of dialectical materialism, nationalism, internationalism, and intercommunalism to the Black Panther Party, see *The Huey P. Newton Reader*, ed. David Hilliard and Donald Weise (New York: Seven Stories Press, 2002).

4 The scandal surrounding the Tuskegee Syphilis Study was caused by revelations that white doctors in Alabama from the US Public Health Service had deceived and withheld treatment from African American male patients who suffered from the illness to advance a research study, over the course of forty years, from 1932 to 1972. See Susan M. Reverby, *Examining Tuskegee: The Infamous Syphilis Study and Its Legacy* (Chapel Hill: University of North Carolina Press, 2009).

CHAPTER 4

1 Neil Smith, *The New Urban Frontier* (New York: Routledge, 1996), xviii.

2 Jamie Peck and Heather Whiteside, "Financializing Detroit," *Economic Geography* 92, no. 3 (2016): 235–68.

3 Laura Pulido, "Flint, Environmental Racism, and Racial Capitalism," *Capitalism Nature Socialism* 27, no. 3 (2016): 1–16.

4 Indeed, if we read this chapter against the timelines in chapter 1, we see that the most recent waves of revanchism sweeping the country rework already-existing structures of racial capitalism, slavery, and settler colonialism on which the US national sovereignty rests. See David Langstaff, "The Inauguration of Fascism? Thinking Violence and Resistance in the Age of Trump," *Abolition*, January 28, 2017, abolitionjournal.org/the-inauguration-of-fascism-thinking-violence-and-resistance-in-the-age-of-trump/.

5 Paige Williams, "Drop Dead, Detroit!" *New Yorker*, January 27, 2014, www.newyorker.com/magazine/2014/01/27/drop-dead-detroit. The full quote reads, "What we're gonna do is turn Detroit into an Indian reservation, where we herd all the Indians into the city, build a fence around it, and then throw in the blankets and corn."

6 Considered to be a model by conservatives for other states, the Mackinac Center has frequently used Detroit as a testing ground

for new policies. See Joshua M. Akers, "Making Markets: Think Tank Legislation and Private Property in Detroit," *Urban Geography* 34, no. 8 (2013): 1070–95.

7   The full text of Emergency Manager Order No. 1 can be seen at www.detroitmi.gov/Portals/0/docs/EM/Order1.pdf.

8   The full text of the complaint can be found at web.archive.org /web/20170103181309/http://sugarlaw.org/wp-content /uploads/2013/05/Complaint-Fed-Ct.pdf.

9   See the full plan at web.archive.org/web/20180404101110/http:// www.d-rem.org:80/peoplesplan/.

10   Christine Ferretti, "For Detroit Retirees, Pension Cuts Become Reality," *Detroit News*, February 27, 2015, www.detroitnews.com /story/news/local/wayne-county/2015/02/27/detroit-retirees -pension-cuts-become-reality/24156301/.

11   Sarah Cwiek, "With Citizen District Councils Eliminated, Detroiters Talk How to Move Forward on Development, Michigan Radio, October 14, 2014, www.michiganradio.org/post/citizens-district-councils-eliminated-detroiters-talk-how-move -forward-development.

12   Michigan's Blighted Area Rehabilitation Act of 1945 simultaneously gave cities a set of new powers related to urban renewal and "blight" clearance and mandated the creation of CDCs in redevelopment areas, which would consult with the city on urban renewal plans. But CDCs were not widely created in Detroit neighborhood (if at all) until the late 1960s, when the City of Detroit passed an ordinance implementing the CDC requirement in the 1945 Blighted Area Rehabilitation Act. Jefferson-Chalmers was one of the first CDCs created in the city, along with Virginia Park. See www. legislature.mi.gov/(S(zma334vcdtcrqvrw1ie3bt45))/documents /mcl/pdf/mcl-Act-344-of-1945.pdf.

13   UN Human Rights Office of the High Commissioner, "Joint Press Statement by Special Rapporteur on Adequate Housing as a Component of the Right to an Adequate Standard of Living and to Right to Non-Discrimination in This Context, and Special Rapporteur on the Human Right to Safe Drinking Water and Sanitation Visit to City of Detroit (United States of America)," October 20, 2014, www.ohchr .org/EN/NewsEvents/Pages/DisplayNews.aspx?NewsID=15188.

14   For the video of Ross's speech, see "Rev. Joan C. Ross, Linda Campbell Speak Out against Anti-Community Benefits Bill (HB 5977) in Detroit City Council Special Session," New North End Woodward Community Coalition, December 8, 2014, www. northendwoodward.org/2014/12/rev-joan-c-ross-linda-campbell -speak-out-against-anti-community-benefits-bill-hb-5977-in -detroit-city-council-special-session/.

15   See "Coalition Turns in Signatures to Place Community Benefits Ordinance on November Ballot" Equitabledetroit.org. Archived at https://web.archive.org/web/20161022162015/http://www. equitabledetroit.org/.

16   Ryan Felton, "EXCLUSIVE: Former Duggan Liaison Heads Dark Money Fund Opposing Detroit Community Benefits Ordinance," *Detroit Metro Times*, October 12, 2016, www.metrotimes.com /news-hits/archives/2016/10/12/exclusive-former-duggan -liaison-heads-dark-money-fund-opposing-detroit-community- benefits-ordinance.

17   Oona Goodin-Smith, "Republicans Block Subpoena for Gov. Rick Snyder's Flint Water Documents," MLive, updated January 24, 2017, www.mlive.com/news/flint/index.ssf/2017/01/committee _denies_request_to_su.html.

18   Avi Selk, "'I Can't Lose My House': Outrage after Flint Sends Foreclosure Warnings over Tainted-Water Bills," *Washington Post*, May 4, 2017, www.washingtonpost.com/news/energy-environment /wp/2017/05/04/the-latest-in-flints-water-crisis-pay-for-it-or-lose

-your-home/?utm_term=.285b0bba5b9f; and Christine Ferretti, "Nearly 18K at Risk as Detroit Water Shutoffs Begin," *Detroit News*, April 19, 2017, www.detroitnews.com/story/news/local /detroit-city/2017/04/19/water-shutoffs-begin-detroit/100661242/.

CHAPTER 5

1   See Asher Ghertner's argument, drawn from India, that urges scholars to look to "mid-level theories," including enclosure, urban revolution, and accumulation by dispossession instead of defaulting to gentrification to describe urban displacement. He chooses these not to be exhaustive but to focus on *causes* and *mechanisms* rather than outcomes. Asher Ghertner, *Rule by Aesthetics: World-Class City Making in Delhi* (New York: Oxford University Press, 2015).

2   Bernadette Atuahene and Timothy R. Hodge, "Stategraft," *Southern California Law Review* 91 (2017): 263–302.

3   Levy's film is available here: vimeo.com/89583583.

4   See Matthew Desmond, *Evicted: Poverty and Profit in the American City* (New York: Broadway Books, 2016).

5   Quoted in Michelle Wilde Anderson, "The New Minimal Cities," *Yale Law Journal* 123, no. 1118 (2014): 166.

6   More information about the community radio station can be found on its website at www.wnuc.org.

7   Reverend Ross's quote of $175,000 is a conservative estimate and is likely referring to the neighborhoods east of Woodward. By 2018, prices for homes in the historically elite Arden Park and Boston-Edison portion of the neighborhood had risen well into the $500,000 range, according to real estate listings on Zillow.com.

8   Since 2008, the Storehouse of Hope has provided emergency food, personal care services, referrals, resources, and education and development activities designed to enhance human dignity and sustain families and individuals living in the North End. In 2015, the scope of their work broadened to include the CLT.

CHAPTER 6

1   Henri Lefebvre, "The Right to the City," *Writings on Cities*, trans. and ed. Eleonore Kofman and Elizabeth Lebas (Oxford: Blackwell).

2   See Kafui A. Attoh, "What Kind of Right Is the Right to the City?" *Progress in Human Geography* 35, no. 5 (2011): 669–85; Don Mitchell, *The Right to the City: Social Justice and the Fight for Public Space* (New York: Guilford Press, 2003); and David Harvey, *Rebel Cities: From the Right to the City to the Urban Revolution* (London: Verso Books, 2012).

3   For a view of the right to the city that accounts for colonialism, racism, and patriarchy, see Stefan Kipfer and Kanishka Goonewardena, "Urban Marxism and the Post-Colonial Question: Henri Lefebvre and 'Colonisation,'" *Historical Materialism* 21, no. 2 (2013): 76–116. David Harvey argues that the right to the city is "one of the most precious yet most neglected of our human rights . . . far more than the individual liberty to access urban resources: it is a right to change ourselves by changing the city. It is, moreover, a common rather than an individual right since this transformation inevitably depends upon the exercise of a collective power to reshape the processes of urbanization." David Harvey, "The Right to the City," *New Left Review* 53 (September–October 2008): 23–40.

4   Mark Purcell, "Possible Worlds: Henri Lefebvre and the Right to the City," *Journal of Urban Affairs* 36, no. 1 (2014): 141–54.

5   The MST full statement responding to Charity Hicks's death can be found here: http://ggjalliance.org/sites/default/files

/solidariedade%20Charity_%20%282%29.pdf.

6   Bob Campbell and David Everett, "Trash, Cash, and Ash: Officials Like Detroit Incinerator Bet, but It's No Sure Thing," *Detroit Free Press*, May 7, 1989.

7   Constance C. Prater, "Troubles Smolder at Detroit's Trash Plant," *Detroit Free Press*, May 20, 1991; Thomas Easton, "Acquisitive Philip Morris May Be on the Prowl," *Baltimore Sun*, September 22, 1991; "Detroit Incinerator Deal Completed," *Detroit Free Press*, October 24, 1991; and "For the Corporate Penske, No Fear of Sharp Turns," *New York Times*, May 26, 1996.

8   Bunyan Bryant and Elaine Hockman, "The Greater Detroit Resource Recovery Facility (the Incinerator)," in Bunyan Bryant, ed., *Michigan: A State of Environmental Justice?* (New York: Morgan James, 2011), 131; "Incinerator Foes Hold Mock Funeral," *Windsor (ON) Star*, April 23, 1990.

9   Sarah Rahal, "Clean Air Advocates Petition to Close Detroit Incinerator," *Detroit News*, May 18, 2018.

10 Environmental Protection Agency, EJ-Screen Report, generated using ejscreen.epa.gov/mapper, and selecting a half-mile radius centered at 42.367559,-83.052270.

11 Wendy Wendland-Bowyer, "Hazards Lurking in Soil as Children Play," *Detroit Free Press*, January 23, 2003; Michigan Department of Environmental Quality, *Renewable Operating Permit Staff Report*, April 2010, www.deq.state.mi.us/aps/downloads/ROP /pub_ntce/M4148/M4148%20Staff%20Report%2009-16-14.doc.

12 Ghassan B. Hamra et al., "Outdoor Particulate Matter Exposure and Lung Cancer: A Systematic Review and Meta-Analysis," *Environmental Health Perspectives* 122, no. 9 (2014): 906–11.

13 Bob Campbell and Constance Prater, "Boiler, Safety Concerns Dog Incinerator's Start," *Detroit Free Press*, April 15, 1989.

14 Elizabeth Karvlin, "We Didn't Screw It Up," *Bond Buyer*, September 29, 2001. See also Campbell and Everett, "Trash, Cash & Ash," *Detroit Free Press*, May 7, 1989; and Angie Cannon, "Wall Street Tells City: Sell Incinerator or Lose Credit Rating," *Detroit News*, August 16, 1991.

15 John Gallagher, "Ex-Detroit Official Defends 2005 Pension Deal Blamed in City's Downfall," *Detroit Free Press*, November 21, 2013.

16 Mary Beth Doyle and Brad Van Guilder, "For a Clean and Safe Detroit: Close the Country's Largest Incinerator," *From the Ground Up* 34, no. 2 (2002): 7–8.

17 Kat Stafford and Kristina Hall, "Controversial Detroit Incinerator Shut Down," Detroit News, March 27, 2019.

18 Breathe Free Detroit Press Release, "Community Celebrates Detroit Incinerator Closure, Step Toward Environmental Justice," March 27, 2019, https://www.ecocenter.org/community -celebrates-detroit-incinerator-closure-step-toward -environmental-justice.

19 Bill Laitner, "Heart and Sole: Detroiter Walks 21 Miles in Work Commute," *Detroit Free Press*, February 1, 2015.

20 Bill Laitner, "Survey: Detroit Has Costliest Car Insurance in U.S," *Detroit Free Press*, February 1, 2015.

21 Kate Zernike, "A Sea of Charter Schools in Detroit Leaves Students Adrift," *New York Times*, June 28, 2016, www.nytimes. com/2016/06/29/us/for-detroits-children-more-school-choice -but-not-better-schools.html.

22 For a first-person account of Warren's experience with the DGEI, see Gwendolyn Warren and Cindi Katz in conversation, vimeo. com/111159306.

23 See Zenobia Jeffries, "In Detroit, Freedom Schools Offer an Alternative to City's Struggling Education System," *Yes!*, September 6, 2016. www.yesmagazine.org/peace-justice/in-detroit -freedom-schools-offer-an-alternative-to-citys-struggling

-education-system-20160906.

24 For more information about People in Education, see www. peopleineducation.org/.

25 Janice E. Hale, *Learning while Black: Creating Educational Excellence for African American Children* (Baltimore: Johns Hopkins University Press, 2011), 111–51.

26 Lindsay Vanhulle, "Duggan: City EMS Response Times Dip below National Average for First Time in Decade," *Crain's Detroit Business*, April 26, 2017.

27 Mike Wilkinson, "Detroit Police Response Times down but Official Numbers Questioned," MLive, November 14, 2015, www. mlive.com/news/detroit/index.ssf/2015/11/tracking_progress_in_ detroit_p.html.

28 The "Big Four" patrols targeted bars and street corners where African Americans used to congregate; Detroit Police Chief James Craig's father was himself a victim of this harassment. See an interview with Detroit chief of police James Craig, www.freep. com/story/news/columnists/rochelle-riley/2017/07/23/detroit-po- lice-chief-craig-riot/497197001/. See also Mark Binelli, "The Fire Last Time," *New Republic*, April 6, 2017. STRESS was known for its use of excessive force and violence, much of which was directed at the Black community. Restore Order featured militarized SWAT style raids that led to numerous arrests of Detroiters in some of the city's poorest districts, and resulted in the killing of Terrance Kellom, though few of these operations ever resulted in charges being filed.

29 Lacino Hamilton, "The Gentrification-to-Prison Pipeline," *Truth- out*, April 30, 2017, www.truth-out.org/news/item/40413-the-gen- trification-to-prison-pipeline.

30 See Kimberley Kinder, *DIY Detroit: Making Do in a City without Services* (Minneapolis: University of Minnesota Press, 2016).

ANOTHER CITY IS POSSIBLE

1 Saskia Sassen, *Expulsions: Brutality and Complexity in the Global Economy* (Cambridge, MA: Harvard University Press, 2014), 15.

2 Cheryl Harris talks about how Black geographies like Detroit are made available for reappropriation. See the following talks in which she uses Detroit as an example: Cheryl Harris, "The Afterlife of Slavery: Markets, Property, and Race," Artists Space Books & Talks, New York, January 19, 2016, www.youtube.com/ watch?v=dQQGndN3BvY&t=1989s.

3 For an example of this critique of alternative food movements, see Julie Guthman, "'If They Only Knew': The Unbearable Whiteness of Alternative Food," in *Cultivating Food Justice: Race, Class, and Sustainability*, ed. Alison Hop Alkon and Julian Agyeman (Cam- bridge, MA: MIT Press, 2011), 263–81.

4 For early articulation of this theme, see James Boggs and Grace Lee Boggs, *Revolution and Evolution in the Twentieth Century* (New York: Monthly Review Press, 1974).

SOURCES FOR SELECTED MAPS AND FIGURES

CHAPTER 1

16–17 Red Sky's Migration Chart

The display at the Museum of Ojibwa Culture was adapted from *The Sacred Scrolls of the Southern Ojibway* by Selwyn Dewdney © University of Toronto Press, 1975. Used with permission from University of Toronto Press and the Museum of Ojibwa Culture. See *The Migration of the Anishinabe—Ojibwe/Waasa-Inaabidaa, We Look in All Directions* (2002), www.ojibwe.org/home/about_migration_hotmap. html and "Migration Story of the Ojibway to the New Land" (Passamaquoddy Tribe at Pleasant Point, 2003), www.wabanaki.com/migration_story.htm.

17 Bellin Map of Detroit, 1764

Jacques Nicolas Bellin, *La Riviere du Detroit Depuis le Lac Sainte Claire jusqu'au Lac Erie* (Paris: Dépôt des Cartes et Plans de la Marine, 1764), Bibliothèque Nationale de France. The Wisconsin Historical Society has made their account, *The Journey of Dollier and Gallinée*, available online at www.americanjourneys.org/aj-049/summary/index.asp.

22 Slavery Landmarks in Detroit

Archival base map: John Farmer, *Map of the City of Detroit in the State of Michigan* (New York: C. B. and J. R. Graham Lithographers, 1835), Stephen S. Clark Library, University of Michigan Library.

22 Elizabeth Denison Forth's House

to make "provisions . . . for the poor" in a house of worship Draft of Elizabeth Denison Forth's will, Forth file, Burton Historical Collection, Detroit Public Library; also quoted in Miles, *The Dawn of Detroit*, 241.

Elizabeth Denison Forth, Home Site, Informational Site, 328 Macomb, Detroit — Wayne County, http://www.mcgi.state.mi.us/hso/sites/15590.htm.

Elizabeth Denison Forth, Last Will and Testament, Forth file, Burton Historical Collection, Detroit Public Library.

Isabella E. Swan, *Lisette*. Gross Isle, MI: Isabella E. Swan, 1965.

Mark E. McPherson, "Lisette's Domestic Legacy," *Michigan Chronicle*, February 10–16, 1999.

Mark E. McPherson, "Lisette In Paris," *Michigan Chronicle*, February 24–March 2, 1999, C6.

Mark E. McPherson, *Looking for Lisette: In a Quest of an American Original* (Dexter, MI: Mage Press-Thomson-Shore, 2001).

"Elizabeth Denison Forth," Salute to Women, *Michigan Chronicle*, February 4–10, 1998, D4.

"Lisette's Legacy of Slavery," *Michigan Chronicle*, February 3, 1999.

"Lisette Gift," *Michigan Chronicle*, March 9, 1999.

"The Enigmatic Lisette: The Quest for Elizabeth Denison Forth," *Michigan Chronicle Compositions*, January 27–February 2, 1999, C1.

23 Elijah Brush's Farm

William B. Blume, ed., "Selected Papers, Supreme Court of Michigan: Case 60, Paper 2, Denison &al: vs. Tucker, September 24, 1807" and "Syllabi of Decisions and Opinions: In the Matter of the Elizabeth

Denison, Et al., September 26, 1807," *Transactions of the Supreme Court of the Territory of Michigan 1805–1814* (Ann Arbor: University of Michigan Press, 1935), 1:134–35, 319–20.

23 William Hull's House
Clarence E. Carter, ed., The Territory of Michigan 1805–1820, vol. X of The Territorial Papers of the United States (Washington: United States Printing Office, 1942), 390.

23 Sainte Anne's Church
Ste. Anne's Church Registers, 1704–1842, Bentley Historical Library, University of Michigan, Ann Arbor, MI.

23 Fort Detroit
"A Company of Negros mounted the Guard"
James Askin to Charles Askin, August 18, 1807, Askin Papers vol. 2, 566, quoted in Tiya Miles, *The Dawn of Detroit*, 192.

23 Whipping Post
"that any justice of the peace"
Laws of the Territory of Michigan: With Marginal Notes And an Index: to Which Are Prefixed, the Ordinance And Several Acts of Congress Relating to This Territory (Detroit: Sheldon & Reed, 1820), 213–14. George B. Catlin, *The Story of Detroit* (Detroit: The Detroit News, 1923), 214.
"where criminals were whipped for petty"
Ephraim S. Williams, "Personal Reminiscences," *Michigan Pioneer and Historical Collections* (Lansing: Thorp & Godfrey, State Printers and Binders, 1886), 8: 235. https://www.cmich.edu/library/clarke /ResearchResources/Michigan_Material_Local/Detroit_Pre_state hood_Descriptions/Entries_by_Date/Pages/1815-18-Williams.aspx.
George B. Catlin, *The Story of Detroit* (Detroit: The Detroit News, 1923), 214.

23 William Macomb's Farm
"Macomb Estate Ledger," *Macomb Family Papers*, R: 2: 1796, Burton Historical Collection, Detroit Public Library, Detroit, Michigan.

23 James May's House
James May Daybook, William D. Robertson, September 6, 1795, and "James May Finding Aid," James May Papers, Burton Historical Collection, Detroit Public Library, Detroit, Michigan.

23 John Askin Farm/Estate
Milo M. Quaife, ed., John Askin Papers, Volume I: 1747–1795 and Volume II: 1796–1820 (Detroit: Detroit Library Commission, 1928). See especially, 1:50-59.

23 Matthew Elliott's House
He owned "dozens" of enslaved Black people "Matthew Elliott Essex County" (York University, Harriet Tubman Institute, Toronto, 2012), 4, 5, quoted in Miles, *The Dawn of Detroit,* 147–48.

24 Traces of Slavery in Present-Day Detroit
"in possession of Settlers"
Transactions of the Supreme Court of Michigan, 1805–1846, vol 1, ed. William Wirt Bloom (Ann Arbor: University of Michigan Press, 1935–40), 395, 414–18. Also, Clever F. Bald, *The Great Fire of 1805* (Detroit: Wayne University Press, 1951), 15–20 and David G. Chardavoyne, "The Northwest Ordinance and Michigan's Territorial Heritage," in Paul Finkelman and Martin J. Hershock, eds. *The History of Michigan Law* (Athens: Ohio University Press, 2006), 21.
Slave owner names sourced from Bill McGraw, "Slavery Is Detroit's Big, Bad Secret?," *Deadline Detroit*, August 27, 2012, www.dead linedetroit.com/articles/1686/slavery_is_detroit_s_big_bad _secret_why_don_t_we_know_anything_about_it; Bill McGraw,

"Slavery Is a Quiet Part of City's Past," *Detroit Free Press,* February 22, 2001, http://mlloyd.org/gen/macomb/text/slave22_20010222.htm; "Native Americans as Slaves, Slave Owners in North," Interview by Michel Martin, *Tell Me More.* Transcript, National Public Radio, January 30, 2012; D. Katzman, "Black Slavery in Michigan," *American Studies* 11, no. 2 (1970): 56–66, https://journals.ku.edu/amerstud/article/view/2447; Edward J. Littlejohn, "Slaves, Judge Woodward, and the Supreme Court of the Michigan Territory," *Michigan Bar Journal,* July 2015, 22–25, www.michbar.org/file/barjournal/article/documents/pdf4article2649.pdf; and David Dill Jr. "Portrait of an Opportunist," *Watertown Daily Times,* September 9, 16, 23, 1990.

26 Detroit and the Underground Railroad
Archival base map: John Farmer, *Map of the City of Detroit in the State of Michigan* (New York: C. B. and J. R. Graham Lithographers, 1835), Stephen S. Clark Library, University of Michigan Library.

33 Detroit and Suburbs Historical Population
Campbell Gibson and Kay Jung, "Historical Census Statistics on Population Totals by Race, 1790 to 1990" (Washington, DC: US Census Bureau, 2005), www.census.gov/population, www.documentation/twps0076/twps0076.html; and Steven Manson, Jonathan Schroeder, David Van Riper, and Steven Ruggles, "Time Series Table A00. Total Population," IPUMS-NHGIS database, http://doi.org/10.18128/D050.V13.0.

40 HOLC Redlining Map of Detroit
Hearne Brothers, *Hearne Brothers Present Polyconic Projection Map of Greater Detroit (Detroit 1939),* Robert K. Nelson, LaDale Winling, Richard Marciano, Nathan Connolly, et al., "Mapping Inequality," *American Panorama,* ed. Robert K. Nelson and Edward L. Ayers,

https://dsl.richmond.edu/panorama/redlining/#loc=11/42.5594/-83.2990&opacity=0.8&city=detroit-mi.

41 DGEI Map of Houses Deteriorating and Dilapidated, 1960
DETROITography blog, December 10, 2014, https://detroitography.com/2014/12/10/Detroit-redlining-map-1939. Map source: William Bunge, *Field Notes: Discussion Paper Number 1,* ed. Ronald J. Horvath and Edward J. Vander Velde (Michigan State University, 1969, 59), https://radicalantipode.files.wordpress.com/2017/01/dgei_fieldnotes-i.pdf.

42–43 Race and Ethnicity in Detroit
2010 Decennial Census Summary File 1, Table P5: Hispanic or Latino Origin by Race, Block level (US Census Bureau, December 21, 2010); and 2011 Canadian Census Ethnicity by Tract, Statistics Canada.

44–45 Wealth and Poverty in Detroit
2008–12 American Community Survey, Table DP03: Selected Economic Characteristics, Blockgroup Level (US Census Bureau, 2013), https://factfinder.census.gov/.

CHAPTER 2

71 Guide map (and subsequent chapter guide maps)
City of Detroit Department of Neighborhoods, 2017, https://data.detroitmi.gov/Government/Detroit-Neighborhoods/5mn6-ihjv/data.

73 Everywhere in Michigan with at Least as much Vacancy as Detroit, 2012
2008–12 American Community Survey, Table S2501: Occupancy Characteristics, Census Designated Place level.

84–85 Land Speculation in the Feedom Freedom Neighborhood

Detroit Parcel database, City of Detroit, City Assessor, 2017; Archival Tax Foreclosures in Detroit, 2002–13, Data Driven Detroit database, 2014, http://portal.datadrivendetroit.org/datasets/9438afd 734d348a694c42a28c4103731_0; and Joshua Akers, Alex B. Hill, and Aaron Petcoff, www.propertypraxis.org.

84 "malignant, cancerous tumor"

Glenda D. Price, Linda Smith, and Dan Gilbert. "A Message from the Chairs" in Detroit Blight Removal Task Force Plan, May 2014, https://web.archive.org/web/20190926133037/ https://datadrivendetroit.org/files/DCPS/CHAPTER%2000.pdf.

91, 93 Black Bottom, 1949 and 1956

Archival neighborhood photographs courtesy of the Burton Historical Collection at Detroit Public Library. Historical aerial photograph from the DTE Historical Aerial Photo Collection at Wayne State University, https://digital.library.wayne.edu/dte_aerial/index.html.

98–99 Detroit Historical Land Cover, circa 1800

"Michigan Circa 1800 Presettlement Vegetation Cover," Michigan Department of Natural Resources, http://gis-midnr.opendata .arcgis.com/datasets/michigan-circa-1800-presettlement -vegetation-cover.

99 "In spite of heavy industry"

Lora Richards, "Urban Dynamics: Detroit River Corridor Preliminary Assessment of Land Use Change," USGS, last modified November 2016, landcover.usgs.gov/urban/detroit/intro.php; and Bruce A. Manny, Thomas A. Edsall, and Eugene Jaworski, "The Detroit River, Michigan: An Ecological Profile," US Fish and Wildlife Service Biological Report 85, 7.17 (1988): 1–86.

CHAPTER 3

120 French Ribbon Farms

Georges-Henri-Victor Collot. Plan Topographique du Détroit et des Eaux qui Forment la Jonction du Lac Erié avec le Lac St Clair, 1796. This version is an adaptation by F. Leesemann and M. A. Heinze of US Engineer Office, Detroit, Michigan, 1965, Office of the Coast Survey (NOAA), https://historicalcharts.noaa.gov /historicals/preview/image/00-00-1796.

121 Pingree Potato Patches

John Conline, Report of Agricultural Committee, Detroit, Mich., of the Cultivation of Idle Land by the Poor and Unemployed (Detroit: Thos. Smith Press, 1896), 16–17, https://babel.hathitrust.org /cgi/pt?id=mdp.39015071615228;view=1up;seq=3.

153 Black Farm Operators in the United States, 1900–2012

Steven Manson, Jonathan Schroeder, David Van Riper, and Steven Ruggles, "U.S. Census of Agriculture Farm Operators by Race," IPUMS-NHGIS database, http://doi.org/10.18128/D050.V13.0.

CHAPTER 4

162 Michigan Cities under Emergency Management

Based on a map by the We the People of Detroit research collective, which is available here: https://wethepeopleofdetroit.com /communityresearch/water/.

172 Olympia Development Area

Detroit Parcel database, City of Detroit, City Assessor, 2017.

184 Detroit Water Department Top Unpaid Water Bills, 2014

Map inspired by Alex B. Hill, "Map: Top 40 Delinquent Commercial Water Accounts in Detroit," Detroitography blog, July 14, 2014, https://detroitography.com/2014/07/14/map-top-40-delinquent -commercial-water-accounts-in-detroit/.

Residential accounts, while accounting for a larger total amount of debt: Detroit Water and Sewerage Department Finance Committee notes, December 12, 2014, dwsd.legistar.com/View.ashx ?M=M&ID=357756&GUID=C2C79B0A-4CB8-4D6D-9823 -5FCF60F1610D.

CHAPTER 5

199 Black Homeownership in Detroit, 1960–2010

Steven Manson, Jonathan Schroeder, David Van Riper, and Steven Ruggles, "Time Series Table AE. Occupied Housing Units by Tenure by Race of Householder (1980–2010); Tables NBT43. Occupied Housing Units by Tenure Status by Race of Occupant (1960) and NT31A and NT31C. Tenure (1970)," IPUMS-NHGIS database, http://doi.org/10.18128/D050.V13.0. The 1960 census dataset only includes a total for all non-white owner-occupants (of any race), but non-Black People of Color accounted for less than 1 percent of Detroit's population in this year, so the non-white owner occupancy data is a reasonable proxy for Black ownership.

200 Wayne County Mortgages Granted by Race of Home Buyer, 2007–2015

Consumer Financial Protection Bureau. Home Mortgage Disclosure Act database, www.consumerfinance.gov/data-research/hmda/. The data shown here include only people who applied for and received home mortgages. The information does not show the number of wealthier people and investors purchasing homes with cash or through using equity on their existing homes, nor do the data include land contracts. Race and ethnicity are as self-reported by mortgage applicants.

202 Asian-American Homeownership in Detroit, 1990–2010

Steven Manson, Jonathan Schroeder, David Van Riper, and Steven Ruggles. "Time Series Table AE. Occupied Housing Units by Tenure by Race of Householder (1980–2010)" IPUMS-NHGIS database, http://doi.org/10.18128/D050.V13.0.

203 Latinx Homeownership in Detroit, 1990–2010

Steven Manson, Jonathan Schroeder, David Van Riper, and Steven Ruggles. "Time Series Table A50. Occupied Housing Units with Hispanic or Latino Householder by Tenure (1970–2010)," IPUMS-NHGIS database, http://doi.org/10.18128/D050.V13.0.

208–9 Property Speculation in Detroit, 2016

Joshua Akers, Alex B. Hill, and Aaron Petcoff, www.propertypraxis.org.

212–13 Housing Insecurity in Detroit

Steven Manson, Jonathan Schroeder, David Van Riper, and Steven Ruggles. "Table DS215: Rent as a Percentage of Household Income in the Past 12 Months (2011–2015 ACS)," IPUMS-NHGIS database, http://doi.org/10.18128/D050.V13.0.

213 DGEI Map of Displacement from the Trumbull Community

William Bunge, Field Notes No. 4: The Trumbull Community, ed. Ronald J. Horvath and Edward J. Vander Velde (Michigan State University, 1972, 25), https://radicalantipode.files.wordpress .com/2017/01/dgei_fieldnotes-iv.pdf.

227–28 Hantz Woodlands Project

Hantz project boundaries show the approximate outlines of the main area of concentration of Hantz property ownership. Detroit Parcel database, City of Detroit, City Assessor, 2017.

233 Wayne County Tax Assessments as a Percentage of Market Value, 2008–15

Mean assessment ratios were calculated based on a trimmed dataset of residential, improved, non-bundled, arms-length transactions.

Detroit residents are being hit twice: Bernadette Atuahene and Timothy Hodge, Stategraft, *Southern California Law Review* 263 (2018): 288–90, https://works.bepress.com/bernadette_atuahene/43/.

Atuahene and Hodge, "Stategraft," 266.

CHAPTER 6

247 Race and Water Shutoffs

2009–13 American Community Survey 5-Year estimates, Table DP01, https://factfinder.census.gov/; "Map of Communities Supplied with Water by DWSD," Detroit Water and Sewerage Department, https://web.archive.org/web/20121026020802; www.dwsd.org:80 /pages_n/map_water_supply.html; and We the People Detroit Research Collective research into shutoff policies.

252–53 Water Shutoffs Timeline

Detroit Water and Sewerage Department Board of Water Commissioners Finance Committee Binder, July 14, 2014, Detroit, https:// web.archive.org/web/20150315025628/http://dwsd .org/downloads_n/about_dwsd/financials/Finance_ Committee_Binder_7-14-2014.pdf; "Emergency Manager Information," Michigan Department of the Treasury, https://web.

archive.org/web/20160102205014/; www.michigan.gov/treasury/0,4679,7-121-1751_51556–201116—,00.html.

261 Environmental Justice in the 48217 Zipcode

Michigan Department of Transportation, 2015, Traffic Volumes. (Lansing: Michigan Department of Transportation), http:// gis-mdot.opendata.arcgis.com/datasets/2015-traffic-volumes ?geometry=-202.676%2C-52.268%2C202.676%2C52.268; 2010 Decennial Census Summary File 1 (U.S. Census Bureau, 2012), https://factfinder.census.gov/; and United States Environmental Protection Agency, Facility Registry Service, www.epa.gov/frs.

266–67 Asthma Rates and Polluters

United States Environmental Protection Agency, Facility Registry Service, www.epa.gov/frs, and Data-Driven Detroit and Michigan Health and Hospital Association, 2007–9; and Asthma Hospitalizations by Zip Code, Tri-County Area (Detroit: Data Driven Detroit, 2012, no longer available online, but see updated asthma rates at portal.datadrivendetroit.org).

274 School Closures

Research by Tom Pedroni, Ruqqayya Maudoodi, and Tim Stallmann.

288–89 Detroiters in Exile and Incarceration Rates in Detroit

United States Department of Homeland Security, Prison Boundaries Vector Digital Data Set (Washington, DC: United States Department of Homeland Security, 2016), "Homeland Infrastructure Foundation Level Data," https://hifld-geoplatform.opendata.arcgis. com/datasets/prison-boundaries; Michigan Department of Corrections, "Offender Tracking Information System," https://mdocweb .state.mi.us/otis2/otis2.html; and Justice Mapping Project. *Justice Atlas of Sentencing and Corrections*, www.justiceatlas.org.

SELECTED BIBLIOGRAPHY

Akers, Joshua. "The Actually Existing Markets of Shrinking Cities." *Metropolitics*, April 18, 2017. www.metropolitiques.eu/IMG/pdf/met-akers2.pdf.

———. "Making Markets: Think Tank Legislation and Private Property in Detroit." *Urban Geography* 34, no. 8 (2013): 1070–95.

Allen, Ernie. "Dying from the Inside: The Decline of the League of Revolutionary Black Workers." In *They Should Have Served That Cup of Coffee: Seven Radicals Remember the '60s*, ed. Dick Cluster. Cambridge, MA: South End Press, 1999.

Amann, Peter. "Vigilante Fascism: The Black Legion as an American Hybrid." *Comparative Studies in Society and History* 25, no. 3 (1983): 490–524.

Amin, Ash, and Philip Howell, eds. *Releasing the Commons: Rethinking the Futures of the Commons*. New York: Routledge, 2016.

Anderson, Michelle Wilde. "The New Minimal Cities." *Yale Law Journal* 123, no. 1118 (2014): 1118–27.

Attoh, Kafui A. "What Kind of Right Is the Right to the City?" *Progress in Human Geography* 35, no. 5 (2011): 669–85.

Atuahene, Bernadette, and Timothy R. Hodge. "Stategraft." *Southern California Law Review* 91, no. 2 (2017): 263–302.

Basso, Keith. *Wisdom Sits in Places: Landscape and Language among the Western Apache*. Albuquerque: University of New Mexico Press, 1996.

Bekkering, Thomas, ed. *Mapping Detroit: Land, Community, and Shaping a City*. Detroit: Wayne State University Press, 2015.

Bernstein, Henry. *Class Dynamics of Agrarian Change*. Vol. 1. West Hartford, CT: Kumarian Press, 2010.

Bhandar, Brenna. *Colonial Lives of Property: Law, Land, and Racial Regimes of Ownership*. Durham, NC: Duke University Press, 2018.

Boggs, Grace Lee. *Living for Change: An Autobiography*. Minneapolis: University of Minnesota, 1998.

Boggs, Grace Lee (with Scott Kurashige). *The Next American Revolution: Sustainable Activism for the Twenty-First Century*. Berkeley: University of California Press, 2011.

Boggs, James, and Grace Lee Boggs. *Revolution and Evolution in the Twentieth Century*. New York: Monthly Review Press, 1974.

Boggs, James, Grace Lee Boggs, Freddy Paine, and Lyman Paine. *Conversations in Maine: Exploring Our Nation's Future*. Minneapolis: University of Minnesota Press, 2018 [1978].

Bryant, Bunyan, and Elaine Hockman. "The Greater Detroit Resource Recovery Facility (the Incinerator)." In *Michigan: A State of Environmental Justice?*, ed. Bunyan Bryant, 127–40. New York: Morgan James, 2011.

Bunge, William. *Fitzgerald: Geography of a Revolution*. Athens: University of Georgia Press, 2011 [1971].

Castellanos, Jorge. "Black Slavery in Detroit." In *Detroit Perspectives: Crossroads and Turning Points*, ed. Wilma Wood Henrickson, 85–93. Detroit: Wayne State University Press, 1991.

Chatterton, Paul. "Seeking the Urban Common: Furthering the Debate on Spatial Justice." *City* 14, no. 6 (2010): 625–28.

Counter Cartographies Collective, Craig Dalton, and Liz Mason-Deese. "Counter (Mapping) Actions: Mapping as Militant Research." *ACME: An International Journal for Critical Geographies* 11, no. 3 (2012): 439–66, www.acme-journal.org/index.php/acme/article/view/941.

Delaney, David. "The Space That Race Makes." *Professional Geographer* 54, no. 1 (2002): 6–14.

Desmond, Matthew. *Evicted: Poverty and Profit in the American City*.

New York: Broadway Books, 2016.

Dewdney, Selwyn. *The Sacred Scrolls of the Southern Ojibway*. Toronto: University of Toronto Press, 1975.

Doyle, Mary Beth, and Brad Van Guilder. "For a Clean and Safe Detroit: Close the Country's Largest Incinerator." *From the Ground Up* 34, no. 2 (2002): 7–8.

Dunnigan, Brian Leigh. *Frontier Metropolis: Picturing Early Detroit, 1701–1838*. Detroit: Wayne State University Press, 2001.

Fine, Sidney. *Violence in the Model City*. East Lansing: Michigan State University Press, 1989.

Finkenbine, Roy. "A Community Militant and Organized: The Colored Vigilant Committee of Detroit." In Frost and Tucker, *A Fluid Frontier*, 154–64.

Foot, Andrew. *Windsor Modern: A Guidebook to Modern Architecture, 1940–1970 in Windsor, Ontario, Canada*. Self-published, 2007.

Freund, David. *Colored Property: State Policy and White Racial Politics in Suburban America*. Chicago: University of Chicago Press, 2007.

Frost, Karolyn Smardz. "Forging Transnational Networks for Freedom: From the War of 1812 to the Blackburn Riots of 1833." In Frost and Tucker, *A Fluid Frontier*, 43–66.

Frost, Karolyn Smardz, and Veta Smith Tucker, eds. *A Fluid Frontier: Slavery, Resistance, and the Underground Railroad in the Detroit River Borderland*. Detroit: Wayne State University Press, 2016.

Georgakas, Dan, and Marvin Surkin. *Detroit, I Do Mind Dying*. Cambridge, MA: South End Press, 1998.

Geschwender, James A. *Class, Race, and Worker Insurgency*. New York: Cambridge University Press, 1977.

Ghertner, Asher. *Rule by Aesthetics: World-Class City Making in Delhi*. New York: Oxford University Press, 2015.

Grigsby, Snow F. *An X-Ray Picture of Detroit*. Detroit: S. F. Grigsby, 1933.

Guthman, Julie. "'If They Only Knew': The Unbearable Whiteness of Alternative Food." In *Cultivating Food Justice: Race, Class, and Sustainability*, ed. Alison Hope Alkon and Julian Agyeman, 263–81. Cambridge, MA: MIT Press, 2011.

Hale, Janice E. *Learning while Black: Creating Educational Excellence for African American Children*. Baltimore: Johns Hopkins University Press, 2011.

Hamra, Ghassan B., Neela Guha, Aaron Cohen, Francine Laden, Ole Raaschou-Nielsen, Jonathan M. Samet, Paolo Vineis, Francesco Forastiere, Paulo Saldiva, Takashi Yorifuji, and Dana Loomis. "Outdoor Particulate Matter Exposure and Lung Cancer: A Systematic Review and Meta-analysis." *Environmental Health Perspectives* 122, no. 9 (2014): 906–91.

Hardt, Michael, and Negri, Antonio. *Commonwealth*. Cambridge, MA: Belknap Press, 2009.

Harney, Stefano, and Fred Moten. *The Undercommons: Fugitive Planning and Black Study*. New York: Minor Compositions, 2013.

Harvey, David. *Rebel Cities: From the Right to the City to the Urban Revolution*. New York: Verso Books, 2012.

———. "The Right to the City." *New Left Review* 53 (2008): 23–40.

Herman, Max. *Fighting in the Streets. Ethnic Succession and Urban Unrest in Twentieth Century America*. New York: Peter Lang, 2005.

Herscher, Andrew. *The Unreal Estate Guide to Detroit*. Ann Arbor: University of Michigan Press, 2012.

Hilliard, David, and Donald Weise, eds. *The Huey P. Newton Reader*. New York: Seven Stories Press, 2002.

Holston, James. "Come to the Street: Urban Protest, Brazil 2013." *Anthropological Quarterly* 87, no. 3 (2014): 887–900.

Huron, Amanda. "Working with Strangers in Saturated Space: Reclaiming and Maintaining the Urban Commons." *Antipode* 47, no. 4 (2015): 963–79.

Kelley, Robin D. G. *Freedom Dreams*. Boston: Beacon Press, 2002.

Kelley, Robin D. G., and Betsy Esch. "Black like Mao." *Souls* 1, no. 4 (1999): 6–41.

Kinder, Kimberley. *DIY Detroit. Making Do in a City without Services.* Minneapolis: University of Minnesota Press, 2016.

Kinney, Rebecca J. *Beautiful Wasteland: The Rise of Detroit as America's Postindustrial Frontier.* Minneapolis: University of Minnesota Press, 2016.

Kipfer, Stefan, and Kanishka Goonewardena. "Urban Marxism and the Post-colonial Question: Henri Lefebvre and 'Colonisation.'" *Historical Materialism* 21, no. 2 (2013): 76–116.

Langstaff, David. "The Inauguration of Fascism? Thinking Violence and Resistance in the Age of Trump." *Abolition*, January 28, 2017. abolitionjournal.org/the-inauguration-of-fascism-thinking-violence-and-resistance-in-the-age-of-trump/.

Lefebvre, Henri. *Writing on Cities*. Trans. and ed. Eleonore Kofman and Elizabeth Lebas. Oxford: Blackwell, 1996.

Lipsitz, George. *How Racism Takes Place*. Philadelphia: Temple University Press, 2011.

———. *The Possessive Investment in Whiteness: How White People Profit from Identity Politics*. Philadelphia: Temple University Press, 2006.

———. "The Racialization of Space and the Spatialization of Race." *Landscape Journal* 26, no. 1 (2007): 10–23.

Lorence, James J. *Organizing the Unemployed: Community and Union Activists in the Industrial Heartland*. Albany, NY: SUNY Press, 1996.

Manning, Thomas June, and Thomas Bekkering, eds. *Mapping Detroit: Land, Community, and Shaping a City*. Detroit: Wayne State University Press, 2015.

Manny, Bruce A., Thomas A. Edsall, and Eugene Jaworski. "The Detroit River, Michigan: An Ecological Profile." *U.S. Fish and Wildlife Service Biological Report* (1988) 85 (7.17).

Mao Tse-tung. "Statement Supporting the American Negroes in Their Just Struggle against Racial Discrimination by U.S. Imperialism." *Peking Review* 9, no. 33 (1966): 24–27.

McKittrick, Katherine. *Demonic Grounds: Black Women and the Cartographies of Struggle*. Minneapolis: University of Minnesota Press, 2006.

———. "On Plantations, Prisons, and a Black Sense of Place." *Social & Cultural Geography* 12, no. 8 (2011): 947–63.

Melamed, Jodi. "Racial Capitalism." *Critical Ethnic Studies* 1, no. 1 (2015): 76–85.

Miles, Tiya. *The Dawn of Detroit: A Chronicle of Slavery and Freedom in the City of the Straits*. New York: New Press, 2017.

———. "Slavery in Early Detroit." *Michigan History*, May–June 2013.

Millington, Gareth. *"Race," Culture and the Right to the City: Centres, Peripheries, Margins*. London: Springer, 2011.

Millington, Nate. "Post-industrial Imaginaries: Nature, Representation, and Ruin in Detroit, Michigan." *International Journal of Urban and Regional Research* 37, no. 1 (2013): 279–96.

Mitchell, Don. *The Right to the City: Social Justice and the Fight for Public Space*. New York: Guilford Press, 2003.

Newman, Andrew. "Gatekeepers of the Urban Commons? Vigilant Citizenship and Neoliberal Space in Multiethnic Paris." *Antipode* 45, no. 4 (2013): 947–64.

Newman, Andrew, and Sara Safransky. "Learning from *Field Notes No.4: The Trumbull Community*: Reflections on the Politics of Urban Land and Participatory Research." Symposium—The Detroit Geographical Expedition and Institute Then and Now: Commentaries on *Field Notes No.4: The Trumbull Community*. Antipode Foundation. radicalantipode.files.wordpress.com/2017/02/dgei-field-notes_newman-and-safransky.pdf.

Ostrom, Elinor. *Governing the Commons*. Cambridge: Cambridge University Press, 2015.

Peck, Jamie, and Heather Whiteside. "Financializing Detroit." *Economic Geography* 92, no. 3 (2016): 235–68.

Peluso, Nancy Lee, and Christian Lund. "New Frontiers of Land Control: Introduction." *Journal of Peasant Studies* 38, no 4 (2011): 667–81.

Perkinson, James W. *Messianism against Christology: Resistance Movements, Folk Arts, and Empire*. New York: Palgrave Macmillan, 2013.

———. *Shamanism, Racism, and Hip-Hop Culture: Essays on White Supremacy and Black Subversion*. New York: Palgrave Macmillan, 2005.

———. *White Theology: Outing Supremacy in Modernity*. New York: Palgrave Macmillan, 2004.

Perry, Keisha-Khan Y. *Black Women against the Land Grab: The Fight for Racial Justice in Brazil*. Minneapolis: University of Minnesota Press, 2013.

Pizzolato, Nicola. "The American Worker and the Forze Nuove: Turin and Detroit at the Twilight of Fordism." *Viewpoint Magazine*, no. 3: Workers' Inquiry, September 25, 2013. www.viewpointmag.com/2013/09/25/the-american-worker-and-the-forze-nuove-turin-and-detroit-at-the-twilight-of-fordism/.

Pothukuchi, Kameshwari. "Five Decades of Community Food Planning in Detroit: City and Grassroots, Growth and Equity." *Journal of Planning Education and Research* 35, no. 4 (2015): 419–34.

Pulido, Laura. "Flint, Environmental Racism, and Racial Capitalism." *Capitalism Nature Socialism* 27, no. 3 (2016): 1–27.

Purcell, Mark. "Excavating Lefebvre: The Right to the City and Its Urban Politics of the Inhabitant." *GeoJournal* 58, nos. 2–3 (2002): 99–108.

———. "Possible Worlds: Henri Lefebvre and the Right to the City." *Journal of Urban Affairs* 36, no. 1 (2014): 141–54.

Quizar, Jessi. "Who Cares for Detroit? Urban Agriculture, Black Self-Determination, and Struggles over Urban Space." PhD diss., University of Southern California, 2014.

Reverby, Susan M. *Examining Tuskegee: The Infamous Syphilis Study and Its Legacy*. Chapel Hill: University of North Carolina Press, 2009.

Robinson, Cedric. *Black Marxism: The Making of the Black Radical Tradition*. Chapel Hill: University of North Carolina Press, 1983.

Rushforth, Brett. *Bonds of Alliance: Indigenous and Atlantic Slaveries in New France*. Chapel Hill: University of North Carolina Press, 2012.

Safransky, Sara. "Greening the Urban Frontier: Race, Property, and Resettlement in Detroit." *Geoforum* 56 (2014): 237–48.

———. "Land Justice as a Historical Diagnostic: Thinking with Detroit." *Annals of the American Association of Geographers* 108, no. 2 (2018): 499–512.

———. "Rethinking Land Struggle in the Postindustrial City." *Antipode* 49, no. 4 (2017): 1079–1100.

Sassen, Saskia. *Expulsions: Brutality and Complexity in the Global Economy*. Cambridge, MA: Harvard University Press, 2014.

Simone, AbdouMaliq, "It's Just the City after All!" *International Journal of Urban and Regional Research* 40, no. 1 (2016): 210–18.

Smedley, Audrey, and Brian D. Smedley. *Race in North America: Origin and Evolution of a Worldview*. New York: Routledge, 2018.

Smith, Neil. *The New Urban Frontier: Gentrification and the Revanchist City*. New York: Routledge, 1996.

Sugrue, Thomas J. *The Origins of the Urban Crisis: Race and Inequality in Postwar Detroit*. Princeton, NJ: Princeton University Press, 2014.

Tayyab, Mahmud. "Debt and Discipline: Neoliberal Political Economy and the Working Classes," *Kentucky Law Journal* 101, no. 1 (2013): 1–54.

Thomas, June, and Henco Bekkering, eds. *Mapping Detroit: Land, Community, and Shaping a City*. Detroit: Wayne State University Press, 2015.

Thompson, Dorothy. *The Essential E. P. Thompson*. New York: New Press, 2001.

Thompson, Edward P. "The Moral Economy of the English Crowd in the Eighteenth Century." *Past & Present* 50 (1971): 76–136.

Thompson, Heather Ann. *Whose Detroit: Politics, Labor, and Race in a Modern American City*. Ithaca, NY: Cornell University Press, 2001.

Tsing, Anna. *Friction: An Ethnography of Global Connection*. Princeton, NJ: Princeton University Press, 2005.

Veracini, Lorenzo. *Settler Colonialism: A Theoretical Overview*. New York: Palgrave Macmillan, 2010.

White, Ben, Saturnino M. Borras Jr., Ruth Hall, Ian Scoones, and Wendy Wolford. "The New Enclosures: Critical Perspectives on Corporate Land Deals." *Journal of Peasant Studies* 39, nos. 3–4 (2012): 619–47.

White, Monica M. "Sisters of the Soil: Urban Gardening as Resistance in Detroit." *Race/Ethnicity: Multidisciplinary Global Contexts* 5, no. 1 (2011): 13–28.

Wigmore, Gregory. "Before the Railroad: From Slavery to Freedom in the Canadian-American Borderland." *Journal of American History* 98 (2011): 437–54.

Wilder, Gary. *Freedom Time: Negritude, Decolonization, and the Future of the World*. Durham, NC: Duke University Press, 2014.

Wilderson, Frank. *Red, White & Black: Cinema and the Structure of U.S. Antagonisms*. Durham, NC: Duke University Press, 2010.

Wolfe, Patrick. "Land, Labor, and Difference: Elementary Structures of Race." *American Historical Review* 106, no. 3 (2001): 866–905.

———. *Settler Colonialism and the Transformation of Anthropology*. New York: Cassell, 1999.

———. "The Settler Complex: An Introduction." *American Indian Culture and Research Journal* 37, no. 2 (2013): 1–22.

Wood, Denis. *Rethinking the Power of Maps*. New York: Guilford Press, 2010.

Zinn, Howard. *A People's History of the United States: 1492–Present*. New York: Routledge, 2015.

CONTRIBUTORS

Gabriela Alcazar is a Detroit resident and immigrant rights activist.

Rhonda Anderson is a Detroit resident and environmental justice activist.

Danielle Atkinson worked as a research assistant with the Uniting Detroiters project. She is the founder and director of Mothering Justice, a statewide organization working to improve the lives of Michigan families by equipping the next generation of mother activists.

Kaisha Brezina is a recent graduate of the College of Literature, Science, and the Arts at the University of Michigan.

Lila Cabbil was president of the Rosa and Raymond Parks Institute for Self-Development and a member and coordinator of Undoing Racism in Detroit's Food System. She passed away in 2019 shortly before this book was completed.

Linda Campbell is a Detroit resident and director of Building Movement Project, Detroit and Detroit People's Platform.

Michelle Cassidy is an assistant professor of history at Central Michigan University.

William Copeland is youth coordinator with the East Michigan Environmental Action Council.

Dessa Cosma is the founder of Detroit Disability Power.

Patrick Crouch is program manager at the Capuchin Soup Kitchen's Earthworks Urban Farm.

Kezia Curtis is a Detroit resident, bicycle mechanic, and activist in youth issues and nonviolent conflict resolution.

Wayne Curtis is codirector of Feedom Freedom Growers.

Michael Darroch is an associate professor of media arts and culture in the School of Creative Arts at the University of Windsor and codirector of the IN/TERMINUS Creative Research Collective based in Windsor, Ontario.

Isra El-beshir worked as a research assistant with the Uniting Detroiters project when she was an anthropology master's student at Wayne State University. El-beshir is now the director of Illinois Art Station at Illinois State University.

Dianne Feeley is a Detroit resident and community activist.

Tanesha Flowers is a Detroit resident and member of the Detroit Action Commonwealth.

Kathleen Foster is a Detroit resident and member of the Riverfront East Congregation Initiative.

Lee Gaddies is a Detroit resident and community activist.

Valerie Glen is a Detroit resident.

Janice Hale was professor emerita at Wayne State University College of Education. She passed away in 2017 before this book was completed.

Aaron Handelsman is a Detroit resident and worked as policy director with the Detroit People's Platform. He currently is a holistic leadership coach for leaders committed to collective liberation.

Imani Harris is a Detroit resident, graduate of Renaissance High School, and a student activist with 482Forward who studies at the Medill School of Journalism at Northwestern University.

Joselyn Fitzpatrick Harris is a Detroit resident and a member of the former Jefferson Chalmers Citizen District Council.

Kaleema Hasan was a poet, activist, and longtime Detroiter. She passed away in 2016 before this book was completed.

Jeanine Hatcher is a native Detroiter and the executive director of GenesisHOPE, a community development corporation for the neighborhood where she grew up—Islandview—where youth are empowered to organize community events, connect people to good food and help local businesses thrive.

Elena Herrada is a lifelong Detroiter, a mother of four daughters, and a grandmother of five children whose family has been in the city for three generations. A graduate of Wayne State University, she is an activist and counternarrator.

Charity Hicks was a Detroit resident, community activist, and member of the People's Water Board. She passed away in 2014 before this book was completed.

Alex B. Hill is a scholar-activist and cartographer who does advocacy work for a number of organizations related to racial justice, food access, and health disparities.

Gloria House is professor emerita in humanities and African American studies at the University of Michigan–Dearborn and associate professor emerita in interdisciplinary studies at Wayne State University. She has been an activist in human rights and social justice causes since her work as a field secretary in the Student Non-Violent Coordinating Committee in Lowndes County, Alabama, in the mid-1960s.

Shea Howell is professor and chair of the Department of Communication and Journalism at Oakland University. She is a founding member and board member of the Boggs Center, a space to nurture the development of visionary organizing rooted in place and history.

Robert Johnson is a doctoral candidate in Wayne State University's Anthropology Department.

Herbert Jones is a Detroit resident and member of the Detroit Action Commonwealth.

Sarah Khan is a recent graduate of the College of Literature, Science, and the Arts at the University of Michigan.

Carmen Malis King is a Detroit-rooted community health worker, doula, writer, and herbalist.

Jaqueline Lacey is a master's student in the Employment and Labor Relations Program at Wayne State University.

Jenny Lee is the director of Allied Media Projects.

Kate Levy is a documentarian who collaborates with communities in pursuit of economic and social justice.

Mark Luborsky is a medical anthropologist at Wayne State University.

Emily Macgillivray is an assistant professor of Native American studies at Northland College.

Jeanette Marble is a Detroit resident and member of the Riverfront East Congregation Initiative.

Vincent Martin is a Detroit resident and environmental justice activist.

Michelle Martinez is an environmental justice activist from Southwest Detroit.

Cecily McClellan is a lifelong resident of Detroit, activist, founding member of We the People of Detroit, Detroit Active and Retired Employee Association, and Woodward Village Neighborhood Association.

Curtis McGuire is a legal worker, photographer, graphic designer, and community organizer. He has lived in Detroit since 2004.

Shanna Merola is a photographer and filmmaker based out of Hamtramck, Michigan. In addition to teaching at Wayne State University and the College for Creative Studies, she is the coordinator for the Legal Observer Program at the Detroit and Michigan Chapter of the National Lawyers Guild and photographer for the Detroit Coalition against Police Brutality.

Tiya Miles is professor of history and Radcliffe Alumnae Professor at Harvard University.

Isaac Ginsberg Miller has taught with InsideOut Literary Arts Project, Detroit Future Schools, and the James and Grace Lee Boggs School.

Andrew Newman is an associate professor of anthropology at Wayne State University.

Gregg Newsom is a Detroit resident who works for Building Movement Project, Detroit and Detroit People's Platform.

Alexandra Passarelli is a recent graduate of the College of Literature, Science, and the Arts at the University of Michigan.

James W. Perkinson is professor of social ethics at the Ecumenical Theological Seminary and an artist on the spoken-word poetry scene in the inner city.

Tova Perlmutter is executive director of Mondoweiss, an independent news operation devoted to informing readers about developments in Israel/Palestine, related US foreign policy, and the struggle for Palestinian human rights.

Tawana "Honeycomb" Petty is a mother, organizer, author, and poet. She is the director of Petty Propolis, director of Data Justice Programming for the Detroit Community Technology Project, a member of the Detroit Digital Justice Coalition, a board member of the James and Grace Lee Boggs Center to Nurture Community Leadership, a Detroit Equity Action Lab Fellow, and a co-founder and editorial board member of *Riverwise* Magazine.

Jessi Quizar is an assistant professor of ethnic studies at Northern Arizona University.

Josiah Rector is an assistant professor of history at the University of Houston.

Lee Rodney is an associate professor of media arts and culture in the School of Creative Arts at the University of Windsor, and codirector of the IN/TERMINUS Creative Research Collective based in Windsor, Ontario.

Paul Rodriguez is a recent graduate of the College of Literature, Science, and the Arts at the University of Michigan.

Zak Rosen is a Detroit-based radio and podcast producer. His stories have aired on NPR, APM, PRI, the BBC, Deutsche Welle, and Radio Helsinki.

Lauren Rosenthal is an artist and cartographer who currently lives and works in Lambertville, New Jersey.

Rev. Joan Ross is the executive director of the Greater Woodward CDC.

Ayana Rubio worked as a research assistant with the Uniting Detroiters project. She is now a data analyst with Data Driven Detroit.

Sara Safransky is a human geographer and assistant professor at Vanderbilt University.

Andrea Sankar is a medical anthropologist at Wayne State University.

Betty A. Scruse is a Detroit resident.

Amy Senese is a documentary photographer based in Detroit.

Yusef "Bunchy" Shakur is a Detroit resident, author, educator, organizer, college graduate, and founder of the Urban Network Bookstore.

Syri Simpson is a Detroit resident and transportation justice activist.

Brother Jerry Smith was the Director of the Capuchin Soup Kitchen until 2017.

Lottie Spady is a Detroit resident, community activist, and poet.

Tim Stallmann is a cartographer based in Durham, North Carolina, and a worker-owner at Research Action Design.

Soh Suzuki is a member of the Detroit Asian Youth Project.

Amelia Wieske is a Detroit resident and occasional gardener.

Deborah Williamson worked with Michigan Roundtable for Diversity and Inclusion and was coordinator of the Riverfront East Congregation Initiative.

Malik Yakini is director of the Community Black Community Food Security Network

INDEX

abandonment, geography of, 298, 299
Abbott, James Sr., 24
Abbott, Pompey, 24
Abbott Street, 24
agriculture. *See* urban agriculture; urban gardens
air pollution, 265–68
Air Products, 260
Ajin, Yousef, 192
Alcazar, Gabriela, 166–68
Alden Park Towers, letter to, 210–11
Allied Media Conference (AMC), and Allied Media Projects, 282–83
Alternative Housing, Alternative Future: A Transatlantic Roundtable, 234
Ambac Assurance, 179
Ambassador Bridge, 70, *108*
Anderson, Rhonda, 258, 259–61, 303
Anishinaabeg migration, 16
Asian American homeownership, 202
Askin, John, 23
asset-based organizing, 222
asthma rates, 267
austerity. *See* Detroit financial crisis

backyard garden, 94–97
Bagley, 94, 186
Bank of America, 177
Basso, Keith, 74
Battle of the Overpass, 32
Belle Isle, state take-over of, 178, 206
Bellin, Jacques-Nicolas, 16–17

Benson, Scott, 174–75, 189
Benson Compromise, 174–75, 189, 190
Bethel African Methodist Episcopal Church, 26
"Big Four," 287
Bing, David, 168, 217
Black Bottom, 38, 70, 87–93, 182
Blackburn, Lucie and Thornton, and Blackburn Rebellion, 27
"Black Day in July" (Merola), 58
Black genocide, 51
Black Government Conference, 50
Black Legion, 35–39
Black militia, 23
Black Panthers, 50, 130–31, 263
Blackrock, 179
block busting, 39
block clubs, 72
Boggs, Grace Lee, 12–13, 51, 62–67, 274
Boggs, James (Jimmy), 12–13, 51, 62–63, 64, 274
bonds, 265–68
Bossett, Ensign, 23
Boston-Edison, 45, 198, 312n7
Bozanich, George, 109
Breathe Free Detroit campaign, 268
Bréhant, René, 17
Brightmoor, 84, 189
Broadband Technologies Opportunities Program, 283
Broder & Sachse, 214
Broken City Lab, 106
Brown, John, 26–27

Brush, Elijah, 23
Brush Park, 23
Building Movement Detroit, 143
Bunche Preparatory Academy, 91
Bunge, William (Bill), 7, 273. *See also* Detroit Geographical Expedition and Institute (DGEI)
Burgess, Ezra, 23
busing, 273

Cabbil, Lila, 136–37, 301–2
Campbell, Linda, 34, 149–54, 170, 214–16, 298
capitalism, 28–34, 298. *See also* racial capitalism
Capuchin Soup Kitchen, 118, 139–40. *See also* Earthworks Urban Farm
carbon forests, 196
Cass Corridor, 239
children, recreational spaces for, 276–77, 278. *See also* education; youth organizing and programs
Chin, Vincent, 286
Chinatown, 202, 274, 286
chronic illness, 191
citizens' district councils (CDCs), 180, 181, 182, 311n12
Citizens Environment Alliance (CEA), 109
City-Wide Citizen's Action Committee, 51
citywide suffrage, 167–68
civil disobedience, 248–51
civil rights
    and globalization from below, 50–51

Grace Lee Boggs and Sterling Toles and, 62–67
Great March to Freedom, 46–53
riots and rebellions, 56–59, 62–63
and Trump's election, 189–90
Civil Rights Congress, 51
Cleage, Albert, 51
coal-power plants, 260
collective landownership, 113
colonization of Detroit, 14–17
Colored Vigilant Committee, 26, 27
commons. *See* urban commons
Community Benefits Agreement (CBA) ordinance, 168, 173–75, 179, 188, 189, 190
community gardens. *See* urban agriculture; urban gardens
community land trusts (CLT), 231–37, 240–41
Connor Kitchen, 140
Consent Agreement with State of Michigan, 161
Cook Eat Talk program, 118, 146–47
Copeland, Diana, 262
Copeland, William, 258, 262–64, 303
Corktown, 94, 95, 96, 200, 290, 294
corporate power, 204–7
Cosma, Dessa, 302
crime and police harassment, 287–90
and Detroit Action Commonwealth, 291–92
and Urban Network, 293–95
cross-border commons, 106–10
Crouch, Patrick, 142–44
Curtis, Kezia, 79–86
Curtis, Wayne, 79, 130–34, 302

Davis, Jesse, 56–57
DeBaptiste, George, 27
debt. *See also* Detroit financial crisis; emergen-

cy management; foreclosures; housing and homeownership
Deferred Action for Childhood Arrivals (DACA), 164, 167–68
deindustrialization, 28, 34, 45–46, 73. *See also* postindustrial city
democracy, 157–61
Detroit People's Platform, 170–71
fight for CBA ordinance, 173–75
and opposition to Public Act 4 (PA4), 163–65
and people power, 181–82
"People's Plan for Restructuring toward a Sustainable Detroit," 176–80
taxation without representation, 186–87, 191
Trump and, 188–92
and undocumented immigrants, 166–68
water shutoffs, 183–85
Denison, Hannah, 23
Denison, Peter, 23
depopulation, 196
"Detroit" (Petty), 193
Detroit Action Commonwealth (DAC), 291–92
Detroit Agricultural Network, 123
Detroit Asian Youth Project, 274, 286
Detroit Black Community Food Security Network (DBCFSN), 124–27, 142
Detroit Chinatown Mural, 286
Detroit Digital Justice Coalition, 283, 306n18
Detroit Economic Growth Corporation, 144
Detroiters Resisting Emergency Management (D-REM), 168–69
Detroit financial crisis. *See also* emergency management
austerity measures, 3, 90, 157, 234, 243
bankruptcy of Detroit, 160, 173, 177, 178
Consent Agreement with State of Michigan, 161

municipal debt, 90, 158, 160, 268
racial politics of, 162
Detroit Food Justice Task Force, 118, 146–47, 151
Detroit Future City (DFC) Strategic Framework, 196, 217–21
Detroit Future Schools, 283–84
Detroit Future Youth Network, 274
Detroit Geographical Expedition and Institute (DGEI), 7, 273, 276–77, 278, 306n20
Detroit Independent Freedom Schools Movement, 274
Detroit Institute of Art, 178
Detroit Jail, 27
Detroit Jobs First, 189
Detroit People's Platform, 154, 170–71, 174, 216, 232
Detroit Renewable Energy, 268
Detroit River, 72, 99, 100–103
Detroit Summer, 63, 274, 281–82, 286
Detroit Water and Sewerage Department (DWSD), 179, 246–47, 249, 251
Detroit Works Project, 217
Detropia, 300
DeVos, Betsy, 160, 192
digital ecology, healthy, 283
dignity, 256
Dillon, Andy, 161, 169
dioxins, 265–68
disinvestment, 238–39
displacement, 70, 195–96. *See also* housing and homeownership; land
and Black homeownership in Detroit, 198–201
and community land trust, 231–37
and corporate power, 204–7
and disinvestment, 238–39

due to urban renewal, 213
of Griswold seniors, 214–16
housing insecurity, 212–13
land speculation, 208–9
letter to Alden Park Towers management, 210–11
Riverfront East Congregation Initiative (RECI), 222–28
and systems change work, 238–41
telling stories of, 112–13
urban sustainability as force of, 217–21
Dodge Main, 32–34
Dodge Revolutionary Union Movement, 32–34
Dollier de Casson, François, 17
Douglass, Frederick, 26–27
Downtown, 74, 123, 168, 196, 200, 214–16, 239, 269, 294
Downtown Development Authority, 172
D-Town Farm, 125
due process, 291–92
Duffield Elementary School, 91
Duggan, Mike, 178, 189
dumping, illegal, 82–83

Earley, Darnell, 34, 273
Earthworks Urban Farm, 142–44
East Michigan Environmental Action Council (EMEAC), 262–64
economy of the community, 222
Ecorse Township, 260
education, 273–78
of African American children, 285
protests under emergency management, 279–80
youth programs, 281–84
Education Social Action, 226

Eight Mile wall, 38
Elliott, Matthew, 23
emergency management. *See also* Detroit financial crisis
attempts to stave off, 2
and corporate power in revitalization of Detroit, 204–7
education and, 273–74, 279–80
EM orders 26 and 36, 180
fight for CBA ordinance, 173–75
Michigan cities affected by, 160–61, 162
and people power, 181–82
"People's Plan for Restructuring toward a Sustainable Detroit," 176–80
and Public Act 4 (PA 4), 163–64
and Public Act 436 (PA 436), 164–65
struggles over imposition of, 157, 168–69
taxation without representation, 186–87, 191
and urban commons and right to the city, 5
and urban revanchism, 3–4
water shutoffs, 183–85
environmental justice, 258
incineration technology and economic crisis, 265–68
and rethinking ourselves and economic realm, 259–61
youth education and organizing, 262–64
environmental racism, 262–64, 265–68
Equitable Detroit Coalition, 174, 189
Equitable Internet Initiative, 240
Evergreen Alliance, 265
Eviction Defense Committee, 77–78
evictions, 210–11
Ewing, Heidi, 300

fallow properties, 209. *See also* vacancies

Farm-A-Lot program, 123, 151
farm operators, Black, 153
federal grants, 177
Federal Housing Administration (FHA), 39, 40
Feeley, Dianne, 76–78
Financial Advisory Board, 161
Financial Guaranty Insurance Co., 185
Finney, Seymour, 27
First Unitarian Universalist Church of Detroit, 49, 57
fishing, 72, 100–103
Fitzgerald, 276–77, 278
Flint water crisis, 157, 158, 169, 179, 185, 188, 189, 192
Flowers, Tanesha, 219, 291–92
food and food justice, 117–18, 146–47, 150–54. *See also* fishing; urban agriculture
Food Warriors Youth Development Program, 125
Ford, 32
Ford, Henry, 32
foreclosures, 69, 77–78, 82, 84, 90, 177, 191, 195, 196, 198, 209, 223, 233, 234, 236, 240
Fort Detroit, 23
Forth, Elizabeth Denison, 22, 24
Foster, Kathleen, 222–26
48217 zip code, 258, 259, 303
48217 zip code, 259–61
Frankensteen, Richard, *30*
Freedom Freedom, 79, 83–86, 131–34
Freedom Schools Movement, 274
Freund, David, 39
frontier culture, 4

Gaddies, Lee, 90
Gardening Angels, 123
Garden Resource Program, 123

gardens. *See* urban agriculture; urban gardens
General Electric, 265
genocide, 51
gentrification, 74, 77, 123, 154, 195–96, 210–11, 287. *See also* displacement; urban renewal
geography of abandonment, 298
Gilbert, Dan, 4, 209
globalization from below, 12, 50–51
governance. *See* democracy; emergency management; revanchism
Grady, Rachel, 300
Grandmont-Rosedale, 198
Granholm, Jennifer, 158
Greater Detroit Resource Recovery, 258, 265–68
Great Lakes Watershed, 104–5
Great March to Freedom, 46–53
Great Society program, 59
Greece, 234
green urbanism, 196
Griswold, 214–16
Grosse Pointe, 38

Hale, Janice, 278
Hamilton, Lacino, 287
Hamtramck, 24
Hamtramck, Jean-François, 24
Handelsman, Aaron, 231–37
Hannah-Attisha, Mona, 188
Hannan Center, 214
Hantz, John and Hantz Farms, 84, 224, 227–28
Hardest Hit Funds, 90
Harmon, M. D., 81
Harris, Imani, 273, 279–80
Harris, Joselyn Fitzpatrick, 181–82
Hatcher, Jeanine, 78
HB5977, 174

Hebron, Jerry, 113–14
Herrada, Elena, 301
Hi Boys (King), 54
Hickey, Bill, 189
Hicks, Charity, 72, 246, 254–57
Highland Park, 160, 238
homelessness, 291–92
Home Mortgage Disclosure Act, 200
Home Owners' Loan Corporation (HOLC), 40
Homes for All (HFA) campaign, 232
Homrich 9, 248–51
Homrich Wrecking Inc., 249–50
housing and homeownership. *See also* displacement; gentrification; land
    Asian American, 202
    Black, 198–201
    defending, 76–78
    deteriorating and dilapidated houses, 1960, 41
    governance and, 186–87
    high-income houses, 45–46
    historical population of Detroit and suburbs, 33
    houses in poverty, 45–46
    housing insecurity, 212–13
    impact on Detroit, 209
    Latinx, 203
    multigenerational, 111–13
    myth of security through, 236
    race and right to, 35–45
    race's impact on, 200–201
    urban renewal's impact on, 88–90
Hull, William, 23
human rights violation, water shutoffs as, 183–85

identification cards, 292
image of Detroit

Detroit as unexceptional, 300–301
Detroit as urban wilderness, 69
    media portrayal, 81
    mythology threatening Detroit, 1
    visions for Detroit's future, 301–3
immigration, 111, 164, 166–68, 192
Immigration and Customs Enforcement (ICE), 166–68, 192
incarceration, 191, 288, 289
incineration technology, 265–68
income tax, 176
Indian Village, 45, 198
indigenous people and societies
    Anishinaabeg migration, 16
    enslavement of, 20–21
    erasure of, 12
individualism, 66–67
industrial capitalism, 28–34
Industrial Workers of the World, 30
infrastructure. *See* education; right to the city; transit; water
Insurrection Act (1807), 56
internet, 240
Islandview, 143, 327

jails, 191, 288, 289
James, C. L. R., 51
James and Grace Lee Boggs Center to Nurture Community Leadership, 63–64, 66
Jefferson Chalmers, 181
Jericho Journey, 271–72
Joe Louis Arena site, 185
Johnson, Lyndon B., 56
Johnson, Ruth, 167
Jones, Brenda, 168, 174, 179
Jones, Herbert, 291–92

Keep Growing Detroit, 123
King, Carmen Malis, 303
King, Henri Umbaji, 54
King, Martin Luther Jr., 46–47, 189–90, 192
Koch Carbon, 82–83
Kowalska, Tamara, 109
Ku Klux Klan, 35–39, 49
Kurtz, Ed, 169

labor movement, 28–34, 278, 298. *See also* League of Revolutionary Black Workers (LRBW); unionization; United Auto Workers (UAW)
Lambert, William, *25, 26, 27*
land, 69–75. *See also* displacement; urban agriculture; urban commons
    accessibility of, 154
    and actions of elected officials, 181–82
    appropriation of, 151–52
    care for, 70, 72, 79–86, 87, 90, 102–3, 223–26
    collective ownership of, 113
    community land trusts (CLT), 231–37, 240–41
    de facto public, 224
    defending, 76–78
    Detroit historical land cover, circa 1800, 98–99
    Detroit River and people's relationship to, 100–103
    and Detroit / Windsor cross-border commons, 106–10
    governance and ownership of, 186–87
    historical land cover, circa 1800, 98–99
    liberated, as means of survival, 130–34
    McClellan's experiences in Black Bottom, 87–92
    multigenerational ownership of, 111–13
    and ongoing displacement, 70

open, 72, 73, 80–81
    potential uses for vacant, 113–15
    and Public Act 436, 163–65
    transfer of publicly held, to private interests, 172–73, 180, 185, 206, 227–28
    Wieske's "Backyard Garden," 94–97
land grabbing, 209, 224–26, 228
land justice, 152, 231–37, 240–41
land speculation, 82–83, 84–85, 208–9
Latinx homeownership, 203
League of Revolutionary Black Workers (LRBW), 34
Lee, Jenny, 274–78, 281–84
Lefebvre, Henri, 4, 243, 244
legacy expenses and liabilities, 177
Levy, Kate, 216
liberated territory, as means of survival, 130–34
Linwood Madonna and Child (King), 54
Little Caesars Arena, 173
Liuzzo, Viola, 49
Live Arts Media Project, 282
local income tax, 176
Lyda et al. v. City of Detroit (2014), 252

M-1 Streetcar (QLine), 238, 239, 269–70, 272
Macomb, Alexander, 24
Macomb, William, 23
Macomb County, 24
mapmaking, 6–7
Marathon Oil, 259–60
Marble, Jeanette, 222–26
Mariner Park, 102–3
Market Value Analysis of Detroit, 217, 220–21
Martin, Trayvon, 264
Martin, Vincent, 258, 259–61
Martinez, Michelle, 111–15

May, James, 23
McClellan, Cecily, 87–92
McGee, Minnie, 38
McGee, Orsel, 38
McGuire, Curtis, 301
McKittrick, Katherine, 12
Meldrum Soup Kitchen, 140
Merola, Shanna, 58
Mexicantown, 203
Michigan Air Pollution Control Commission (MAPCC), 268
Michigan Department of Environmental Quality, 188
Michigan Water as a Human Right Bill Package, 252
Midtown, 74, 182, 195, 196, 200, 216, 238, 239, 269, 294. *See also* Cass Corridor
migration. *See also* immigration
    Anishinaabeg migration, 16
    The Great Migration, 32, 33, 39, 80, 91, 112, 122, 186
    outmigration from Detroit, 59
    of whites from American South, 76
Miliken v. Bradley (1974), 273
Miller, Isaac Ginsberg, 129
Miller High School, 91
mobility, 269–72. *See also* transit
Montreal, 234
Moroun, Manuel "Matty," 81, 209
mortgages, race and approval for, 200–201. *See also* foreclosures; subprime mortgages and crisis
Movimento dos Trabalhadores Rurais Sem Terra; Landless Workers Movement (MST), 257
Muchmore, Dennis, 169
municipal bonds, 265–68

Murphy, Frank, 122
mythology, threatening Detroit, 1

National Organization for an American Revolution (NOAR), 63
1967 rebellion, 56–59, 205
North End, 238–39
North End Community Garden, 114
North End Woodward Community Coalition (NEWCC), 168, 238, 239–40
Nsoroma Institute, 126, 127, 131

Oakwood Heights, 259
Obama, Barack, 167
Occupy Detroit, 77–78
Olympia Development, 172, 173, 239
Order No. 1, 168
Orozco, Hector, 164
Orr, Kevyn, 34, 168, 178, 179, 180
outmigration, 59

Packard Motor Company, 32
palenques, 113
Palmer Woods, 45
Patterson, L. Brooks, 158
pension obligation certificates (POCs), 90
Penske, Roger, 265
People's Institute for Survival and Beyond, 137
"People's Plan for Restructuring toward a Sustainable Detroit," 176–80
People's Water Board, 254–55
Perkinson, James, 246, 249–53
Perlmutter, Tova, 163–64
Petty, Tawana "Honeycomb," 193
Philip Morris, USA, 265
Pingree, Hazen, 121

Pingree Potato Patches, 121
place-based ministry, 222
Plataforma de Afectados por la Hipoteca; Platform for People Affected by Mortgages (PAH), 234, 235
Poleski, Earl, 174
Poletown, 38
police, 287–95
polluting industries, 259–61
population of Detroit, 33, 304n1
postindustrial city, 12, 35, 117, 195, 298
potato patches, 121
poverty, 45–46, 139–40, 255
prisons, 191, 288, 289
property taxes, 78, 81, 84, 90, 177, 233. *See also* tax foreclosures
Proposal A (Community Benefits Agreement), 174–75, 189
Public Act 4 (PA4), 157, 160, 163–65
Public Act 436 (PA 436), 164, 165
Purcell, Mark, 244

QLine (M-1 Streetcar), 238, 239, 269–70, 272
Quizar, Jessi, 79–86

race, racism, and ethnicity
    and children's spaces, 276, 278
    and corporate power in revitalization of Detroit, 204–7
    and crime and police harassment, 287
    in Detroit, 42–43
    and education, 285
    erasure of Black people, 12
    and governance in Detroit, 186–87
    and homeownership, 198–201
    and Public Act 436 vote, 165

and right to housing, 35–45
and right to the city, 243
spatial racism, 196, 236
and urban agriculture, 124–27, 130–34, 136–37
and water shutoffs, 246–47, 250–51
racial capitalism, 5
    geography of abandonment and, 298
    Grace Lee Boggs and Sterling Toles and, 62–67
    housing and, 33, 35–45, 76–77, 84
racial citizenship, 5
    and labor struggles, 30, 32–34
    and urban sustainability as force of displacement, 217–19
radio, 238, 241
Randolph, A. Philip, 32
recreational facilities, 276–77, 278
Rector, Josiah, 258
redlining, 33, 39, 40–41
Red Sky, James, 16
Red Wings, 173
Reinvestment Fund, 221
rental insecurity, 212
Republic of New Afrika, 50
restaurants, 154
"Resurget Cineribus" (Miller), 129
Reuther, Walter, *30*, 32
revanchism, 3–4, 157–61
    and challenging racial capitalism, 5
    corporate power and, 204–7
    Detroit People's Platform, 170–71
    fight for CBA ordinance, 173–75
    and opposition to Public Act 4 (PA4), 163–65
    and people power, 181–82
    "People's Plan for Restructuring toward a

Sustainable Detroit," 176–80
taxation without representation, 186–87, 191
Trump and, 188–92
and undocumented immigrants, 166–68
water shutoffs, 183–85
revenue sharing, 176–77
Revolution and Evolution (Boggs and Boggs), 63, 67
Revolutionary Action Movement, 51
Rhodes, Steven, 180, 185, 252
ribbon farms, 120
Richburg, Keith B., 81
right to the city, 243–44
education, 273–86
environmental justice, 258–68
freedom from crime and police harassment, 287–95
mobility, 269–72
as neglected human right, 312n3
urban commons and, 4–5
water, 246–57
Right to the City Alliance (RTC), 231, 232, 236
riots and rebellions, 56–59, 62–63, 205
Rise Together Detroit, 189
River Fishing Association of Detroit, 100
Riverfront East Congregation Initiative (RECI), 222–28
River Rats Fishing Association (RRFA), 101–3
Robertson, James, 269
Robinson, Cedric, 5
Romney, George W., 56
Ross, Rev. Joan, 174, 188, 238–41, 312n7
Rouge Park, 125

Sainte Anne's Church, 23
Samyn, Rick, 142

Sassen, Saskia, 298
schools, 89, 273
Score, Mike, 224
Scruse, Betty A., 210–11
Second Baptist Church, 26
senior citizens, displacement of, 214–16
Senior Housing Preservation, 214, 216
settler colonialism, 70, 305–6n16
Shakur, Yusef "Bunchy," 226, 293–95
Shamba Organic Garden Collective, 127
sickouts, 34, 279–80
Side Lot Program, 239
Sidney D. Miller High School, 91
Sierra Club, 260
Simpson, Syri, 269, 271–72
sit-down strikes, 32
slavery, 20–21
and collective landownership, 113
in early republic, 18–19
landmarks in Detroit, 22–23
traces in present-day Detroit, 24
Underground Railroad, 20, 25–27
Smith, Brother Jerry, 139–40, 301
Smith, John, 35
Smith, Neil, 3, 157
Snyder, Rick, 158, 168, 169, 192
socialism, 51
soup kitchens, 118, 139–40
Southwest Detroit, 43, 70, 82–83, 87, 112, 114, 123, 164, 167, 200, 260
Spady, Lottie, 146–47, 302
spatial racism, 196, 236
St. Matthew's Episcopal Church, 26
Storehouse of Hope, 240–41, 312n8
street courts, 290, 291–92
structural changes in Detroit, 154, 157–58, 160–61

subprime mortgages and crisis, 2, 70, 84, 89–90
suffrage, 167–68, 169, 291, 292
Sugar Law Center, 163
Suzuki, Soh, 286
Sweet, Gladys and Ossian, 35, 38, 76–77
Sweet, Zachary, 280
Syncora, 180

taxation without representation, 186–87, 191
tax foreclosures, 69, 78, 82, 84, 177, 191, 196, 209, 233, 234, 236, 240
Temperance Hotel, 27
Thompson, E. P., 6, 308n26
Thompson, Myrtle Curtis, 79, 84
thrift gardens, 122
Toles, Sterling, 12–13, 64–67
Tootsie's Park, 87
transit, 238, 239, 269–72
Trump, Donald, 160, 188–92
Truth, Sojourner, 38
Tsing, Anna, 4
Tucker, Catherine, 23, 24
Tuskegee Syphilis Study, 310n4

UHURU, 51
Ujamaa Food Co-op, 125
Underground Railroad, 20, 25–27
undocumented immigrants, 164, 166–68
Undoing Racism in Detroit's Food System, 117–18, 125–26, 136–37
Unemployed Councils, 30–32
unemployment, 57, 251, 298
unionization, 28–34, 298
United Auto Workers (UAW), 32, 34
United Detroiters workshop map, 74–75
United Nations, 183–85

Uniting Detroiters, 2
urban agriculture, 117–19, 123. *See also* urban
    gardens
    Capuchin Soup Kitchen, 139–40
    Detroit Black Community Food Security
        Network (DBCFSN), 124–27
    Earthworks Urban Farm, 142–44
    food justice, 146–47
    liberated territory as means of survival,
        130–34
    Linda Campbell on, 149–54
    Pingree Potato Patches, 121
    "Resurget Cineribus" (Miller), 129
    ribbon farms, 120
    thrift gardens, 122
    Undoing Racism in Detroit's Food System,
        117–18, 125–26, 136–37
urban commons, 69–75
    and civil rights movement, 46
    cross-border, between Detroit and Windsor,
        106–10
    defense of land, 76–78
    Detroit historical land cover, circa 1800,
        98–99
    and environmental justice, 111–15
    Great Lakes Watershed, 104–5
    McClellan's recollections of Black Bottom,
        87–93
    ownership and care of land, 79–86
    and right to the city, 4–5
    and River Rats, 100–103
    sites associated with Underground Railroad,
        27
    and Undoing Racism in the Detroit Food
        System, 137
    Wieske's "Backyard Garden," 94–97

urban gardens
    control and distribution of land, 113–14
    Earthworks Urban Farm, 142–44
    importance of, 224
    land speculation in Freedom Freedom, 84–86
    ownership and care of land, 79
    Pingree Potato Patches, 121
    ribbon farms, 120
    thrift gardens, 122
    Wieske's "Backyard Garden," 94–97
Urban Network, 293–95
urban renewal, 88–90, 93, 180, 182, 186–87, 195,
    213, 273, 311n12. *See also* displacement;
    gentrification
urban strategy, 244
urban sustainability, as force of displacement,
    217–21
USB, 177
US Social Forum, 263

vacancies, 72, 73, 78, 80–81, 113–15, 178, 204,
    223–26
Veterans Administration, 39
Vietnam War, 50
voting, 167–68, 169, 291, 292

wage theft, 191
Walk to Freedom, 46–53
Warren, Gwendolyn, 7, 273
Washington, Melvin, 209
water
    and environmental justice, governance, and
        civic-minded communities, 254–56
    Flint crisis, 157, 158, 169, 179, 185, 188, 189,
        192
    right to, 246–48

shutoffs, 157, 179, 183–85, 246–53
wealth, extracted from Detroit, 186–87, 191
wealth disparity, 45–46
Weaver, Karen, 188
Webb, William, 26–27
"We Charge Genocide: The Crime of Government
    against the Negro People," 51
We the People of Detroit Research Collective, 251
whipping post, 23
white flight, 59, 205
white supremacy, 5, 69, 118, 126, 137, 189–90
Wieske, Amelia, 94–97
Wigmore, Gregory, 20
Wilder, Gary, 304n6
Williams, Ephraim S., 23
Williams, Robert, 51
Williamson, Deborah, 222–26
Winchester, Hank, 250
Windsor, Ontario, 105, 106–10
Windsor Youth Center (WYC), 109–10
WNUC, 238, 241
Wobblies, 30
Woodbridge, 195
Woodward, Augustus B., 24
Woodward Avenue, 24
Woolworth's, 32

Yakini, Malik, 124–27, 302
Young, Coleman, 59, 88, 123, 158, 204, 265
Young Educators Alliance, 263
youth organizing and programs, 258, 262–64, 278,
    281–84

Zinn, Howard, 6
Zone 8, 293